Financial Accounting

An Introduction

Financial Accounting
An Introduction

Tony Davies
and
Tony Boczko

The **McGraw·Hill** Companies

London   Boston   Burr Ridge, IL   Dubuque, IA   Madison, WI   New York   San Francisco
St. Louis   Bangkok   Bogotá   Caracas   Kuala Lumpur   Lisbon   Madrid   Mexico City
Milan   Montreal   New Delhi   Santiago   Seoul   Singapore   Sydney   Taipei   Toronto

Financial Accounting: An Introduction
Tony Davies and Tony Boczko
ISBN-10: 0-07-710940-6
ISBN-13: 978-0-07-710940-0

Education

Published by McGraw-Hill Education
Shoppenhangers Road
Maidenhead
Berkshire
SL6 2QL
Telephone: 44 (0) 1628 502 500
Fax: 44 (0) 1628 770 224
Website: www.mcgraw-hill.co.uk

British Library Cataloguing in Publication Data
A catalogue record for this book is available from the British Library

Library of Congress Cataloguing in Publication Data
The Library of Congress data for this book has been applied for from the Library of Congress

Acquisitions Editor: Mark Kavanagh
Development Editor: Rachel Crookes
Senior Marketing Manager: Marca Wosoba
Senior Production Editor: Eleanor Hayes

Text Design by Jonathan Coleclough
Cover design by Fielding Design Ltd
Typeset by Mathematical Composition Setters Ltd, Salisbury, Wiltshire
Printed and bound in Great Britain by CPI Bath Press

Dedication

I dedicate this book with love and thanks
to my parents
Regina and Philip

Brief Table of Contents

Detailed Table of Contents

Appendices

Features

Case Studies

Press Extracts

Figures

Preface

Introduction

Financial Accounting: An Introduction has two key aims. One aim is to provide undergraduates, post-graduates, and others with a book about financial accounting in a practical business context that is clear and easy to understand. In *Financial Accounting* we have maintained a rigorous approach and full coverage of all the theoretical and technical aspects of accounting, together with their practical application. At the same time, we have tried to remove the fear and intimidation that sometimes accompanies this subject, by making it more user-friendly and a little more fun to study.

The other aim is to provide a comprehensive and flexible teaching and learning resource, with a wide range of study and assessment material supported by an 'easy to use' accessible website. There are links between each of the chapters, which follow a structure that has been designed to facilitate effective teaching and learning of financial accounting in a progressive way. Alternatively, each chapter may be used on a standalone basis; chapters may also be excluded if they relate to subjects that are not essential for a specific module. Basic bookkeeping is a topic that may or may not be a requirement of some modules and so it has been placed in an appendix towards the end of the text.

Accounting is of critical importance in the support of all business activities. The formal study of accounting is exciting because it introduces a toolkit that enables a better understanding of the performance of businesses, and the decisions and problems they face. These issues are discussed daily by managers and in the media. This textbook provides you with the toolkit and shows you how to apply it in practice, utilising a comprehensive range of learning features, illustrative examples and assessment material to support and reinforce your study.

This textbook is aimed primarily at students who are not majoring in accounting, but who are undertaking an introductory-level module as part of their degree or diploma course in business management, economics or any other subject. *Financial Accounting* is a tightly-written, clear and engaging text which distils the core principles of financial accounting for those students who may not have the luxury of devoting all their time to its study.

Content and structure

Each topic in *Financial Accounting* has been carefully researched to closely follow the typical current requirements of introductory undergraduate and MBA modules. The text assumes no prior knowledge of the subject, starting at square one and taking you step-by-step through the concepts and application of techniques, with clear explanations and numerous worked examples.

This textbook is primarily about financial accounting, which is broadly concerned with the recording and analysis of historical financial data, the presentation of financial information, and compliance with current legislation, and accounting rules and standards. Another branch of accounting, management accounting, uses financial and non-financial information and also provides information for the costing of products for the valuation of stocks, the pricing of products and services, and the planning, control, and decision-making functions. It is mainly involved in the support of the management of an organisation in dealing with current problems and in the evaluation of the future outcomes of various different scenarios and decisions.

Financial Accounting includes coverage of some contemporary issues and topics of growing importance, for example:

- the international approach to the development of a common set of accounting rules to be used by businesses in groups of countries, for example the European Union
- the up-to-date position regarding corporate governance, and the responsibilities of directors, primarily in the UK
- the reporting of corporate social responsibility (CSR) by companies

The first three chapters deal with the three key financial statements: balance sheet; profit and loss account; cash flow statement, and in particular those relating to limited companies. In most respects these also apply to other profit-making and not-for-profit organisations in both the private and public sectors.

Chapter 2 begins with an introduction to the preparation of simple financial statements and then goes on to consider the balance sheet in detail.

Chapter 3 looks in detail at the profit and loss account. It looks at how to recognise that a profit (or loss) has been made and how it is linked with the balance sheet and cash flow.

Chapter 4 deals with the cash flow statement, which shows from where an organisation has received cash during an accounting period and how cash was used.

Chapter 5 is headed *Business performance analysis*. The three financial statements provide information about business performance and its financial position. Much more may be gleaned about the performance of the business through further analysis of the financial statements, using financial ratios and other techniques, for example trend analysis, industrial and inter-firm analysis.

Chapter 6 looks at the analysis and interpretation of the published accounts of a business. It uses the report and accounts for the year ended 31 March 2004 of Johnson Matthey plc to illustrate the type of financial and non-financial information provided by a major UK public company.

In Chapter 7 we broaden the scope of our study of accounting to provide an introduction to corporate governance, a topic that is becoming increasingly important, as the responsibilities of directors continue to increase. The burden lies with management to run businesses in strict compliance with statutory, regulatory and accounting requirements, so it is crucial that directors are aware of the rules and codes of practice in place to regulate the behaviour of directors of limited companies.

Chapter 8 deals primarily with long-term, external sources of business finance for investment in businesses. This relates to the various types of funding available to business, including the raising of funds from the owners of the business (the shareholders) and from lenders external to the business. Chapter 8 also shows how the costs of the alternative sources of capital are used in the calculation of the overall cost of capital that may be used by companies as the discount rate to evaluate proposed investments in capital projects, and in the calculation of economic value added (EVA) to evaluate company performance.

Chapter 9 is about IT and accounting, and emphasises how the continuing development of IT has resulted in changes in the role of the accounting and finance function, and a broadening of the range of other business disciplines in which it is now involved. It explains how IT has impacted on every area within a business: design; engineering; manufacturing; human resources management; purchasing; distribution; sales; marketing, and how these operational areas have increasingly become totally integrated with the accounting and finance function. The spreadsheet has now become an indispensable tool in every aspect of business life. Accounting Excel spreadsheet applications are fully illustrated in worked examples and chapter-end assessment material.

This text has been written primarily for non-specialist students, and so each chapter aims to help students understand the broader context and relevance of financial accounting in the business environment. Every chapter provides comprehensive examples and commentary on company activity, including at least one press extract. Companies featured include: Microsoft; easyJet; Marks & Spencer; Corus; Shearings; Tyco International; Network Rail. In addition, two of the chapters feature extracts and analysis of the Report and Accounts 2004 of Johnson Matthey plc.

Using this book

To support your study and reinforce the topics covered, we have included a comprehensive range of learning features and assessment material in each chapter, including:

- learning objectives
- introduction
- highlighted key terms
- fully-worked examples
- Excel spreadsheet worked examples
- integrated progress checks
- key points summary
- questions
- discussion points
- exercises
- Excel spreadsheet exercises.

Within each chapter we have also included numerous diagrams and charts that illustrate and reinforce important concepts and ideas. The double-page *Guided tour* that follows on pages xxi–xxii summarises the purpose of these learning features and the chapter-end assessment material. To gain maximum benefit from this text and to help you succeed in your study and exams, you are encouraged to familiarise yourself with these elements now, before you start the first chapter.

Accounting is essentially a 'hands-on' subject; just reading about it is not enough. Believe us, from our own experience we know that repeated practice of examples and exercises is the only way to become proficient in its techniques. You may think that reading through this book or your lecture notes, highlighting the odd sentence and gliding through the worked examples, progress checks and chapter-end questions and exercises, will instil the knowledge and expertise required to pass your exams. This would be a big mistake. Active learning needs to be interactive: if you haven't followed a topic or an example, go back and work through it again; try to think of other examples to which particular topics may be applied. The only way to check you have a comprehensive understanding of things is to attempt all the integrated progress checks and worked examples, and the chapter-end assessment material, and then compare your solutions with the text and answers provided. Full solutions are given for each worked example, and solutions to 45% of the chapter-end exercises (those with their numbers in colour) are provided in Appendix 3. The book's supporting website (www.mcgraw-hill.co.uk/textbooks/davies) provides an extensive range of learning and teaching resources (see page xxiii). Additional self-assessment material is available in the student centre of the website.

Case studies

This book includes three case studies that may be tackled either individually or as a team. The case studies are a little more weighty than the chapter-end exercises; in addition, they integrate many of the topics included in the chapters in each part of the text to which they relate, although not exclusively. Each case study therefore gives you an opportunity to apply the knowledge and techniques gained from each part of the book, and to develop these together with the analytical skills and judgement required to deal with real-life business problems. Additional cases are provided on the accompanying website.

We hope that this textbook will put a sparkle into your study of financial accounting and enhance your interest, and increase your understanding and skills. Above all, relax, learn and enjoy!

Online learning centre (OLC)

The website accompanying this text

www.mcgraw-hill.co.uk/textbooks/davies

includes an extensive range of chapter-based student and lecturer resources, and comprises three main sections:

Information centre

- Textbook contents
- Preface
- Guided tour
- Sample chapter
- About the authors
- Author interview
- What the reviewers say

Student centre

- Additional chapter-based exercises
- Excel spreadsheet solutions to worked examples
- Additional case studies
- Self-testing multiple-choice questions organised by chapter with automatic grading
- Revision notes organised by chapter
- Glossary of key terms
- The press room
- Useful weblinks
- International and UK accounting standards

Lecturer centre

- Solutions to all chapter-based exercises
- Excel spreadsheet solutions to chapter-based exercises
- Debriefings to all case studies
- Large multiple-choice questions test bank
- PowerPoint lecture slides
- Textbook figures
- PageOut

Remember to check the website frequently throughout your studies, as these resources will be regularly updated.

Acknowledgements

Thank you to the following lecturers who were involved in either the initial market research and/or in providing useful review comments and technical checks of the draft chapters during the development phase of this project:

- Graham Ball
- Mike Barker
- Tariq Bashir
- Bruce Bowhill
- Mary Canny
- Giovanni Cozzi
- Cedric McCallum
- Ian Crawford
- Robert Devlin
- Barbara Dexter
- Graham Diggle
- Steve Dungworth
- Steward Hughes
- Carolyn Isaaks
- Chris Knight
- Danny Leiwy
- John Lyons
- Jenny Maynard
- Rona O'Brien
- Gary Owen
- Richard Pike
- Graeme Reid
- Mark Richer
- Clare Roberts
- Zeljko Seviç
- Jon Simon
- Chris Simpson
- John Syer
- Brian Telford
- Tony Wall
- Pauline Willis

Thank you to CIMA (the Chartered Institute of Management Accountants) for their permission to include extracts from their Management Accounting Official Terminology 2000 edition.

Thank you to *Accountancy Age*, *The Daily Telegraph*, *The Times*, and *The Guardian* for their permission to use extracts from their publications, and to *HSBC Bank Group Archives* for their permission to use photographic images.

Thank you to Johnson Matthey plc for permission to use extracts of their Report and Accounts 2004 as an excellent example of the information provided to shareholders by a major UK plc.

Thank you to systems analyst, Norrette Moore, for her invaluable review comments with regard to the chapter about IT and accounting.

Thank you to Mark Kavanagh for his support and encouragement in the writing of this book.

Guided Tour

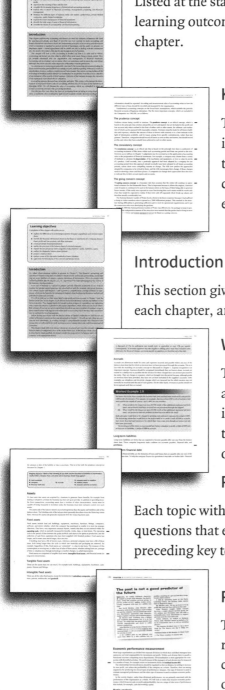

Learning objectives

Listed at the start of each chapter, these bullet points identify the core learning outcomes you should have acquired after completing each chapter.

Key terms

These are colour highlighted the first time they are introduced, alerting you to the core concepts and techniques in each chapter. A full explanation is contained in the glossary of key terms section at the end of the book.

Introduction

This section gives you a brief overview of the coverage and purpose of each chapter, and how it links to the previous chapter.

Worked examples

The numerous worked examples in each chapter provide an application of the learning points and techniques included within each topic. By following and working through the step-by-step solutions, you have an opportunity to check your knowledge at frequent intervals.

Progress checks

Each topic within each chapter includes one or more of these short questions that enable you to check and apply your understanding of the preceding key topics before you progress to the next one in the chapter.

Press extracts

These topical extracts used in every chapter feature real company examples from the press, including commentary that highlights the practical application of accounting and finance in the business environment.

Summary of key points

Following the final section in each chapter there is a comprehensive summary of the chapter topics. These allow you to check that you understand all the main points covered before moving on to the next chapter.

Questions

These are short narrative-type questions that encourage you to review and check your understanding of all the key topics. There are typically 8 to 11 of these questions at the end of each chapter.

Discussion points

This section typically includes 2 to 4 thought-provoking ideas and questions that encourage you to critically apply your understanding and/or further develop some of the topics introduced in each chapter, either individually or in team discussion.

Exercises

These comprehensive examination-style questions are graded by their level of difficulty, as well as by the time typically required to complete them. Designed to assess your knowledge and application of the principles and techniques covered in a chapter, there are typically 7 to 10 exercises at the end of each chapter. Full solutions to the colour-highlighted exercise numbers are provided in Appendix 3 to allow you to self-assess your progress.

Online Learning Centre (OLC)

After completing each chapter, log on to the supporting Online Learning Centre website. Take advantage of the study tools offered to reinforce the material you have read in the text, and to develop your knowledge of business accounting and finance in a fun and effective way.

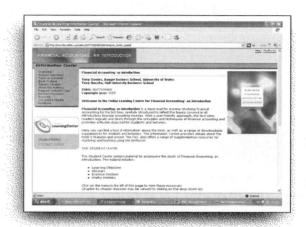

Resources for students include:

- Additional chapter-based exercises

- Excel spreadsheet solutions to worked examples

- Additional case studies

- Self-testing multiple-choice questions organised by chapter with automatic grading

- Revision notes organised by chapter

- Glossary of key terms

- The press room

- Useful weblinks

- International and UK accounting standards

Additionally available for lecturers:

- Solutions to all chapter-based exercises

- Excel spreadsheet solutions to chapter-based exercises

- Debriefings to all case studies

- Large multiple-choice questions test bank

- PowerPoint lecture slides

- Textbook figures

- PageOut

1

Financial accounting: the building blocks

Contents

Learning objectives

Completion of this chapter will enable you to:

- outline the uses and purpose of accounting and the practice of accountancy
- explain the development of the conceptual frameworks of accounting
- outline the contents of the UK Statement of Principles (SOP)
- explain the main UK accounting concepts and accounting and financial reporting standards
- appreciate the meaning of true and fair view
- consider the increasing importance of international accounting standards
- explain what is meant by financial accounting, management accounting, and financial management
- illustrate the different types of business entity: sole traders, partnerships, private limited companies, public limited companies
- explain the nature and purpose of financial statements
- identify the wide range of users of financial information
- consider the issues of accountability and financial reporting.

Introduction

This chapter explains why accounting and finance are such key elements of business life. Both for aspiring accountants, and those of you who may not continue to study accounting and finance beyond the introductory level, the fundamental principles of accounting and the ways in which accounting is regulated to protect owners of businesses, and the public in general, are important topics. A broad appreciation will be useful not only in dealing with the subsequent text, but also in the context of the day-to-day management of a business.

This chapter will look at why accounting is needed and how it is used and by whom. Accounting and finance are wide subjects, which often mean many things to many people. They are broadly concerned with the organisation and management of financial resources. Accounting and accountancy are two terms which are sometimes used to mean the same thing, although they more correctly relate separately to the subject and the profession.

Accounting and accountancy are generally concerned with measuring and communicating the financial information provided from accounting systems, and the reporting of financial results to shareholders, lenders, creditors, employees and Government. The owners or shareholders of the wide range of business entities that use accounting may be assumed to have the primary objective of maximisation of the wealth of their business. Directors of the business manage the resources of the business to meet shareholders' objectives.

Accounting operates through basic principles and rules. This chapter will examine the development of conceptual frameworks of accounting, which in the UK are seen in the Statement of Principles (SOP). We will discuss the rules of accounting, which are embodied in what are termed accounting concepts and accounting standards.

Over the past few years there has been an increasing focus on trying to bring together the rules, or standards, of accounting that apply in each separate country, into one set of accounting standards. For example, with effect from January 2005 all the large companies within the European Union are required to comply with one such set of accounting standards relating to the way in which they report financial information. We will discuss how this may affect the topics we shall be covering in this book.

We will consider the processes used in accounting and look at an overview of the financial statements used in financial reporting, and the way in which financial reporting is used to keep shareholders informed. The timely and accurate disclosure of truthful information is a fundamental requirement in the preparation of appropriate statements of the financial performance and the financial position of a business. Directors and managers are responsible for running businesses and their accountability to shareholders is maintained through their regular reporting on the activities of the business.

A large number of accounting concepts and terms are used throughout this book, the definitions of which may be found in the glossary of key terms at the end of the book.

What is accounting, and its uses and purposes?

The original, basic purposes of **accounting** were to classify and record monetary transactions (see Appendix 1) and present the financial results of the activities of an entity, in other words the scorecard that shows how the business is doing. The accounting profession has evolved and accounting techniques have been developed for use in a much broader business context. To look at the current nature of accounting and the broad purposes of accounting systems we need to consider the three questions these days generally answered by accounting information:

- how are we doing, and are we doing well or badly?
- which problems should be looked at?
- which is the best alternative for doing a job?

a scorecard (like scoring a game of cricket, for example)
attention-directing
problem solving.

Although accountants and the accounting profession have retained their fundamental roles they have grown into various branches of the profession, which have developed their own specialisms and responsibilities.

Accounting is a part of the information system within an organisation (see Appendix 1, which explains double-entry **bookkeeping**, and how data is identified, recorded and presented as information in the ways required by the users of financial information). Accounting also exists as a service function, which ensures that the financial information that is presented meets the needs of the users of financial information. To achieve this, accountants must not only ensure that information is accurate, reliable and timely but also that it is relevant for the purpose for which it is being provided, consistent for comparability, and easily understood (see Fig. 1.1).

In order to be useful to the users of financial information, the accounting data from which it is prepared, together with its analysis and presentation must be:

- accurate – free from error of content or principle
- reliable – representing the information that users believe it represents
- timely – available in time to support decision-making

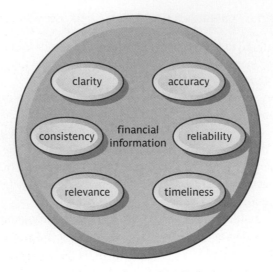

Figure 1.1 Features of useful financial information

- relevant – applicable to the purpose required, for example a decision regarding a future event or to support an explanation of what has already happened
- consistent – the same methods and standards of measurement of data and presentation of information to allow like-for-like comparison
- clear – capable of being understood by those for whom the information has been prepared.

In the next few sections we will see just how important these features are, and in the ways they are included in the development of various **conceptual frameworks of accounting**, and the accounting policies selected by companies.

The conceptual frameworks of accounting

How can the credibility and usefulness of accounting and financial information be ensured? Accounting operates within a framework. This framework is constantly changing and evolving as new problems are encountered, as new practices and techniques are developed, and the objectives of users of financial information are modified and revised.

The search for a definitive conceptual framework, a theoretical accounting model, which may deal with any new accounting problem that may arise, has resulted in many conceptual frameworks having been developed in a number of countries worldwide. The basic assumption for these conceptual frameworks is that **financial statements** must be useful. The general structure of conceptual frameworks deals with the following six questions:

1. What is the purpose of financial statement reporting?
2. Who are the main users of accounting and financial information?
3. What type of financial statements will meet the needs of these users?
4. What type of information should be included in financial statements to satisfy these needs?
5. How should items included in financial statements be defined?
6. How should items included in financial statements be recorded and measured?

In 1989 the **International Accounting Standards Board (IASB)** issued a conceptual framework that largely reflected the conceptual frameworks of USA, Canada, Australia, and UK. This was based on the ideas and proposals made by the accounting profession since the 1970s in both the USA and UK. In 1999 the **Accounting Standards Board (ASB)** in the UK published its own conceptual framework called the **Statement of Principles (SOP) for Financial Reporting**.

> **Progress check 1.1 What is meant by a conceptual framework of accounting?**

The Statement of Principles (SOP)

The 1975 Corporate Report was the first UK attempt at a conceptual framework. This, together with the 1973 Trueblood Report published in USA, provided the basis for the conceptual framework issued by the IASB in 1989, referred to in the previous section. It was followed by the publication of the SOP by the ASB in 1999. The SOP is a basic structure for determining objectives, in which there is a thread from the theory to the practical application of accounting standards to transactions that are reported in published accounts. The SOP is not an accounting standard and its use is not mandatory, but it is a statement of guidelines; it is, by virtue of the subject, constantly in need of revision.

The SOP identifies the main users of financial information as:

- investors
- lenders
- employees
- suppliers and creditors
- customers and debtors
- Government
- the general public.

The SOP focuses on the interests of investors and assumes that each of the other users of financial information is interested in or concerned about the same issues as investors.

The SOP consists of eight chapters that deal with the following topics:

1. The objectives of financial statements, which are fundamentally to provide information that is useful for the users of that information.
2. Identification of the entities that are required to provide financial statement reporting by virtue of the demand for the information included in those statements.
3. The qualitative characteristics required to make financial information useful to users:
    - materiality (inclusion of information that is not material may distort the usefulness of other information)
    - relevance
    - reliability
    - comparability (enabling the identification and evaluation of differences and similarities)
    - comprehensibility.
4. The main elements included in the financial statements – the 'building blocks' of accounting such as assets and liabilities.
5. When transactions should be recognised in financial statements.
6. How assets and liabilities should be measured.
7. How financial statements should be presented for clear and effective communication.

8. The accounting by an entity in its financial statements for interests in other entities.

The UK SOP can be seen to be a very general outline of principles relating to the reporting of financial information. The SOP includes some of the basic concepts that provide the foundations for the preparation of financial statements. These accounting concepts will be considered in more detail in the next section.

> **Progress check 1.2** **What are the aims of the UK Statement of Principles how does it try to achieve these aims?**

UK accounting concepts

The accounting framework revolves around the practice of accountancy and the accounting profession, which is bounded by rules, or concepts (see Fig. 1.2, in which the five most important concepts are shown shaded) of what data should be included within an accounting system and how that data should be recorded.

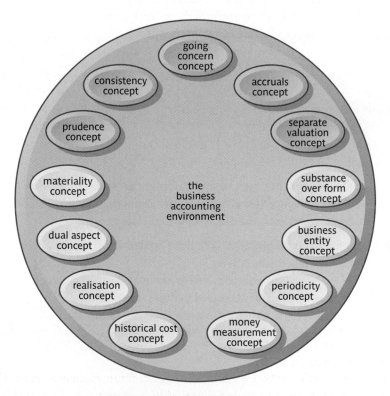

Figure 1.2 Accounting concepts

Accounting concepts are the principles underpinning the preparation of accounting information relating to the ethical rules, boundary rules, and recording and measurement rules of accounting. Ethical rules, or principles, are to do with limiting the amount of judgement (or indeed creativity) that may be used in the reporting of financial information. Boundary rules are to do with which types of data, and the amounts of each, that should be held by organisations, and which elements of financial information should be reported. Recording and measurement rules of accounting relate to how the different types of data should be recorded and measured by the organisation.

Fundamental accounting concepts are the broad basic assumptions, which underlie the periodic financial accounts of business enterprises. The five most important concepts, which are included in the Companies Act 1985/89, are as follows:

The prudence concept

Prudence means being careful or cautious. The **prudence concept** is an ethical concept, which is based on the principle that revenue and profits are not anticipated, but are included in the profit and loss account only when realised in the form of either cash or other assets, the ultimate cash realisation of which can be assessed with reasonable certainty. Provision must be made for all known liabilities and expenses, whether the amount of these is known with certainty or is a best estimate in the light of information available, and for losses arising from specific commitments, rather than just guesses. Therefore, companies should record all losses as soon as they are known, but should record profits only when they have actually been achieved in cash or other assets.

The consistency concept

The **consistency concept** is an ethical rule that is based on the principle that there is uniformity of accounting treatment of like items within each accounting period and from one period to the next. However, as we will see in Chapter 3, judgement may be exercised as to the application of accounting rules to the preparation of financial statements. For example, a company may choose from a variety of methods to calculate the **depreciation** of its machinery and equipment, or how to value its stocks of a product. Until recently, once a particular approach had been adopted by a company for one accounting period then this approach should normally have been adopted in all future accounting periods, unless there were compelling reasons to change. The ASB now prefers the approaches adopted by companies to be revised by them, and the ASB encourages their change, if those changes result in showing a truer and fairer picture. If companies do change their approaches then they have to indicate this in their annual reports and accounts.

The going concern concept

The **going concern concept** is a boundary rule that assumes that the entity will continue in operational existence for the foreseeable future. This is important because it allows the original, historical costs of assets to continue to be used in the balance sheet on the basis of their being able to generate future income. If the entity was expected to cease functioning then such assets would be worth only what they would be expected to realise if they were sold off separately (their break-up values) and therefore usually considerably less.

The National Botanic Garden of Wales faced a threat to its future existence because it had suffered a slump in visitor numbers since it opened as a 2000 Millennium project. This resulted in the attraction having difficulties in generating sufficient cash to meet its operational requirements and to pay the contractors who were developing the gardens.

In March 2004 the National Botanic Garden of Wales was offered a £2.3m package to keep it open. However, the independent trustees of the attraction were warned that the garden had to bring in more money from visitors and private sponsors to secure its future as a going concern.

A going concern or an expensive failure?

Trustees for the National Botanic Garden of Wales are to meet today to decide whether it should be put into liquidation after the Welsh Assembly's refusal to provide £3 million to keep it open.

The attraction, in Llanarthne, Carmarthenshire, is funded by the Millennium Commission. It was opened by the Prince of Wales three years ago and was Britain's first national botanic garden for 200 years.

Visitor numbers are down, however, and it may close within days. In a statement, the Prince, a patron, said he hoped 'a situation can be found to allow the garden to remain open'. The trustees said last night that only a 'last-minute miracle' could save it.

A spokesman said liquidation, in which assets would be sold to recoup money for creditors, was the most likely outcome of today's meeting.

The garden was a showpiece Millennium project, using National Lottery funds. The commission is expected to call back the £21 million given to the garden if it is liquidated.

Brian Charles, deputy chairman of the trustees, said closure would be a tragedy. 'It's an outstanding attraction for Wales. We will open the doors today, but it will be up to the administrators whether they open again'.

Carwyn Jones, the Welsh Assembly rural affairs minister, said the garden was in the wrong place and should have been opened in Cardiff.

A report by an independent panel sponsored by the Wales Tourist Board said it had no commercial future.

National botanic garden on brink of liquidation, by Richard Savill

© *Daily Telegraph*, 15 December 2003

The accruals concept

The **accruals concept** (or the matching concept) is a recording and measurement rule that is based on the principle that revenues and costs are recognised as they are earned or incurred, are matched with one another, and are dealt with in the profit and loss account of the period to which they relate, irrespective of the period of receipt or payment. It would be misleading to report profit as the difference between cash received and cash paid during a period because some trading and commercial activities of the period would be excluded, since many transactions are based on credit.

Most of us are users of electricity. We may use it over a period of three months for heating, lighting, and running our many home appliances, before receiving an invoice from the electricity supplier for the electricity we have used. The fact that we have not received an invoice until much later doesn't mean we have not incurred a cost for each month. The costs have been accrued over each of those months, and we will pay for them at a later date.

The separate valuation concept

The **separate valuation concept** is a recording and measurement rule that relates to the determination of the aggregate amount of any item. In order to determine the aggregate amount of an asset or a liability, each individual asset or liability that comprises the aggregate must be determined separately. This is important because material items may reflect different economic circumstances. There must be a review of each material item to comply with the appropriate accounting standards:

- FRS 11 (Impairment of Fixed Assets and Goodwill)

- FRS 12 (Provisions, Contingent Liabilities and Contingent Assets)
- FRS 15 (Tangible Fixed Assets).

(See the later section, which discusses UK accounting standards called **Financial Reporting Standards (FRSs)**, and **Statements of Standard Accounting Practice (SSAPs)**.)

Note the example of the Millennium Dome 2000 project, which was developed in Greenwich, London, throughout 1999 and 2000 and cost around £800m. At the end of the year 2000 a valuation of the individual elements of the attraction resulted in a total of around £100m.

The further eight fundamental accounting concepts are:

The substance over form concept

Where a conflict exists, the **substance over form concept**, which is an ethical rule, requires the structuring of reports to give precedence to the representation of financial or economic reality over strict adherence to the requirements of the legal reporting structure. This concept is dealt with in another accounting standard FRS 5 Reporting the Substance of Transactions. An example of this is where a company leases an asset, for example a machine, and discloses it in its balance sheet even though not holding legal title to the asset, whilst also disclosing separately in its balance sheet the amount that the company still owes on the machine. The reason for showing the asset in the balance sheet is because it is being used to generate income for the business, in the same way as a purchased machine. The substance of this accounting transaction (treating a leased asset as though it had been purchased) takes precedence over the form of the transaction (the lease itself).

The business entity concept

The **business entity concept** is a boundary rule that ensures that financial accounting information relates only to the activities of the business entity and not to the other activities of its owners. An owner of a business may be interested in sailing and may buy a boat and pay a subscription as a member of the local yacht club. These activities are completely outside the activities of the business and such transactions must be kept completely separate from the accounts of the business.

The periodicity concept

The **periodicity concept** (or time interval concept) is a boundary rule. It is the requirement to produce financial statements at set time intervals. This requirement is embodied, in the case of UK companies, in the Companies Act 1985/1989 (all future references to the Companies Act will relate to the Companies Act 1985/1989 unless otherwise stated). Both annual and interim financial statements are required to be produced by **public limited companies (plcs)** each year.

Internal reporting of financial information to management may take place within a company on a monthly, weekly, daily, or even an hourly basis. But owners of a company, who may have no involvement in the running of the business or its internal reporting, require the external reporting of their company's accounts on a six-monthly and yearly basis. The owners of the company may then rely on the regularity with which the reporting of financial information takes place, which enables them to monitor company performance, and compare figures year on year.

The money measurement concept

The **money measurement concept** is a recording and measurement rule that enables information relating to transactions to be fairly compared by providing a commonly-accepted unit of converting quantifiable amounts into recognisable measures. Most quantifiable data is capable of being converted, using a common denominator of money, into monetary terms. However, accounting deals only with those items capable of being translated into monetary terms, which imposes a limit on the scope of accounting reporting to such items. You may note, for example, that in a University's balance sheet there is no value included for its human resources, that is its lecturers, its managers, and secretarial and support staff.

The historical cost concept

The **historical cost concept** is a recording and measurement rule that relates to the practice of valuing assets at their original acquisition cost. For example, you may have bought a mountain bike two years ago for which you were invoiced and paid £150, and may now be wondering what it is currently worth. One of your friends may consider it to be worth £175 because they feel that the price of new mountain bikes has increased over the past two years. Another friend may consider it to be worth only £100 because you have used it for two years and its condition has deteriorated. Neither of your friends may be incorrect, but their views are subjective and they are different. The only measure of what your bike is worth on which your friends may agree is the price shown on your original invoice, its historical cost.

   Although the historical cost basis of valuation may not be as realistic as using, for instance, a current valuation, it does provide a consistent basis for comparison and almost eliminates the need for any subjectivity.

The realisation concept

The **realisation concept** is a recording and measurement rule and is the principle that increases in value should only be recognised on realisation of assets by arms-length sale to an independent purchaser. This means, for example, that sales revenue from the sale of a product or service is recognised in accounting statements only when it is realised. This does not mean when the cash has been paid over by the customer; it means when the sale takes place, that is when the product or service has been delivered, and ownership is transferred, to the customer. Very often, sales persons incorrectly regard a 'sale' as the placing of an order by a customer because they are usually very optimistic and sometimes forget that orders can get cancelled. Accountants, being prudent individuals, correctly record a sale by issuing an invoice when services or goods have been delivered (and installed).

The dual aspect concept

The **dual aspect concept** is the recording and measurement rule that provides the basis for double-entry bookkeeping. It reflects the practical reality that every transaction always includes both the giving and receiving of value. For example, a company may pay out cash in return for a delivery into its warehouse of a consignment of products, which it subsequently aims to sell. The company's reduction in its cash balance is reflected in its increase in its stock of products.

The materiality concept

Information is material if its omission or misstatement could influence the economic decisions of users taken on the basis of the financial statements. Materiality depends on the size of the item or error judged, its significance, in the particular circumstances of its omission or misstatement. Thus, materiality provides a threshold or cut-off point rather than being a primary qualitative characteristic that information must have if it is to be useful. The **materiality concept** is the overriding recording and measurement rule, which allows a certain amount of judgement in the application of all the other accounting concepts. The level of materiality, or significance, will depend on the size of the organisation and the type of revenue or cost, or asset or liability being considered. For example, the cost of business stationery is usually charged as an expense regardless of whether or not all the items have been used; it would be pointless to try and attribute a value to such relatively low-cost unused items.

True and fair view

The term **true and fair view** was introduced in the Companies Act 1947, requiring that companies' reporting of their accounts should show a true and fair view. It was not defined in that Act and has not been defined since. Some writers have suggested that conceptually it is a dynamic concept but over the years it could be argued that it has failed, and various business scandals and collapses have occurred without users being alerted. The concept of true and fair was adopted by the European Community Council in its fourth directive, implemented by the UK in the Companies Act 1981, and subsequently in the implementation of the seventh directive in the Companies Act 1989 (section 226 or 227). Conceptually the directives require additional information where individual provisions are insufficient.

In practice true and fair view relates to the extent to which the various principles, concepts, and standards of accounting have been applied. It may therefore be somewhat subjective and subject to change as new accounting rules are developed, old standards replaced and new standards introduced. It may be interesting to research the issue of derivatives and decide whether the true and fair view concept was invoked by those companies that used or marketed these financial instruments, and specifically consider the various collapses or public statements regarding losses incurred over the past few years. Before derivatives, the issue which escaped disclosure in financial reporting under true and fair view was leasing.

UK accounting and financial reporting standards

A number of guidelines, or standards (some of which we have already discussed), have been developed by the accounting profession to ensure truth, fairness, and consistency in the preparation and presentation of financial information.

A number of bodies have been established to draft accounting policy, set accounting standards, and to monitor compliance with standards and the provisions of the Companies Act. The Financial Reporting Council (FRC), whose chairman is appointed by the Department of Trade and Industry (DTI) and the Bank of England, develops accounting standards policy and gives guidance on issues of public concern. The ASB, which is comprised of members of the accountancy profession, and on which the Government has an observer status, has responsibility for development, issue, and withdrawal of accounting standards.

The accounting standards are called Financial Reporting Standards (FRSs). Up to 1990 the **accounting standards** were known as Statements of Standard Accounting Practice (SSAPs), and were issued by the Accounting Standards Committee (ASC), the forerunner of the ASB. Although some SSAPs have now been withdrawn there are, in addition to the new FRSs, a large number of SSAPs that are still in force. A list of all FRSs and SSAPs that are currently in force may be found in Appendix 2 at the end of this book. The website accompanying this book contains the up-to-date position with regard to changes in accounting standards.

The ASB is supported by the Urgent Issues Task Force (UITF). Its main role is to assist the ASB in areas where an accounting standard or Companies Act provision exists, but where unsatisfactory or conflicting interpretations have developed or seem likely to develop. The UITF also deals with issues that need to be resolved more quickly than through the issuing of an accounting standard. A recent example of this was the Y2K problem, which involved ensuring that computerised accounting transactions were not corrupted when we moved from the year 1999 to the year 2000.

The Financial Reporting Review Panel (FRRP) reviews comments and complaints from users of financial information. It enquires into the annual accounts of companies where it appears that the requirements of the Companies Act, including the requirement that annual accounts shall show a true and fair view, might have been breached. The Stock Exchange rules covering financial disclosure of publicly quoted companies require such companies to comply with accounting standards and reasons for non-compliance must be disclosed.

Pressure groups, organisations and individuals may also have influence on the provisions of the Companies Act and FRSs (and SSAPs). These may include some Government departments (for example Inland Revenue, HM Customs & Excise, Office of Fair Trading) in addition to the DTI and employer organisations such as the Confederation of British Industry (CBI), and professional bodies like the Law Society, Institute of Directors, and Chartered Management Institute.

There are therefore many diverse influences on the form and content of company accounts. In addition to legislation, standards are continually being refined, updated and replaced and further enhanced by various codes of best practice. As a response to this the UK Generally Accepted Accounting Practices (UK GAAP), first published in 1989, includes all practices that are considered to be permissible or legitimate, either through support by statute, accounting standard or official pronouncement, or through consistency with the needs of users and of meeting the fundamental requirement to present a true and fair view, or even simply through authoritative support in the accounting literature. UK GAAP is therefore a dynamic concept, which changes in response to changing circumstances.

➡   Within the scope of current legislation, best practice and accounting standards, each company needs to develop its own specific **accounting policies**. Accounting policies are the specific accounting bases selected and consistently followed by an entity as being, in the opinion of the management, appropriate to its circumstances and best suited to present fairly its results and financial position. Examples are the various alternative methods of valuing stocks of materials, or charging the cost of a machine over its useful life, that is, its depreciation.

The accounting standard that deals with how a company chooses, applies and reports on its accounting policies is called FRS 18, Accounting Policies, and was issued in 2000 to replace SSAP 2, Disclosure of Accounting Policies. FRS 18, clarified when profits should be recognised (the realisation concept), and the requirement of 'neutrality' in financial statements in neither overstating gains nor understating losses (the prudence concept). This standard also emphasised the increased importance of the going concern concept and the accruals concept. The aims of FRS 18 are:

- to ensure that companies choose accounting policies that are most suitable for their individual circumstances, and incorporate the key characteristics stated in chapter 3 of the SOP
- to ensure that accounting policies are reviewed and replaced as necessary on a regular basis
- to ensure that companies report accounting policies, and any changes to them, in their annual reports and accounts so that users of that information are kept informed.

Whereas FRS 18 deals with the disclosure by companies of their accounting policies, FRS 3, Reporting Financial Transactions, deals with the reporting by companies of their financial performance. Financial performance relates primarily to the profit and loss account, whereas financial position relates primarily to the balance sheet. FRS 3 aims to ensure that users of financial information get a good insight into the company's performance during the period to which the accounts relate. This is in order that decisions made about the company may be made on an informed basis. FRS 3 requires the following items to be included in company accounts to provide the required level of reporting on financial performance (which will all be discussed in greater detail in Chapter 3 which is about the profit and loss account and Chapter 6 which looks at published reports and accounts):

- analysis of turnover, cost of sales, operating expenses, and profit before interest
- exceptional items
- extraordinary items
- statement of recognised gains and losses (a separate financial statement along with the balance sheet, profit and loss account, and cash flow statement).

> **Progress check 1.3** What is meant by accounting concepts and accounting standards, and why are they needed? Give some examples.

International accounting standards

The International Accounting Standards Committee (IASC) set up in 1973, which is supported by each of the major professional accounting bodies, fosters the harmonisation of accounting standards internationally. To this end each UK FRS (Financial Reporting Standard) includes a section explaining its relationship to any relevant international accounting standard.

There are wide variations in the accounting practices that have been developed in different countries. These reflect the purposes for which financial information is required by the different users of that information, in each of those countries. There is a different focus on the type of information and the relative importance of each of the users of financial information in each country. This is because each country may differ in terms of:

- who finances the businesses – individual equity shareholders, institutional equity shareholders, debenture holders, banks, etc.
- tax systems either aligned with or separate from accounting rules
- the level of government control and regulation
- the degree of transparency of information.

The increase in international trade and globalisation has led to a need for convergence, or harmonisation, of accounting rules and practices. The IASC was created in order to develop international accounting standards, but these have been slow in appearing because of the difficulties in bringing together differences in accounting procedures. Until 2000 these standards were called **International Accounting Standards (IASs)**. The successor to the IASC, the IASB (International Accounting Standards Board) was set up in April 2001 to make financial statements more comparable on a worldwide basis. The IASB publishes its standards in a series of pronouncements called **International Financial Reporting Standards (IFRSs)**. It has also adopted the body of standards issued by the IASC, which continue to be designated IASs.

The chairman of the IASB, Sir David Tweedie, has said that 'the aim of the globalisation of accounting standards is to simplify accounting practices and to make it easier for investors to compare the financial statements of companies worldwide'. He also said that 'this will break down barriers to investment and trade and ultimately reduce the cost of capital and stimulate growth'

(*Business Week*, 7 June 2004). On 1 January 2005 there was convergence in the mandatory application of the IFRSs by listed companies within each of the European Union member states. The impact of this should be negligible with regard to the topics covered in this book, since UK accounting standards have already moved close to international standards. The reason for this is that the UK SOP was drawn up using the 1989 IASB conceptual framework for guidance. A list of current IFRSs and IASs is shown in Appendix 2 at the end of this book.

At the time of writing this book, major disagreements continued about convergence from 1 January 2005. For example, there was disagreement by European banks and insurers concerning the IASB rules requiring listed companies to record the gains and losses of various derivatives at fair market value in their published reports and accounts. The French banks, in particular, feared that the IASB may be imposing Anglo-Saxon views of accounting on the rest of the world! (See 'When bankers kept saying NON', *Business Week*, 1 March 2004).

> **Progress check 1.4 What is the significance of the International Financial Reporting Standards (IFRS) that have been issued by the IASB?**

Worked Example 1.1

Young Gordon Brown decided that he would like to start to train to become an accountant. Some time after he had graduated (and after an extended backpacking trip across a few continents) he registered with The Chartered Institute of Management Accountants (CIMA). At the same time Gordon started employment as part of the graduate intake in the finance department of a large engineering group. The auditors came in soon after Gordon started his job and he was intrigued and a little confused at their conversations with some of the senior accountants. They talked about accounting concepts and this standard and that standard, SSAPs and FRSs, all of which meant very little to Gordon. Gordon asked his boss, the Chief Accountant Angela Jones, if she could give him a brief outline of the framework of accounting one evening after work over a drink.

Angela's outline might have been something like:

- Accounting is supported by a number of rules, or concepts, that have evolved over many hundreds of years, and by accounting standards to enable consistency in reporting through the preparation of financial statements.
- Accounting concepts relate to the framework within which accounting operates, ethical considerations and the rules relating to measurement of data.
- A number of concepts relate to the boundaries of the framework: business entity; going concern; periodicity.
- A number of concepts relate to accounting principles or ethics: consistency; prudence; substance over form.
- A number of concepts relate to how data should be measured and recorded: accruals; separate valuation; money measurement; historical cost; realisation; dual aspect; materiality.
- Accounting standards are formulated by a body comprised of members of the accounting institutes (Accounting Standards Board – ASB) and are guidelines which businesses are recommended to follow in the preparation of their financial statements.

- The original standards were the Statements of Standard Accounting Practice (SSAPs) which have been and continue to be superseded by the Financial Reporting Standards (FRSs).
- The aim of the SSAPs/FRSs is to cover all the issues and problems that are likely to be encountered in the preparation of financial statements and they are the authority to ensure that 'financial statements of a reporting entity give a true and fair view of its state of affairs at the balance sheet date and of its profit or loss for the financial period ending on that date' (as quoted from the ASB foreword to *Accounting Standards*).
- SSAPs were promulgated by the Accounting Standards Committee (ASC).
- FRSs are promulgated by the ASB.

Financial accounting, management accounting, and financial management

The provision of a great deal of information, as we shall see as we progress through this book, is mandatory; it is needed to comply with, for example, the requirements of Acts of Parliament, the Inland Revenue, and HM Customs & Excise. However, there is a cost of providing information that has all the features that have been described, which therefore renders it potentially useful information. The benefits from producing information, in addition to mandatory information, should therefore be considered and compared with the cost of producing that information to decide on which information is 'really' required.

Accountants may be employed by accounting firms, which provide a range of accounting-related services to individuals, companies, public services and other organisations. Alternatively, accountants may be employed within companies, public services, and other organisations. Accounting firms may specialise in **audit**, corporate taxation, personal taxation, VAT, or consultancy (see the right hand column of Fig. 1.3). Accountants within companies, public service organisations etc., may be employed in the main functions of **financial accounting**, **management accounting**, and **treasury**

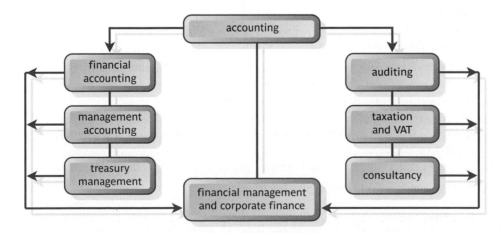

Figure 1.3 Branches of accounting

➡ **management** (see the left hand column of Fig. 1.3), and also in general management. Accounting
➡ skills may also be required in the areas of **financial management**, and corporate finance. Within companies this may include responsibility for investments, and the management of cash and foreign currency risk. External to companies this may include advice relating to mergers and acquisitions, and
➡ Stock Exchange **flotations**.

Financial accounting

Financial accounting is primarily concerned with the first question answered by accounting information, the scorecard function. Taking a car-driving analogy, financial accounting makes greater use of
the rear-view mirror than the windscreen; financial accounting is primarily concerned with historical
information.

Financial accounting is the function responsible in general for the reporting of financial information to the owners of a business, and specifically for preparation of the periodic external reporting of
financial information, statutorily required, for shareholders. It also provides similar information as
required for Government and other interested third parties, such as potential investors, employees,
lenders, suppliers, customers, and financial analysts. Financial accounting is concerned with the
➡ three key financial statements: the **balance sheet**; **profit and loss account**; **cash flow statement**. It
assists in ensuring that financial statements are included in published reports and accounts in a way
that provides ease of analysis and interpretation of company performance.

The role of financial accounting is therefore concerned with maintaining the scorecard for the
entity. Financial accounting is concerned with the classification and recording of the monetary transactions of an entity in accordance with established concepts, principles, accounting standards and
legal requirements and their presentation, by means of profit and loss accounts, balance sheets and
➡ cash flow statements, during and at the end of an **accounting period**.

Within most companies, the financial accounting role usually involves much more than the preparation of the three main financial statements. A great deal of analysis is required to support such
statements and to prepare information both for internal management and in preparation for the
➡ annual audit by the company's external **auditors**. This includes sales analyses, bank reconciliations,
and analyses of various types of expenditure.

A typical finance department has the following additional functions within the financial
➡ accounting role: control of **accounts payable** to suppliers (the purchase ledger); control of **accounts
receivable** from customers (the sales ledger), and credit control; control of cash (and possible wider
treasury functions) including cash payments, cash receipts, managers' expenses, petty cash, and
banking relationships. The financial accounting role also usually includes responsibility for payroll,
whether processed internally or by an external agency. However, a number of companies elect to
transfer the responsibility for payroll to the personnel, or human resources department, bringing
➡ with it the possibility of loss of **internal control**.

The breadth of functions involved in financial accounting can require the processing of high
volumes of data relating to purchase invoices, supplier payments, sales invoices, receipts from customers, other cash transactions, petty cash, employee expense claims, and payroll data. Control and
monitoring of these functions therefore additionally requires a large number of reports generated by
the accounting systems, for example:

- analysis of accounts receivable (debtors): those who owe money to the company – by age of debt
- analysis of accounts payable (creditors): those to whom the company owes money – by age of
  invoice

- sales analyses
- cheque and automated payments
- records of fixed assets
- invoice lists.

Management accounting

Past performance is never a totally reliable basis for predicting the future. However, the vast amount of data required for the preparation of financial statements, and maintenance of the further subsidiary accounting functions, provides a fertile database for use in another branch of accounting, namely management accounting.

Management accounting is primarily concerned with the provision of information to managers within the organisation for product costing, planning and control, and decision-making, and is to a lesser extent involved in providing information for external reporting.

The functions of management accounting are wide and varied. Whereas financial accounting is primarily concerned with past performance, management accounting makes use of historical data, but focuses almost entirely on the present and the future. Management accounting is involved with the scorecard role of accounting, but in addition is particularly concerned with the other two areas of accounting, namely problem solving and attention directing. These include cost analysis, decision-making, sales pricing, forecasting and budgeting.

Financial management

Financial management has its roots in accounting, although it may also be regarded as a branch of applied economics. It is broadly defined as the management of all the processes associated with the efficient acquisition and deployment of both short- and long-term financial resources. Financial management assists an organisation's operations management to reach its financial objectives. This may include, for example, responsibility for corporate finance and treasury management, which is concerned with cash management, and the management of interest rate and foreign currency exchange rate risk.

The management of an organisation generally involves the three overlapping and inter-linking roles of strategic management, risk management, and operations management. Financial management supports these roles to enable management to achieve the financial objectives of the shareholders. Financial management assists in the reporting of financial results to the users of financial information, for example shareholders, lenders, and employees.

The responsibility of the finance department for financial management includes the setting up and running of reporting and control systems, raising and managing funds, the management of relationships with financial institutions, and the use of information and analysis to advise management regarding planning, policy and capital investment. The overriding requirement of financial management is to ensure that the financial objectives of the company are in line with the interests of the shareholders; the underlying fundamental objective of a company is to maximise shareholder wealth.

Financial management, therefore, includes both accounting and treasury management. Treasury management includes the management and control of corporate funds, in line with company policy. This includes the management of banking relationships, borrowings, and investment. Treasury management may also include the use of the various financial instruments, which may be used to hedge the risk to the business of changes in interest rates and foreign currency exchange rates, and advising on how company strategy may be developed to benefit from changes in the economic environment and the market in which the business operates.

As management accounting continues to develop its emphasis on decision-making and strategic management, and broaden the range of activities that it supports, the distinction between management accounting and financial management is slowly disappearing.

Worked Example 1.2

A friend of yours is thinking about pursuing a career in accounting and would like some views on the major differences between financial accounting, management accounting and financial management.

The following notes provide a summary that identifies the key differences.

Financial accounting: The financial accounting function deals with the recording of past and current transactions, usually with the aid of computerised accounting systems. Of the various reports prepared, the majority are for external users, and include the profit and loss account, balance sheet, and the cash flow statement. In a plc, such reports must be prepared at least every six months, and must comply with current legal and reporting requirements.

Management accounting: The management accounting function works alongside the financial accounting function, using a number of the day-to-day financial accounting reports from the accounting system. Management accounting is concerned largely with looking at current issues and problems and the future in terms of decision-making and forecasting, for example the consideration of 'what if' scenarios during the course of preparation of forecasts and budgets. Management accounting outputs are mainly for internal users, with much confidential reporting, for example to the directors of the company.

Financial management: Financial management may include responsibilities for corporate finance and the treasury function. This includes the management and control of corporate funds, within parameters specified by the board of directors. The role often includes the management of company borrowings, investment of surplus funds, the management of both interest rate and exchange rate risk, and giving advice on economic and market changes and the exploitation of opportunities. The financial management function is not necessarily staffed by accountants. Plcs report on the treasury activities of the company in their periodic reporting and financial review.

The article on page 19, which appeared in the *Daily Telegraph*, illustrates some of the important applications of accounting and financial management. These include:

- the planning activities, particularly with regard to restructuring of the business
- negotiations with bankers
- evaluation of investments in new steelworks
- union negotiations
- costs of compliance with environmental requirements.

In February 2004 St Modwen Properties announced it had purchased some of the Corus surplus property, the former Llanwern steelworks site in Wales. They also revealed plans to invest more than £200m in the site over the next 10 years. The project would create 7,000 jobs and lead to a total end

Accounting and financial management in action

Corus, the troubled steel producer, is quietly marketing around 7,000 acres of surplus property in a bid to raise funds and streamline its business as it prepares for a radical restructuring of its UK operations.

Corus, formed though a merger of British Steel and Hoogovens of the Netherlands in 1999, requires around £250m to pay for redundancies and investments in its plan to turn around its ailing UK business.

Corus is unable to put a value on its surplus property because of the expensive cleaning up which some sites may require. Corus is legally liable to carry out the remediation work which can sometimes cost more than the value of the site.

Since the merger, Corus has cut around 10,000 jobs in the UK and is planning to cut a further 1,100 as it closes more unprofitable plants. The number of redundancies could rise by another 2,000 if its Teesside steel plant cannot be brought into profit.

However, the company intends to invest in modernising two or three steelworks in the UK in order to boost its output.

Earlier this month Corus announced that it had secured a new £800m debt facility, but the £250m needed for the UK restructuring is likely to come from either a rights issue or from fresh loans.

It is also planning to dispose of most of its US business after years of poor performance.

Philippe Varin, the new Corus chief executive who was appointed three months ago from the French aluminium producer Pechiney, has said the money is required 'the sooner the better'.

Despite selling several smaller portfolios earlier this year – including one to Threadneedle, the fund manager, for £48m in July – realising the value of its property portfolio is likely to be a slow process.

The company won planning permission in April to redevelop the 1,125 acre site of the former Ravenscraig steelworks in Scotland more than 11 years after the last steel was poured there.

Corus puts land up for sale to raise funds for rescue package, by Edward Simkins and Mary Fagan

© *Daily Telegraph*, 24 August 2003

value of £750m and they hoped to be on site towards the end of 2005. The acquisition of the Llanwern site was the fifth major land deal St Modwen completed with Corus, which retained a further 1,500 acres at Llanwern, including the operational steelworks.

Progress check 1.5 What are the main differences between financial accounting, management accounting, and financial management?

Accounting and accountancy

Accounting is sometimes referred to as a process of identifying, measuring and communicating economic information to permit informed judgements and decisions by users of the information, and also to provide information, which is potentially useful for making economic and social decisions. The term 'accounting' may be defined as:

- the classification and recording of monetary transactions
- the presentation and interpretation of the results of those transactions in order to assess performance over a period and the financial position at a given date
- the monetary projection of future activities arising from alternative planned courses of action.

Accounting processes are concerned with how data is measured and recorded and how the accounting function ensures the effective operation of accounting and financial systems. Accounting processes follow a system of recording and classification of data, followed by summarisation of financial information for subsequent interpretation and presentation. An accounting system is a series of tasks and records of an entity by which the transactions are processed as a means of maintaining financial records. Such systems identify, assemble, analyse, calculate, classify, record, summarise and report transactions.

Most companies prepare an accounting manual that provides the details and responsibilities for each of the accounting systems. The accounting manual is a collection of accounting instructions governing the responsibilities of persons, and the procedures, forms and records relating to preparation and use of accounting data.

There may be separate accounting manuals for the constituent parts of the accounting system, for example:

■ financial accounting manual – general ledger and coding
■ management accounting manual – budget and cost accounting
■ financial management/treasury manual – bank reconciliations and foreign currency exposure management.

Accountancy is defined as the practice of accounting. A **qualified accountant** is a member of the accountancy profession, and in the UK is a member of one of the six professional accountancy bodies (see Fig. 1.4). An accountant becomes qualified within each of these institutes through passing a large number of extremely technically-demanding examinations and completion of a mandatory period of three years' practical training. The examination syllabus of each of the professional bodies tends to be very similar; each body provides additional emphasis on specific areas of accounting.

Chartered Management Accountants (qualified member of CIMA) receive their practical training in industrial and commercial environments, and in the public sector, for example the NHS. They are

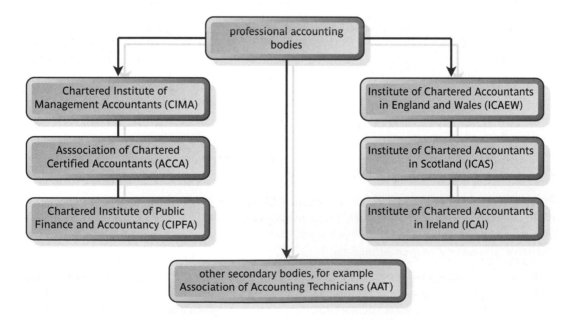

Figure 1.4 The professional accounting bodies

involved in practical accounting work and development of broader experience of strategic and operational management of the business. Certified Accountants (qualified members of ACCA) and Chartered Accountants (qualified members of ICAEW, ICAS, or ICAI) usually receive training while working in a practising accountant's office, which offers services to businesses and the general public, but may also receive training while employed in industrial and commercial organisations. Training focuses initially on auditing, and may then develop to include taxation and general business advice. Many accountants who receive training while specialising in central and local government usually, but not exclusively, are qualified members of CIPFA.

There are also a number of other accounting bodies like the Association of Accounting Technicians (AAT), Association of International Accountants, and Association of Authorised Public Accountants. The AAT, for example, provides bookkeeping and accounting training through examination and experience to a high level of competence, but short of that required to become a qualified accountant. Treasury management is served by the Association of Corporate Treasurers (ACT). This qualification has tended to be a second qualification for accountants specialising in corporate funding, cash and working capital management, interest rate and foreign currency exchange rate risk management. In the same way, the Institute of Taxation serves accountants who are tax specialists.

> **Progress check 1.6** What services does accounting offer and why do businesses need these services?

Worked Example 1.3

Of which professional bodies are accountants likely to be members if they are employed as auditors, or if they are employed in the industrial and commercial sectors, or if they are employed in local government?

The following list of each of the types of professional accounting bodies links them with the sort of accounting they may become involved in.

Chartered Institute of Management Accountants (CIMA): management accounting and financial accounting roles with a focus on management accounting in the industrial and commercial sectors, and strategic and operational management

Institutes of Chartered Accountants (ICAEW, ICAS, ICAI): employment within a firm of accountants, carrying out auditing, investigations, taxation and general business advice – possible opportunities to move into an accounting role in industry

Chartered Institute of Public Finance and Accountancy (CIPFA): accounting role within central government or local government

Association of Chartered Certified Accountants (ACCA): employment either within a firm of accountants, carrying out auditing etc., or management accounting and financial accounting roles within commerce/industry

Association of Corporate Treasurers (ACT): commercial accounting roles with almost total emphasis on treasury issues: corporate finance; funding; cash management; working capital management; financial risk management

Types of business entity: sole traders; partnerships; limited companies; public limited companies

Business entities are involved either in manufacturing (for example, food and automotive components) or in providing services (for example retailing, hospitals or television broadcasting). Such entities include profit-making and not-for-profit organisations, and charities. The main types of entity, and the environments in which they operate, are represented in Fig. 1.5. The four main types of profit-making organisations are explained in the sections that follow.

The variety of business entities can be seen to range from quangos (quasi-autonomous non-government organisations) to partnerships to limited companies. Most of the topics covered in this book apply to any type of business organisation that has the primary aim of maximising the wealth of their owners: limited liability companies, both private (Ltd) companies and public (plc) limited companies, sole traders, and partnerships.

> **Progress check 1.7** **What are the different types of business entity? Can you think of some examples of each?**

Sole traders

A sole trader entity is applicable for most types of small business. It is owned and financed by one individual, who receives all the profit made by the business, even though more than one person may work in the business.

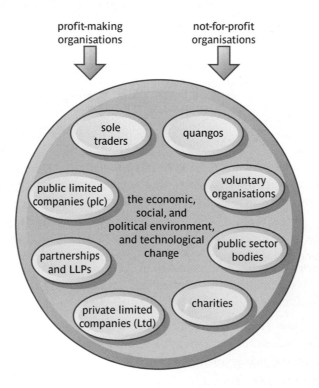

Figure 1.5 Types of business entity

The individual sole trader has complete flexibility regarding:

- the type of (legal) activities in which the business may be engaged
- when to start up or cease the business
- the way in which business is conducted.

The individual sole trader also has responsibility for:

- financing the business
- risk-taking
- decision-making
- employing staff
- any debts or loans that the business may have (the responsibility of which is unlimited, and cases of financial difficulty may result in personal property being used to repay debts).

A sole trader business is simple and cheap to set up. There are no legal or administrative set-up costs as the business does not have to be registered since it is not a legal entity separate from its owner. As we shall see, this is unlike the legal position of owners, or shareholders, of limited companies who are recognised as separate legal entities from the businesses they own.

Accounting records are needed to be kept by sole traders for the day-to-day management of the business and to provide an account of profit made during each tax year. Unlike limited companies, sole traders are not required to file a formal report and accounts each year with the **Registrar of Companies**. However, sole traders must prepare accounts on an annual basis to provide the appropriate financial information for inclusion in their annual Tax Return for submission to the Inland Revenue.

Sole traders normally remain quite small businesses, which may be seen as a disadvantage. The breadth of business skills is likely to be lacking since there are no co-owners with which to share the management and development of the business.

Partnerships

Partnerships are similar to sole traders except that the ownership of the business is in the hands of two or more persons. The main differences are in respect of how much each of the partners puts into the business, who is responsible for what, and how the profits are to be shared. These factors are normally set out in formal partnership agreements, and if the partnership agreement is not specific then the provisions of the Partnership Act 1890 apply. There is usually a written partnership agreement (but this is not absolutely necessary) and so there are initial legal costs of setting up the business.

A partnership is called a firm and is usually a small business, although there are some very large partnerships, for example firms of accountants like PriceWaterhouseCoopers. Partnerships are formed by two or more persons and, apart from certain professions like accountants, architects and solicitors, the number of persons in a partnership is limited to 20.

A partnership:

- can carry out any legal activities agreed by all the partners
- is not a legal entity separate from its partners.

The partners in a firm:

- can all be involved in running the business
- all share the profits made by the firm

- are all jointly and severally liable for the debts of the firm
- all have unlimited liability for the debts of the firm (and cases of financial difficulty may result in personal property being used to repay debts)
- are each liable for the actions of the other partners.

Accounting records are needed to be kept by partnerships for the day-to-day management of the business and to provide an account of profit made during each tax year. Unlike limited companies, partnership firms are not required to file a formal report and accounts each year with the Registrar of Companies, but they must submit annual accounts for tax purposes to the Inland Revenue.

A new type of legal entity was established in 2001, the limited liability partnership (LLP). This is a variation on the traditional partnership, and has a separate legal identity from the partners, which therefore protects them from personal bankruptcy.

One of the main benefits of a partnership is that derived from its broader base of business skills than that of a sole trader. A partnership is also able to share risk-taking, decision-making, and the general management of the firm.

Limited companies

A **limited company** is a legal entity separate from the owners of the business, which may enter into contracts, own property, and take or receive legal action. The owners limit their obligations to the amount of finance they have put into the company by way of the share of the company they have paid for. Normally, the maximum that may be claimed from shareholders is no more than they have paid for their shares, regardless of what happens to the company. Equally, there is no certainty that shareholders may recover their original investment if they wish to dispose of their shares or if the business is wound up, for whatever reason.

A company with unlimited liability does not give the owners, or members, of the company the protection of limited liability. If the business were to fail, the members would be liable, without limitation, for all the debts of the business.

The legal requirements relating to the registration and operation of limited companies is contained within the Companies Act 1985 as amended by the Companies Act 1989. Limited companies are required to be registered with the Registrar of Companies as either a private limited company (designated Ltd) or a public limited company (designated plc).

Private limited companies (Ltd)

Private limited companies are designated as Ltd. There are legal formalities involved in setting up a Ltd company which result in costs for the company. These formalities include the drafting of the company's Memorandum and Articles of Association (M and A) that describe what the company is and what it is allowed to do, registering the company and its director(s) with the Registrar of Companies, and registering the name of the company.

The shareholders provide the financing of the business in the form of share capital, of which there is no minimum requirement, and are therefore the owners of the business. The shareholders must appoint at least one director of the company, who may also be the company secretary, who carries out the day-to-day management of the business. A Ltd company may only carry out the activities included in its M and A.

Limited companies must regularly produce annual accounts for their shareholders and file a copy with the Registrar of Companies, and therefore the general public may have access to this information. A Ltd company's accounts must be audited by a suitably qualified accountant, unless it is exempt from this requirement, currently (with effect from 30 March 2004) by having annual sales of less then £5.6m and a balance sheet total of less than £2.8m. The exemption is not compulsory and having no audit may be a disadvantage: banks, financial institutions, customers and suppliers may rely on information from Companies House to assess creditworthiness and they are usually reassured by an independent audit. Limited companies must also provide copies of their annual accounts for the Inland Revenue and also generally provide a separate computation of their profit on which corporation tax is payable. The accounting profit of a Ltd company is adjusted for:

- various expenses that may not be allowable in computing taxable profit
- tax allowances that may be deducted in computing taxable profit.

Limited companies tend to be family businesses and smaller business with the ownership split among a few shareholders, although there have been many examples of very large private limited companies. The shares of Ltd companies may be bought and sold but they may not be offered for sale to the general public. Since ownership is usually with family and friends there is rarely a ready market for the shares and so their sale usually requires a valuation of the business.

Public limited companies (plc)

Public limited companies are designated as plc. A plc usually starts its life as a Ltd company and then becomes a plc by applying for a listing of its shares on the Stock Exchange or the Alternative Investment Market, and making a public offer for sale of shares in the company. Plcs must have a minimum issued share capital of (currently) £50,000. The offer for sale, dealt with by a financial institution and the company's legal representatives, is very costly. The formalities also include the re-drafting of the company's M and A, reflecting its status as a plc, registering the company and its director(s) with the Registrar of Companies, and registering the name of the plc.

The shareholders must appoint at least two directors of the company, who carry out the day-to-day management of the business, and a suitably qualified company secretary to ensure the plc's compliance with company law. A plc may only carry out the activities included in its M and A.

Plcs must regularly produce annual accounts, which they copy to their shareholders. They must also file a copy with the Registrar of Companies, and therefore the general public may have access to this information. The larger plcs usually provide printed glossy annual reports and accounts which they distribute to their shareholders and other interested parties. A plc's accounts must be audited by a suitably qualified accountant, unless it is exempt from this requirement by (currently) having annual sales of less then £5.6m and a balance sheet total of less than £2.8m. The same drawback applies to having no audit as applies with a Ltd company. Plcs must also provide copies of their annual accounts for the Inland Revenue and also generally provide a separate computation of their profit on which corporation tax is payable. The accounting profit of a plc is adjusted for:

- various expenses that may not be allowable in computing taxable profit
- tax allowances that may be deducted in computing taxable profit.

The shareholders provide the financing of the plc in the form of share capital and are therefore the owners of the business. The ownership of a plc can therefore be seen to be spread amongst many shareholders (individuals and institutions like insurance companies and pension funds), and the shares may be freely traded and bought and sold by the general public.

Worked Example 1.4

Ike Andoowit is in the process of planning the setting up of a new residential training centre.

Ike has discussed with a number of his friends the question of registering the business as a limited company, or being a sole trader. Most of Ike's friends have highlighted the advantages of limiting his liability to the original share capital that he would need to put into the company to finance the business. Ike feels a bit uneasy about the whole question and decides to obtain the advice of a professional accountant to find out:

(i)   the main disadvantages of setting up a limited company as opposed to a sole trader
(ii)   if Ike's friends are correct about the advantage of limiting one's liability
(iii)   what other advantages there are to registering the business as a limited company.

The accountant may answer Ike's questions as follows:

Setting up as a sole trader is a lot simpler and easier than setting up a limited company. A limited company is bound by the provisions of the Companies Act 1985 as amended by the Companies Act 1989, and for example, is required to have an independent annual audit. A limited company is required to be much more open about its affairs.

The financial structure of a limited company is more complicated than that of a sole trader. There are also additional costs involved in the setting up, and in the administrative functions of a limited company.

Running a business as a limited company requires registration of the business with the Registrar of Companies.

As Ike's friends have pointed out, the financial obligations of a shareholder in a limited company are generally restricted to the amount he/she has paid for his/her shares. In addition, the number of shareholders is potentially unlimited, which widens the scope for raising additional capital.

It should also be noted that:

- a limited company is restricted in its choice of business name
- if its annual sales exceed £1m, a limited company is required to hold an annual general meeting (AGM)
- any additional finance provided for a company by a bank is likely to require a personal guarantee from one or more shareholders.

Progress check 1.8 **There are some differences between those businesses that have been established as sole traders and those established as partnerships, and likewise there are differences between private limited companies and public limited companies. What are these differences, and what are the similarities?**

An introduction to financial statement reporting

Limited companies produce financial statements for each accounting period to provide adequate information about how the company has been doing. There are three main financial statements – balance sheet, profit and loss account (or income statement), and cash flow statement. Companies are also obliged to provide similar financial statements at each year end to provide information for their shareholders, the Inland Revenue, and the Registrar of Companies. This information is frequently used by City analysts, investing institutions and the public in general.

After each year end companies prepare their **annual report and accounts** for their shareholders.   ←
Copies of the annual report and accounts are filed with the Registrar of Companies and copies are available to other interested parties such as financial institutions, major suppliers and other investors. In addition to the profit and loss account and cash flow statement for the year and the balance sheet as at the year end date, the annual report and accounts includes notes to the accounts, and much more financial and non-financial information such as company policies, financial indicators, corporate governance compliance, directors' remuneration, employee numbers, business analysis, and segmental analysis. The annual report also includes an operating and financial review of the business, a report of the auditors of the company, and the chairman's statement.

The auditors' report states compliance or otherwise with accounting standards and that the accounts are free from material misstatement, and that they give a true and fair view prepared on the assumption that the company is a going concern. The chairman's statement offers an opportunity for the chairman of the company to report in unquantified and unaudited terms on the performance of the company during the past financial period and on likely future developments. However, the auditors would object if there was anything in the chairman's statement that was inconsistent with the audited accounts.

Progress check 1.9 What are the three main financial statements reported by a business? How are business transactions ultimately reflected in financial statements?

Worked Example 1.5

Gordon Brown soon settled into his graduate trainee role in the finance department of the large engineering group, and pursued his CIMA studies with enthusiasm. Although Gordon was more interested in business planning and getting involved with new development projects, his job and his studies required him to become totally familiar with, and to be able to prepare, the financial statements of a company. Gordon was explaining the subject of financial statements and what they involved to a friend of his, Jack, another graduate trainee in human resources. Where? – you've guessed it – over an after-work drink.

Gordon explained the subject of financial statements to Jack, bearing in mind that he is very much a non-financial person.

Limited companies are required to produce three main financial statements for each accounting period with information about company performance for:

- shareholders
- the Inland Revenue
- banks
- City analysts
- investing institutions
- the public in general.

The three key financial statements are the:

(a)   Balance sheet

(b)   Profit and loss account (or income statement)

(c)   Cash flow statement.

(a)   **Balance sheet:** a financial snapshot at a moment in time, or the financial position of the company comparable with pressing the 'pause' button on a DVD. The DVD in 'play' mode shows what is happening as time goes on second by second, but when you press 'pause' the DVD stops on a picture; the picture does not tell you what has happened over the period of time up to the pause (or what is going to happen after the pause). The balance sheet is the consequence of everything that has happened up to the balance sheet date. It does not explain how the company got to that position.

(b)   **Profit and loss account:** this is the DVD in 'play' mode. It is used to calculate whether or not the company has made a gain or deficit on its operations during the period, its financial performance, through producing and selling its goods or services. Net earnings or net profit is calculated from revenues derived throughout the period between two 'pauses', minus costs incurred in deriving those revenues.

(c)   **Cash flow statement:** this is the DVD again in 'play' mode, but net earnings is not the same as cash flow, since revenues and costs are not necessarily accounted for when cash transfers occur. Sales are accounted for when goods or services are delivered and accepted by the customer but cash may not be received until some time later. The profit and loss account does not reflect non-trading events like an issue of shares or a loan that will increase cash but are not revenues or costs. The cash flow statement summarises cash inflows and cash outflows and calculates the net change in the cash position for the company throughout the period between two 'pauses'.

Figure 1.6 Users of financial and accounting information

Users of accounting and financial information

Financial information is important to a wide range of groups both internal and external to the organisation. Such information is required, for example, by individuals outside the organisation to make decisions about whether or not to invest in one company or another, or by potential suppliers who wish to assess the reliability and financial strength of the organisation. It is also required by managers within the organisation as an aid to decision-making. The main users of financial information are shown in Fig. 1.6.

> **Progress check 1.10** How many users of financial information can you think of and in what ways do you think they may use this information?

Worked Example 1.6

Kevin Green, a trainee accountant, has recently joined the finance department of a newly formed public limited company. Kevin has been asked to work with the company's auditors who have been commissioned to prepare some alternative formats for the company's annual report.

As part of his preparation for this, Kevin's manager has asked him to prepare a draft report about who is likely to use the information contained in the annual report, and how they might use such information.

Kevin's preparatory notes for his report included the following:

- **Competitors** as part of their industry competitive analysis studies to look at market share, and financial strength
- **Customers** to determine the ability to provide a regular, reliable supply of goods and services, and to assess customer dependence
- **Employees** to assess the potential for providing continued employment and assess levels of remuneration
- **General public** to assess general employment opportunities, social, political and environmental issues, and to consider potential for investment
- **Government** VAT and corporate taxation, Government statistics, grants and financial assistance, monopolies and mergers
- **Investment analysts** investment potential for individuals and institutions with regard to past and future performance, strength of management, risk versus reward
- **Lenders** the capacity and the ability of the company to service debt and repay capital
- **Managers/directors** to a certain extent an aid to decision-making, but such relevant information should already have been available internally
- **Shareholders/investors** a tool of accountability to maintain a check on how effectively the directors/managers are running the business, to assess the financial strength and future developments
- **Suppliers** to assess the long-term viability and whether the company is able to meet its obligations and pay suppliers on an ongoing basis.

Accountability and financial reporting

When we talk about companies we are generally referring to limited companies, as distinct from sole traders and partnerships (or firms – although this term is frequently wrongly used to refer to companies). As we have discussed, limited liability companies have an identity separate from their owners, the shareholders, and the liability of shareholders is limited to the amount of money they have invested in the company, that is their shares in the company. Ownership of a business is separated from its stewardship, or management, by the shareholders' assignment to a board of directors the responsibility for running the company. The directors of the company are accountable to the shareholders, and both parties must play their part in making that accountability effective.

The directors of a limited company may comprise one or more professionally qualified accountants (usually including a finance director). The directors of the company necessarily delegate to middle managers and junior managers the responsibility for the day-to-day management of the business. It is certainly likely that this body of managers, who report to the board of directors, will include a further one or more qualified accountants responsible for managing the finance function.

Accountability is maintained by reporting on the financial performance and the financial position of the business to shareholders on both a yearly and an interim basis. The reporting made in the form of the financial statements includes the balance sheet, profit and loss account, and cash flow statement.

You may question why all the accounting regulation that we have discussed in the earlier sections of this chapter is necessary at all. Well, there are a number of arguments in favour of such regulation:

- It is very important that the credibility of financial statement reporting is maintained so that actual and potential investors are protected as far as possible against inappropriate accounting practices.
- Generally, being able to distinguish between the good and not so good companies also provides some stability in the financial markets.
- The auditors of companies must have some rules on which to base their true and fair view of financial position and financial performance, which they give to the shareholders and other users of the financial statements.

External auditors are appointed by, and report independently to, the shareholders. They are professionally qualified accountants who are required to provide objective verification to shareholders and other users that the financial statements have been prepared properly and in accordance with legislative and regulatory requirements; that they present the information truthfully and fairly; and that they conform to the best accounting practice in their treatment of the various measurements and valuations.

The audit is defined by the Auditing Practices Board (APB) as 'an independent examination of, and expression of an opinion on, the financial statements of the enterprise'. There is a requirement for all companies registered in the UK to have an annual audit, except for those companies that (currently) have an annual turnover of less than £5.6m and a balance sheet total of less than £2.8m.

The financial reporting of the company includes preparation of the financial statements, notes and reports, which are audited and given an opinion on by the external auditors. A regulatory framework exists to see fair play, the responsibility for which is held jointly by the Government, and the private sector, including the accountancy profession and the Stock Exchange.

The Government exercises influence through bodies such as the Department of Trade and Industry (DTI) and through Parliament by the enactment of legislation, for example the Companies Act. Such legal regulation began with the Joint Stock Companies Act of 1844.

Subsequent statutes exerted greater influence on company reporting: the Companies Acts 1948, 1967, and 1981. The provisions included in these Acts were consolidated into the Companies Act 1985, which was then amended in 1989. The Companies Act 1985, as amended in 1989, contains the overall current legal framework.

It may be argued that the increasing amount of accounting regulation itself stifles responses to changes in economic and business environments, and discourages the development of improved financial reporting. We have already seen that the development of various conceptual frameworks indicates that there is wide disagreement about what constitutes accounting best practice. The resistance to acceptance of international accounting standards may be for political reasons, the rules perhaps reflecting the requirements of specific interest groups or countries.

It is also true that despite increasing accounting regulation there have been an increasing number of well-publicised financial scandals in the USA in particular, where the accounting systems are very much 'rule-based', as well as in the UK, Italy, and Japan. However, these scandals have usually been the result of fraudulent activity. This leads to another question as to why the auditors of such companies did not detect or prevent such fraud. The answer is that, despite the widespread perception of the general public to the contrary, auditors are not appointed to detect or prevent fraud. Rather, they are appointed by the shareholders to give their opinion as to whether the financial statements show a true and fair view and comply with statutory, regulatory, and accounting and financial reporting standards requirements.

Progress check 1.11 In what ways may the reliability of financial reporting be ensured?

Worked Example 1.7

You are thinking of changing jobs (within marketing) and moving from a local, well-established retailer that has been in business for over 20 years. You have been asked to attend an interview at a new plc that started up around two years ago. The plc is a retailer via the Internet. Your family has suggested that you investigate the company thoroughly before your interview, paying particular attention to its financial resources. There is a chance the plc may not be a going concern if its business plan does not succeed.

You will certainly want to include the following questions at your interview.

(a) Are any published accounts available for review?
(b) What is the share capital of the company (for example, is it £10,000 or £1,000,000)?
(c) Is the company profitable?
(d) Does the company have loan commitments?
(e) Is the company working within its bank overdraft facilities?
(f) Are any press analyses of the company available?
(g) What is the current customer base?

The answers may suggest whether the company can continue trading for the foreseeable future.

Summary of key points

- The three main purposes of accounting are: to provide records of transactions and a score-card of results; to direct attention to problems; to evaluate the best ways of solving problems.
- Accountancy is the practice of accounting.
- Conceptual frameworks of accounting have been developed in many countries and the UK conceptual framework is embodied in the Statement of Principles (SOP).
- The framework of accounting is bounded by concepts (or rules) and standards, covering what data should be included within an accounting system and how that data should be recorded.
- International accounting standards have been developed, which should be adopted by listed companies within the European Union by 1 January 2005.
- The main branches of accounting within commercial and industrial organisations are financial accounting, management accounting, treasury management, financial management and corporate finance.
- The main services, in addition to accounting, that are provided by accountants to commercial and industrial organisations are auditing, corporate taxation, personal taxation, VAT advice, and consultancy.
- The large variety of types of business entity includes profit and not-for-profit organisations, both privately and Government owned, involved in providing products and services.
- The four main types of profit-making businesses in UK are sole traders, partnerships, limited companies (Ltd), and public limited companies (plc).
- Accounting processes follow a system of recording and classifying data, followed by a summarisation of financial information for subsequent interpretation and presentation.
- The three main financial statements that appear within a business's annual report and accounts, together with the chairman's statement, directors' report, and auditors' report, are the balance sheet, profit and loss account, and cash flow statement.
- There is a wide range of users of financial information external and internal to an organisation. External users include: potential investors; suppliers; financial analysts. Internal users include: managers; shareholders; employees.
- Accountability is maintained by the reporting to shareholders on a yearly and half-yearly basis of sales and other activities and profits or losses arising from those activities, and the audit function.

Assessment material

Questions

Q1.1   (i)   How many different types of business entity can you think of?

(ii)   In what respect do they differ fundamentally?

Q1.2   (i)   Why are accountants required to produce financial information?

(ii)   Who do they produce it for and what do they do with it?

Q1.3 Describe the broad regulatory, professional, and operational framework of accounting.

Q1.4 What are conceptual frameworks of accounting?

Q1.5 (i) What are accounting concepts?

    (ii) What purpose do they serve?

Q1.6 What is the UK Statement of Principles (SOP)?

Q1.7 (i) What is accountancy?

    (ii) What is an accountant?

    (iii) What do accountants do?

Q1.8 What do accountants mean by SSAPs and FRSs, and what are they for?

Q1.9 What are IASs and IFRSs and why are they important?

Q1.10 (i) What is financial management?

    (ii) How does financial management relate to accounting and perhaps other disciplines?

Q1.11 How do financial statements ensure accountability for the reporting of timely and accurate information to shareholders is maintained?

Discussion points

D1.1 The managing director of a large public limited company stated: 'I've built up my business over the past 15 years from a one man band to a large plc. As we grew we seemed to spend more and more money on accountants, financial managers, and auditors. During the next few months we are restructuring to go back to being a private limited company. This will be much simpler and we can save a fortune on accounting and auditing costs.' Discuss.

(Hint: You may wish to research Richard Branson and, for example, Virgin Air on the Internet, to provide some background for this discussion.)

D1.2 The managing director of a growing private limited company stated: 'All these accounting concepts and standards seem like a lot of red tape to me, and we've got financial accountants and management accountants as well as auditors. Surely all I need to know at the end of the day is how much have we made.' Discuss.

D1.3 Is accounting objective? Discuss with reference to at least six different accounting concepts.

Exercises

Exercises E1.1 to E1.10 require an essay-type approach. You should refer to the relevant sections in Chapter 1 to check your solutions.

Level I

E1.1 *Time allowed – 15 minutes*

Discuss the implications of preparation of the profit and loss account if there were no accounting concepts.

E1.2 *Time allowed – 30 minutes*

At a recent meeting of the local branch of the Women's Institute they had a discussion about what sort of organisation they were. The discussion broadened into a general debate about all types of organisation, and someone brought up the term 'business entity'. Although there were many opinions, there was little sound knowledge about what business entities are. Jane Cross said that her husband was an accountant and she was sure he wouldn't mind spending an hour one evening to enlighten them on the subject. Chris Cross fished out his text books to refresh his knowledge of the subject and came up with a schedule of all the different business entities he could think of together with the detail of their defining features and key points of difference and similarity.

Prepare the sort of schedule that Chris might have drafted for his talk and identify the category that the Women's Institute might fall into.

E1.3 *Time allowed – 30 minutes*

Mary Andrews was an accountant but is now semi-retired. She has been asked by her local comprehensive school careers officer to give a talk entitled 'What is an accountant and what is accounting, its use and its purpose?'

Prepare a list of bullet points that covers everything necessary for Mary to give a comprehensive and easy-to-understand presentation to a group of sixth formers at the school.

Level II

E1.4 *Time allowed – 30 minutes*

Accounting standards in general are reasonably clear and unambiguous.

Are there any major areas where accountants may disagree in balance sheet accounting?

E1.5 *Time allowed – 30 minutes*

Financial statements are produced each year by businesses, using prescribed formats.

Should major plcs be allowed to reflect their individuality in their own financial statements?

E1.6 *Time allowed – 45 minutes*

Professionals in the UK, for example, doctors, solicitors, accountants etc., normally work within partnerships. Many tradesmen, such as plumbers, car mechanics, carpenters, and so on, operate as sole traders. Software engineers seem to work for corporations and limited companies.

Consider the size of operation, range of products, financing, the marketplace, and the geographical area served, to discuss why companies like Microsoft and Yahoo should operate as plcs.

E1.7 *Time allowed – 60 minutes*

Bill Walsh has just been appointed Finance Director of a medium-sized engineering company, Nutsan Ltd, which has a high level of exports and is very sensitive to economic changes throughout the UK and the rest of the world. One of the tasks on Bill's action list is a review of the accounting and finance function.

What are the senior financial roles that Bill would expect to be in place and what are the important functions for which they should be responsible?

E1.8 *Time allowed – 60 minutes*

The Millennium Dome was opened to the general public in the UK for the year 2000 and was planned to close at the end of 2000 for the site to be used for some other purpose. There were problems financing the construction and the general day-to-day operations. There were many crises reported in the press during 2000. A proposed takeover of the site fell through in September 2000, with various reasons given by the potential acquirer.

You are required to research into the Dome using the BBC, *Financial Times* and the other serious newspapers, and the Internet, and summarise the financial aspects of the project that you gather. You should focus on the attitudes expressed by the general public, select committees of MPs, Government ministers, the Opposition, the Dome's management, and consider examples of bias, non-timeliness, and lack of transparency.

E1.9 *Time allowed – 60 minutes*

Conceptual frameworks of accounting have been developed over many years and in many countries.

Explain how these culminated in the publication of the UK Statement of Principles (SOP) in 1999, and discuss the implications of each of the eight chapters.

E1.10 *Time allowed – 60 minutes*

The International Accounting Standards Board (IASB) decreed the adoption of the International Financial Reporting Standards (IFRSs) by all listed companies within the European Union mandatory with effect from 1 January 2005.

Discuss the practical and political issues surrounding this decision.

2

Financial statements of limited companies – balance sheet

Contents

Learning objectives

Completion of this chapter will enable you to:

- explain the differences in accounting treatment of capital expenditure and revenue expenditure
- identify the financial information shown in the financial statements of a company: balance sheet; profit and loss account; cash flow statement
- construct simple financial statements
- outline the structure of the balance sheet of a limited company
- classify the broad balance sheet categories of shareholders' equity, liabilities, assets
- outline the alternative balance sheet formats
- prepare a balance sheet
- evaluate some of the alternative methods of asset valuation
- appreciate the limitations of the conventional balance sheet.

Introduction

We talked about business entities in general in Chapter 1. The financial accounting and reporting of limited companies are similar to those of sole traders and partnerships, except that they are more detailed and require a greater disclosure of information. This is to comply with current legislation and the requirements for reporting of financial information to the owners of the business (the shareholders).

Each type of business is required to prepare periodic financial statements in one form or another for internal control purposes, the shareholders and, for example, the Inland Revenue. The current chapter and Chapters 3 and 4 provide a comprehensive coverage of financial statements, which are the basis for the subsequent chapters about business performance analysis and published reports and accounts.

We will be looking in a little more detail at the profit and loss account in Chapter 3 and the balance sheet later in this chapter. Each of these financial statements includes expenditure of one form or another. This chapter begins by broadly looking at types of expenditure and explaining what is meant by revenue expenditure and capital expenditure. Most items may be clearly identified in terms of revenue or capital expenditure, but there are also a number of uncertain areas in these classifications with regard to the rules used in accounting and in the way that expenditure may be analysed for taxation purposes.

Before dealing specifically with the balance sheets of limited companies we will discuss the subject of financial statements that was introduced in Chapter 1. We will see how these are constructed and interrelated, by working through a comprehensive example that illustrates how transactions are reflected in the profit and loss account, balance sheet and cash flow statement of a business.

This chapter deals with how balance sheets are structured and how the accounts within the balance sheet are categorised. Each of the items within each of the balance sheet categories will be described in detail and form the basis to enable the preparation of a balance sheet of a limited company in the appropriate format.

The chapter closes by illustrating the subjective nature of the balance sheet and considers one of the areas in which this is apparent through looking at examples of the alternative methods for valuation of assets that are available to companies.

Capital expenditure and revenue expenditure

Expenditure made by an entity falls generally within two types:

- revenue expenditure
- capital expenditure.

Revenue expenditure relates to expenditure incurred in the manufacture of products, the provision of services or in the general conduct of the company, which is normally charged to the profit and loss account in the accounting period in which it is incurred or when the products and services are sold. This expenditure includes repairs and depreciation of fixed assets as distinct from the provision of these assets. Revenue expenditure relates to expenditure on those items where the full benefit is received within the normal accounting period. The accruals (matching) concept says that sales must be recognised in the period in which they are earned, and the costs incurred in achieving those sales must also be recognised in the same period. Therefore the costs of revenue expenditure appear under the appropriate headings within the profit and loss account of the period in which the benefits are consumed and the costs are therefore incurred.

In some circumstances expenditure, which would normally be treated as revenue expenditure, is not written off in one period. This is called deferred revenue expenditure and relates to, for example, extensive expenditure on an advertising campaign over a period of months.

Capital expenditure (not to be confused with share capital or capital account, which are something completely different) relates to the cost of acquiring, producing or enhancing fixed assets. Capital expenditure is extremely important because it is usually much higher in value and follows the appropriate authorisation of expenditure on items of plant or equipment, or on a specific project. Such expenditure is usually expected to generate future earnings for the entity, protect existing revenue or profit levels, or provide compliance with, for example, health and safety or fire regulation requirements. Capital expenditure does not necessarily relate directly to sales derived in the period that the expenditure was made. It relates to expenditure on those items where the benefit from them is received over a number of future accounting periods. Therefore, capital expenditure items are held and carried forward to subsequent accounting periods until such time as their costs must be matched with sales or other benefits derived from their use. Accordingly, such items should appear in the balance sheet under the heading fixed assets. The values of these items are reduced during each subsequent accounting period as the appropriate portions of their cost are charged to the profit and loss account to match the sales or other benefits deriving from their use. Receipts from the disposal of fixed assets also appear under the fixed assets heading in the balance sheet. They are not treated as sales in the profit and loss account.

Control over capital expenditure is maintained through procedures for authorisation and subsequent monitoring of capital expenditure. Capital expenditure proposals are formal requests for authority to incur capital expenditure. Organisations usually require capital expenditure proposals to be supported by detailed qualitative and quantitative justifications for the expenditure, in accordance with the company's capital investment criteria. Levels of authority for expenditure must be clearly defined. The reporting structure of actual expenditure must also be aligned with the appropriate authority levels.

In addition to the actual plant or equipment cost some revenue-type expenditure such as delivery and installation costs may also, where appropriate, be treated as capital expenditure. Such expenditure is described as being capitalised. In many circumstances revenue items must be capitalised as they are considered part of the acquisition cost, and in other circumstances revenue items may optionally be capitalised as part of the acquisition cost. In many circumstances it is not always possible to provide a clear ruling.

The general rule is that if the expenditure is as a result of: (a) a first-time acquisition, delivery, and commissioning of a fixed asset; or relates to (b) improving the asset from when it was first acquired, then it is capital expenditure. If the expenditure is neither of these two types then it is normally revenue expenditure. The following examples of expenditure illustrate some of the circumstances that may prompt the question 'is it revenue or capital expenditure?'.

Repairs are usually treated as revenue expenditure, but if, for example, some second-hand plant is purchased and some immediate repair costs are incurred necessary to make it efficient for the company's purpose, then such repairs become capital expenditure and are therefore added to the plant cost as part of the acquisition cost. Salaries and wages are revenue items. However, salaries and wages paid to employees to erect and fit some new machinery that has been acquired must be considered as an addition to the cost of the machinery.

Legal expenses are usually treated as revenue expenditure. But the legal expenses of conveyancing when purchasing a factory must be treated as part of the cost of the factory. Finance charges incurred during, say, the building of a factory or installation of plant and machinery may be capitalised so long as such a policy is applied consistently.

Apportionment of expenditure

Some items of expenditure require an apportionment of costs. This means that part of the cost is charged as capital expenditure and the balance is written off immediately as revenue expenditure. This is frequently the case within the uncertain area of improvements, alterations, and extensions to plant and buildings. Capitalisation of the whole may not be prudent, since the value of the plant or building may not be enhanced to anything near the amount of money that may have been spent. The prudent policy may be not to permanently capitalise any expenditure that is not represented by assets, although legally this may be acceptable.

You may question why the distinction between capital and revenue expenditure is so important. We have already touched on the prudence concept and the consistency concept. The matching concept requires a company to match income, sales or turnover, and costs as closely as possible to the time period to which they relate. If the expected life of a fixed asset acquired to generate income is, say, 5 years then the costs of that asset should be spread over 5 years to match the realisation of the income it generates. It is therefore important to ensure that all the costs associated with the acquisition, installation and commissioning of the asset are included as part of its capitalised cost.

The amount of corporation tax that a company must pay on the profits it has generated is not computed simply as a percentage of profit. Depending on the tax rules currently in force, many revenue items may be disallowable expenses so far as taxable profit is concerned. In a similar way the treatment of capital expenditure in terms of allowances against taxation also has an impact on the amount of tax payable by the company.

Worked Example 2.1

The following table illustrates how various items of expenditure are normally classified as either capital expenditure or revenue expenditure.

Revenue expenditure	**Capital expenditure**
Wages and salaries	Computer software
Interest payable	Goodwill
Travel expenses	Enhancement of a moulding machine
Repairs to the factory building	Patents
Professional fees	Office desk

Financial statements of limited companies

In Chapter 1 we introduced the topic of the financial statements that businesses need to prepare for each accounting period to provide adequate information about the financial performance and the financial position of the business.

We will now look in more detail at the three key financial statements (see Fig. 2.1): balance sheet, profit and loss account (or income statement), and cash flow statement.

Balance sheet

The balance sheet summarises the financial position of the business; it is a financial snapshot at a moment in time. It may be compared to looking at a DVD. In 'play' mode the DVD is showing what is happening as time goes on second by second. If you press 'pause' the DVD stops on a picture. The picture does not tell you what has happened over the period of time up to the pause (or what is going to happen after the pause). The balance sheet is the financial position of the company at the 'pause' position. It is the consequence of everything that has happened up to that time. It does not explain how the company got to that position, it just shows the results of financial impacts of events and decisions up to the balance sheet date. The year end may be 31 December, but other dates may be chosen. A company's year end date is (normally) the same date each year.

The balance sheet comprises a number of categories, within the three main elements (see Fig. 2.2), which are labelled **assets**, **liabilities** or shareholders' equity (usually referred to as just

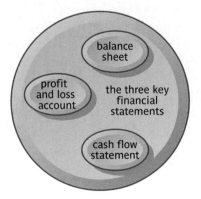

Figure 2.1 The three key financial statements

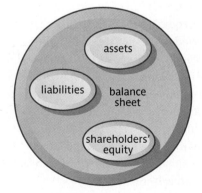

Figure 2.2 The main elements of the balance sheet

equity). The assets are debit balances and the liabilities and shareholders' equity are credit balances. (Note: the concepts of debit and credit, and double-entry bookkeeping are fully covered in Appendix 1.) The balance sheet is always in balance so that

$$\text{total assets (TA)} = \text{equity (E)} + \text{total liabilities (TL)}$$

The balance sheet is a summary of the **general ledger** in which the total assets equal the shareholders' equity plus total liabilities.

If the balance sheet is the financial snapshot at a moment in time – the 'pause' on the DVD – the two other financial statements are the equivalent of what is going on throughout the accounting period – the 'play' mode on the DVD.

Profit and loss account

The profit and loss account and income statement are two terms that really mean the same thing. Profit (or loss) may be considered in two ways, which both give the same result.

The profit and loss account shows the change in wealth of the business over a period. The wealth of the business is the amount it is worth to the owners, the shareholders. The accumulation of the total change in wealth since the business began, up to a particular point in time, is reflected within the equity section of the balance sheet under the heading 'retained profits'. The profit and loss account measures the change in the balance sheet from one 'pause' to another. An increase in equity is a profit and a decrease in equity is a loss.

The profit and loss account may also be considered in its measurement of the trading performance of the business (see Fig. 2.3). The profit and loss account calculates whether or not the company has made a profit or loss on its operations during the period, through producing and selling its goods or services. The result, the net earnings or **net profit** (or loss), is derived from deducting expenses incurred from revenues derived throughout the period between two 'pauses'. The profit and loss account is dealt with in detail in Chapter 3.

The total of the expenses (debits) and revenues (credits) accounts within the general ledger comprise the profit and loss account. The total of these may be a net debit or a net credit. A net debit represents a loss and a net credit represents a profit. The net profit or loss is reflected in the balance sheet of the business under the heading 'retained profits', which is part of 'shareholders' equity'. All the other accounts within the general ledger, other than expenses and revenues, may be summarised into various other non-profit and loss account categories and these represent all the other balances that complete the overall balance sheet of the business.

There are three main points to consider regarding the profit and loss account and how it differs from the cash flow statement. First, revenues (or **sales** or income) and expenses (or costs or expenditure) are not necessarily accounted for when cash transfers occur. Sales are normally accounted for when goods or services are delivered and accepted by the customer. Cash will rarely be received immediately from the customer, except in businesses like high-street retailers and supermarkets; it is normally received weeks or months later.

Second, the profit and loss account does not take into account all the events that impact on the financial position of the company. For example, an issue of new **shares** in the company, or a loan to the company, will increase cash but they are neither revenue nor expenses.

Third, non-cash flow items, for example depreciation and bad debts, reduce the profit, or increase the loss, of the company but do not represent outflows of cash. These topics will be covered in detail in the next chapter.

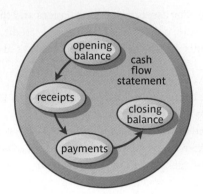

Figure 2.3 The main elements of the profit and loss account   **Figure 2.4** The main elements of the cash flow statement

Therefore it can be seen that net profit is not the same as cash flow. A company may get into financial difficulties if it suffers a severe **cash** shortage even though it may have positive net earnings (profit).

Cash flow statement

Between them, the balance sheet and profit and loss account show a company's financial position at the beginning and at the end of an accounting period and how the profit or loss has been achieved during that period.

The balance sheet and profit and loss account do not show or directly analyse some of the key changes that have taken place in the company's financial position, for example:

- How much capital expenditure (for example, equipment, machinery and buildings) has the company made, and how did it fund the expenditure?
- What was the extent of new borrowing and how much **debt** was repaid?
- How much did the company need to fund new **working capital** (which includes, for example, an increase in **debtors** and **stock** requirements as a result of more business activity)?
- How much of the company's funding was met by funds generated from its trading activities, and how much by new external funding (for example, from banks and other lenders, or new shareholders)?

The profit and loss account and the cash flow statement (see Fig. 2.4) are the two 'DVDs' which are running in parallel between the two 'pauses' – the balance sheets at the start and the finish of an accounting period. However, the cash flow statement goes further in answering the questions like those shown above. The aim of the cash flow statement is to summarise the cash inflows and outflows and calculate the net change in the cash position for the company throughout the period between two 'pauses'.

> **Progress check 2.1** Explain the fundamental differences between the types of information presented in each of the three key financial statements.

Construction and use of financial statements

An example will best illustrate how financial statements may be constructed. We will use the example of Mr Bean's business, Ayco (see also Example A1.1, Appendix 1), to track how some simple transactions are reflected in the profit and loss account, cash flow statement, and balance sheet.

Worked Examples 2.2 to 2.5 will look at the four one-week periods during Ayco's first month of trading and show the profit and loss account reflecting the trading transactions of the business. The result, the change in wealth of the business, is shown as the resources held at the end of each period and reflected in the balance sheet. The example will show the cash flow statement as movements in cash and changes to the cash balance, which is reflected in the balance sheet that gives a summary of the financial position of the company at the end of each period.

Worked Example 2.2

Mr Bean decides to set up a wholesale business, Ayco, on 1 January 2005. He has his own cash resources for the purpose of setting up the business and has estimated that an initial £50,000 would be required for this purpose. During the first four-week period in business, January 2005, **Ayco** will enter into the following transactions:

		£
Week 1	Receipt of cheque from Mr Bean	50,000
Week 1	Purchase for cash the freehold of a shop	30,000
Week 1	Purchase for cash the shop fittings	5,000
Week 2	Cash paid for printing and stationery used	200
Week 3	Purchases of stock, from Beeco Ltd, of Aymen toys, payable two months later (12,000 toys at £1 each)	12,000
Week 3	Sales of Aymen toys to Ceeco Ltd for cash (1,000 toys at £2 each)	2,000
Week 4	Sales of Aymen toys to Deeco Ltd, receivable one month later (8,000 toys at £2 each)	16,000

		Week 1 £	Total £
Profit and loss account	Sales	0	0
	Cost of sales	0	0
	Gross profit	0	0
	Expenses	0	0
	Profit/(loss)	0	0
	Cumulative profit/(loss)	0	0
Cash flow statement	Opening balance	0	0
	Cash received ex Mr Bean	50,000	50,000
	Cash received from customers	0	0
	Cash paid for shop freehold	(30,000)	(30,000)

Balance sheet	Cash paid for shop fittings	(5,000)	(5,000)
	Cash paid for stationery	0	0
	Closing balance	15,000	15,000
	Cash closing balance	15,000	15,000
	Freehold shop	30,000	30,000
	Shop fittings	5,000	5,000
	Stocks	0	0
	Debtors	0	0
	Creditors	0	0
	Total wealth	50,000	50,000
	Represented by:		
	Mr Bean's original capital	50,000	50,000
	Profit/(loss) to date	0	0
	Total capital	50,000	50,000

The statement above shows that no trading took place during the first week of January. Mr Bean paid £50,000 of his personal funds into the bank account of Ayco, representing his capital invested in Ayco. The company immediately used £35,000 of this to purchase the freehold of a shop together with shop fittings.

We can summarise the financial position at the end of the first week as follows:

■ There was neither a profit nor a loss.

■ Cash has been increased by Mr Bean's capital invested, less payments for the shop and fittings, to give a closing cash (bank) balance of £15,000.

■ The wealth of the business at the end of the first week was Mr Bean's original capital of £50,000. Wealth had not been increased or decreased as there was no profit or loss.

The wealth was represented by the shop, its fittings, and the closing bank balance. Totals for the month to date are of course the same as for week 1.

Let's look at the subsequent three weeks' accounting periods, one week at a time, beginning with week 2.

Worked Example 2.3

		Week 1	Week 2	Total
		£	£	£
Profit and loss account	Sales	0	0	0
	Cost of sales	0	0	0
	Gross profit	0	0	0
	Expenses	0	(200)	(200)

	Profit/(loss)	0	(200)	(200)
	Cumulative profit/(loss)	0	(200)	(200)
Cash flow statement	Opening balance	0	15,000	0
	Cash received ex Mr Bean	50,000	0	50,000
	Cash received from customers	0	0	0
	Cash paid for shop freehold	(30,000)	0	(30,000)
	Cash paid for shop fittings	(5,000)	0	(5,000)
	Cash paid for stationery	0	(200)	(200)
	Closing balance	15,000	14,800	14,800
Balance sheet	Cash closing balance	15,000	14,800	14,800
	Freehold shop	30,000	30,000	30,000
	Shop fittings	5,000	5,000	5,000
	Stocks	0	0	0
	Debtors	0	0	0
	Creditors	0	0	0
	Total wealth	50,000	49,800	49,800
	Represented by:			
	Mr Bean's original capital	50,000	50,000	50,000
	Profit/(loss) to date	0	(200)	(200)
	Total capital	50,000	49,800	49,800

We can summarise the financial position at the end of the second week as follows:

- There was still no trading but printing and stationery had been used, and there was a charge for their expense to the profit and loss account, therefore there was a loss for the week. The cumulative two weeks is obtained by adding across each line in the profit and loss account, which is also the sum of the totals, to give a cumulative two-week loss of £200.
- Cash was reduced in week 2 by the cash paid for printing and stationery expenses to give a closing balance of £14,800. It can be seen that the two-week cumulative cash position is calculated by starting with the week 1 opening balance and then adding across all the payment and receipt elements. The sum of the total column will give the same closing balance as that shown for week 2.
- The wealth of the business at the end of the second week was Mr Bean's original capital reduced by the cumulative loss of £200 to give £49,800. The wealth was represented by the shop, its fittings, and the closing bank balance.

Note that the cumulative balance sheet at the end of week 2 is exactly the same as that shown in the week 2 column and not the totals of each of the elements added across in weeks 1 and 2. This is always true for however many weeks or any other period we may be looking at, which is what we would expect since the balance sheet does show the financial position at a point in time, in this example the position at the end of week 2.

Progress check 2.2 How can a business have made a loss during an accounting period if it hasn't been involved in any trading during the period?

Worked Example 2.4

Let's now look at accounting period week 3.

		Week 1	Week 2	Week 3	Total
		£	£	£	£
Profit and loss account	Sales	0	0	2,000	2,000
	Cost of sales	0	0	(1,000)	(1,000)
	Gross profit	0	0	1,000	1,000
	Expenses	0	(200)	0	(200)
	Profit/(loss)	0	(200)	1,000	800
	Cumulative profit/(loss)	0	(200)	800	800
Cash flow statement	Opening balance	0	15,000	14,800	0
	Cash received ex Mr Bean	50,000	0	0	50,000
	Cash received from customers	0	0	2,000	2,000
	Cash paid for shop freehold	(30,000)	0	0	(30,000)
	Cash paid for shop fittings	(5,000)	0	0	(5,000)
	Cash paid for stationery	0	(200)	0	(200)
	Closing balance	15,000	14,800	16,800	16,800
Balance sheet	Cash closing balance	15,000	14,800	16,800	16,800
	Freehold shop	30,000	30,000	30,000	30,000
	Shop fittings	5,000	5,000	5,000	5,000
	Stocks	0	0	11,000	11,000
	Debtors	0	0	0	0
	Creditors	0	0	(12,000)	(12,000)
	Total wealth	50,000	49,800	50,800	50,800
	Represented by:				
	Mr Bean's original capital	50,000	50,000	50,000	50,000
	Profit/(loss) to date	0	(200)	800	800
	Total capital	50,000	49,800	50,800	50,800

We can summarise the financial position at the end of the third week as follows:

- There was some trading, which gave a profit for the week of £1,000. The cumulative three weeks is obtained by adding across each line in the profit and loss account, which is also the sum of the totals, to give a cumulative three-week profit of £800.

- Cash was increased in week 3 by the cash received from customers, and with no cash payments the closing balance was £16,800. It can be seen that the three-week cumulative cash position is calculated by starting with the week 1 opening balance and then adding across all the payment and receipt elements. The sum of the total column will give the same closing balance as that shown for week 3.
- The wealth of the business at the end of the third week was Mr Bean's original capital increased by the cumulative profit of £800 to give £50,800. The wealth was represented by the shop, its fittings, the closing bank balance, plus stocks less creditors (two new categories introduced in this example). The first category is stocks. Stocks had been purchased in the month, but had been reduced by the amount used in trading. The second new category is the result of the purchase of stock for £12,000, which had not yet been paid out in cash but nevertheless was a claim against the company. This claim is an amount due to be paid to suppliers, or creditors of the business, and therefore a reduction in the wealth of the company.

The amount of stocks used in trading to provide the sales of £2,000 is called **cost of sales**, which in this example is £1,000. Note again that the cumulative balance sheet at the end of week 3 is exactly the same as that shown in the week 3 column and not the totals added across each of the elements in weeks 1, 2 and 3.

Worked Example 2.5

Let's now look at the final accounting period, week 4.

		Week 1 £	Week 2 £	Week 3 £	Week 4 £	Total £
Profit and loss account	Sales	0	0	2,000	16,000	18,000
	Cost of sales	0	0	(1,000)	(8,000)	(9,000)
	Gross profit	0	0	1,000	8,000	9,000
	Expenses	0	(200)	0	0	(200)
	Profit/(loss)	0	(200)	1,000	8,000	8,800
	Cumulative profit/ (loss)	0	(200)	800	8,800	8,800
Cash flow statement	Opening balance	0	15,000	14,800	16,800	0
	Cash received ex Mr Bean	50,000	0	0	0	50,000
	Cash received from customers	0	0	2,000	0	2,000
	Cash paid for shop freehold	(30,000)	0	0	0	(30,000)
	Cash paid for shop fittings	(5,000)	0	0	0	(5,000)

	Cash paid for stationery	0	(200)	0	0	(200)
	Closing balance	15,000	14,800	16,800	16,800	16,800
Balance sheet	Cash closing balance	15,000	14,800	16,800	16,800	16,800
	Freehold shop	30,000	30,000	30,000	30,000	30,000
	Shop fittings	5,000	5,000	5,000	5,000	5,000
	Stocks	0	0	11,000	3,000	3,000
	Debtors	0	0	0	16,000	16,000
	Creditors	0	0	(12,000)	(12,000)	(12,000)
	Total wealth	50,000	49,800	50,800	58,800	58,800
	Represented by:					
	Mr Bean's original capital	50,000	50,000	50,000	50,000	50,000
	Profit/(loss) to date	0	(200)	800	8,800	8,800
	Total capital	50,000	49,800	50,800	58,800	58,800

We can summarise the final financial position at the end of the fourth week as follows:

■ There was further trading, which gave a profit for the week of £8,000. The cumulative four weeks is obtained by adding across each line in the profit and loss account, which is also the sum of the totals, to give a cumulative four-week profit of £8,800.

■ No cash was received or paid during week 4, and so the closing balance remained at £16,800. It can be seen that the four-week cumulative cash position is calculated by starting with the week 1 opening balance and then adding across all the payment and receipt elements. The sum of the total column will give the same closing balance as that shown for week 4.

■ The wealth of the business at the end of the fourth week was Mr Bean's original capital increased by the cumulative profit of £8,800 to give £58,800. The wealth was represented by the shop, its fittings, closing bank balance, stock, less creditors, and now another additional element: debtors. Sales of £16,000 had been made in the month, none of which had been paid in cash. The amount remaining due from customers, the debtors of the company, at the end of the week was £16,000 which represented an element of the wealth of Ayco. The stock used for those sales had reduced the stock from the end of the previous week £11,000 to £3,000 at the end of week 4.

Note again that the cumulative balance sheet at the end of week 4 is exactly the same as that shown in the week 4 column and not the totals of each of the elements added across in weeks 1, 2, 3 and 4.

Progress check 2.3 **Why is there usually a difference between profit and cash in an accounting period?**

Examples 2.2 to 2.5 introduced a number of terms relating to financial statements. Whilst they gave an introduction to the principles and put things in context they were by no means exhaustive. In this chapter and the next two, we will consider each of the financial statements in more detail, beginning with the balance sheet.

What does the balance sheet tell us?

In theory the balance sheet of a private limited company or a public limited company should be able to tell us all about the company's financial structure and liquidity – the extent to which its assets and liabilities are held in cash or in a near cash form (for example, bank accounts and deposits). It should also tell us about the assets held by the company, the proportion of **current assets** and the extent to which they may be used to meet current obligations. In later chapters we will look at many of the important ratios used to evaluate the strength of a company's balance sheet. We will also see how the balance sheet tells us about the financial structure of companies and the sources of such financing.

An element of caution should be noted in analysing balance sheet information. The balance sheet is an historical document. It may have looked entirely different six months or a year ago, or even one week ago. There is not always consistency between the information included in one company's balance sheet with that of another company. Two companies even within the same industry are usually very difficult to compare. Added to that, very often different analysts use the same ratios in different ways.

We will look at some of the variety of methods used to value the various items contained in the balance sheet. However, in addition to the wide choice of valuation methods, the information in a typical published balance sheet does not tell us anything about the quality of the assets, their real value in money terms or their value to the business.

'**Off balance sheet financing**' and '**window dressing**' are two terms that often crop up in discussions about the accuracy of balance sheet information. The former relates to the funding of operations in such a way that the relevant assets and liabilities are not disclosed in the balance sheet of the company concerned. The latter is a **creative accounting** practice in which changes in short-term funding have the effect of disguising or improving the reported liquidity (cash and near cash) position of the reporting organisation.

Structure of the balance sheet

Assets are acquired by a business to generate future benefits, for example from trading or whatever activities the business has been set up to provide. To acquire assets the business must first raise the necessary funds. In doing so the claims or obligations are created in the form of shareholders' equity or liabilities.

Shareholders' equity and both long-term and **current liabilities** represent claims, or obligations, on the company to provide cash or other benefits to a third party. Equity, or capital, represents a claim by the owners, or shareholders, of the business against the business.

Liabilities represent claims by persons other than the owners of the business, against the business. These claims arise from transactions relating to the provision of goods or services, or lending money to the business.

An example of a balance sheet format adopted by a limited company, Flatco plc, is shown in Fig. 2.5. It is shown in what is termed an horizontal format in order to illustrate the grouping of the assets categories, the total of which equal the total of the liabilities and equity categories. UK companies invariably adopt the vertical format (see Fig. 2.7), rather than the horizontal format balance sheet, which we shall discuss in a later section of this chapter.

Flatco plc
Balance sheet as at 31 December 2005

Figures in £000

	Assets			Liabilities		
	Fixed assets			**Capital and reserves** (shareholders' equity)		
operational	Intangible	416		Capital	1,200	financial
operational	Tangible	1,884		Premiums	200	financial
operational	Financial	248		Profit and loss account	1,594	financial
			2,548			2,994
				Long-term liabilities (over one year)		
				Financial debt	173	financial
				Creditors	154	operational
				Provisions	222	operational
						549
	Current assets			**Current liabilities** (less than one year)		
operational	Stocks	311				
operational	Debtors	573		Financial debt	50	financial
operational	Prepayments	589		Creditors	553	operational
financial	Cash	327		Accruals	202	operational
			1,800			805
			4,348			4,348

Figure 2.5 A typical horizontal balance sheet format showing the balancing of assets with liabilities

The detail of each of the categories within the balance sheet will be explained in the sections that follow. As we have shown in Fig. 2.5, each balance sheet category, both assets and liabilities, may be described as either financial or operational. Capital and **reserves** and financial debt are financial resources, whereas **fixed assets**, stocks, debtors, **prepayments**, long-term liabilities and short-term liabilities are operational, relating to the manufacturing, commercial and administrative activities of the company. Cash, which is also financial, represents the temporary difference between the financial resources and its uses.

We will now look at each of the balance sheet categories in detail, beginning with shareholders' equity and liabilities.

Capital and reserves or shareholders' equity

Shareholders' equity is usually simply called 'equity'. It represents the total investment of the shareholders in the company, the total wealth. Equity comprises capital, premiums, and retained earnings. The cost of shareholders' equity is generally regarded as the **dividends** paid to shareholders, the level of which is usually dependent on how well the company has performed during the year.

Capital

The nominal value of a share is the value of each share, decided at the outset by the promoters of the company. The nominal value is the same for each of the shares and may be, for example, 25p, 50p, or

£1 (the usual maximum). The initial **share capital** is the number of shares in the company multiplied by the nominal value of the shares (for example, 2 million shares at 50p per share is £1,000,000, or at £1 per share is £2,000,000). Each share is a title of ownership on the assets of the company. This is an important issue in respect of control and growth of the company.

Worked Example 2.6

Arthur King is setting up a small limited company, Round Table Ltd, for which he needs initial capital of £10,000. Arthur creates 100 shares each having a nominal value of £100. Arthur decides to start off as king of his empire and keep 90% of the shares for himself and so buys 90 shares at £100 each and pays £9,000 out of his personal account into the bank account of the new company, Round Table Ltd. The remaining 10 shares are purchased by ten of Arthur's friends, each for £100. Arthur owns 90% of the company, and each friend owns 1% of the company, has 1% of the voting rights at shareholders' meetings and will receive 1% of dividends paid by the company.

Round Table Ltd does well and after some time Arthur considers that he needs additional capital of a further £10,000 to fund its growth. Arthur may issue 100 new shares at £100 each.

We may discuss the implications for Arthur if he is unable to afford any additional shares himself and the new shares are sold to new investors. The total number of shares will become 200 of which he will own 90, that is 45%.

Because Arthur will have less than 50% of the shares we may say that he therefore loses control of the company. There are two main considerations regarding the issue of shares and control.

The first point is that the founder of a growing business must face a difficult dilemma: growing, but losing control, or keeping control but losing growth opportunities. An alternative may be to go to the bank and fund growth with a loan. However, along with this goes a vulnerability to failure at the first cash crisis the company may face.

The second point is that the issue of new shares at the same price as the existing original shares may be considered unfair. When Round Table Ltd was created it was worth only the money that the original shareholders invested in it. The company's credibility has now been built up through successful operations and an understanding of the market. Surely this must have a value so that the new share issue should be made at a higher price? The difference in price between the original nominal value and the price new investors will have to pay is the share premium.

Premiums

The **share premium** may be best illustrated with an example.

Worked Example 2.7

Using the company in Worked Example 2.6, let's assume that for potential investors the value of one share is now £400. This means that 25 shares of £400 would be needed to raise additional capital of £10,000.

We will look at how these new shares should appear in the company's balance sheet.

(i)   These new shares cannot appear in the balance sheet with a nominal value of £400 because it would then mean that legally the shareholders would have voting and dividend rights four times those of the £100 nominal shares.

(ii)   The capital in the balance sheet will need to be increased by 25 × £100, the nominal value of the shares, that is £2,500.

(iii) A new category, share premiums, is required on the balance sheet.

(iv)   Share premiums will have a value of 25 × (£400 – £100), that is £7,500.

Retained earnings

Retained earnings is the final element within the equity of the company. The profit or net earnings generated from the operations of the company belongs to the shareholders of the company. It is the shareholders who decide how much of those earnings are distributed to shareholders as dividends, the balance being held and reinvested in the business. The retained earnings of the company are increased by the annual net profit less any dividends payable; they are part of the shareholders' wealth and therefore appear within the equity of the company. Similarly, any losses will reduce the retained earnings of the company.

Liabilities

Current, or short-term, liabilities

Short-term liabilities are items that are expected to become payable within one year from the balance sheet date. These comprise trade **creditors** (or accounts payable) within one year, financial debts, **accruals**, tax, and dividends.

Short-term financial debt

Short-term financial debts are the elements of overdrafts, loans and leases that are payable within one year of the balance sheet date.

Trade creditors or accounts payable

Whereas there is a cost associated with equity and financial debt in the form of dividends and interest payable, creditors are sometimes considered 'free' of such cost. This, however, is not really true. Creditors payable within one year comprise taxes, national insurance, VAT, etc. as well as accounts payable to suppliers of materials, goods and services provided to the company. Accounts payable, for example, are not free debt.

Worked Example 2.8

A supplier may offer to a company payment terms of three months from delivery date.

We will look at the effect of the company proposing to the supplier payment terms of two months from delivery date, for which the supplier may for example offer 1% or 2% early settlement discount.

A discount of 1% for settlement one month early is equivalent to over 12% per annum. Consequently, it becomes apparent that the supplier's selling price must have included some allowance for financial charges; accounts payable to suppliers are therefore not a free debt.

Accruals

Accruals are allowances made for costs and expenses incurred and payable within one year of the balance sheet date but for which no invoices have yet been processed through the accounts. This is in line with the matching (or accruals) concept we discussed in Chapter 1. Expense recognition is an important concept. Expenses should be recognised immediately they are known about. Accruals are treated in a similar way to payables but the invoices for these charges have not yet been processed by the entity. They are charges or expenses, which are brought into the period because, although goods (or services) have been provided, they have not yet been included in the supplier's accounts. Some examples are telephone and electricity charges which are incurred but for which invoices may not normally be received until the end of each quarter. On the other hand, revenues or profits should not be recognised until they are earned.

Worked Example 2.9

We know that in the Ayco example the business had used and had been invoiced for and paid for £200 worth of stationery. If we assume, for example, that more than £200 worth of stationery had been used in the month of January, say £1,000, we can consider:

(i)   What would be the impact on Ayco if £500 worth of the additional stationery had been used, and an invoice had been received but not processed through the ledgers?

(ii)   What would be the impact on Ayco if £300 worth of the additional stationery had been used, and an invoice had not yet been received but was still in the mail?

Both amounts would have to be charged to printing and stationery expenses for a total of £800. The balancing entries that would have to be made would be to credit a total of £800 to accruals. Ayco knew they had used stationery for which there was a cost even though an invoice may not have been processed.

The net impact of the above on Ayco would have been a reduction in profit, a debit of £800 and an increase in liabilities, a credit of £800 to accruals.

Long-term liabilities

Long-term liabilities are items that are expected to become payable after one year from the balance sheet date. These comprise long-term trade creditors (or accounts payable), financial debt, and **provisions.**

Long-term financial debt

Long-term financial debts are the elements of loans and leases that are payable after one year of the balance sheet date. To help the company finance its operations it may take on further debt – financial debt for a limited period of time. The company has to pay interest on financial debt, over the period of the loan, regardless of how well or not the company performs, that is, regardless of whether it has made a profit or a loss.

Financial debt, provided by various financial institutions such as banks, may take the form of over-drafts, loans, **debentures** and leases. Interest rates vary according to the risk of the investment. The level of interest payable, and thus the choice of which type of debt the company may wish to take on, will be determined by how risky the potential lender regards this particular company.

A banker or investor may wish to invest in Government securities, which are risk free, and receive the low rate of return offered by such investments. For a company, which is not risk free, the investor will expect a higher rate of interest as an incentive or compensation for the risk being taken. The higher the risk of a security, the higher the expected rate of return (see Fig. 2.6).

The difference between the interest rate paid on Government securities and the interest rate that a company pays on loans is called the risk premium. Shareholders' equity is even riskier than shorter-term corporate debt (for example, a loan made to the company). Therefore, the company should not only make a profit but the level of profit should be such that the shareholders get a return in line with their level of risk. This should be the return on Government securities plus a risk premium which is even higher than the risk premium payable on the corporate debt.

Long-term trade creditors or accounts payable

Creditors payable after one year mainly comprise accounts payable to suppliers of goods and services provided to the company that may typically, for example, relate to capital projects taking place over an extended period.

Provisions

Provisions are amounts charged against profit to provide for an expected liability or loss even though

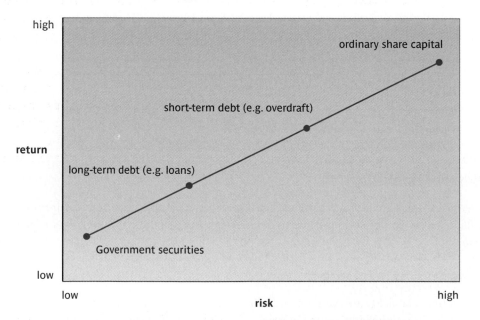

Figure 2.6 An illustration of the relationship between risk and return

the amount or date of the liability or loss is uncertain. This is in line with the prudence concept we discussed in Chapter 1.

Progress check 2.4 Which of the following do you think may be classified as liabilities or shareholders' equity within a balance sheet, and under which headings should they appear?

- bank overdraft
- computer
- five-year bank loan

- accruals

- amounts owed to suppliers
- ordinary shares
- amounts owed by customers

Assets

We have seen that assets are acquired by a business to generate future benefits, for example from trading or whatever activities the business has been set up to provide. In addition to providing benefits from transactions, accounting assets have a number of other characteristics. Assets must be capable of being measured in monetary units; the business must have exclusive control over such assets.

The assets side of the balance sheet is more homogeneous than the equity and liabilities side of the balance sheet. The liabilities side of the balance sheet generally describes where the financing comes from, whereas the assets side generally represents how the money has been used.

Fixed assets

Fixed assets include land and buildings, equipment, machinery, furniture, fittings, computers, software, and motor vehicles, which the company has purchased to enable it to meet its strategic objectives. They have a very important common feature, namely that they are not renewed within the **operating cycle**, which is normally measured in months, weeks, days, or even hours. The operating cycle is the period of time between the point at which cash starts to be spent on production, and the collection of cash from customers who have been supplied with finished product. Fixed assets last longer, and in most cases much longer, than one year.

A building may have a life of twenty years, whereas a personal computer may have a life of three years, both being longer than the cycle in which raw materials and packaging are renewed, for example. Regardless of this, fixed assets are 'consumed' on a day-to-day basis. The measure of this consumption or wearing out, or other loss of value of these assets, whether arising from use, passage of time or obsolescence through technology or market changes, is called depreciation.

Fixed assets are comprised of tangible fixed assets, **intangible fixed assets**, and financial assets (or long-term investments).

Tangible fixed assets

These are the assets that one can touch, for example land, buildings, equipment, machinery, computers, fixtures and fittings.

Intangible fixed assets

These are all the other fixed assets, except for investments in **subsidiary companies**, and include software, patents, trademarks, and **goodwill**.

Balance sheet formats

The summary balance sheet that we saw in Fig. 2.5 is known as the horizontal format. Although now rarely used in practice within businesses, it was a conventional format in which assets are shown in one column and liabilities (and equity) in the other column. Such a presentation clearly illustrated how total assets equalled the total of liabilities (and equity).

The horizontal balance sheet format can be represented by the equation

$$\text{total assets (TA)} = \text{equity (E)} + \text{total liabilities (TL)}$$
$$TA = E + TL$$

or

$$\text{fixed assets (FA)} + \text{current assets (CA)}$$
$$= \text{equity (E)} + \text{long-term liabilities (LTL)} + \text{current liabilities (CL)}$$
$$FA + CA = E + LTL + CL$$

An alternative, more commonly used format is the vertical format. The vertical format simply rearranges the above equation to become

$$FA + (CA - CL) - LTL = E$$

Each element in the equation is represented vertically with total assets less total liabilities equal to, or represented by, the equity of the company.

Using the data from Fig. 2.5 the balance sheet for Flatco plc is shown in a vertical format in Fig. 2.7. The vertical format balance sheet has some advantages over the horizontal format. It shows a balance sheet total, that is the equity, or total capital, of the business; it is the total wealth that is represented by the **net assets** of the business. A balance sheet is probably easier to read down the page rather than across, and the vertical format does clearly highlight each of the main sections of the balance sheet.

The Companies Act requires comparative figures for the previous year for each line in the balance sheet (not shown in the Flatco plc balance sheet example). These are normally shown in a column to the right of the current year's figures.

In Appendix 1, the concept of the **trial balance**, and its links with the profit and loss account and balance sheet are examined in detail. Worked Example 2.11 uses the trial balance of Perfecto Ltd to identify the various categories of assets, and liabilities and equity (the debits and the credits).

Worked Example 2.11

The balances extracted from the trial balance of Perfecto Ltd at 30 September 2005 are presented in an alphabetical list:

	£000
Accruals	100
Bank and cash balances	157
Creditors due within one year	277
Creditors due after one year	77
Debtors	284
Intangible fixed assets	203

Long-term loans	85
Prepaid expenses and accrued income	295
Profit and loss account year to 30 September 2005 (profit)	130
Provisions	103
Retained earnings at 30 September 2004	525
Share capital	600
Share premium	105
Stocks of finished goods	95
Stocks of materials	37
Tangible fixed assets	902
Work in progress	29

It should be noted that a provision is similar to an accrual. If the total of the debit balances is equal to the total of the credit balances it may be assumed that the information is complete.

First, we need to identify which are assets (debit balances) and which are liabilities and equity (credit balances). Second, we can check that the trial balance is actually in balance, and if there is any missing information. Third, we can prepare a balance sheet for Perfecto Ltd as at 30 September 2005 using a vertical format.

	Assets (debits) £000	Liabilities and equity (credits) £000
Accruals		100
Bank and cash balances	157	
Creditors due within one year		277
Creditors due after one year		77
Debtors	284	
Intangible fixed assets	203	
Long-term loans		85
Prepaid expenses and accrued income	295	
Profit and loss account year to 30 September 2005 (profit)		130
Provisions		103
Retained earnings at 30 September 2004		525
Share capital		600
Share premium		105
Stocks of finished goods	95	
Stocks of materials	37	
Tangible fixed assets	902	
Work in progress	29	
Total	2,002	2,002

The total of the assets is £2,002,000, which is equal to the total of the liabilities plus equity. The trial balance is therefore in balance and there doesn't appear to be any information missing. However, errors of omission, for example, or transposed figures, may not be spotted from the information given. There could be equal and opposite debit and credit balances that have been excluded from the list in error.

Given that the data is correct, an accurate balance sheet for Perfecto Ltd as at 30 September 2005 may be prepared.

Perfecto Ltd
Balance sheet as at 30 September 2005

	£000	£000	£000
Fixed assets			
Intangible			203
Tangible			902
			1,105
Current assets			
Stocks [95 + 37 + 29]	161		
Debtors	284		
Prepayments	295		
Cash	157		
		897	
Current liabilities (less than one year)			
Creditors	277		
Accruals	100		
		377	
Net current assets (working capital)			520
Total assets less current liabilities			1,625
less			
Long-term liabilities (over one year)			
Financial debt	85		
Creditors	77		
			162
less			
Provisions			103
Net assets			1,360
Capital and reserves			
Capital			600
Premiums			105
Profit and loss account [130 + 525]			655
			1,360

> **Progress check 2.6** What does the horizontal format balance sheet tell us? Why is the vertical format balance sheet preferred by most UK companies?

Many of the larger businesses in the UK consist of a number of companies rather than just one company. The control of such companies, or groups of companies, rests with a parent company, which is called the holding company. The other companies within the group are called subsidiaries. The holding company holds the required number of shares in each of the subsidiaries to give it the required control.

Businesses operate in a group structure for a variety of reasons. It may be because they cover different countries, different products, or different market sectors; it may be to provide independence, or separate accountability, or may very often be a result of successive takeovers or mergers of businesses.

The Companies Act 1985/1989 requires group accounts to be prepared for the holding company in addition to the accounts that are required to be prepared for each of the individual companies within the group. These '**consolidated accounts**' exclude all transactions between companies within the group, for example inter-company sales and purchases, to avoid double counting of transactions. In most other respects, the group consolidated accounts reflect an amalgamation of each of the components of the balance sheets of all the companies within the group.

Valuation of assets

The question of valuation of assets at a specific balance sheet date arises in respect of choosing the most accurate methods relating to fixed assets, stocks and debtors (and similarly creditors), which support the fundamental requirement to give a true and fair view.

Companies must be very careful to ensure that their assets are valued in a way that realistically reflects their ability to generate future cash flows. This applies to both current assets such as stocks, and fixed assets such as land and buildings. The balance sheets of companies rarely reflect either the current market values of fixed assets, or their future earnings potential, since they are based on historical costs. During 2004, Marks and Spencer plc was facing a takeover bid from entrepreneur Philip Green (see the press extract below). The directors of Marks and Spencer plc prepared to fight off the takeover bid on the basis that the offer price was a long way short of the value of its assets. Marks and Spencer was revaluing its portfolio of freehold property, which the directors felt was worth £2bn more than stated in its balance sheet.

Marks and Spencer's revaluation of its property portfolio was a measure to protect it against takeover. Directors of companies must take care in such valuation increases that reflect the impact of property price inflation, which may not be sustained, and ignore the future earning potential of the assets. Marks and Spencer was also carrying out a review of its underperforming businesses, headed by Lifestore, the home furnishings shop, so that the company could decide on what changes needed to be made.

Differences between the methods chosen to value various assets (and liabilities) at the end of accounting periods may have a significant impact on the results reported in the profit and loss account for those periods. Examples of this may be seen in:

- fixed assets and depreciation
- stocks valuations and cost of sales
- valuations of accounts payable and accounts receivable denominated in foreign currencies
- provisions for doubtful debts.

The real value of a company's assets

Retail entrepreneur Philip Green is this week expected to table a fresh bid for Marks & Spencer, as the high street giant considers ditching its flagship £15m homeware store.

Mr Green, who owns Top Shop and BHS, is preparing to raise his offer for M&S, following the board's near-instant rejection of his previous bid earlier this month.

Insiders expect the new offer – tabled through bid vehicle Revival – to be worth up to £8.8 billion. It would value the company's shares at between 380p and 390p, and would offer current M&S shareholders the opportunity to hold equity in the new company, so as to reap any returns made by Mr Green.

The previous bid of 290p–310p in cash plus a 25 pc stake in Revival was rejected within hours by the M&S board, under its newly appointed chief executive Stuart Rose. A number of M&S insiders, as well as city analysts, do not expect an offer below 400p to be accepted, although Mr Green has indicated that this is more than he regards the company is worth.

M&S is preparing to fight off a new bid by revaluing its portfolio of freehold property, which some reckon is worth up to £4 billion – £2 billion more than its valuation in the group's accounts. Mr Rose has brought in close adviser Charles Wilson to help mastermind the retail group's recovery.

Paul Myners has been drafted in as a temporary replacement for chairman Luc Vandevelde. It emerged yesterday that Mr Vandevelde's private equity fund, Change Capital Partners, is one of the bidders for £200m retailer Pets at Home.

Yesterday, Mr Rose was working at the company's Baker Street headquarters on a review of M&S's underperforming businesses. Top of the list is Lifestore, the home furnishings shop launched by ousted clothing chief Vittorio Radice. M&S has admitted that the pioneer Gateshead store is not meeting performance targets, but a spokesman warned yesterday that its fate may take some time to be decided.

'Stuart and Charles have only been at the company for 10 days,' he said. 'It will take a certain amount of time for them to decide what needs changing and what doesn't. Lifestore is clearly not performing well at the moment so it is the subject of a review. Our revaluing of the property portfolio is already under way, and we should have the results in a matter of weeks.'

The spokesman played down suggestions that the value of the properties would be released and passed on to shareholders. 'We need to be able to point to the inherent value of the company if there is another bid,' he said. 'For the moment, though, our main tactic here is to wait and see what Philip Green does next.'

Mr Green is expected to return from his home in Monaco this afternoon to put the finishing touches to the new bid. Yesterday he said: 'All I'm going to say at the moment is that we are considering our position. Other than that I can't make any comment.'

The M&S spokesman said Mr Rose was unavailable to talk to the press.

Green to bid £8.8bn as M&S considers selling flagship Lifestore, by Edmund Conway

© *Daily Telegraph*, 14 June 2004

The valuation of assets and liabilities will all be covered in detail in Chapter 3 when we look at the profit and loss account. The rules applicable to the valuation of balance sheet items are laid down in the Companies Act 1985, as amended by the Companies Act 1989. These rules allow companies to prepare their financial statements under the historical cost convention (the gross value of the asset being the purchase price or production cost), or alternative conventions of historical cost modified to include certain assets at a revalued amount or current cost.

Under alternative conventions, the gross value of the asset is either the market value at the most recent valuation date or its current cost: tangible fixed assets should be valued at market value or at current cost; investments (fixed assets) are valued at market value or at any value considered appropriate by the directors; investments (current assets) are valued at current cost; stocks are valued at current cost. If a reduction in value of any fixed assets is expected to be permanent then provision for this must be made. The same applies to investments even if the reduction is not expected to be permanent.

Fixed assets with finite lives are subject to depreciation charges. Current assets must be written down to the amount for which they could be disposed of (their **net realisable value**), if that value is lower than cost or an alternative valuation. It should be noted that provisions for reductions in value no longer considered necessary must be written back to the profit and loss account.

There is an element of choice between alternative valuation methods that may be adopted by businesses. Because of this, difficulties may arise in trying to provide consistent comparisons of the performance of companies even within the same industrial sectors. If changes in accounting policies have been introduced, further inconsistencies arise in trying to provide a realistic comparison of just one company's performance between one accounting period and another.

The Companies Act 1985/1989, accounting concepts, and the accounting standards (SSAPs and FRSs) lay down certain rules for the valuation of balance sheet items. We will look at some of the most important valuation rules in respect of fixed assets and current assets.

Fixed assets

Capital expenditure on fixed assets is defined in the Companies Act 1985 as those assets intended for use on a continuing basis in the company's activities. As we have already discussed, fixed assets comprise tangible assets, intangible assets, and investments (financial assets). Within tangible fixed assets there are various categories of asset: land and buildings (freehold, long leasehold and short leasehold); plant and machinery; fixtures, fittings, tools and equipment; assets in the course of construction.

Capital expenditure relates to acquisition of fixed assets and includes all the costs of putting an asset into service with the company so that the company will benefit from the services of the asset for more than one trading period.

Interest charges incurred in the financing of the production of an asset may be added to and included in the total cost of the asset. Such charges are said to have been capitalised, and if they are included in the total fixed asset cost this must be disclosed in a note to the financial statements.

Which other acquisition costs should be added to the asset price to give the total acquisition cost? The total amount recorded in the accounts of a company, the capitalised cost, for each category of fixed asset, should include various acquisition costs in addition to the purchase price of the asset, as follows:

- land
  - agent's commissions
  - legal fees
  - survey fees
  - draining, clearing, landscaping, demolition costs
- buildings
  - repair, alteration and improvement costs
- other assets
  - freight costs
  - customs duty
  - installation charges
- building construction
  - subcontract work
  - materials costs
  - labour costs
  - direct construction overheads
  - excavation costs
  - construction offices
  - professional fees
- own-built plant and machinery
  - materials costs
  - labour costs
  - production overheads.

Overheads that may be capitalised relate to costs of wages, salaries and expenses not directly incurred in the construction of buildings or machinery, but which nevertheless are necessary costs incurred to enable construction to take place. Examples may be a proportion or the full costs of management and supervision of projects, and a share of electricity or similar charges incurred on such projects.

Worked Example 2.12

We have been asked to decide which of the following items should be disclosed in the balance sheet and which should be disclosed in the profit and loss account.

	£
1. Extension to the factory	500,000
2. New plant	100,000
3. Architect's fee for supervising the building of the extension	10,000
4. Haulier's invoice for delivering the plant	5,000
5. Invoice from decorators for painting the reception area	2,000
6. Insurance premium for twelve months on new cars	15,000
7. Invoice from garage for ten new cars	200,000

The disclosure should be as follows:

	£
1. Balance sheet – fixed assets	500,000
2. Balance sheet – fixed assets	100,000
3. Balance sheet – fixed assets	10,000
4. Balance sheet – fixed assets	5,000
5. Profit and loss account – repairs	2,000
6. Profit and loss account – insurance	15,000
7. Balance sheet – fixed assets	200,000

A valuation problem arises with regard to fixed assets because such assets have been 'consumed' over time and will currently be worth less than at the time of acquisition. The total cost of using a fixed asset over its life is generally defined as the original investment less a portion of its cost recovered (its residual value) at the end of the asset's useful life. Depreciation is allocated to charge a fair proportion of the total cost (or valuation) of the asset to each accounting period expected to benefit from its use. The net fixed asset figure reported in each period's balance sheet will reflect the reduction to the historical cost, or revalued amount, of the asset using the depreciation calculated for each period.

Intangible assets include: deferred development costs; concessions; patents; licences; trademarks; goodwill; brand names. Investments (financial assets) primarily include shares and loans in non-consolidated group companies.

> **Progress check 2.7** Does it really matter if the year-end balance sheet of a company shows fixed assets at cost, less depreciation, but ignores any change in their value? This should be discussed from the points of view of an investor and a lender as two major users of financial statements.

Brand names

Some organisations have included brand names for products like chocolate bars and beers in their balance sheets as intangible assets, therefore inflating the totals of their balance sheets. Examples of companies that have capitalised brand names have been:

- Ranks Hovis McDougall (1991) capitalised non-purchased brand names
- Guinness (1993) capitalised purchased brand names.

Brands purchased by a company may be capitalised, whereas non-purchased brands may not normally be capitalised. The ASB have viewed the inclusion of non-purchased brands as undesirable because of the difficulty in ascertaining historical costs and the inappropriateness of trying to capitalise the earnings or cash flows that have been generated by the brand names. Capitalisation of purchased brand names is permitted under FRS 10. Purchased brands have proved to be as desirable as traditional tangible fixed assets, and so should be disclosed in the balance sheet.

Goodwill

FRS 10 defines goodwill as the difference between the value of the business as a whole and the aggregate of the fair values of its separable net assets. It can only appear on the balance sheet if a business has been acquired for a value in either cash or shares, so a company may not capitalise internally generated goodwill. FRS 10 requires purchased goodwill to be capitalised, along with all other purchased fixed assets. It may be **amortised** (depreciated) through the profit and loss account over its useful economic life, or left in the balance sheet at its purchased cost indefinitely, and justified annually.

Research and development costs

Development costs do not include research costs. A development cost is defined in SSAP 13 as the cost of scientific or technical knowledge in order to produce new or substantially improved materials, devices, products or services; to install new processes or systems prior to the commencement of commercial production or commercial applications; or to improve substantially those already produced or installed. Development expenditure on new products or services is normally undertaken with an expectation of future commercial benefits, either from increased profits or reduced costs, and so to the extent that such costs are recoverable they may be matched against the future revenues.

Pure research costs are defined in SSAP 13 as the costs of experimental or theoretical work undertaken primarily to acquire new scientific or technical knowledge and understanding, not primarily directed towards any specific practical aim or application. Applied research costs are the costs of original or critical investigation undertaken in order to gain new scientific or technical knowledge and directed towards a specific practical aim or objective. In general, no one particular period rather than any other will be expected to benefit and so these costs should be charged to the profit and loss account as they are incurred.

Stocks

Problems arise in the area of valuation of stocks for three main reasons. First, homogeneous items within various stock categories are purchased continuously and consumed continuously in the manufacturing processes. The purchase prices of these homogeneous items may vary considerably. How do we know the specific prices of each item as we take them from stock and use them?

The general rule is that stocks must be valued at the lower of purchase cost (or production cost) and their net realisable value. The Companies Act 1985/1989 allows a number of alternative methods to be used to determine the cost of stock, the most common being FIFO (first in first out, where the oldest items of stock or their costs are assumed to be the first to be used), LIFO (last in first out, where the most recently acquired items of stock or their costs are assumed to be the first to be used), average cost, and market value. LIFO is not permitted in the UK by the accounting standard for Stocks and Long-term Contracts, SSAP 9, and is not acceptable for taxation purposes.

Second, materials may be purchased from a variety of geographical locations. Additional costs such as duty, freight, and insurance may be incurred. How should these be accounted for? The costs of stocks should comprise the expenditure that has been incurred in the normal course of business in bringing the product or service to its present location and condition.

Third, as materials, packaging and other consumable items are used during the production processes to manufacture work in progress, partly finished product and fully finished product, how should costs be correctly apportioned to give a true cost? Which costs should be included and which should be excluded?

Stocks are disclosed as a main heading in the balance sheet and comprise raw materials and consumables, work in progress, finished goods, and long-term contracts. SSAP 9 requires that companies must disclose accounting policies adopted in respect of stocks and work in progress.

Debtors

Debtors, or accounts receivable, are normally paid to the company according to contractual terms of trading agreed at the outset with each customer. However, economic and trading circumstances may have changed. Can the company be sure that it will receive payment in full against all outstanding receivables? If not, what is a more realistic valuation of such debtors?

Accounts receivable may need to be reduced by an assessment of debts that will definitely not be paid (bad debts), or debts that are unlikely ever to be paid (doubtful debts). Bad and doubtful debts and their impact on the profit and loss account will be examined in detail in Chapter 3 which looks at the profit and loss account.

When goods or services are supplied to a customer they are invoiced at the agreed price and on the trading terms that have been contracted. The trading terms may be, for example, 30 days. In this case the sales value will have been taken into the current period profit and loss account but the debt, or the account receivable, will remain unpaid in the **sales ledger** account until it is settled after 30 days.

Foreign currency transactions

A general factor that may impact on the valuation of all asset types (and liabilities) is foreign currency exchange rate risk. For example, a customer in the USA may insist on being invoiced by the company in US$, say 10,000 US$. At the time of delivery of the goods or services the value of the US$ sale in £ at the exchange rate on the day will be, say, £6,250 (£ = 1.60 US$). The sales invoice may be issued a few days later and the exchange rate may have changed, for example £6,173 (£ = 1.62 US$). The customer may have agreed payment for two months later and the exchange rate may have moved again, say £5,714 (£ = 1.75 US$). What value should have been attributed to the account receivable at the balance sheet date?

The value attributed to a sales invoice is its £ value on the day if invoiced in £ sterling. If a sales invoice is rendered in foreign currency SSAP 20 requires it to be valued at the exchange rate at the date of the transaction, or at an average rate for the period if exchange rates do not fluctuate significantly.

If the transaction is to be settled at a contracted exchange rate then the exchange rate specified in the contract should be used. Such a trading transaction is then said to be covered by a matching forward contract.

> **Progress check 2.8** UK International Ltd invoiced a customer in the USA for goods to the value of 100,000 US$ on 31 December 2005. The US$ cheque sent to UK International by the customer was received on 31 January 2006 and was converted into £ sterling by the bank at 1.45 US$ to £1. Discuss the two transactions, the invoice and its settlement, and their impact on UK International's profit and loss account and its balance sheet as at 31 December 2005.

A foreign exchange forward contract is a contract, for example between a company and a bank, to exchange two currencies at an agreed exchange rate. Note also the foreign exchange forward option contract which extends this idea to allow the bank or the company to call for settlement of the contract, at two days' notice, between any two dates that have been agreed between the bank and the company at the time of agreeing the contract.

At the end of each accounting period, all debtors denominated in foreign currency should be translated, or revalued, using the rates of exchange ruling at the period-end date, or, where appropriate, the rates of exchange fixed under the terms of the relevant transactions. Where there are related or matching forward contracts in respect of trading transactions, the rates of exchange specified in those contracts may be used. A similar treatment should be applied to all monetary assets and liabilities denominated in a foreign currency, that is, cash and bank balances, loans, and amounts payable and receivable.

An exchange gain or loss will result during an accounting period if a business transaction is settled at an exchange rate which differs from that used when the transaction was initially recorded, or, where appropriate, that used at the last balance sheet date. An exchange gain or loss will also arise on unsettled transactions if the rate of exchange used at the balance sheet date differs from that used previously. Such gains and losses are recognised during each accounting period and included in the profit or loss from ordinary activities.

Summary of key points

- Items of expenditure may be generally classified as either capital expenditure or revenue expenditure, although some items may need to be apportioned between the two classifications.
- Limited companies are required to prepare periodically three main financial statements: balance sheet; profit and loss account; cash flow statement.
- Financial statements are required for the shareholders and the Registrar of Companies, and are also used by, for example, analysts, potential investors, customers, suppliers.
- Categories within the balance sheet are classified into shareholders' equity, liabilities, and assets.
- The structure of the balance sheet lends itself to two main formats: horizontal format and vertical format, the latter being the most popular and having many advantages.
- Valuation of the various items within the balance sheet is covered by the Companies Act 1985 as amended by the Companies Act 1989, and accounting concepts and standards, but nevertheless gives rise to problems and differences in approach.
- Within the rules alternative methods may be used to value the different categories of assets (and liabilities) within the balance sheet.

■ There are limitations to the conventional balance sheet arising not only from the fact that it is an historical document, but also from inconsistencies in its preparation between companies and industries, the employment of various asset valuation methods, off-balance sheet financing, and window dressing.

Questions

Q2.1   (i)   What are the three main financial statements?

       (ii)   What is their purpose?

Q2.2   Consider two ways of looking at the profit of a business: an increase in the wealth of the company; and the net result of the company's trading operations (sales less expenses). What do these terms mean, and is the result different using the two approaches?

Q2.3   Explain the vertical format structure of the balance sheet for a typical limited company.

Q2.4   Explain what assets, liabilities and shareholders' equity are, and give some examples of each.

Q2.5   Illustrate the difference between current liabilities and long-term liabilities with some examples of each.

Q2.6   (i)   What accounting convention is generally used in the valuation of fixed assets?

       (ii)   What additional costs may sometimes be included and to which assets may these be applied?

Q2.7   Why are current assets and fixed assets shown under different balance sheet classifications?

Q2.8   Describe what are meant by intangible assets and give some examples of their valuation.

Q2.9   What factors influence the accurate valuation of a company's debtors?

Q2.10 Why should a potential investor exercise caution when analysing the balance sheets of potential companies in which to invest?

Discussion points

D2.1 'Surely the purchase of fixed assets is expenditure just like spending on stationery or photocopy expenses so why should it appear as an entry in the balance sheet?' Discuss.

D2.2 'It has often been said that the value of every item in a balance sheet is a matter of opinion and the cash balance is the one and only number that can truly be relied upon.' Discuss.

Exercises

Solutions are provided in Appendix 3 to all exercise numbers highlighted in colour.

Level I

E2.1 *Time allowed – 30 minutes*

Mr IM Green – Manager Ian admired the sign on the door to his new office, following his appointment as manager of the human resources department. The previous manager left fairly suddenly to join another company but had left Ian with some papers about costs of his department, which showed a total of £460,000 together with a list of items of expenditure. This seemed rather a high figure to Ian for a department of five people. Ian's boss muttered something to him about capital expenditure and revenue expenditure, but this was an area about which Ian had never been very clear. The list left with Ian by his predecessor was as follows:

	£
Legal fees	42,000
5 personal computers	15,000
Specialist software	100,000
3 laser printers	10,000
Salaries	158,000
National Insurance costs	16,000
Pension costs	14,000
Building repairs	25,000
Equipment repairs	8,000
Health and safety costs	20,000
Staff recruitment fees	10,000
Training costs	20,000
Subsistence and entertaining	10,000
Office furniture	12,000
	460,000

Assume that you are the finance manager whom Ian has asked for advice and provide him with a list that separates the items into capital and revenue expenditure.

E2.2 *Time allowed – 30 minutes*
The balances in the accounts of Vertico Ltd at 31 July 2005 are as follows:

	£000
Accrued expenses	95
Bank overdraft	20
Debtors	275
Plant and equipment	309
Finished product	152
Computer system	104
Petty cash	5
Share capital	675
Trade creditors	293
Final payment on computer system due 1 September 2006	52
Loan for a factory building	239
Buildings	560
Raw materials	195

(i) **An important number has been omitted. What is that?**
(ii) **Using the data provided and the missing data prepare a balance sheet for Vertico Ltd as at 31 July 2005 in a vertical format.**

E2.3 *Time allowed – 45 minutes*
You are required to prepare a balance sheet for Trainer plc as at 31 December 2005 using the trial balance at 31 December 2005 and the additional information shown below.

Trial balance at 31 December 2005	Debit	Credit
	£000	**£000**
Bank	73	
Ordinary share capital		320
Land and buildings at cost	320	
Plant and machinery at cost	200	
Cumulative depreciation provision (charge for year 2005 was £20,000)		80
Stocks	100	
Sales		1,000
Cost of sales	600	
Operating expenses	120	
Depreciation	20	
Bad debts written off	2	
Debtors	100	
Accruals		5
Trade creditors		130
	1,535	1,535

Additional information: The company will be paying £20,000 for corporation tax on the 2005 profits during 2006.

E2.4 *Time allowed – 45 minutes*
The following information relates to Major plc at 31 December 2005, and the comparative numbers at 31 December 2004.

	2004	2005
	£000	**£000**
Accruals	800	1,000
Bank overdraft		16,200
Cash at bank	600	
Plant and machinery at cost	17,600	23,900
Debentures (interest at 15% per annum)	600	750
Plant and machinery depreciation	9,500	10,750
Proposed dividends	3,000	6,000
Ordinary share capital	5,000	5,000
Preference share capital	1,000	1,000
Prepayments	300	400
Profit and loss account	3,000	10,100
Stocks	5,000	15,000
Taxation	3,200	5,200
Trade creditors	6,000	10,000
Trade debtors	8,600	26,700

Prepare a balance sheet in the format adopted by most of the leading UK plcs showing the previous year comparative figures.

E2.5 *Time allowed – 60 minutes*

From the trial balance of Gremlins plc at 31 March 2005 identify the assets and expenses (debit balances) and income, liabilities and equity (credit balances), confirm that the trial balance is in balance, then prepare a balance sheet for Gremlins plc as at 31 March 2005 using a vertical format.

	£000
Depreciation on office equipment and furnishings (administrative expenses)	156
Bank overdraft	609
Accountancy and audit fees	30
Electricity paid in advance	45
Computer system (net book value)	441
Advertising and promotion	135
Share premium account	240
Interest received	15
Plant and equipment (net book value)	927
Amount for final payment on factory machine due March 2007	252
Trade debtors	1,110
Goodwill	204
12-year lease on factory	330
Rents received	63
Prepaid expenses	885
Interest paid	120
Office electricity	66
Retained earnings at 31 March 2004	513
Stocks of materials at 31 March 2005	585
Telephone	87
Distribution costs	162
Other office utilities	72
Cost of goods sold	1,659
Administrative salaries	216
Sales salaries	267
Furniture and fixtures (net book value)	729
Sales	3,267
Office rent	165
Finished product at 31 March 2005	84
Debenture	750
Trade creditors	1,257
Cash	51
Share capital	1,560

Level II

E2.6 *Time allowed – 60 minutes*

Prepare a balance sheet in vertical format as at 31 December 2004 for Gorban Ltd based on the following trial balance, and the further information shown below.

Learning objectives

Completion of this chapter will enable you to:

- describe what is meant by profit (or loss)
- outline the structure of the profit and loss account (income statement) of a limited company
- classify the categories of income and expenditure that comprise the profit and loss account
- appreciate the alternative profit and loss account formats
- prepare a profit and loss account
- explain the links between the profit and loss account and the balance sheet, particularly with regard to the valuation of fixed assets and depreciation, stock and cost of sales, and debtors and the doubtful debt provision
- explain the links between the profit and loss account and cash flow
- appreciate the subjective aspects of profit measurement.

Introduction

In Chapter 2 we looked at how to prepare simple financial statements from transactions carried out by a business during an accounting period. We then looked in a little more detail at the first of these financial statements, namely the balance sheet. This chapter will be concerned with the second of the financial statements, the profit and loss account (or income statement). Although profit and loss accounts are prepared by all forms of business entity, this chapter, in a similar way to Chapter 2, deals primarily with the profit and loss accounts of limited companies, both private and public.

This chapter deals with how profit and loss accounts are structured and how the accounts within the profit and loss account are categorised. Each of the items within each of the profit and loss account categories will be described in detail and form the basis to enable the preparation of a profit and loss account of a limited company in the appropriate format.

We will look at the relationship between the profit and loss account and the balance sheet and provide an introduction to the relationship between profit (or loss) and cash flow. Like the balance sheet, the profit and loss account is subjective largely because of the impact on costs of the variety of approaches that may be taken to the valuation of assets and liabilities.

What does the profit and loss account tell us?

The profit and loss account of a private limited company or a public limited company should be able to tell us all about the results of the company's activities over specified accounting periods. The profit and loss account shows us what revenues have been generated and what costs incurred in generating those revenues, and therefore the increase or decrease in wealth of the business during the period.

The same note of caution we mentioned in Chapter 2 that should be exercised in the analysis of balance sheet information, applies to profit and loss account information. The profit and loss account is an historical statement and so it does not tell us anything about the ability of the business to sustain or improve upon its performance over subsequent periods.

There is not always consistency between the information included in one company's profit and loss account and that of another company. As with the balance sheet, the profit and loss accounts of two companies even within the same industry may be very difficult to compare. This will be illustrated in the wide variety of methods of depreciation calculations and stock valuation methods examined in this chapter. In addition, the bases of financial ratios (to be examined in detail in Chapter 5) used by analysts in looking at a company's profit and loss account may often be different.

It is often said of profit and loss statements, as well as of balance sheets, that the value of every item included in them is a matter of opinion. This is due not only to the alternative stock valuation and depreciation methods, but also because of the subjective assessment of whether the settlement of a customer account is doubtful or not, and the sometimes imprecise evaluation of accruals and provisions.

What is profit?

We saw from the worked examples in Chapter 2 that profit (or loss) may be considered from two perspectives. We may consider these perspectives to illustrate the links between the profit and loss account and the balance sheet.

The first perspective, which is not suggested as a method for calculating profit in practice, compares the balance sheet of an entity at the start of an accounting period with the balance sheet at the end of the accounting period. We may see from these that the values of each of the components of the balance sheet may have changed. For example, levels of stocks, debtors, creditors, cash, fixed assets, and accruals may have changed during an accounting period. We have seen that the net value of the assets and liabilities in the balance sheet represents the capital, or equity, or the wealth of the business at a point in time. The change in wealth over an accounting period between the beginning and end of the accounting period is the profit or loss for the period reflected in the retained earnings category in the balance sheet.

Profit (or loss) considered in this way can be represented in the equation:

total assets (TA) − total liabilities (TL) = equity (E) + profit (P)

Worked Example 3.1

Using the opening balance sheet 1 March 2005 below and the further transactions (a) and (b), we are able to:

(i) show how the balance sheet will change after these transactions/events have taken place
(ii) identify the profit which the shareholders should consider is potentially distributable as a dividend.

Opening balance sheet 1 March 2005	£
Fixed assets	100,000
Current assets	100,000

Net profit for the 12 months to 31 December 2005 for Squirrel Ltd is therefore:

Sales	£1,200,000	[£1,300,000 less £100,000]
less Expenses	£975,000	[£1,000,000 plus £5,000 less £60,000 plus £30,000]
which equals	£225,000	

There must be an application of concepts and standard practices in arriving at net profit, otherwise users of financial information would not have reasonable confidence in the amounts being shown in the accounts reported by companies, large or small.

In this chapter we will look at the profit and loss account from the second perspective. We will look at how a profit and loss account is constructed and prepared by deducting total costs from total revenues, as the second of the three key financial statements that are required to be prepared by a limited company.

> **Progress check 3.1 Explain the perspectives from which we may consider the profit (or loss) of a business.**

Structure of the profit and loss account

As we have seen previously, the profit and loss account measures whether or not the company has made a profit or loss on its operations during the period, through producing or buying and selling its goods or services. It measures whether total sales or revenues are higher than the total costs (profit), or whether total costs are higher than total sales or revenues (loss).

The total revenue of a business is generated from the provision of goods or services and may be, for example, in the form of:

- sales (goods)
- interest received (on loans)
- rents (from property)
- subscriptions (to TV channels)
- fees (professions)
- royalties (books, CDs).

The total costs of a business include the expenditure incurred as a result of the generation of revenue. The total costs of a business include, for example:

- costs of goods purchased for resale
- costs of manufacturing goods for sale
- transport and distribution costs
- advertising
- promotion
- insurance
- costs of the 'consumption' of fixed assets over their useful lives (depreciation)

- wages and salaries
- interest paid
- stationery costs
- photocopy costs
- communications costs
- electricity
- water and effluent costs
- travel expenses
- entertaining expenses
- postage.

Each of the above examples of costs (by no means an exhaustive list) incurred in the generation of revenue by a business appears itself as a separate heading, or is grouped within one or other of the other main headings within the profit and loss account. Figure 3.2 shows each of the levels of profit that are derived after allowing for the various categories of revenues and expenses.

We will look at how a basic profit and loss account is constructed to arrive at the profit on ordinary activities after taxation (or net profit) for the company. Net profit is also sometimes called net earnings, from which may be deducted dividends payable to ordinary shareholders. The net result is then the retained profit for the financial year.

Figure 3.3 shows an example of the profit and loss account format adopted by a public limited company, Flatco plc.

Each of the categories of revenue and cost within the profit and loss account (see Fig. 3.4) can be examined in a little more detail.

Turnover

The main source of income for a company is its **turnover**, primarily comprised of sales of its products and services to third-party customers. Revenues and costs are not necessarily accounted for when

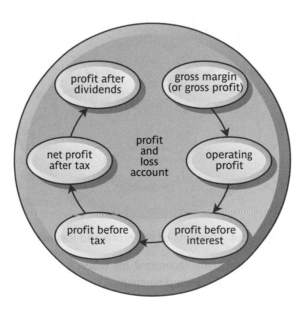

Figure 3.2 Levels of profit within the profit and loss account

Distribution costs and administrative expenses include all expenses related to the 'normal' operations of the company, except those directly related to manufacturing like the costs of the purchasing department, logistics department, and quality department. They also exclude the share of overhead costs, for example, heating and lighting, business rates, water and effluent costs, relating to manufacturing activities. Administrative expenses exclude financial expenses and revenues, because these are really a function of the financial structure of the company (the extent of its funding by owners' share capital and by lenders' debt, or loans), and any other non-operational expenses and revenues.

Other operating income

Other operating income includes all other revenues that have not been included in other parts of the profit and loss account. It does not include sales of goods or services, reported turnover, or any sort of interest receivable, reported within the net interest category.

Operating profit (OP)

Operating profit (see Fig. 3.2 and Fig. 3.3), or

$$\text{OP} = \text{turnover} - \text{COS} - \text{other operating expenses} + \text{other operating income}$$

The operating profit is the net of all operating revenues and costs, regardless of the financial structure of the company and whatever exceptional events occurred during the period that resulted in exceptional costs. Operating profit is not required to be disclosed according to the Companies Act 1985/1989, but its disclosure is one of the specific recommendations within the standard on Reporting Financial Performance, FRS 3. It is therefore an extremely important profit/loss subtotal because it allows inter-firm comparisons of companies operating in the same markets but having different financial policies.

Income from other fixed asset investments

Income from other fixed asset investments specifically excludes interest receivable, but includes dividends receivable from subsidiary or fellow subsidiary companies and from **non-related companies**.

Profit before interest and tax (PBIT)

Profit before interest and tax, or

$$\text{PBIT} = \text{OP} + \text{income from other fixed asset investments}$$

PBIT is a measure of the profitability of the operations of a company regardless of the amount of interest payable and receivable on overdrafts and loans, and regardless of the amount of corporation tax it may have to pay.

Net interest

Net interest is the difference between financial revenues and charges, interest receivable and payable, and includes other financial costs like bank charges, and costs of transferring funds. The overall level of cost (or revenue) will be dependent on the type of company and level of interest rates and debt/equity mix within the funding of the company.

Profit before tax (PBT)

Profit before tax, or

$$\text{PBT} = \text{PBIT} +/- \text{net interest}$$

Tax on profit on ordinary activities

Corporation tax is payable on profits of limited companies. The companies, as entities, are responsible for the tax, rather than individuals as with sole traders and partnerships. Tax is shown in the profit and loss accounts, balance sheets and cash flow statements of limited companies.

The corporation tax shown on the face of the profit and loss account will have been based on a computation carried out prior to the exact amount payable having been agreed with the Inland Revenue. There may therefore be some differences from year to year between the tax payable numbers reported and tax actually paid.

Profit after tax (PAT)

PAT, or net profit, is the profit on ordinary activities after tax. The final charge that a company has to suffer, provided it has made sufficient profits, is therefore corporate taxation.

$$\text{PAT} = \text{PBT} - \text{corporation tax}$$

> **Progress check 3.2 What exactly do we mean by cost of sales? What types of expense does cost of sales include and what types of expense does it exclude?**

The net profit has resulted from the following processes. The assets, owned by the shareholders, have generated the operating profit. Operating profit has been used to pay interest to bankers and other lenders, and corporation tax to the Inland Revenue. What is left belongs to the owners of the assets, the shareholders. The net profit is the increase in wealth of the company.

The directors propose how much will be distributed to shareholders in dividends, and how much will be held as retained earnings as part of the equity of the company and reinvested in the operations of the company. The shareholders vote on whether to accept or reject the directors' proposal. The net profit is used to provide the shareholders' returns, the dividends they receive from their total investment in the equity of the company. So, not only does the net profit have to be positive, but it has to be high enough to reward the risk the shareholders took in investing in the company. In some circumstances a dividend may be paid out of retained earnings, even though the company may have made a loss during the period. This is obviously only acceptable in the short term and cannot be continued for successive accounting periods.

Dividends

The Companies Acts do not have a specific requirement for dividends to be shown in the profit and loss account, but both the Acts and FRS 3 imply that dividends are usually deducted from the profit or loss for the financial year in arriving at the profit or loss retained for the year. The dividend line in the profit and loss account includes any interim payment that may have been made and any final dividend proposed by the directors to be paid to shareholders later in the year.

and loss account. A company's ordinary activities have now been defined so broadly that extraordinary items have now effectively disappeared from the face of the profit and loss account.

The costs resulting from the complete destruction of a factory may be sufficiently extraordinary to warrant the appearance of extraordinary items as a separate item on the profit and loss account.

2. Exceptional items

Exceptional items are items of abnormal size and incidence, which are derived from the ordinary activities of the business. FRS 3 requires exceptional items to be included under the statutory format headings to which they relate and disclosed on the face of the profit and loss account if necessary to give a true and fair view.

3. Earnings per share

FRS 3 also refers to earnings per share, which would normally be disclosed after the retained profit for the year (not shown in the Flatco plc example).

4. Reconciliation of the movement in shareholders' funds

The movement in shareholders' funds for Flatco plc, disclosed in accordance with the requirements of FRS 3, is shown in Fig. 3.5. The actual report would of course include the previous year 2004 comparative figures.

Figure 3.6 shows the profit and loss account for Flatco plc restated in line with format 1 and illustrating the provisions of FRS 3. The Companies Act requires comparative figures for the previous year for each line in the profit and loss account (not shown in the example), usually shown in a column to the right of the current year's figures.

Worked Example 3.3

The relevant profit and loss account balances, representing the costs and revenues for the year to date as extracted from the trial balance of Perfecto Ltd at 30 September 2005, are presented below in an alphabetical list:

	£000
Advertising and promotion	54
Corporation tax	70
Costs of administration departments	146
Costs of production departments	277
Costs of purchasing and logistics department	77
Depreciation on factory machinery	284
Depreciation on office equipment	35
Direct labour cost of sales	203
Freight out costs	230
Interest paid	20
Interest received	10

Materials cost of sales	611
Rent and utilities (2/3 factory, 1/3 office)	48
Sales	2,279
Warehousing and goods outward costs	84

We will prepare a profit and loss account for Perfecto Ltd for the year to 30 September 2005, using format 1, and which complies as far as possible with the provisions included in FRS 3.

Perfecto Ltd
Profit and loss account for the year ended 30 September 2005

Figures in £000

Turnover		2,279
Cost of sales [277 + 77 + 284 + 203 + 611 + 32 (2/3 of 48)]		(1,484)
Gross profit		795
Distribution costs [54 + 230 + 84]	(368)	
Administrative expenses [146 + 35 + 16 (1/3 of 48)]	(197)	
		(565)
Operating profit		230
Net interest [20 − 10]		(10)
Profit before tax		220
Tax on profit on ordinary activities		(70)
Profit on ordinary activities after tax		150

The Companies Act 1985/1989 requires group accounts to be prepared for the holding company in addition to the accounts that are required to be prepared for each of the individual companies within the group. Consolidated accounts exclude all transactions between companies within the group, for example inter-company sales and purchases. In most other respects the group consolidated accounts reflect an amalgamation of each of the components of the profit and loss accounts of all the companies within the group.

> **Progress check 3.4 There are four profit and loss account formats that comply with the requirements of the Companies Act 1985/1989. How do formats 1 and 3 differ from formats 2 and 4? Which format appears to be favoured by the majority of UK companies?**

Profit and loss and the balance sheet

The balance sheet and the profit and loss account, whilst they are both historical statements, are not alternatives or competing options. They show different financial information, as we have discussed. The balance sheet shows the financial position at the start and at the end of an accounting period, and the profit and loss account shows what has happened during the period, the financial performance.

Worked Example 3.7

Consider a company van, which cost £20,000 to purchase new. Its residual value is considered to be zero at the end of its useful life of 5 years. The rate of inflation is 10% and the cost of capital is 15%.

The depreciation for the first year and the net book value (NBV) at the end of year 1 may be evaluated using six alternative methods, including straight line depreciation.

		Depreciation in year 1	NBV at end of year 1
1. Straight line depreciation over 5 years, i.e. 20% per annum using an historical cost of £20,000	£20,000 at 20%	£4,000	£16,000
2. Constant purchasing power, which means allowing for an inflationary price increase (in this case 10%), and using straight line depreciation at 20% per annum	£20,000 × 1.10 at 20%	£4,400	£17,600
3. Replacement value for an identical one-year-old van based on used van market value of say £17,000. Depreciation would be £20,000 − £17,000 = £3,000		£3,000	£17,000
4. Replacement cost of a new van less one year's depreciation based on an estimated replacement cost of say	£21,600 at 20%	£4,320	£17,280
5. Net realisable value – net proceeds from a trade auction say £16,000. Depreciation would be £20,000 − £16,000 = £4,000		£4,000	£16,000
6. Economic value using estimated net cash flow from using the van for each year 1: £6,000; 2: £6,000; 3: £6,000; 4: £6,000 present values of future cash flows, using a cost of capital of 15% per annum (a **discounted cash flow (DCF)** technique). $£6,000/1.15 + £6,000/1.15^2 + £6,000/1.15^3 + £6,000/1.15^4$ Depreciation will be £20,000 − £17,160		£2,840	£17,160

Whichever method of depreciation is used, it must be consistent from one accounting period to another. The depreciation method adopted must be disclosed within the company's accounting policies that accompany the financial statements and include the depreciation rates applied to each of the categories of fixed asset.

> **Progress check 3.6** What are the various methods that may be used to depreciate an asset? Describe two of the most commonly used methods.

The amount of depreciation calculated for an accounting period is charged as a cost in the profit and loss account, the depreciation charge. A corresponding amount is also reflected in an account in the balance sheet, the cumulative depreciation provision account, the effect of which is to reduce the original cost of the fixed assets at the end of each accounting period.

The difference between depreciation cost and other costs such as wages is that it is not a cash expense, that is it will generate no cash inflow or outflow. The only cash outflow relating to depreciation took place when the asset was originally purchased. The depreciation is really only the 'memory' of that earlier cash outflow.

> **Progress check 3.7** Why are assets depreciated and what factors influence the decision as to how they may be depreciated?

Cost of sales

As we saw in Chapter 2, stocks of **raw materials**, **work in progress**, **finished product**, and consumable stores, pose problems in their valuation for three main reasons:

- raw materials may be purchased from a variety of geographical locations, and additional costs such as duty, freight, and insurance may be incurred – the costs of stocks should comprise the expenditure that has been incurred in the normal course of business in bringing the product or service to its present location and condition
- packaging and other consumable items, in addition to raw materials, are used during the production processes to manufacture work in progress, partly finished product and fully finished product, and such costs must be correctly apportioned to give a true cost – stocks are disclosed as a main heading in the balance sheet and comprise raw materials and consumables, work in progress, finished goods, and long-term contracts
- homogeneous items within various stock categories are purchased continuously and consumed continuously in the manufacturing processes and the purchase prices of these homogeneous items may vary considerably – stocks must be valued at the lower of purchase cost (or production cost) and their net realisable value.

There are many alternative methods that may be used to determine the cost of stock. The four methods that are most commonly used by businesses are:

- **first in first out (FIFO)**
- **last in first out (LIFO)**
- average cost
- market value.

February opening stock	400	1,200	Sales	1,400	16,800
Purchases	1,200	5,200			
	1,600	6,400			
February closing stock	200	600			
Cost of goods sold	1,400	5,800			
Gross profit		11,000			
		16,800			16,800

There were 400 units in stock at the beginning of January that cost £3 each and then 600 units were purchased at £4 each and then 800 purchased at £5 each. On a LIFO basis it is assumed that the 1,400 units sold in January used the 800 last purchased at £5 each and then the 600 units purchased at £4 each. The cost of these units was $(800 \times £5) + (600 \times £4) = £6,400$. The 400 units of stock remaining at the end of January (which becomes the opening stock at the beginning of February) are the 400 units left from opening stock at £3 each and so are valued at £1,200. Using the same basis, the cost of the 1,400 units sold in February was $(1,000 \times £4) + (200 \times £6) + (200 \times £3) = £5,800$. The 200 units of stock remaining at the end of February are the 200 units left from the opening stock of 400 units at £3 each and so are valued at £600.

The result is a gross profit of £10,400 for January and £11,000 for February.

Average cost – smoothing of revenues and stock values, assuming that individual units purchased cannot be followed through to actual sales so total purchases combined to calculate an average cost per unit

	Units	£		Units	£
January opening stock	400	1,200	Sales	1,400	16,800
Purchases	1,400	6,400			
	1,800	7,600			
January closing stock	400	1,689			
Cost of goods sold	1,400	5,911			
Gross profit		10,889			
		16,800			16,800

$$\text{Average cost per unit for January} = \frac{(1,200 + 6,400)}{(400 + 1,400)} = \frac{7,600}{1,800} = £4.222$$

$$\text{January closing stock} = 400 \times \frac{7,600}{1,800} = £1,689$$

	Units	£		Units	£
February opening stock	400	1,689	Sales	1,400	16,800
Purchases	1,200	5,200			
	1,600	6,889			
February closing stock	200	861			
Cost of goods sold	1,400	6,028			
Gross profit		10,772			
		16,800			16,800

$$\text{Average cost per unit for February} = \frac{(1,689 + 5,200)}{(400 + 1,200)} = \frac{6,889}{1,600} = £4.305$$

$$\text{February closing stock} = 200 \times \frac{6,889}{1,600} = £861$$

The result is a gross profit of £10,889 for January and £10,772 for February

The lower of FIFO or market value

	Units	£		Units	£
January opening stock	400	1,200	Sales	1,400	16,800
Purchases	1,400	6,400			
	1,800	7,600			
January closing stock	400	2,000			
Cost of goods sold	1,400	5,600			
Gross profit		11,200			
		16,800			16,800
February opening stock	400	2,000	Sales	1,400	16,800
Purchases	1,200	5,200			
	1,600	7,200			
February closing stock	200	600			
Cost of goods sold	1,400	6,600			
Gross profit		10,200			
		16,800			16,800

January closing stock using FIFO is £2,000. Using market value, January closing stock is 400 units at £6 per unit – £2,400. Using the lower value, stock at the end of January is £2,000. February closing stock using FIFO is £800. Using market value, February closing stock is 200 units at £3 per unit – £600. Using the lower value, stock at the end of February is £600.

Worked Example 3.9

Trade debtors on the books of Sportswear Wholesalers Ltd at 31 January 2005 were £429,378: current month £230,684, month 2 £93,812, 3 to 6 months £64,567, over 6 months £40,315. On 18 January 2005 one of Sportswear's customers, Road Runner Ltd, had gone into liquidation owing Sportswear £15,342, which had been invoiced over 6 months previously. Sportswear's policy was to provide for doubtful debts on the basis of 3 to 6 months' debts 5%, and over 6 months' debts 10%.

Let's consider what entries would appear in Sportwear's cumulative profit and loss account to January 2005 and its balance sheet at 31 January 2005 in respect of bad and doubtful debts. We may assume that no other debts have been written off during the year to date.

Road Runner Ltd has gone into liquidation owing Sportswear £15,342, of which it is assumed there is no chance of any recovery, therefore it must be written off as a bad debt in the profit and loss account in January 2005.

The effect of the bad debt write off is to reduce trade debtors by £15,342, and the debts over 6 months old will reduce down to £24,973 [£40,315 – £15,342].

The doubtful debt provision at 31 January in line with Sportswear's policy is

5% × £64,567   = £3,228
10% × £24,973   = £2,497
Total   = £5,725 (assuming no opening doubtful debt provision at 1 January 2005)

Profit and loss account for the year to 31 January 2005:

Bad and doubtful debts

Road Runner Ltd write off 31/01/05	£15,342
Doubtful debt provision at 31/01/05	£5,725
Balance at 31 January 2005	£21,067

Balance sheet as at 31 January 2005:

Trade debtors:

Balance per accounts receivable at 31/01/05	£429,378
Road Runner Ltd write off 31/01/05	£15,342
Balance at 31 January 2005	£414,036

Doubtful debt provision:

Doubtful debt provision at 31/01/05	£5,725
Balance at 31 January 2005	£5,725

Trade debtors in Sportswear's balance sheet as at 31 January 2005 would be £408,311 [£414,036 – £5,725]

Such bad and doubtful debt entries would not be individually apparent from inspection of Sportswear Wholesalers Ltd's financial statements. Bad and doubtful debt charges are normally included under the profit and loss account heading *Distribution Costs*, and the corresponding balance sheet entries are reflected within the total *Trade Debtors* heading.

Profit and loss and cash flow

During the last decade of the twentieth century there was a great deal of activity in the birth and growth of so-called dot.com companies. Their aim was to exploit the use of the Internet to provide opportunities to sell products and services in wider markets and on an increasingly global basis. The apparent success of the majority of these businesses was initially based on growth of potential in both market share and profitability reflected in the numbers of subscribers attracted to their websites. Actual and potential profitability do not necessarily inevitably result in a healthy cash position. Such companies invariably required large amounts of cash for them to continue operating for extended periods prior to achieving profitability and to generate their own cash flows. Many dot.com businesses from that era failed to survive and flourish, but there were also many successes, for example, Amazon.com, Sportingbet.com, and Lastminute.com.

In Chapter 2 we discussed how profit and cash flow do not mean the same thing. In fact, the profit earned and the net cash generated during an accounting period are usually very different, and often significantly different. How often do we see cases reported of businesses in serious financial difficulties because of severe cash shortages, even though they may appear to be trading profitably?

However, it is invariably the reported profits, or more usually estimated profits, that are closely monitored by investors and financial analysts. It is these numbers on which analysts base their business forecasts, and which influence investor confidence in a business, and therefore its share price.

June 2004 saw a severe profits warning from the budget airline easyJet (see the *Accountancy Age* extract below). easyJet's chief executive actually gave a full year profit forecast for 2004 that indicated that it was likely to be 50% worse than analysts had expected. This had a huge impact on the share price, which fell by 19%.

Nevertheless, cash flow is very important. There is a relationship between cash and profit, and it is possible to identify and quantify the factors within this relationship. The profit or loss made by a business during an accounting period differs from the net cash inflows and outflows during the period because of:

■ cash expected to be paid or received relating to transactions during a period may in fact not be paid or received until the following or subsequent periods

Profits warning – the writing on the wall

Chris Walton, the finance director of troubled budget airline EasyJet, has come under pressure from shareholders to step down over the manner in which the company communicated its recent profit warnings.

The Independent reported that institutional shareholders have raised the issue with the airline's non-executive directors although Sir Colin Chandler, chairman of EasyJet, has backed his FD, saying the company was not contemplating any board changes 'at the moment'.

Last week EasyJet warned that rising fuel prices and fare cuts could hurt fiscal 2004 earnings sending the share price tumbling by 19% – the company's share price has almost halved in value since the beginning of May.

EasyJet founder and its biggest shareholder Stelios Haji-Ioannou, who has a 41% stake in the airline, has also been critical of the manner in which the warnings have been handled saying there was 'room for improvement'.

Easyjet FD under threat

© *Accountancy Age*, 14 June 2004

- cash may have been paid or received in advance of goods or services being received or provided and invoices being received or issued
- cash may have been paid or received relating to non-manufacturing, non-trading, or non-profit items – for example, cash received for shares in the business, and cash paid out on capital expenditure
- profit will have been calculated to include the impact of non-cash items such as depreciation.

When we look at the cash flow statement in the next chapter we shall see that one of the schedules that is required to be prepared in support of the cash flow statement is in fact a reconciliation of operating profit to net cash flow.

Prior to that, we can consider the following example, which is not in strict compliance with the cash flow reconciliation schedule requirement, but will serve to illustrate how profit and cash flow are linked and how the links may be identified.

Worked Example 3.10 shows that despite making a profit of £10,000 during an accounting period the company in fact had a shortfall of cash of £45,000 for the same period. After adjusting profit for the non-cash item of depreciation and adding the increase in share capital it effectively had an increase in funds during the month of £25,000. It then had to finance the purchase of fixed assets of £20,000 and finance an increase in its working capital requirement of £50,000 (stocks £34,000 plus debtors £18,000 less creditors £2,000). This resulted in its cash deficit for the month of £45,000. The company therefore went from having a positive cash balance of £6,000 at the start of the month to an overdraft of £39,000 at the end of the month.

Worked Example 3.10

In Worked Example 3.4 we saw that Ronly Bonly Jones Ltd made a profit of £10,000 during the month of January 2005. A summary of its balance sheet at 1 January 2005, and the 31 January 2005 balance sheet that we derived, are as follows:

	1 January 2005	31 January 2005
	£000	**£000**
Fixed assets at cost	130	150
Depreciation provision	(20)	(25)
Stocks	45	79
Debtors	64	82
Cash and bank	6	–
	225	286
Creditors	(87)	(89)
Bank overdraft	–	(39)
Share capital	(50)	(60)
Profit and loss account	(88)	(98)
	(225)	(286)

We can provide a reconciliation of Ronly Bonly Jones Ltd's profit for the month of January with the cash flow for the same period.

	January 2005
	£000
Profit for the month	10
Add back non-cash item	
Depreciation for month	5
	15
Cash gained from	
Increase in creditors	2
Additional share capital	10
	27
Cash reduced by	
Purchase of fixed assets	(20)
Increase in stocks	(34)
Increase in debtors	(18)
	(72)
Cash outflow for month	(45)
Cash and bank 1 January 2005	6
Cash outflow for month	(45)
Cash and bank 31 January 2005	(39)

Both the company and its bankers would obviously need to monitor RBJ Ltd's performance very closely over future months! A company will normally continuously review its cash, overdraft, accounts payable, and accounts receivable position. The bank manager will regularly review a company's balances and require advance notice of potential breaches of its overdraft limits.

> **Progress check 3.11 In what ways does the profit earned by a business during an accounting period differ from the cash generated during the same period? In what ways are profit and cash affected by the settlement (or not) of their accounts by the customers of the business?**

Summary of key points

- Profit and loss account and income statement are two terms usually used to mean the same thing.
- The profit (or loss) of an entity may be considered from two perspectives: by considering the change in wealth between the start and end of an accounting period; by deducting total costs from total revenues (sales) generated during the accounting period.

- Categories within the profit and loss account are classified into turnover, cost of sales, other operating costs, other operating income, net interest, taxation, and dividends.
- There are four alternative profit and loss account formats permitted by the Companies Act 1985/1989, and in line with the provisions of FRS 3; format 1 is the most widely used by the majority of limited companies.
- The profit and loss account is closely linked with the balance sheet in two ways: they both reflect the change in wealth of the business; most transactions are reflected once in the profit and loss account and once in the balance sheet.
- Valuation of the various items within the balance sheet in accordance with the Companies Act 1985/1989, accounting concepts and standards, has a significant impact on the level of profit (or loss) earned by a business during an accounting period.
- The profit (or loss) earned during an accounting period is not the same as the cash flow generated during the period, but the links between the two measures may be quantified and reconciled.
- There are limitations to the profit and loss account, which like the balance sheet is an historical document, primarily due to the impact on costs of the employment of alternative methods of valuation of assets and liabilities.

Questions

Q3.1   How would you define the profit (or loss) earned by a business during an accounting period?

Q3.2   Outline a profit and loss account showing each of the main category headings.

Q3.3   (i)   What are the requirements that determine the format of the profit and loss account of a limited company?

(ii)   Which accounting standard contains provisions relating to the format of the profit and loss account?

(iii)   What are the main requirements relevant to the formats?

Q3.4   The profit and loss account and the balance sheet report on different aspects of a company's financial status. What are these different aspects and how are they related?

Q3.5   (i)   Why are the methods used for the valuation of the various types of assets so important?

(ii)   Describe the three main categories of asset that are most relevant.

Q3.6   What is depreciation and what are the problems encountered in dealing with the depreciation of fixed assets?

Q3.7   Describe the three most commonly used methods of accounting for depreciation.

Q3.8   Describe the four most commonly used methods of valuing stocks.

Q3.9   How does the valuation of trade debtors impact on the profit and loss account of a business?

Q3.10   Profit does not equal cash, but how can the one be reconciled with the other for a specific accounting period?

Discussion points

D3.1 'My profit for the year is the total of my pile of sales invoices less the cash I have paid out during the year.' Discuss.

D3.2 'The reason why companies make a provision for depreciation on their fixed assets is to save up enough money to buy new ones when the old assets reach the end of their lives.' Discuss.

D3.3 Why is judgement so important in considering the most appropriate method to use for valuing stocks? What are the factors that should be borne in mind and what are the pros and cons of the alternative methods? (Hint: Research Marks and Spencer plc and Laura Ashley plc to collect background material for this discussion.)

Exercises

Solutions are provided in Appendix 3 to all exercise numbers highlighted in colour.

Level I

E3.1 *Time allowed – 30 minutes*

Mr Kumar's chemist shop derives income from both retail sales and from prescription charges made to the NHS and to customers. For the last 2 years to 31 December 2003 and 31 December 2004 his results were as follows:

	2003	**2004**
	£	**£**
Sales and prescription charges to customers	196,500	210,400
Prescription charges to the NHS	48,200	66,200
Purchases of stocks	170,100	180,600
Opening stock at the start of the year	21,720	30,490
Closing stock at the end of the year	30,490	25,300
Wages	25,800	27,300
Mr Kumar drawings*	20,500	19,700
Rent and rates	9,400	13,200
Insurance	1,380	1,620
Motor vehicle expenses	2,200	2,410
Other overheads	14,900	15,300

* Note that Mr Kumar's drawings are the amounts of money that he has periodically taken out of the business for his own use and should be shown as a deduction from the profits earned by the business rather than an expense in the profit and loss account.

Rent for the year 2003 includes £2,400 paid in advance for the half year to 31 March 2004, and for 2004 includes £3,600 paid in advance for the half year to 31 March 2005. Other overheads for 2003 do not include the electricity invoice for £430 for the final quarter (included in 2004 other overheads). There is a similar electricity invoice for £510 for 2004. Depreciation may be ignored.

(i)   Prepare a profit and loss account for the two years to 31 December.

(ii)   Why do you think that there is a difference in the gross profit to sales % between the two years?

(iii) Using Mr Kumar's business as an example, explain the accruals accounting concept and examine whether it has been complied with.

E3.2 *Time allowed – 30 minutes*

Discuss the concepts that may apply and practical problems that may be encountered when accounting for:

(i)   the acquisition of desktop personal computers, and

(ii)   popular brands of products supplied by retailers

with specific comments regarding their depreciation charged to the profit and loss account and their net book values shown in the balance sheet.

E3.3 *Time allowed – 30 minutes*

A friend of yours owns a shop selling CDs and posters for the 12–14-year-old market. From the following information advise him on the potential problems that may be encountered in the valuation of such items for balance sheet purposes:

(i)   greatest hits compilation CDs have sold consistently over the months and cost £5,000 with a retail value of £7,000

(ii)   sales of specific group CDs, which ceased recording in the previous year, have now dropped off to zero and cost £500 with a total retail value of £700

(iii) specific group CDs, which are still constantly recording and selling in the shop every week, cost £1,000 with a total retail value of £1,400

(iv)   specific artist posters are currently not selling at all (although CDs are), and cost £50 with a retail value of £100.

E3.4 *Time allowed – 30 minutes*

The Partex company began trading in 2002, and all sales are made to customers on credit. The company is in a sector that suffers from a high level of bad debts, and a provision for doubtful debts of 4% of outstanding debtors is made at each year end.

Information relating to 2002, 2003 and 2004 was as follows:

	Year to 31 December		
	2002	**2003**	**2004**
Outstanding debtors at 31 December*	£88,000	£110,000	£94,000
Bad debts to be written off during year	£4,000	£5,000	£4,000

* before bad debts have been written off

You are required to state the amount that will appear:

(i)   in the balance sheet for debtors, and

(ii)   in the profit and loss account for bad debts.

E3.5 *Time allowed – 45 minutes*

Tartantrips Ltd, a company in Scotland, operates several ferries and has a policy of holding several in reserve, due to the weather patterns and conditions of various contracts with local authorities. A ferry costs £5 million and has an estimated useful life of 10 years, at which time its realisable value is expected to be £1 million.

Calculate and discuss three methods of depreciation available to the company:

(i)   sum of the digits
(ii)   straight line
(iii) reducing balance.

E3.6 *Time allowed – 60 minutes*
From the following profit and loss information that has been provided by Lazydays Ltd, for the year ended 31 March 2005 (and the corresponding figures for the year to 31 March 2004), construct a profit and loss account, using the format adopted by the majority of UK plcs, including comparative figures.

	2005	**2004**
	£	**£**
Administrative expenses	22,000	20,000
Depreciation	5,000	5,000
Closing stock	17,000	15,000
Distribution costs	33,000	30,000
Dividends paid	32,000	30,000
Dividends received from non-related companies	5,000	5,000
Interest paid	10,000	10,000
Interest received	3,000	3,000
Opening stock	15,000	10,000
Purchases	99,000	90,000
Redundancy costs	5,000	
Sales	230,000	200,000
Taxation	25,000	24,000

(a)   Depreciation is to be included in the administrative expenses
(b)   Redundancy costs are to be regarded as an exceptional item

Level II

E3.7 *Time allowed – 60 minutes*
Llareggyb Ltd started business on 1 January 2005 and its year ended 31 December 2005. Llareggyb entered into the following transactions during the year.

Received funds for share capital of £25,000
Paid suppliers of materials £44,000
Purchased 11,000 units of materials at £8 per unit, one of which was required in one unit of finished goods
Heating and lighting costs paid for cash £16,000
Further heating and lighting costs £2,400 were incurred within the year, but still unpaid at 31 December 2005
Mr D Thomas loaned the company £80,000 on 1 January 2005 at 8% per annum
Loan interest was paid to Mr Thomas for January to June 2005
8,000 finished goods units were sold to customers at £40 each
Customers paid £280,000 to Llareggyb for sales of finished goods

Rent on the premises £60,000 was paid for 18 months from 1 January 2005, and business rates for the same period of £9,000 were also paid

Salaries and wages were paid for January to November amounting to £132,000 but the December payroll cost of £15,000 had not yet been paid

A lorry was purchased for £45,000 on 1 January 2005 and was expected to last for 5 years after which it could be sold for £8,000

The company uses the straight line method of depreciation

Prepare a profit and loss account for Llareggyb Ltd for the year ended 31 December 2005.

E3.8 *Time allowed – 60 minutes*

From the trial balance of Retepmal Ltd at 31 March 2004 prepare a profit and loss account for the year to 31 March 2004 and a balance sheet as at 31 March 2004 using the vertical formats used by most UK companies.

	£
Premises (net book value)	95,000
Trade debtors	75,000
Purchases of stocks	150,000
Retained earnings at 31 March 2003	130,000
Stocks at 31 March 2003	15,000
Furniture and fixtures	30,000
Sales	266,000
Distribution costs and administrative expenses	90,000
Trade creditors	54,000
Motor vehicles (net book value)	40,000
Cash and bank	35,000
Share capital	80,000

Additional information:

(a)   Stocks at 31 March 2004 were £25,000.

(b)   Dividend proposed for 2004 was £7,000.

(c)   An accrual for expenses of £3,000 was required at 31 March 2004.

(d)   A prepayment of expenses of £5,000 was required at 31 March 2004.

(e)   Corporation tax estimated to be payable on 2003/2004 profits was £19,000.

(f)   Annual depreciation charges on premises and motor vehicles for the year to 31 March 2004 are included in administrative expenses and distribution costs respectively, and in the cumulative depreciation provisions used to calculate the net book values of £95,000 and £40,000, shown in the trial balance at 31 March 2004.

The furniture and fixtures balance of £30,000 relates to purchases of assets during the year to 31 March 2004. The depreciation charge to administrative expenses and the corresponding depreciation provision are not included in the trial balance at 31 March 2004. They are required to be calculated for a full year to 31 March 2004, based on a useful economic life of eight years and an estimated residual value of £6,000.

4

Financial statements of limited companies – cash flow statement

Contents

financial position. We will see in this chapter how the cash flow statement addresses this shortfall of information provided by the other two key financial statements, by answering questions like:

- How much capital expenditure (for example, machines and buildings) has the company made, and how did it fund the expenditure?
- What was the extent of new borrowing and how much debt was repaid?
- How much did the company need to fund new **working capital requirements** (for example, increases in debtors and stock requirements as a result of more business activity)?
- How much of the company's funding was met by funds generated from its trading activities, and how much was met by new external funding (for example, from banks and other lenders, or new shareholders)?

We introduced the DVD analogy in Chapters 2 and 3 with regard to the balance sheet and the profit and loss account. In the same way as profit (or loss), cash represents the dynamic DVD of changes in the cash position of the business throughout the period between the two 'pauses' – the balance sheets at the start and the finish of an accounting period. The cash flow statement summarises the cash inflows and outflows and calculates the net change in the cash position throughout the period. In this way it provides answers to the questions shown above. Analysis and summary of the cash inflows and outflows of the period answers those questions by illustrating:

- changes in the level of cash between the start and end of the period
- how much cash has been generated, and from where
- for what purpose cash has been used.

Structure of the cash flow statement

The basic purpose of a cash flow statement, as we saw in Chapter 2, is to report the cash receipts and cash payments that take place within an accounting period (see Fig. 4.1), and to show how the cash balance has changed from the start of the period to the balance at the end of the period. This can be seen to be objective and clearly avoids the problems of allocation associated with the preparation of a conventional profit and loss account.

However, a more useful presentation would describe:

- how the company generated or lost cash

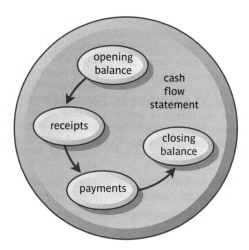

Figure 4.1 The main elements of the cash flow statement

- how the company financed its growth and investments
- the extent to which the company was funded by debt and equity.

The cash flow statement is covered in FRS 1, Cash Flow Statements, and its objective is to ensure that **reporting entities** fall within its scope:

- for companies to report their cash generation and cash absorption for a period by highlighting the significant components of cash flow in a way that facilitates comparison of the cash flow performances of different businesses
- for companies to provide information that assists in the assessment of their liquidity, solvency and financial adaptability.

SSAP 10, Statements of Source and Application of Funds, was the original accounting standard that required companies to provide a statement of source and application of funds. This statement was difficult to understand and did not provide a clear explanation of the cash flows of the company. SSAP 10 was replaced in September 1991 by the ASB with FRS 1, requiring companies to publish a cash flow statement. FRS 1 was subsequently revised in 1996. FRS 1 requires that the company's cash flow statement should list its cash flows for the period, and be classified under standard headings. These headings arc represented in Fig. 4.2.

> Progress check 4.1 Explain what is meant by a cash flow statement.

The headings under which cash inflows and outflows for the period are itemised follow a particular order. We will look at explanations of each of the headings and how they are put together to provide an analysis of the cash movements of the business over an accounting period.

> Progress check 4.2 What are the aims and purposes of the cash flow statement?

Figure 4.2 Cash inflows and cash outflows reflected in the cash flow statement

Creditors due within one year	(305)	(312)
Bank overdraft	(153)	(222)
Equity	(308)	(555)
	(766)	(1,089)

The indirect method may be used to calculate the net cash flow from operating activities:

Calculation of depreciation	£000
Fixed assets at the start of the year were	385
Additions during the year were	290
Disposals during the year were	zero
	675
Fixed assets at the end of the year were	525
Therefore, depreciation for the year was	150

Indirect Ltd
Cash flow statement for the year ended 30 June 2005
Reconciliation of operating profit to net cash inflow from operating activities

	£000
Operating profit	247
Depreciation charges	150
Increase in stocks [277 – 157]	(120)
Increase in debtors [287 – 224]	(63)
Increase in creditors due within 1 year [312 – 305]	7
Net cash inflow from operating activities	221

The above worked example shows how the net cash inflow from operating activities of £221,000 was calculated by starting with the operating profit for the year of £247,000 and adjusting for changes in depreciation and working capital over the year.

The only other cash activity during the year appears to be the acquisition of fixed assets totalling £290,000. If we deduct that from the net cash inflow from operating activities of £221,000 we get a net cash outflow of £69,000. This agrees with the movement in the cash and bank balances, which have worsened from an overdraft of £153,000 at the beginning of the year to an overdraft of £222,000 at the end of the year.

Progress check 4.5 Describe the direct and the indirect cash flow methods that may be used to derive net operating cash flow, their differences and their purpose.

Cash flow statement formats

There is no statutory requirement for companies to prepare a cash flow statement. FRS 1 requires all reporting entities that prepare financial statements, intended to give a true and fair view of their financial position and profit and loss, to include a cash flow statement as a primary statement within their financial statements, except for small companies which are specifically exempted.

There is one standard format for the cash flow statement prescribed by FRS 1, which includes the headings we have discussed above. The cash flow statement actually comprises a number of statements:

- reconciliation of operating profit to net operating cash flows (Fig. 4.4)
- cash flow statement of cash inflows and outflows (Fig. 4.5)
- reconciliation of net cash flow to movement in **net debt** (Fig. 4.6)
- note on gross cash flows (Fig. 4.7)
- note on analysis of changes in net debt (Fig. 4.8).

Figures 4.4 to 4.8 illustrate the format of the cash flow statements and have been prepared from the balance sheet and profit and loss account for Flatco plc included in Chapter 2 and Chapter 3.

The comparative figures for the previous year (not shown in the Flatco plc illustrations, Figs 4.3 to 4.8) are usually reported in columns to the right of the current year's figures. Each of the statements shown in Figs 4.4 to 4.8 is important for the following reasons:

- the reconciliation of operating profit to net cash flow from operating activities (Fig. 4.4) shows how the net cash flow from operating activities is derived from adjusting operating profit for non-cash items and movements in working capital
- the cash flow statement (Fig. 4.5) reports the net cash flow for an accounting period, derived from the net cash flow from operating activities and adjusted for all non-operating categories of cash inflows and outflows
- the reconciliation of net cash flow to movement in net debt (Fig. 4.6) shows how the net cash flow for an accounting period is the difference between the net debt at the beginning of the period and the net debt at the end of the period
- note 1 – gross cash flows (Fig. 4.7) provides more detail with regard to the non-operating cash inflows and outflows used in the cash flow statement (Fig. 4.5)
- note 2 – analysis of changes in net debt (Fig. 4.8) analyses the net debt movement shown in Fig. 4.6 in greater detail to show each of the categories that comprise net debt.

Flatco plc
Cash flow statement for the year ended 31 December 2005
Reconciliation of operating profit to net cash flow from operating activities

	£000
Operating profit	550
Depreciation charges	345
Increase in stocks	(43)
Increase in debtors	(28)
Increase in creditors	112
Net cash inflow from operating activities	936

Figure 4.4 Reconciliation of operating profit to net cash flow from operating activities

Cash flow statement	
	£000
Net cash inflow from operating activities	936
Returns on investments and servicing of finance (note 1)	40
Taxation	(44)
Capital expenditure (note 1)	(299)
	633
Equity dividends paid	(67)
	566
Management of liquid resources (note 1)	–
Financing (note 1)	373
Increase in cash	939

Figure 4.5 Cash flow statement

Reconciliation of net cash flow to movement in net debt/funds (note 2)	
	£000
Increase in cash for the period	939
Cash inflow from increase in long-term debt	(173)
Change in net debt	766
Net debt at 1 January 2005	(662)
Net funds at 31 December 2005	104

Figure 4.6 Reconciliation of net cash flow to movement in net debt/funds

Note 1 to the cash flow statement – gross cash flows		
	£000	**£000**
Returns on investments and servicing of finance		
Income from investments	100	
Interest received	11	
Interest paid	(71)	
		40
Capital expenditure		
Payments to acquire tangible fixed assets	(286)	
Payments to acquire intangible fixed assets	(34)	
Receipts from sales of tangible fixed assets	21	
		(299)
Management of liquid resources		
Purchase of Government bills (short-term investments)	(200)	
Sale of Government bills (short-term investments)	200	
		–
Financing		
Issue of ordinary share capital	200	
Debenture loan	173	
		373

Figure 4.7 Note 1 – gross cash flows

Note 2 to the cash flow statement – analysis of change in net debt/funds			
	At 1 January 2005 £000	Cash flows £000	At 31 December 2005 £000
Cash in hand and at bank	17	310	327
Overdraft	(679)	629	(50)
Debenture	–	(173)	(173)
Total (debt)/funds	662	766	104

Figure 4.8 Note 2 – analysis of change in net debt/funds

Worked Example 4.3

The reconciliation of operating profit to net cash flow from operating activities shown below is an extract from the published accounts of Tomkins plc, which is a diversified multinational UK plc with interests in the UK, USA and other parts of the world. Tomkins had been acquisitive in the past, but sold off activities it wished not to develop in the future.

We can use this table to comment on the working capital movements for the year 2000.

Figures in £m	2000	1999
Operating profit	519.1	495.3
Depreciation	197.9	175.0
Profit/(loss) on sale of fixed assets	(1.0)	(6.1)
(Increase)/decrease in stocks	(64.4)	4.7
(Increase)/decrease in debtors	(73.2)	7.2
Increase/(decrease) in creditors	(0.9)	(89.7)
Other	0.5	1.3
Net cash inflow from operating activities	578.0	587.7

Operating profits may initially be considered to be on a plateau, but as the group is not solely involved in one industrial sector, further analysis is difficult.

The stocks movement of £64.4m is quite significant and the company may be expected to explain what activity or decision brought this about.

The debtors movement of £73.2m is also worthy of separate comment to assist users of the cash flow statement to make their economic judgement.

The creditors movement of £0.9m is most unexpected as many companies would use creditors in part to finance increases in stocks and debtors.

Net cash inflows for the two years are so similar that the company may have set internal targets to ensure sufficient cash flows were achieved, allowing for acquisitions, disposals and trading.

Worked Example 4.4

The extract from a leading UK supermarket retailer's cash flow statement shown below is its net debt note for the year to February 2000.

Figures in £m	Opening balance 1 Mar 1999	Cash flow	Closing balance 28 Feb 2000
Cash at bank	127	(39)	88
Overdrafts	(31)	(4)	(35)
	96	(43)	53
Liquid resources	201	57	258
Short-term loans	(799)	(13)	(812)
Long-term loans	(1,218)	(341)	(1,559)
Net debt	(1,720)	(340)	(2,060)

We will discuss each of the elements in the net debt note and comment briefly on the cash flow movements over the year.

(a) Both cash and overdraft balances have contributed to the increase in net debt. This apparent policy of reducing cash balances and increasing overdrafts may be questioned. The actual policy can be established by looking at the trends over several years and any comments made by the company in its published report and accounts.

(b) The liquid resources were in fact increased, possibly to take advantage of the increase in interest rates being paid in the UK. The company was actually publicly criticised in late 2000 by the UK Government for holding on to suppliers' funds for too long.

(c) The company is obviously using short-term funds to finance the business. The users of financial information usually require information on the timing of repayments of loans (in this case the bulk of the £812 million short-term debt is owed to banks), which plcs are required by the Companies Act to disclose in their published reports and accounts.

(d) All major UK plcs provide an overview of their treasury activities in their published reports and accounts, which links current policies with the components of net debt (for example, banking facilities).

(e) The financial press sometimes comment on net debt movement. This may vary from year to year and from analyst to analyst. A typical comment might be 'the £340 million increase has pushed net borrowings of the company to over £2 billion for the first time'.

The Companies Act 1985/1989 requires group accounts to be prepared for the holding company in addition to the accounts that are required to be prepared for each of the individual companies within the group. These 'consolidated accounts' exclude all transactions between companies within the group, for example inter-company sales and purchases. Undertakings preparing consolidated financial statements should prepare a consolidated cash flow statement and related notes; they are not then required to prepare an entity cash flow statement.

> **Progress check 4.6** What are the schedules that are used to support the main cash flow statement and what is their purpose?

Worked Example 4.5

We may use the following data, extracted from the financial records of Zap Electronics plc, to prepare a cash flow statement in compliance with the provisions of FRS 1, together with the appropriate notes and reconciliations. The data relate to the financial statements prepared for the year ended 31 July 2005.

	£000
Dividends paid on ordinary shares	49
Purchase of Government bills (short-term investments)	200
Issue of ordinary share capital	100
Reduction in stocks	25
Corporation tax paid	120
Interest paid	34
Operating profit	830
Bank and cash balance 31 July 2005	527
Purchase of machinery	459
Sale of Government bills	100
Interest received	18
Purchase of a copyright (intangible fixed asset)	78
Depreciation charge for the year	407
Purchase of a building	430
Sale of a patent (intangible fixed asset)	195
Increase in trade debtors	35
Reduction in trade creditors (due within 1 year)	85
Bank and cash balance 1 August 2004	342

Zap Electronics plc
Cash flow statement for the year ended 31 July 2005
Reconciliation of operating profit to net cash flow from operating activities

	£000
Operating profit	830
Depreciation charge	407
Reduction in stocks	25
Increase in debtors	(35)
Reduction in creditors	(85)
Net cash inflow from operating activities	**1,142**

Cash flow statement

	£000
Net cash inflow from operating activities	1,142
Returns on investments and servicing of finance (note 1)	(16)
Taxation	(120)
Capital expenditure (note 1)	(772)
	234
Equity dividends paid	(49)
	185
Management of liquid resources (note 1)	(100)
Financing (note 1)	100
Increase in cash	185

Reconciliation of net cash flow to movement in net debt/net funds (note 2)

	£000
Increase in cash for the period	185
Change in net debt	185
Net funds at 1 August 2004	342
Net funds at 31 July 2005	527

Note 1 to the cash flow statement – gross cash flows

	£000	£000
Returns on investments and servicing of finance		
Interest received	18	
Interest paid	(34)	
		(16)
Capital expenditure		
Payments to acquire intangible fixed assets	(78)	
Payments to acquire tangible fixed assets [430 + 459]	(889)	
Receipts from sales of intangible fixed assets	195	
		(772)
Management of liquid resources		
Purchase of Government bills	(200)	
Sale of Government bills	100	
		(100)
Financing		
Issue of ordinary share capital		100

Note 2 to the cash flow statement – analysis of change in net debt/funds

	At 1 August 2004	Cash flows	At 31 July 2005
	£000	£000	£000
Bank and cash	342	185	527
Overdraft	–	–	–
	342	185	527

Worked Example 4.6

Perfecto Ltd
Profit and loss account for the year ended 30 September 2005

	£000	£000
Turnover		2,279
Cost of sales		(1,484)
Gross profit		795
Distribution costs	(368)	
Administrative expenses	(197)	
		(565)
Operating profit		230
Net interest		(10)
Profit before tax		220
Tax on profit on ordinary activities		(70)
Profit on ordinary activities after tax		150
Dividends [20 + 20]		(40)
Retained profit for the financial year		110

Perfecto Ltd
Balance sheet as at 30 September 2005

	2005	2004
	£000	£000
Fixed assets		
Intangible	203	193
Tangible	902	1,071
	1,105	1,264
Current assets		
Stocks	161	142
Debtors	284	193
Prepayments	295	278
Cash	157	–
	897	613

Current liabilities (less than one year)

Bank overdraft	–	20
Creditors	187	231
Corporation tax	70	55
Proposed dividend	20	20
Accruals	100	81
	377	407
Net current assets	520	206
Total assets less current liabilities	1,625	1,470
less		
Long-term liabilities (over one year)		
Creditors	77	184
Financial debt	85	126
Provisions	103	185
	265	495
Net assets	1,360	975
Capital and reserves		
Capital	600	450
Premiums	105	–
Profit and loss account	655	525
	1,360	975

During the year Perfecto Ltd acquired new plant and machinery for £150,000, bought a patent for £10,000, and made no disposals of either tangible or intangible fixed assets.

Perfecto Ltd paid an interim dividend of £20,000 during the year and declared a final dividend of £20,000. Interest paid was £20,000 and interest received was £10,000. The company paid corporation tax of £55,000 during the year.

We have all the data required to prepare a cash flow statement for the year ended 30 September 2005 complying with FRS 1, including all supporting reconciliations and notes.

	£000
Fixed assets at the start of the year were	1,264
Additions during the year were	160 [150 + 10]
Disposals during the year were	zero
	1,424
Fixed assets at the end of the year were	1,105
Therefore, depreciation for the year was	319

	30 Sep 2004	30 Sep 2005	Difference
	£000	£000	£000
Stocks	142	161	19 increase
Debtors and prepayments	471 [193 + 278]	579 [284 + 295]	108 increase
Creditors, accruals, and provisions	681 [231 + 81 + 184 + 185]	467 [187 + 100 + 77 + 103]	214 decrease

Perfecto Ltd
Cash flow statement for the year ended 30 September 2005
Reconciliation of operating profit to net cash flow from operating activities

	£000
Operating profit	230
Depreciation charges	319
Increase in stocks	(19)
Increase in debtors	(108)
Reduction in creditors	(214)
Net cash inflow from operating activities	208

Cash flow statement

	£000
Net cash inflow from operating activities	208
Returns on investments and servicing of finance (note 1)	(10)
Taxation	(55)
Capital expenditure (note 1)	(160)
	(17)
Equity dividends paid	(20)
	(37)
Management of liquid resources (note 1)	–
Financing (note 1)	214
Increase in cash	177

Reconciliation of net cash flow to movement in net debt/funds (note 2)

	£000
Increase in cash for the period	177
Cash outflow from decrease in long-term debt	41
Change in net debt	218
Net debt at 30 September 2004	(146)
Net funds at 30 September 2005	72

Note 1 to the cash flow statement – gross cash flows

	£000	£000
Returns on investments and servicing of finance		
Interest received	10	
Interest paid	(20)	
		(10)
Capital expenditure		
Payments to acquire tangible fixed assets	(150)	
Payments to acquire intangible fixed assets	(10)	
		(160)
Financing		
Issue of ordinary share capital [600 + 105 – 450]	255	
Repayment of loans [126 – 85]	(41)	
		214

Note 2 to the cash flow statement – analysis of change in net debt/funds

	At 30 September 2004 £000	Cash flows £000	At 30 September 2005 £000
Cash	–	157	157
Bank overdraft	(20)	20	–
Long-term debt	(126)	41	(85)
Total (debt)/funds	(146)	218	72

Cash flow links to the balance sheet and profit and loss account

The diagram shown in Fig. 4.9 is a representation of some simple links between cash flow and the profit and loss account, and the relationship with the balance sheet. It shows how, for example:

- a purchase of fixed assets for cash of £50 has
  - increased fixed assets in the balance sheet from the opening balance of £100 to the closing balance of £150
  - decreased the opening cash balance by £50
- a profit of £100, that has been realised in cash, has
  - increased by £100 the opening cash balance of £100 which, less the outflow of £50 for fixed assets, gives a closing balance of £150
  - increased the profit and loss account from the opening balance of £100 to the closing balance of £200.

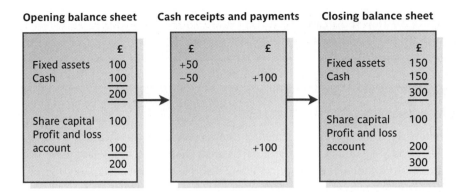

Figure 4.9 Some simple links between cash flow and the profit and loss account, and the balance sheet

The effect of the above transactions is

- cash has increased by £50
- fixed assets have been increased by £50
- profit has increased by £100
- the balance sheet is still in balance with increased total assets and total liabilities.

We may see from the more detailed information given as part of cash flow statement reporting how cash flow may be appreciated in the context of the information given by the balance sheet and the profit and loss account. The accounting standard FRS 1, Cash Flow Statements requires companies to provide two reconciliations included as part of the cash flow statement reporting, between:

- operating profit and the net cash flow from operating activities

and between:

- the net cash flow during the period and the movement in net debt.

These reconciliations do not form part of the cash flow statement but each is provided in a supporting schedule and in a separate note. The links between cash flow and the profit and loss account may therefore be observed by way of the operating profit adjusted for non-cash items and the changes in working capital, to arrive at net cash flow from operating activities.

Opening and closing balances of cash do not appear on the face of the cash flow statement and so do not provide a direct link with the corresponding numbers reported in the balance sheet. It is for this reason that the increase or decrease in cash that appears in the cash flow statement must be reconciled with the opening and closing balance sheet numbers – the movement in net debt.

Usually this reconciliation is a simple matter of adding the increase or decrease in cash during the accounting period to the opening balance of cash and cash equivalents to agree the closing balance of cash. However, there are some situations when, in addition to the cash flows of the entity, the movement in net debt has to identify specific items, which must be reconciled to the opening and closing balance sheet amounts:

- the acquisition or disposal of subsidiaries (excluding cash balances)
- other non-cash charges
- the recognition of changes in market value and exchange rate movements.

Progress check 4.7 How is the cash flow statement of a business related to its other financial statements, the profit and loss account and the balance sheet?

Worked Example 4.7

Detailed below are the cash flow statement and direct cash flow analysis for Ronly Bonly Jones Ltd for the month of January 2005, and its balance sheet as at 1 January 2005. Rather than deriving a cash flow statement from a profit and loss account and a balance sheet this example aims to derive the following information from a cash flow statement:

(i)   reconciliation of the cash flow for the month with the profit for the month
(ii) derivation of the profit and loss account for the month
(iii) derivation of the changes in the balance sheet during the month from the 1 January balance sheet
(iv) preparation of the balance sheet as at 31 January 2005.

Figures in £000

Reconciliation of operating profit to net cash flow from operating activities

Operating profit	10
Depreciation charges	5
Increase in stocks	(34)
Increase in debtors	(18)
Increase in creditors	2
Net cash outflow from operating activities	(35)

Cash flow statement

Net cash outflow from operating activities	(35)
Capital expenditure – tangible fixed asset additions	(20)
	(55)
Financing – increase in equity share capital	10
Decrease in cash	(45)

Direct method

Operating activities	
Net cash received from customers	632
Cash payments to suppliers	(422)
Cash paid to and on behalf of employees	(190)
Other cash payments	(55)
Net cash outflow from operating activities	(35)

Balance sheet as at 1 January 2005

	£000
Fixed assets at cost	130
Depreciation provision	(20)
Stocks	45
Debtors	64
Cash and bank	6
	225
Creditors	(87)
Share capital	(50)
Profit and loss account	(88)
	(225)

We may reconcile the cash flow for the month with the profit for the month as follows:

January 2005

	£000	
Increase in debtors during the month	18	
Cash received from customers	632	
Sales for the month	650	
Increase in stocks during the month	(34)	
Purchases of materials from suppliers	424	[increase in creditors 2 + cash payments to suppliers 422]
Cost of goods sold in the month	390	
Depreciation charge in the month	5	
Cash paid to and on behalf of employees	190	
Other cash payments	55	
Expenses for the month	245	

Therefore the profit and loss account for January 2005 is

	£000
Sales	650
Cost of goods sold	(390)
Depreciation	(5)
Expenses	(245)
Profit for January	10

Let's derive the 31 January 2005 balance sheet from the information that has been provided:

Figures in £000	Fixed assets	Depn	Stocks	Debtors	Cash	Creditors	Equity	Profit/loss account
1 January 2005	130	(20)	45	64	6	(87)	(50)	(88)
Sales				650				(650)
Cash from customers				(632)	632			0
Purchases			424			(424)		0
Cash to creditors					(422)	422		0
Stock sold			(390)					390
Depreciation		(5)						5
Expenses					(245)			245
Fixed asset additions	20				(20)			0
Issue of shares					10		(10)	0
31 January 2005	150	(25)	79	82	(39)	(89)	(60)	(98)

Therefore the balance sheets at 1 January 2005 and at 31 January 2005 are as follows:

	1 January 2005 £000	31 January 2005 £000
Fixed assets at cost	130	150
Depreciation provision	(20)	(25)
Stocks	45	79
Debtors	64	82
Cash and bank	6	(39)
	225	247
Creditors	(87)	(89)
Share capital	(50)	(60)
Profit and loss account	(88)	(98)
	(225)	(247)

In Worked Example 4.7, we have

- used the cash flow statement to derive the profit and loss account for the month

and we have then used the

- 1 January 2005 balance sheet
- profit and loss account for the month of January 2005
- non-profit and loss items also shown in the January cash flow statement

to derive the balance sheet for 31 January 2005.

In this way, we can see how the balance sheet, profit and loss account and cash flow statement of a business are inextricably linked.

Worked Example 4.8

We can use the cash flow reconciliation statement to provide an explanation of the net cash outflow of £45,000, shown in Worked Example 4.7, to shareholders in Ronly Bonly Jones Ltd.

During January 2005 there was a profit before depreciation of £15,000 (£10,000 + £5,000). This, together with the increase in share capital of £10,000, provided a total cash inflow for the month of £25,000. However, there was a net outflow of cash on increased working capital of £50,000 (£34,000 + £18,000 − £2,000) and capital expenditure of £20,000. This all resulted in a net cash outflow of £45,000 (£25,000 − £50,000 − £20,000).

The net cash outflow may be in line with what the company had planned or forecast for January 2005. Alternatively, the outflow may not have been expected. Changes in trading circumstances and/or management decisions may have been the reason for the difference between the actual and expected cash flow for January 2005.

The shareholders of Ronly Bonly Jones Ltd need to be reassured that the current cash position is temporary, and under control, and within the overdraft facility agreed with the company's bankers. The shareholders must also be reassured that the company is not in financial difficulty or that if problems are being experienced then the appropriate remedial actions are in place.

Summary of key points

- Cash flow includes not only cash in hand but also deposits and overdrafts, repayable on demand with any bank or other financial institutions.
- The cash flow statement lists the inflows and outflows of cash for a period classified under the standard headings of: operating activities; returns on investments and servicing of finance; taxation; capital expenditure and financial investment; acquisitions and disposals; equity dividends paid; management of liquid resources; financing.
- The preparation of a cash flow statement is not a legal requirement. However, FRS 1 requires all reporting entities which prepare financial statements intended to give a true and fair view of their financial position and profit and loss to include a cash flow statement as a primary statement within their financial statements, unless specifically exempted.
- There is only one standard format for the cash flow statement prescribed by FRS 1, comprising a main statement of cash inflows and outflows, supported by schedules and notes reconciling net operating cash flow to operating profit and reconciling net cash flow to changes in net debt.
- Net cash flow from operating activities may be derived using the direct method or the indirect method, with both methods giving the same result.
- The cash flow statement is directly related to both the profit and loss account and the balance sheet and the links between them may be quantified and reconciled.
- The preparation of the cash flow statement is a highly objective exercise, in which all the headings and amounts are cash based and therefore easily measured.
- The cash flow generated during an accounting period is a matter of fact and does not rely on judgement or the use of alternative conventions or valuation methods.

Questions

Q4.1 (i) How would you define cash generated by a business during an accounting period?

(ii) Which accounting standard deals with cash flow?

Q4.2 Give an example of the main cash flow statement showing each of the main categories.

Q4.3 Give an example of the reconciliations and notes that are prepared in support of the main cash flow statement.

Q4.4 Describe the ways in which both the direct method and the indirect method may be used to derive the net operating cash flow during an accounting period of a business.

Q4.5 (i) Which reconciliation statement is used to link the cash flow statement to the profit and loss account?

(ii) How does it do that?

Q4.6 (i) Which reconciliation statement is used to link the cash flow statement to the balance sheet?

(ii) What are the links?

Q4.7 Why is cash so important, compared to the other assets used within a business?

Q4.8 (i) What questions does the cash flow statement aim to answer?

(ii) How far does it go towards answering them?

Discussion points

D4.1 Why is the information disclosed in the profit and loss account and the balance sheet not considered sufficient for users of financial information? What was so important about cash flow that it was considered necessary for the Accounting Standards Board to issue FRS 1 (Cash Flow Statements) in 1991, which was subsequently revised in 1996?

D4.2 'Forget your profit and loss accounts and balance sheets, at the end of the day it's the business's healthy bank balance that is the measure of its increase in wealth.' Discuss.

Exercises

Solutions are provided in Appendix 3 to all exercise numbers highlighted in colour.

Level I

E4.1 *Time allowed – 60 minutes*

Candice-Marie James and Flossie Graham obtained a one-year lease on a small shop which cost them £15,000 for the year 2005, and agreed to pay rent of £4,000 per year payable one year in advance. Candyfloss started trading on 1 January 2005 as a florist, and Candice and Flossie bought a second-hand, white delivery van for which they paid £14,500. The business was financed by Candice and Flossie each providing £9,000 from their savings and an interest free loan from Candice's uncle of £3,000. Candice and Flossie thought they were doing OK over their first six months but they weren't sure how to measure this. They decided to try and see how they were doing financially and looked at the transactions for the first six months:

	£
Cash sales of flowers	76,000
Rent paid	4,000
Wages paid	5,000
Payments for other operating expenses	7,000
Purchases of stocks of flowers for resale	59,500
Legal expenses paid for the lease acquisition	1,000

In addition, at 30 June 2005 they owed a further £4,000 for the purchase of flowers and £1,000 for other operating expenses. Customers had purchased flowers on credit and the sum still owed amounted to £8,000. One customer was apparently in financial difficulties and it was likely that the £1,500 owed would not be paid. Stocks of flowers at 30 June 2005 valued at cost were £9,500. They estimated that the van would last four years, at which time they expected to sell it for £2,500, and that depreciation would be spread evenly over that period.

(i)   **Prepare a cash flow statement for Candyfloss for the first 6 months of the year 2005 using the direct method.**

(ii)   **Prepare a conventional profit and loss account statement for Candyfloss, on an accruals basis.**

(iii)   **Why is the profit different from the cash flow?**

(iv)   **Which statement gives the best indication of the first 6 months' performance of Candyfloss?**

E4.2 *Time allowed – 60 minutes*

Using the information from Exercise E4.1 prepare a cash flow statement for Candyfloss for the first six months of the year 2005, using the indirect method.

E4.3 *Time allowed – 60 minutes*

Jaffrey Packaging plc have used the following information in the preparation of their financial statements for the year ended 31 March 2005.

	£000
Dividends paid	25
Issue of a debenture	200
Reduction in stocks	32
Corporation tax paid	73
Interest paid	28
Operating profit for the year	450
Bank and cash balance 31 March 2005	376
Purchase of factory equipment	302
Dividends payable at 31 March 2005	25
Interest received	5
Depreciation charge for the year	195
Purchase of a new large computer system	204
Sale of a patent (intangible fixed asset)	29
Increase in trade debtors	43
Reduction in short-term creditors	62
Bank and cash balance 1 April 2004	202

You are required to prepare a cash flow statement in compliance with the provisions of FRS 1, together with the appropriate supporting schedules and reconciliations.

E4.4 *Time allowed – 60 minutes*

From the profit and loss account for the year ended 31 December 2004 and balance sheets as at 31 December 2003 and 31 December 2004, prepare a complete cash flow statement for Medco Ltd for the year to 31 December 2004.

During the year 2004 the company:

(i)   acquired new fixed assets that cost £12,500

(ii) issued new share capital for £5,000

(iii) sold fixed assets for £2,000 that had originally cost £3,000 and had a net book value of £2,500

(iv) depreciated its fixed assets by £2,000.

Figures in £

	2004
Profit and loss account	
Operating profit	2,500
Interest	(100)
Profit before tax	2,400
Tax	(500)
Profit on ordinary activities after tax	1,900
Interim dividend	(300)
Final dividend	(600)
Retained profit	1,000

Balance sheet as at 31 December	**2004**	**2003**
Fixed assets	28,000	20,000
Current assets		
Stocks	6,000	5,000
Debtors	4,000	3,000
Investments	5,100	3,000
Cash and bank	2,150	5,000
Creditors due in less than one year		
Overdraft	(6,000)	(2,000)
Trade creditors	(4,000)	(6,000)
Taxation	(500)	(400)
Dividend (proposed)	(600)	(450)
Creditors due in over one year		
Loan	(2,000)	(1,000)
Net assets	32,150	26,150
Capital and reserves		
Ordinary shares	14,000	10,000
Share premium	6,000	5,000
Profit and loss account	12,150	11,150
	32,150	26,150

Level II

E4.5 *Time allowed – 90 minutes*

Llareggyb Ltd started business on 1 January 2005 and its year ended 31 December 2005. Llareggyb made the following transactions during the year.

Received funds for share capital of £25,000

Paid suppliers of materials £44,000

Purchased 11,000 units of materials at £8 per unit, one of which was required in one unit of finished goods

Heating and lighting costs paid for cash £16,000

Further heating and lighting costs £2,400 were incurred within the year, but unpaid at 31 December 2005

Mr D Thomas loaned the company £80,000 on 1 January 2005 at 8% per annum

Loan interest was paid to Mr Thomas for January to June 2005

8,000 finished goods units were sold to customers at £40 each

Customers paid £280,000 to Llareggyb for sales of finished goods

Rent on the premises £60,000 was paid for 18 months from 1 January 2005, and business rates of £9,000 for the same period were also paid

Salaries and wages were paid for January to November amounting to £132,000 but the December payroll cost of £15,000 had not been paid

A lorry was purchased for £45,000 on 1 January 2005 and was expected to last for 5 years after which it could be sold for £8,000. The company uses the straight line method of depreciation.

You are required to:

(i)   **prepare a balance sheet for Llareggyb Ltd as at 31 December 2005**

(ii) **prepare a cash flow statement for Llareggyb Ltd for the year ended 31 December 2005.**

(Note: you may use the profit or loss figure calculated in Exercise E3.7 to complete this exercise.)

E4.6 *Time allowed – 90 minutes*

The balance sheets for Victoria plc as at 30 June 2003 and 30 June 2004 are shown below:

Victoria plc
Balance sheet as at 30 June

Figures in £000	2003	2004
Fixed assets		
Cost	6,900	9,000
Depreciation provision	(900)	(1,100)
	6,000	7,900
Current assets		
Stocks	2,600	4,000
Trade debtors	2,000	2,680
Cash and bank	200	–
	4,800	6,680

Creditors due within one year

Overdraft	–	600
Trade creditors	2,000	1,800
Tax payable	300	320
Dividend payable	360	480
	2,660	3,200
Net current assets	2,140	3,480
Total assets less current liabilities	8,140	11,380
less		
Creditors due in over one year		
10% Debentures	(1,000)	(1,000)
Net assets	7,140	10,380
Capital and reserves		
Ordinary share capital	4,000	5,500
Share premium	–	1,240
Profit and loss account	3,140	3,640
	7,140	10,380

The following information is also relevant:

1. During the years 2003 and 2004 Victoria plc disposed of no fixed assets.
2. Interim dividends were not paid during the years ended 30 June 2003 and 2004.
3. Debenture interest was paid on 10 February in each year.

You are required to:

(i)   calculate:

      (a)   **profit before tax for the year ended 30 June 2004**

      (b)   **operating profit for the year ended 30 June 2004**

(ii)   **prepare a cash flow statement for Victoria plc for the year to 30 June 2004 that includes all supporting schedules and an analysis of change in net debt.**

E4.7 *Time allowed – 90 minutes*

Sparklers plc have completed the preparation of their profit and loss account for the year ended 31 October 2004 and their balance sheet as at 31 October 2004. During the year Sparklers sold for £2m some fixed assets that had originally cost £11m. The cumulative depreciation on those assets at 31 October 2003 was £7.6m.

You have been asked to prepare a full cash flow statement for the same period in compliance with the provisions contained in FRS 1. The directors are concerned about the large bank overdraft at 31 October 2004 which they believe is due mainly to the increase in trade debtors as a result of apparently poor credit control. What is your assessment of the reasons for the increased overdraft?

Sparklers plc
Profit and loss account for the year ended 31 October 2004

	2004	2003
	£m	£m
Operating profit	41.28	18.80
Interest paid	(0.56)	–
Interest received	0.08	0.20
Profit before tax	40.80	19.00
Tax on profit on ordinary activities	(10.40)	(6.40)
Profit after tax	30.40	12.60
Dividends		
Preference paid	(0.20)	(0.20)
Ordinary: interim paid	(4.00)	(2.00)
final proposed	(12.00)	(6.00)
Retained profit for the financial year	14.20	4.40

Sparklers plc
Balance sheet as at 31 October 2004

	2004	2003
	£m	£m
Fixed assets		
Tangible at cost	47.80	35.20
Depreciation	(21.50)	(19.00)
	26.30	16.20
Current assets		
Stocks	30.00	10.00
Debtors	53.40	17.20
Prepayments	0.80	0.60
Cash and bank	–	1.20
	84.20	29.00
Current liabilities (less than one year)		
Overdraft	32.40	–
Creditors	20.00	12.00
Accruals	2.00	1.60
Dividends	12.00	6.00
Taxation	10.40	6.40
	76.80	26.00
Net current assets	7.40	3.00
Total assets less current liabilities	33.70	19.20
less		
Long-term liabilities (over one year)		
Debenture	1.50	1.20
Net assets	32.20	18.00

Capital and reserves

£1 ordinary shares	10.00	10.00
£1 preferences shares 10%	2.00	2.00
Profit and loss account	20.20	6.00
	32.20	18.00

E4.8 *Time allowed – 90 minutes*

Dimarian plc's profit and loss account for the year ended 31 December 2004, and its balance sheets as at 31 December 2004 and 2003, are shown below. Dimarian plc issued no new ordinary shares during the year.

   During 2004 Dimarian plc spent £100,000 on fixed assets additions. There were no fixed assets disposals during 2004.

Dimarian plc
Profit and loss account for the year ended 31 December 2004

Figures in £000

Turnover	850
Cost of sales	(500)
Gross profit	350
Distribution and administrative costs	(120)
	230
Other operating income	20
Operating profit	250
Interest receivable	10
	260
Interest payable	(30)
Profit before tax	230
Tax on profit on ordinary activities	(50)
Profit on ordinary activities after tax	180
Retained profit 1 January 2004	230
	410
Proposed dividends	(80)
Retained profit 31 December 2004	330

Dimarian plc
Balance sheet as at 31 December 2004

Figures in £000	**2004**	**2003**
Fixed assets		
Intangible	40	50
Tangible	750	800
	790	850

Current assets		
Stocks	50	60
Debtors	170	160
Prepayments	20	40
Cash and bank	20	10
	260	270
Current liabilities (less than one year)		
Overdraft	20	10
Creditors	40	60
Accruals	30	20
Dividends	80	70
Taxation	50	30
	220	190
Net current assets	40	80
Total assets less current liabilities	830	930
less		
Long-term liabilities (over one year)		
Debenture	100	300
Net assets	730	630
Capital and reserves		
Share capital	260	260
Share premium	50	50
Revaluation reserve	90	90
Profit and loss account	330	230
	730	630

Required:

(i) Prepare an operating cash flow reconciliation statement for the year to 31 December 2004.

(ii) Prepare a cash flow statement for the year ended 31 December 2004, in the format used by UK plcs.

(iii) Include an analysis of change in net debt/funds from 31 December 2003 to 31 December 2004.

5

Business performance analysis

Contents

Learning objectives

Completion of this chapter will enable you to:

- carry out a performance review of a business, including the use of SWOT analysis
- critically evaluate the limitations of the performance review process
- differentiate between divisional manager performance measurement and economic performance measurement
- analyse business performance through the use of ratio analysis of profitability; efficiency; liquidity; investment; financial structure
- use both profit and cash flow in the measurement of business performance
- critically compare the use of cash flow versus profit as the best measure in the evaluation of financial performance
- use earnings before interest, tax, depreciation and amortisation (EBITDA) as a close approximation of a cash flow performance measure.

Introduction

Chapters 2, 3, and 4 introduced us to the financial statements of limited companies. This chapter is concerned with how the performance of a business may be reviewed through analysis and evaluation of the balance sheet, the profit and loss account, and the cash flow statement. Business performance may be considered from outside or within the business for a variety of reasons. The performance review process provides an understanding of the business which, together with an analysis of all the relevant information, enables interpretation and evaluation of its financial performance during successive accounting periods and its financial position at the end of those accounting periods.

The chapter begins with an outline of the steps involved in the performance review process and also considers the limitations of such a process. The main body of this chapter is concerned with ratio analysis. Financial ratio analysis looks at the detailed use of profitability, efficiency, liquidity, investment, and financial structure ratios in the evaluation of financial performance.

The chapter closes with a discussion about which is the best measure of performance – cash or profit. The use of earnings per share and cash flow in performance measurement are discussed along with the measurement of earnings before interest, tax, depreciation and amortisation (EBITDA) as an approximation of cash flow. The debate continues as to whether cash flow or profit represents the best basis for financial performance measurement.

In Chapter 6 we shall build on the knowledge gained from the current chapter when we examine the published report and accounts of a major UK plc, Johnson Matthey.

The performance review process

A performance review using financial statements may be undertaken for a number of reasons, for example:

- to assist in investment decisions

- to identify possible takeover targets
- to evaluate the financial strength of potential or existing customers or suppliers.

The main aim of a performance review is to provide an understanding of the business, and, together with an analysis of all the relevant information, provide an interpretation of the results. A performance review is generally undertaken using a standard format and methodology. The most effective performance review is provided from a balanced view of each of the activities of the organisation, which necessarily involves the close cooperation of each role: marketing; research and development; design; engineering; manufacturing; sales; logistics; finance; human resources management.

The performance review process begins with a **SWOT analysis** and works through a number of steps to the conclusions, as outlined in Fig. 5.1. A SWOT analysis includes an internal analysis of the company, and an analysis of the company's position with regard to its external environment.

1. SWOT analysis

SWOT is shorthand for strengths, weaknesses, opportunities and threats. The first look at a company's performance usually involves listing the key features of the company by looking internally at its particular strengths and weaknesses, and externally at risks or threats to the company and opportunities that it may be able to exploit. The SWOT analysis may give some indication of, for example, the strength of the company's management team, how well it is doing on product quality, and areas as yet untapped within its marketplace.

To keep the analysis focused, a cruciform chart may be used for SWOT analysis. An example is outlined in Fig. 5.2, relating to a fictitious company in the 1990s which manufactured components for supply to automotive manufacturers.

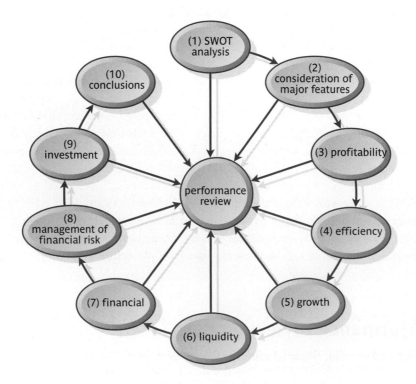

Figure 5.1 The stages of performance review

STRENGTHS	WEAKNESSES
Market share Part of a large diversified group	Slow product development Products designed not easy to manufacture
OPPORTUNITIES	THREATS
European joint ventures Market share of Japanese manufacturers	Japanese transplant manufacturers European economic recession

Figure 5.2 An example of a SWOT analysis

2. Consideration of major features

The increasing amount of information now provided in published financial statements enables the analyst to look in detail at the various industrial and geographical sectors of the business, the trends within these and the business in general. Further background information may be extracted from the accounting policies, the auditors' report, chairman's report and details of any significant events that have been highlighted.

3. Profitability

A number of financial indicators and ratios may be considered to assess the profitability of the company, which include:

- **ROCE (return on capital employed)**, or **ROI (return on investment)**
- return on sales (ROS)
- gross margin to sales
- asset turnover
- earnings per share (eps)
- **dividend cover**
- **price earnings ratio (P/E)**.

4. Efficiency

The efficiency of the company may be considered in terms of:

- its operating cycle – its **debtor days**, **creditor days**, and **stock days**
- its **operating gearing**
- **vertical analysis** of its profit and loss account (which we will look at in Chapter 6).

In a vertical analysis of the profit and loss account (which may also be applied to the balance sheet) each item is expressed as a percentage of the total sales. The vertical analysis provides evidence of structural changes in the accounts such as increased profitability through more efficient production.

5. Growth

Growth of the organisation may relate to sales growth and gross margin growth. **Horizontal analysis** (which we will look at in Chapter 6), or common size analysis, of the profit and loss account allows a line-by-line analysis of the accounts compared with those of the previous year. It may provide over a number of years a trend of changes showing either growth or decline in these elements of the accounts by calculation of annual percentage growth rates in profits, sales, stock or any other item.

6. Liquidity

Liquidity is concerned with the short-term solvency of the company. It is assessed by looking at a number of key ratios:

- **current ratio**
- **acid test**
- **defensive interval**
- cash ROCE
- **cash interest cover**.

7. Finance

How the company is financed is concerned with the long-term solvency of the company. It is assessed by looking at a number of other key ratios:

- **gearing** – the proportion of capital employed financed by lenders rather than shareholders, expressed in a number of ways, for example the **debt/equity ratio** (long-term loans and preference shares/ordinary shareholders' funds)
- dividend cover (eps/dividend per share)
- **interest cover** (PBIT/interest payable)
- various forms of off balance sheet financing.

Off balance sheet financing is defined as the funding or refinancing of a company's operations in such a way that, under legal requirements and existing accounting conventions, some or all of the finance may not be disclosed in its balance sheet. The Accounting Standards Board (ASB) has tried (and indeed continues to try) to introduce regulations forcing the inclusion of this type of financing.

8. Management of financial risk

The global market is here. Companies increasingly trade multinationally with greater levels of sophistication in products, operations, and finance. Risk assessment and the management of risk are therefore now assuming increasing importance. The main areas of risk are the areas of investment, foreign currency exchange rates and interest rates, and levels of trade credit.

9. Investment

Investment ratios examine whether or not the company is undertaking sufficient investment to ensure its future profitability. These ratios include, for example:

- capital expenditure/sales
- capital expenditure/depreciation
- capital expenditure/gross fixed assets.

10. Conclusions

The conclusion of the performance review will include consideration of the company's SWOT analysis and the main performance features. It will consider growth and profitability and whether or not this is maintainable, as well as levels of finance and investment, and whether there is sufficient cash flow, and the future plans of the business.

All performance reviews must use some sort of benchmark. Comparisons may be made against past periods and against budget; they may also be made against other companies and using general data relating to the industry within which the company operates. Later in this chapter we will look in more detail at the use of profitability, efficiency, liquidity, and investment ratios, and ratios relating to financial structure.

> **Progress check 5.1 Describe each of the stages in a business performance review process.**

Limitations of the performance review process

There are many obvious limitations to the above approach. In comparing performance against other companies (and sometimes within the company in comparing past periods), or looking at industrial data, it should be borne in mind that:

- there may be a lack of uniformity in accounting definitions and techniques
- the balance sheet is only a snapshot in time, and only represents a single estimate of the company's position
- there may actually be no standards for comparison
- changes in the environment and changes in money values, together with short-term fluctuations, may have a significant impact
- the past should really not be relied on as a good predictor of the future.

The volatility and unpredictability of the computer games market is well understood by John Menzies who enjoyed considerable success with their sales of Pokemon games. The press extract on p. 150 indicates that John Menzies did not assume that they would continue indefinitely to be profitable in that market.

As the extract illustrates, John Menzies decided (as a likely result of a strategic review of their business) that it may not continue its distribution agreement with Nintendo, the maker of games consoles and the Pokemon games, and may also dispose of its toyshop chain the Early Learning Centre.

Diversified companies present a different set of problems. Such companies by their very nature are comprised of companies engaged in various industrial sectors, each having different market conditions, financial structures and expectations of performance. The notes to the accounts, which appear in each company's annual report and accounts, invariably present a less than comprehensive picture of the company's position.

As time goes by, and accounting standards and legislation get tighter and tighter, the number of

> **Progress check 5.2 What are the main limitations encountered in carrying out the performance review of a business?**

loopholes which allow any sort of window dressing of a company's results are reduced. Inevitably, however, there will always remain the possibility of the company's position being presented in ways that may not always represent the 'truth'. We will now look at the type of information that may be used and the important financial ratios and their meaning and relevance.

The past is not a good predictor of the future

Pikachu, the cuddly Pokémon character, helped to propel John Menzies, the distribution, retail and aviation services group, to pre-tax profits of £15.7 million before exceptionals, compared with just £4.1 million last time.

But David Mackay, John Menzies' chief executive, believes the Pokémon craze is dying out and the company will not extend the exclusive distribution agreement with Nintendo, maker of games consoles and Pokémon games.

Mr Mackay said: 'Pokémon was a unique and wonderful phenomenon but it is on the decline.' He added that the games market was volatile, unpredictable and about to suffer intense competition.

John Menzies is in the throes of being transformed into an aviation services business and, unsurprisingly, a raft of exceptionals clouded its interim account.

A £2.5 million gain on one disposal was more than offset by a £26.4 million loss on another, resulting in a pre-tax loss after exceptionals of £8.2 million.

A fall in operating losses at the Early Learning Centre, the toyshop chain, means that its disposal is likely.

Mr Mackay said: 'We are on track to be in profit this year but there will be no fire sale.'

John Menzies bought Ogden Ground Services, a major airport services group, for £76 million last November and will seek a reclassification from distribution to support services once ELC has been sold.

Robin Althaus, an analyst at Seymour Pierce, said: 'Menzies cannot be faulted so far in its re-invention but it is still an emerging picture.'

The interim dividend rises to 5.5p a share from 5p. The shares rose $5\frac{1}{2}$p to $426\frac{1}{2}$p yesterday.

Pokémon helps to lift Menzies, by Mark Court

© *The Times*, London, 24 January 2001

Economic performance measurement

Most large organisations are divided into separate divisions in which their individual managers have autonomy and total responsibility for investment and profit. Within each division there is usually a functional structure comprising many departments. Divisionalisation is more appropriate for companies with diversified activities. The performance of the managers of each division may be measured in a number of ways, for example return on investment (ROI) and **residual income (RI)**.

The relationships between divisions should be regulated so that no division, by seeking to increase its own profit, can reduce the profitability of the company as a whole. Therefore, there are strong arguments for producing two broad types of performance measure. One type of measure is used to evaluate managerial performance and the other type of measure is used to evaluate economic performance.

In the current chapter, rather than divisional performance, we are primarily concerned with the performance of the organisation as a whole. We will look at ratios that measure economic performance, which focus not only on profit and profitability, but on a range of other areas of performance that include, for example, cash and working capital.

Ratio analysis

The reasons for a performance review may be wide and varied. Generally, it is required to shed light on the extent to which the objectives of the company are being achieved. These objectives may be:

- to earn a satisfactory return on capital employed (ROCE)
- to maintain and enhance the financial position of the business with reference to the management of working capital, fixed assets and bank borrowings
- to achieve cost targets and other business targets such as improvements in labour productivity.

Ratio analysis is an important area of performance review. It is far more useful than merely considering absolute numbers, which on their own may have little meaning. Ratios may be used:

- for a subjective assessment of the company or its constituent parts
- for a more objective way to aid decision-making
- to provide **cross-sectional analysis** and **inter-firm comparison**
- to establish models for loan and credit ratings
- to provide equity valuation models to value businesses
- to analyse and identify underpriced shares and takeover targets
- to predict company failure.

There are various models that may be used to predict company failure such as those developed by John Argenti (*Corporate Collapse – the Causes and Symptoms*, 1976), and Edward Altman (*Corporate Financial Distress – A Complete Guide to Predicting, Avoiding and Dealing with Bankruptcy*, 1983). Altman's model is sometimes used for prediction of corporate failure by calculating what is called a *Z score* for each company. For a public industrial company if the *Z score* is greater than 2.99 then it is unlikely to fail, and if the score is less than 1.81 then it is likely to fail. Statistical analyses of financial ratios may further assist in this area of prediction of corporate failure, using for example time series and line of business analyses.

As we saw in our examination of the performance review process, the key ratios include the following categories:

- profitability
- efficiency
- liquidity
- investment
- financial structure.

The financial structure, or gearing, of the business will also be considered in further detail in Chapter 8 when we look at sources of finance and the cost of capital. In the current chapter we will use the financial statements of Flatco plc, an engineering company, shown in Figs. 5.3 to 5.9, to illustrate the calculation of the key financial ratios. The profit and loss account and cash flow statement are for the year ended 31 December 2005 and the balance sheet is as at 31 December 2005. Comparative figures are shown for 2004.

Profitability ratios

It is generally accepted that the primary objective for the managers of a business is to maximise the wealth of the owners of the business. To this end there are a number of other objectives, subsidiary to the main objective. These include:

- survival
- stability
- growth
- maximisation of market share
- maximisation of sales

Flatco plc
Balance sheet as at 31 December 2005

Figures in £000	2005	2004
Fixed assets		
Intangible	416	425
Tangible	1,884	1,921
Financial	248	248
	2,548	2,594
Current assets		
Stocks	311	268
Debtors	573	517
Prepayments	589	617
Cash	327	17
	1,800	1,419
Current liabilities (less than one year)		
Financial debt	50	679
Creditors	553	461
Taxation	50	44
Dividends	70	67
Accruals	82	49
	805	1,300
Net current assets	995	119
Total assets		
less current liabilities	3,543	2,713
less		
Long-term liabilities		
Financial debt	173	–
Creditors	154	167
	327	167
less		
Provisions	222	222
Net assets	2,994	2,324
Capital and reserves		
Capital	1,200	1,000
Premiums	200	200
Profit and loss account	1,594	1,124
	2,994	2,324

Figure 5.3 Flatco plc balance sheet as at 31 December 2005

- maximisation of profit
- maximisation of return on capital.

Each group of financial ratios is concerned to some extent with survival, stability, growth and maximisation of shareholder wealth. We will first consider ratios in the broad area of profitability (see Fig. 5.10), which give an indication of how successful the business has been in its achievement of the wealth maximisation objective.

$$\text{gross margin } \% = \frac{\text{gross margin}}{\text{sales}} = \frac{\text{sales} - \text{cost of sales (COS)}}{\text{sales}}$$

Flatco plc
Profit and loss account for the year ended 31 December 2005

Figures in £000		2005		2004
Turnover				
Continuing operations		3,500		3,250
Discontinued operations		–		–
		3,500		3,250
Cost of sales		(2,500)		(2,400)
Gross profit		1,000		850
Distribution costs	(300)		(330)	
Administrative expenses	(155)		(160)	
Other operating costs				
Exceptional items: redundancy costs	(95)		–	
		(550)		(490)
Other operating income		100		90
Operating profit				
Continuing operations	550		450	
Discontinued operations	–		–	
		550		450
Income from other fixed asset investments		100		80
Profit before interest and tax		650		530
Net interest		(60)		(100)
Profit before tax		590		430
Tax on profit on ordinary activities		(50)		(44)
Profit on ordinary activities after tax		540		386
Dividends		(70)		(67)
Retained profit for the financial year		470		319

Additional information
Authorised and issued share capital 31 December 2005, 1,200,000 £1 ordinary shares
(1,000,000 in 2004).
Total assets less current liabilities 31 December 2003, £2,406,000.
Trade debtors 31 December 2003, £440,000.
Market value of ordinary shares in Flatco plc 31 December 2005, £2.75 (£3.00, 2004).
Tangible fixed assets depreciation provision 31 December 2005, £1,102,000 (£779,000, 2004).

Figure 5.4 Flatco profit and loss account for the year ended 31 December 2005

Flatco plc
Cash flow statement for the year ended 31 December 2005
Reconciliation of operating profit to net cash flow from operating activities

Figures in £000	2005	2004
Operating profit	550	450
Depreciation charges	345	293
Increase in stocks	(43)	(32)
Increase in debtors and prepayments [– 573 + 517 – 589 + 617]	(28)	(25)
Increase in creditors and accruals [553 – 461 + 82 – 49 + 154 – 167]	112	97
Net cash inflow from operating activities	936	783

Figure 5.5 Reconciliation of operating profit to net cash flow from operating activities

Cash flow statement

Figures in £000

	2005	2004
Net cash inflow from operating activities	936	783
Returns on investments and servicing of finance (note 1)	40	(20)
Taxation	(44)	(40)
Capital expenditure (note 1)	(299)	(170)
	633	553
Equity dividends paid	(67)	(56)
	566	497
Management of liquid resources (note 1)	–	–
Financing (note 1)	373	290
Increase in cash	939	787

Figure 5.6 Cash flow statement

Reconciliation of net cash flow to movement in net debt (note 2)

Figures in £000

	2005	2004
Increase in cash for the period	939	787
Cash inflow from increase in long-term debt	(173)	–
Change in net debt	766	787
Net debt at 1 January [17 – 679 – 0]	(662)	(1,449)
Net funds/net debt at 31 December [327 – 50 – 173]	104	(662)

Figure 5.7 Reconciliation of net cash flow to movement in net debt

Note 1 to the cash flow statement – gross cash flows

Figures in £000

	2005	2004
Returns on investments and servicing of finance		
Income from investments	100	80
Interest received	11	–
Interest paid	(71)	(100)
	40	(20)
Capital expenditure		
Payments to acquire tangible fixed assets	(286)	(170)
Payments to acquire intangible fixed assets	(34)	–
Receipts from sales of tangible fixed assets	21	–
	(299)	(170)
Management of liquid resources		
Purchase of treasury bills	(200)	–
Sale of treasury bills	200	–
	–	–
Financing		
Issue of ordinary share capital	200	300
Debenture loan	173	–
Expenses paid in connection with share issues	–	(10)
	373	290

Figure 5.8 Note 1 – gross cash flows

Note 2 to the cash flow statement – analysis of change in net debt/funds			
Figures in £000	**At 1 January 2005**	**Cash flows**	**At 31 December 2005**
Cash in hand and at bank	17	310	327
Overdraft	(679)	629	(50)
Debenture	–	(173)	(173)
Total (debt)/funds	(662)	766	104
	At 1 January 2004	**Cash flows**	**At 31 December 2004**
Cash in hand and at bank	–	17	17
Overdraft	(1,449)	770	(679)
Total (debt)/funds	(1,449)	787	(662)

Figure 5.9 Note 2 – analysis of change in net debt/funds

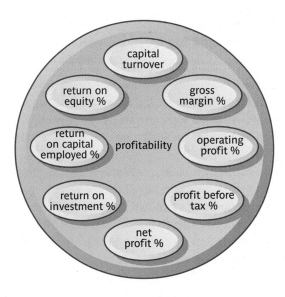

Figure 5.10 Profitability ratios

This is used to gain an insight into the relationship between production/purchasing costs and sales revenues. The gross margin needs to be high enough to cover all other costs incurred by the company, and leave an amount for profit. If the gross margin percentage is too low then sales prices may be too low, or the purchase costs of materials or production costs may be too high.

$$\text{operating profit } \% = \frac{\text{operating profit}}{\text{sales}} = \frac{\text{sales} - \text{COS} - \text{other operating expenses}}{\text{sales}}$$

The operating profit (or profit before interest and tax (PBIT) excluding other operating income) ratio is a key ratio that shows the profitability of the business before incurring financing costs. If the numerator is not multiplied by 100 to give a percentage, it shows the profit generated by each £1 of turnover.

$$\text{profit before tax (PBT) } \% = \frac{\text{profit before tax}}{\text{sales}} = \frac{\text{operating profit } +/- \text{ net interest}}{\text{sales}}$$

This is the profit ratio that uses profit after financing costs, that is, having allowed for interest payable and interest receivable. It should be remembered that profit before tax (PBT) is a profit measure that goes further than dealing with the trading performance of the business, in allowing for financing costs. It provides an indication of pre-tax profit-earning capability from the sales for the period.

$$\text{net profit } \% = \frac{\text{net profit}}{\text{sales}} = \frac{\text{profit before tax (PBT) } - \text{ corporation tax}}{\text{sales}}$$

This is the final profit ratio after allowing for financing costs and corporation tax. Net profit or return on sales (ROS) is the profit available for distribution to shareholders in the form of dividends and/or future investment in the business.

$$\frac{\text{return on investment (ROI)}}{\text{or return on capital employed (ROCE) } \%} = \frac{\text{operating profit}}{\text{total assets } - \text{ current liabilities}}$$
$$\text{(usually averaged)}$$

This is a form of return on capital employed (using pre-tax profit) which compares income with the operational assets used to generate that income. Profit is calculated before financing costs and tax. This is because the introduction of interest charges introduces the effect of financing decisions into an appraisal of operating performance, and tax levels are decided by external agencies (governments).

The average cost of the company's finance (equity, debentures, loans), weighted according to the proportion each element bears to the total pool of capital, is called WACC, the **weighted average cost of capital.** The difference between a company's ROI and its WACC is an important measure of the extent to which the organisation is endeavouring to optimise its use of financial resources. In their 1999 annual report, Tomkins plc reported on the improvement in their ROI versus WACC gap and stated that 'to be successful a company must consistently deliver a return on investment (ROI) above its weighted cost of capital (WACC) and must actively manage both variables'. A company manages its ROI through monitoring its operating profit as a percentage of its capital employed. A company manages its WACC by planning the proportions of its financing through either equity (ordinary shares) or debt (loans), with regard to the relative costs of each, dividends and interest.

In looking at acquisitions the importance of WACC is emphasised in the Tomkins plc 1999 annual report : 'Tomkins' strategy is to focus on strategic business activities and within this only to make acquisitions which add to shareholder value by enhancing earnings in the first year and deliver an ROI above the WACC hurdle rate (internal cost of capital) within three years.' This refers to the importance of WACC as a factor used in the evaluation of investment in projects undertaken (or not) by a business (see Chapter 8).

$$\text{return on equity (ROE)} = \frac{\text{profit after tax}}{\text{equity}}$$

Another form of return on capital employed, ROE measures the return to the owners on the book value of their investment in a company. The return is measured as the residual profit after all expenses and charges have been made, and the equity is comprised of share capital and reserves.

$$\text{capital turnover} = \frac{\text{sales}}{\text{average capital employed in year}}$$

The capital turnover expresses the number of times that capital is turned over in the year, or alternatively the sales generated by each £1 of capital employed. This ratio will be affected by capital additions that may have taken place throughout a period but have not impacted materially on the performance for that period. Further analysis may be required to determine the underlying performance.

The profitability performance measures discussed above consider the general performance of organisations as a whole. It is important for managers also to be aware of particular areas of revenue or expenditure that may have a significant importance with regard to their own company and that have a critical impact on the net profit of the business. Companies may, for example:

- suffer large warranty claim costs
- have to pay high royalty fees
- receive high volumes of customer debit notes (invoices) for a variety of product or service problems deemed to be the fault of the supplier.

All managers should fully appreciate such key items of cost specific to their own company and be innovative and proactive in identifying ways that these costs may be reduced and minimised.

Managers should also be aware of the general range of costs for which they may have no direct responsibility, but nevertheless may be able to reduce significantly by:

- improved communication
- involvement
- generation of ideas for waste reduction, increased effectiveness and cost reduction.

Such costs may include:

- the cost of the operating cycle
- costs of warehouse space
- project costs
- costs of holding stock
- depreciation (as a result of capital expenditure)
- warranty costs
- repairs and maintenance
- stationery costs
- telephone and fax costs
- photocopy costs.

The relative importance of these costs through their impact on profitability will of course vary from company to company.

Worked Example 5.1

We will calculate the profitability ratios for Flatco plc for 2005 and the comparative ratios for 2004, and comment on the profitability of Flatco plc.

Gross margin, GM

$$\text{gross margin \% 2005} = \frac{\text{gross margin}}{\text{sales}} = \frac{£1{,}000 \times 100\%}{£3{,}500} = 28.6\%$$

$$\text{gross margin \% 2004} = \frac{£850 \times 100\%}{£3{,}250} = 26.2\%$$

Profit before interest and tax, PBIT

$$\text{PBIT \% 2005} = \frac{\text{PBIT}}{\text{sales}} = \frac{£650 \times 100\%}{£3{,}500} = 18.6\%$$

$$\text{PBIT \% 2004} = \frac{£530 \times 100\%}{£3{,}250} = 16.3\%$$

Net profit, PAT (return on sales, ROS)

$$\text{PAT \% 2005} = \frac{\text{net profit}}{\text{sales}} = \frac{£540 \times 100\%}{£3{,}500} = 15.4\%$$

$$\text{PAT \% 2004} = \frac{£386 \times 100\%}{£3{,}250} = 11.9\%$$

Return on capital employed, ROCE (return on investment, ROI)

$$\text{ROCE \% 2005} = \frac{\text{operating profit}}{\substack{\text{total assets} - \text{current liabilities} \\ \text{(average capital employed)}}} = \frac{£550 \times 100\%}{(£3{,}543 + £2{,}713)/2}$$

$$= \frac{£550 \times 100\%}{£3{,}128} = 17.6\%$$

$$\text{ROCE \% 2004} = \frac{£450 \times 100\%}{(£2{,}713 + £2{,}406)/2} = \frac{£450 \times 100\%}{£2{,}559.5} = 17.6\%$$

Return on equity, ROE

$$\text{ROE \% 2005} = \frac{\text{PAT}}{\text{equity}} = \frac{£540 \times 100\%}{£2{,}994} = 18.0\%$$

$$\text{ROE \% 2004} = \frac{£386 \times 100\%}{£2{,}324} = 16.6\%$$

Capital turnover

$$\text{capital turnover 2005} = \frac{\text{sales}}{\text{average capital employed in year}} = \frac{£3{,}500 \times 100\%}{£3{,}128} = 1.1 \text{ times}$$

$$\text{capital turnover } 2004 = \frac{£3,250 \times 100\%}{£2,559.5} = 1.3 \text{ times}$$

Report on the profitability of Flatco plc

Sales for the year 2005 increased by 7.7% over the previous year, partly through increased volumes and partly through higher selling prices.

Gross margin improved from 26.2% to 28.6% of sales, as a result of increased selling prices but also lower costs of production.

PBIT improved from 16.3% to 18.6% of sales (and operating profit improved from 13.8% to 15.7%). If the one-off costs of redundancy of £95,000 had not been incurred in the year 2005 operating profit would have been £645,000 (£550,000 + £95,000) and the operating profit ratio would have been 18.4% of sales, an increase of 4.6% over 2004. The underlying improvement in operating profit performance (excluding the one-off redundancy costs) was achieved from the improvement in gross margin and from the benefits of lower distribution costs and administrative expenses.

ROCE was static at 17.6% because the increase in capital employed as a result of additional share capital of £200,000 and long-term loans of £173,000 was matched by a similar increase in operating profit.

Return on equity increased from 16.6% to 18%, despite the increase in ordinary share capital. This was because of improved profit after tax (up 3.5% to 15.4%) arising from increased income from fixed asset investments and lower costs of finance. Corporation tax was only marginally higher than the previous year despite higher pre-tax profits.

Capital turnover for 2005 dropped to 1.1 times from 1.3 times in 2004. The new capital introduced into the company in the year 2005 to finance major new projects is expected to result in significant increases in sales levels over the next few years, which will see improvements in capital turnover over and above 2004 levels.

> **Progress check 5.3** **How may financial ratio analysis be used as part of the process of review of business performance?**

Efficiency ratios

The regular monitoring of efficiency ratios by companies is crucial because they relate directly to how effectively business transactions are being converted into cash. For example, if companies are not regularly paid in accordance with their terms of trading:

- their profit margins may be eroded by the financing costs of funding overdue accounts
- cash flow shortfalls may put pressure on their ability to meet their day-to-day obligations to pay employees, replenish stocks, etc.

Despite the introduction of legislation to combat slow payment of suppliers, the general situation in the UK is poor in comparison with other European countries (see the following extract from *Accountancy Age*).

Companies that fail to pay suppliers on time

UK businesses could be losing up to £20bn every year in unpaid invoices, according to a report out today.

Intrum Justitia's UK Payment Index estimates that almost half (47%) of UK invoices are overdue – on average 18 days late – and 1.9% of total revenues are never paid at all.

The credit management service provider said the results of the survey clearly illustrated that payment delays put British businesses at risk. The increasing debt-to-income ratios significantly reduced profitability for companies – particularly SMEs who are vulnerable to variations in cash flow and often rely on a limited number of customers, it said.

Compared with Europe, the UK ranked poorly for payment delays, according to the company. The average 18 day UK payment delay is two days longer than in Ireland or the EU.

The research also reveals that UK creditors believe that one of the principal reasons for late payment is a deliberate decision on the part of debtors to use them as a 'source of free finance'. Another key reason cited was 'debtors' financial problems'.

'The consequence of payment delays on the public purse is also worrying – the UK government could be losing up to £10bn each year in lost VAT and corporation tax – the equivalent of the entire UK transport budget,' the report found.

Late payment costs UK companies £20bn, by Damian Wild

© *Accountancy Age*, 26 June 2004

The range of efficiency ratios is illustrated in Fig. 5.11.

Efficiency generally relates to the maximisation of output from resources devoted to an activity or the output required from a minimum input of resources. Efficiency ratios measure the efficiency with which such resources have been used.

$$\textbf{debtor days} = \frac{\textbf{trade debtors} \times \textbf{365}}{\textbf{sales}}$$

Debtor days indicate the average time taken, in calendar days, to receive payment from credit

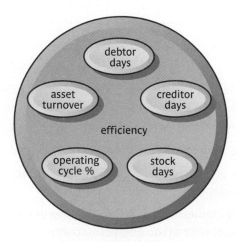

Figure 5.11 Efficiency ratios

customers. Adjustment is needed if the ratio is materially distorted by VAT (or other taxes). This is because sales invoices to customers, and therefore trade debtors (accounts receivable), include the net sales value plus VAT. However, sales are reported net of VAT. To provide a more accurate ratio, VAT may be eliminated from the trade debtors' figures as appropriate. (Note: for example, export and zero-rated sales invoices, which may be included in debtors, do not include VAT and so an adjustment to total trade debtors by the standard percentage rate for VAT may not be accurate.)

$$\text{creditor days} = \frac{\text{trade creditors} \times 365}{\text{cost of sales}} \quad \textbf{(or purchases)}$$

Creditor days indicate the average time taken, in calendar days, to pay for supplies received on credit. For the same reason, as in the calculation of debtor days, adjustment is needed if the ratio is materially distorted by VAT or other taxes.

$$\text{stock days} = \frac{\text{stock value}}{\text{average daily cost of sales in period}}$$

Stock days (or stock turnover) are the number of days that stocks could last at the forecast or most recent usage rate. This may be applied to total stocks, finished goods, raw materials, or work in progress. The weekly internal efficiency of stock utilisation is indicated by the following ratios:

$$\frac{\textbf{finished goods}}{\substack{\textbf{average weekly} \\ \textbf{despatches}}} \qquad \frac{\textbf{raw materials}}{\substack{\textbf{average weekly raw} \\ \textbf{material usage}}} \qquad \frac{\textbf{work in progress}}{\substack{\textbf{average weekly} \\ \textbf{production}}}$$

These ratios are usually calculated using values but may also be calculated using quantities where appropriate.

$$\text{stock weeks} = \frac{\text{total stock value}}{\text{average weekly cost of sales}} \textbf{(total COS for the year divided by 52)}$$

Financial analysts usually only have access to published accounts and so they often use the stock weeks ratio using the total closing stocks value in relation to the cost of sales for the year.

$$\textbf{operating cycle (days) = stock days + debtor days – creditor days}$$

We discussed the operating cycle, or working capital cycle, in Chapter 2 when we looked at the balance sheet. It is the period of time which elapses between the point at which cash begins to be expended on the production of a product, and the collection of cash from the customer. The operating cycle may alternatively be calculated as a percentage using:

$$\textbf{operating cycle \%} = \frac{\textbf{working capital requirement (stocks + debtors – creditors)}}{\textbf{sales}}$$

$$\textbf{asset turnover (times)} = \frac{\textbf{sales}}{\textbf{total assets}}$$

Asset turnover measures the performance of the company in generating sales from the assets under its control. The denominator may alternatively be average net total assets.

Worked Example 5.2

We will calculate the efficiency ratios for Flatco plc for 2005 and the comparative ratios for 2004, and comment on the working capital performance of Flatco plc.

Debtor days

$$\text{debtor days } 2005 = \frac{\text{trade debtors} \times 365}{\text{sales}} = \frac{£573 \times 365}{£3,500} = 60 \text{ days}$$

$$\text{debtor days } 2004 = \frac{£517 \times 365}{£3,250} = 58 \text{ days}$$

Creditor days

$$\text{creditor days } 2005 = \frac{\text{trade creditors} \times 365}{\text{cost of sales}} = \frac{£553 \times 365}{£2,500} = 81 \text{ days}$$

$$\text{creditor days } 2004 = \frac{£461 \times 365}{£2,400} = 70 \text{ days}$$

Stock days (stock turnover)

$$\text{stock days } 2005 = \frac{\text{stock value}}{\text{average daily cost of sales in period}} = \frac{£311}{£2,500/365}$$

$$= 45 \text{ days (6.5 weeks)}$$

$$\text{stock days } 2004 = \frac{£268}{£2,400/365} = 41 \text{ days (5.9 weeks)}$$

Operating cycle days

$$\text{operating cycle } 2005 = \text{stock days} + \text{debtor days} - \text{creditor days}$$

$$= 45 + 60 - 81 = 24 \text{ days}$$

$$\text{operating cycle } 2004 = 41 + 58 - 70 = 29 \text{ days}$$

Operating cycle %

$$\text{operating cycle \% } 2005 = \frac{\text{working capital requirement}}{\text{sales}}$$

$$= \frac{(£311 + £573 - £553) \times 100\%}{£3,500} = 9.5\%$$

$$\text{operating cycle \% } 2004 = \frac{(£268 + £517 - £461) \times 100\%}{£3,250} = 10.0\%$$

Asset turnover

$$\text{asset turnover } 2005 = \frac{\text{sales}}{\text{total assets}} = \frac{£3,500}{£4,348} = 0.80 \text{ times} \qquad [2,548 + 1,800]$$

$$\text{asset turnover } 2004 = \frac{\text{£3,250}}{\text{£4,013}} = 0.81 \text{ times} \qquad [2,594 + 1,419]$$

Report on the working capital performance of Flatco plc

The major cash improvement programme introduced late in the year 2005 began with the implementation of new cash collection procedures and a reinforced credit control department. This was not introduced early enough to see an improvement in the figures for the year 2005. Average customer settlement days actually worsened from 58 to 60 days.

The purchasing department negotiated terms of 90 days with a number of key large suppliers. This had the effect of improving the average creditors settlement period from 70 to 81 days.

A change in product mix during the latter part of the year 2005 resulted in a worsening of the average stock turnover period from 41 to 45 days. This is expected to be a temporary situation. An improved just in time (JIT) system and the use of **vendor managed inventory (VMI)** with two main suppliers in the year 2006 are expected to generate significant improvements in stock turnover.

Despite the poor stock turnover, the operating cycle improved from 29 days to 24 days (operating cycle % from 10.0% to 9.5%). Operating cycle days are expected to be zero or better by the end of year 2006.

Asset turnover dropped from 0.81 in 2004 to 0.80 times in the year 2005. The new capital introduced into the company in 2005 to finance major new projects is expected to result in significant increases in sales levels over the next few years which will see improvements in asset turnover over and above 2004 levels.

Progress check 5.4 What do the profitability and efficiency ratios tell us about the performance of a business?

Liquidity ratios

The degree to which assets are held in a cash or near-cash form is determined by the level of obligations that need to be met by the business. Liquidity ratios (see Fig. 5.12) reflect the health or otherwise of the cash position of the business and its ability to meet its short-term obligations.

$$\textbf{current ratio (times)} = \frac{\textbf{current assets}}{\textbf{current liabilities}}$$

The current ratio is an overall measure of the liquidity of the business. It should be appreciated that this ratio will be different for different types of business. For example, an automotive manufacturer may have a higher ratio because of its relatively high level of stock (mainly work in progress) compared with a supermarket retailer which holds a very high percentage of fast-moving stocks.

$$\textbf{acid test (times)} = \frac{\textbf{current assets} - \textbf{stocks}}{\textbf{current liabilities}}$$

The acid test (or quick ratio) indicates the ability of the company to pay its creditors in the short term. This ratio may be particularly meaningful for supermarket retailers because of the speed with which their stocks are converted into cash.

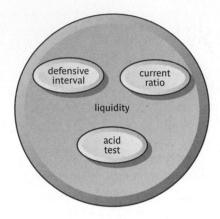

Figure 5.12 Liquidity ratios

$$\text{defensive interval (days)} = \frac{\text{quick assets}}{\text{average daily cash from operations}} \quad \text{(current assets – stocks)}$$

The defensive interval shows how many days a company could survive at its present level of operating activity if no inflow of cash were received from sales or other sources.

Worked Example 5.3

We will calculate the liquidity ratios for Flatco plc for 2005 and the comparative ratios for 2004, and comment on the liquidity of Flatco plc.

Current ratio

$$\text{current ratio 2005} = \frac{\text{current assets}}{\text{current liabilities}} = \frac{£1{,}800}{£805} = 2.2 \text{ times}$$

$$\text{current ratio 2004} = \frac{£1{,}419}{£1{,}300} = 1.1 \text{ times}$$

Acid test (quick ratio)

$$\text{quick ratio 2005} = \frac{\text{current assets – stocks}}{\text{current liabilities}} = \frac{£1{,}800 - £311}{£805} = 1.8 \text{ times}$$

$$\text{quick ratio 2004} = \frac{£1{,}419 - £268}{£1{,}300} = 0.9 \text{ times}$$

Defensive interval

$$\text{defensive interval 2005} = \frac{\text{quick assets}}{\text{average daily cash from operations}}$$

$$\frac{}{(\text{opening debtors} + \text{sales} - \text{closing debtors})/365}$$

$$= \frac{£1{,}800 - £311}{(£517 + £3{,}500 - £573)/365} = 158 \text{ days}$$

$$\text{defensive interval 2004} = \frac{£1{,}419 - £268}{(£440 + £3{,}250 - £517)/365} = 132 \text{ days}$$

Report on the liquidity of Flatco plc

Net cash flow from operations improved from £783,000 in 2004 to £936,000 in 2005. Investments in fixed assets were more than covered by increases in long-term finance in both years. Therefore, the operational cash flow improvement was reflected in the net cash flow of £939,000 (£787,000 2004).

The improved cash flow is reflected in increases in the current ratio (1.1 to 2.2 times) and the quick ratio (0.9 to 1.8 times). The increase in the defensive interval from 132 to 158 days has strengthened the position of the company against the threat of a possible downturn in activity.

Although there has been a significant improvement in cash flow, the increase in investment in working capital is a cause for concern. Actions have already been taken since the year end to try and maximise the returns on investment: reduction in stock levels (noted above); further reductions in trade debtors and prepayments; investment of surplus cash in longer term investments.

> **Progress check 5.5 What are liquidity ratios and why are they so important?**

Investment ratios

Investment ratios (see Fig. 5.13) generally indicate the extent to which the business is undertaking capital expenditure to ensure its survival, and stability and its ability to sustain current revenues and generate future increased revenues.

$$\text{earnings per share} = \frac{\text{profit after tax} - \text{preference share dividends}}{\text{number of ordinary shares in issue}}$$

Earnings per share, or eps, measures the return per share of earnings available to shareholders. The eps of companies may be found in the financial pages sections of the daily press.

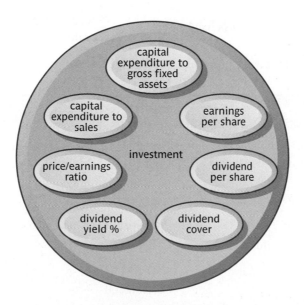

Figure 5.13 Investment ratios

$$\text{dividend per share} = \frac{\text{total dividends paid to ordinary shareholders}}{\text{number of ordinary shares in issue}}$$

Dividend per share is the total amount declared as dividends per each ordinary share in issue. It is the dividend per share actually paid in respect of the financial year. The amount must be adjusted if additional equity shares are issued during the financial year.

$$\text{dividend cover} = \frac{\text{earnings per share}}{\text{dividend per share}}$$

This shows the number of times the profits attributable to equity shareholders cover the dividends payable for the period.

$$\text{dividend yield \%} = \frac{\text{dividend per share}}{\text{share price}}$$

The dividend yield shows the dividend return on the market value of the shares, expressed as a percentage.

$$\text{price/earnings ratio} = \frac{\text{current share price}}{\text{eps}}$$

The price/earnings or P/E ratio shows the number of years it would take to recoup an equity investment from its share of the attributable equity profit. The P/E ratio values the shares of the company as a multiple of current or prospective earnings, and therefore gives a market view of the quality of the underlying earnings.

$$\text{capital expenditure to sales \%} = \frac{\text{capital expenditure for year}}{\text{sales}}$$

This ratio gives an indication of the level of capital expenditure incurred to sustain a particular level of sales.

$$\text{capital expenditure to gross fixed assets \%} = \frac{\text{capital expenditure for year}}{\text{gross value of tangible fixed assets}}$$

This is a very good ratio for giving an indication of the replacement rate of new for old fixed assets.

Worked Example 5.4

We will calculate the investment ratios for Flatco plc for 2005 and the comparative ratios for 2004, and comment on the investment performance of Flatco plc.

Earnings per share, eps

$$\text{eps 2005} = \frac{\text{profit after tax} - \text{preference share dividends}}{\text{number of ordinary shares in issue}} = \frac{£540,000 \times 100}{1,200,000} = 45\text{p}$$

$$\text{eps 2004} = \frac{£386,000 \times 100}{1,000,000} = 38.6\text{p}$$

Dividend per share

$$\text{dividend per share } 2005 = \frac{\text{total dividends paid to ordinary shareholders}}{\text{number of ordinary shares in issue}}$$

$$= \frac{\pounds 70{,}000}{1{,}200{,}000} = 5.8\text{p per share}$$

$$\text{dividend per share } 2004 = \frac{\pounds 67{,}000}{1{,}000{,}000} = 6.7\text{p per share}$$

Dividend cover

$$\text{dividend cover } 2005 = \frac{\text{earnings per share}}{\text{dividend per share}}$$

$$= \frac{45\text{p}}{5.8\text{p}} = 7.8\text{ times}$$

$$\text{dividend cover } 2004 = \frac{38.6\text{p}}{6.7\text{p}} = 5.8\text{ times}$$

Dividend yield %

$$\text{dividend yield } 2005 = \frac{\text{dividend per share}}{\text{share price}}$$

$$= \frac{5.8\text{p} \times 100\%}{\pounds 2.75} = 2.11\%$$

$$\text{dividend yield } 2004 = \frac{6.7\text{p} \times 100\%}{\pounds 3.00} = 2.23\%$$

Price/earnings ratio, P/E

$$\text{P/E ratio } 2005 = \frac{\text{current share price}}{\text{eps}} = \frac{\pounds 2.75}{45\text{p}} = 6.1\text{ times}$$

$$\text{P/E ratio } 2004 = \frac{\pounds 3.00}{38.6\text{p}} = 7.8\text{ times}$$

Capital expenditure to sales %

$$\text{capital expenditure to sales } 2005 = \frac{\text{capital expenditure for year}}{\text{sales}} = \frac{\pounds 286 \times 100\%}{\pounds 3{,}500} = 8.2\%$$

$$\text{capital expenditure to sales } 2004 = \frac{\pounds 170 \times 100\%}{\pounds 3{,}250} = 5.2\%$$

Capital expenditure to gross fixed assets %

$$\text{capital expenditure to gross fixed assets } 2005 =$$

$$\frac{\text{capital expenditure for year}}{\text{gross value of tangible fixed assets}} = \frac{\pounds 286 \times 100\%}{(\pounds 1{,}884 + \pounds 1{,}102)} = 9.6\%$$

$$\text{net book value} + \text{cumulative depreciation}$$
$$\text{provision}$$

$$\text{capital expenditure to gross fixed assets } 2004 = \frac{£170 \times 100\%}{(£1,921 + £779)} = 6.3\%$$

Report on the investment performance of Flatco plc

The improved profit performance was reflected in improved earnings per share from 38.6p to 45p. However, the price/earnings ratio dropped from 7.8 to 6.1 times.

The board of directors reduced the dividend for the year to 5.8p per share from 6.7p per share in 2004, establishing a dividend cover of 7.8 times. The dividend yield reduced from 2.23% at 31 December 2004 to 2.11% at 31 December 2005. The increase in the capital expenditure to sales ratio from 5.2% to 8.2% indicates the company's ability to both sustain and improve upon current sales levels.

The increase in the capital expenditure to gross fixed assets ratio from 6.3% to 9.6% demonstrates the policy of Flatco for ongoing replacement of old assets for new in order to keep ahead of the technology in which the business is engaged.

> **Progress check 5.6 What are investment ratios and what is their purpose?**

Financial ratios

Financial ratios (see Fig. 5.14) are generally concerned with the relationship between debt and equity capital, the financial structure of an organisation. This relationship is called gearing. Gearing is discussed in detail in Chapter 8. The ratios that follow are the two most commonly used. Both ratios relate to financial gearing, which is the relationship between a company's borrowings, which includes both prior charge capital and long-term debt, and its shareholders' funds (share capital plus reserves).

$$\text{gearing} = \frac{\text{long-term debt}}{\text{equity} + \text{long-term debt}}$$

and

$$\text{debt/equity ratio} \atop \text{or leverage} = \frac{\text{long-term debt}}{\text{equity}}$$

These ratios are both equally acceptable in describing the relative proportions of debt and equity used to finance a business. Gearing calculations can be made in other ways, and in addition to those based on capital values may also be based on earnings/interest relationships, for example:

$$\text{dividend cover (times)} = \frac{\text{earnings per share (eps)}}{\text{dividend per share}}$$

This ratio indicates the number of times the profits attributable to the equity shareholders covers the actual dividends paid and payable for the period. Financial analysts usually adjust their calculations for any exceptional or extraordinary items of which they may be aware.

$$\text{interest cover (times)} = \frac{\text{profit before interest and tax}}{\text{interest payable}}$$

This ratio calculates the number of times the interest payable is covered by profits available for such payments. It is particularly important for lenders to determine the vulnerability of interest payments to a drop in profit.

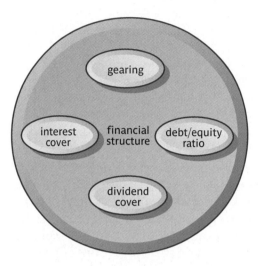

Figure 5.14 Financial ratios

Worked Example 5.5

We will calculate the financial ratios for Flatco plc for 2005 and the comparative ratios for 2004, and comment on the financial structure of Flatco plc.

Gearing

$$\text{gearing } 2005 = \frac{\text{long-term debt}}{\text{equity} + \text{long-term debt}} = \frac{£173 \times 100\%}{(£2,994 + £173)} = 5.5\%$$

$$\text{gearing } 2004 = \frac{£0 \times 100\%}{(£2,324 + £0)} = 0\%$$

Debt/equity ratio

$$\text{debt/equity ratio } 2005 = \frac{\text{long-term debt}}{\text{equity}} = \frac{£173 \times 100\%}{£2,994} = 5.8\%$$

$$\text{debt/equity ratio } 2004 = \frac{£0 \times 100\%}{£2,324} = 0\%$$

Dividend cover

$$\text{dividend cover } 2005 = \frac{\text{earnings per share (eps)}}{\text{dividend per share}} = \frac{45p}{5.8p} = 7.8 \text{ times}$$

$$\text{dividend cover } 2004 = \frac{38.6p}{6.7p} = 5.8 \text{ times}$$

Interest cover

$$\text{interest cover } 2005 = \frac{\text{profit before interest and tax}}{\text{interest payable}} = \frac{£650}{£71} = 9.2 \text{ times}$$

$$\text{interest cover } 2004 = \frac{£530}{£100} = 5.3 \text{ times}$$

Report on the financial structure of Flatco plc

In 2004 Flatco plc was financed totally by equity, reflected in its zero gearing and debt/equity ratios for that year. Flatco plc was still very low geared in 2005, with gearing of 5.5% and debt/equity of 5.8%. This is because its debt of £173,000 at 31 December 2005 is very small compared with its equity of £2,994,000 at the same date.

Earnings per share increased by 16.6% in 2005 compared with 2004. However, the board of directors reduced the dividend, at 5.8p per share for 2005, by 13.4% from 6.7p per share in 2004. This resulted in an increase in dividend cover from 5.8 times in 2004 to 7.8 times in 2005.

Interest payable was reduced by £29,000 in 2005 from the previous year, but PBIT was increased by £120,000 year on year. The result was that interest cover was nearly doubled from 5.3 times in 2004 to 9.2 times in 2005.

> **Progress check 5.7** What are financial ratios and how may they be used to comment on the financial structure of an organisation?

In this chapter we have looked at most of the key ratios for review of company performance and their meaning and relevance. However, the limitations we have already identified generally relating to performance review must always be borne in mind. In addition, it should be noted that the calculations used in business ratio analysis are based on past performance. These may not, therefore, reflect the current position of an organisation. Performance ratio analyses can also sometimes be misleading if their interpretation does not also consider other factors that may not always be easily quantifiable, and may include non-financial information, for example customer satisfaction, and delivery performance. There may be inconsistencies in some of the measures used in ratio analysis. For example, sales numbers are reported net of VAT, but debtors and creditors numbers normally include VAT. Extreme care should therefore be taken with the conclusions used in any performance review to avoid reaching conclusions that may perhaps be erroneous.

If all the financial literature were thoroughly researched the number of different ratios that would be discovered would run into hundreds. It is most helpful to use a limited set of ratios and to fully understand their meaning. The ratios will certainly help with an understanding of the company but do not in themselves represent the complete picture.

Calculation of the ratios for one company for one year is also very limited. It is more relevant to compare companies operating in the same market and to analyse how a company has changed over the years. However, difficulties inevitably arise because it is sometimes impossible to find another company that is strictly comparable with the company being analysed. In addition, the company itself may have changed so much over recent years as to render meaningless any conclusions drawn from changes in ratios.

The best performance measure – cash or profit?

The importance of cash flow versus profit (or earnings per share) as a measure of company performance has increased over the past few years. The advantages and disadvantages in the use of each are shown in Figs. 5.15 and 5.16.

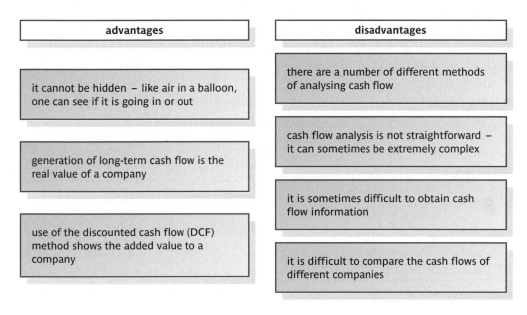

advantages	disadvantages
it cannot be hidden – like air in a balloon, one can see if it is going in or out	there are a number of different methods of analysing cash flow
generation of long-term cash flow is the real value of a company	cash flow analysis is not straightforward – it can sometimes be extremely complex
use of the discounted cash flow (DCF) method shows the added value to a company	it is sometimes difficult to obtain cash flow information
	it is difficult to compare the cash flows of different companies

Figure 5.15 The advantages and disadvantages of using cash flow as a measure of company performance

Worked Example 5.6

We will calculate the cash ROCE % for Flatco plc for 2005 and the comparative ratio for 2004, and compare with the equivalent profit ratio for Flatco plc.

Cash ROCE %

$$\text{cash ROCE \% 2005} = \frac{\text{net cash flow from operations}}{\text{average capital employed}} = \frac{£936 \times 100\%}{(£3,543 + £2,713)/2}$$

$$= \frac{£936 \times 100\%}{£3,128} = 29.9\%$$

$$\text{cash ROCE \% 2004} = \frac{£783 \times 100\%}{(£2,713 + £2,406)/2} = \frac{£783 \times 100\%}{£2,559.5} = 30.6\%$$

Report on the cash and profit ROCE of Flatco plc

Whilst the profit ROCE % was static at 17.6% for 2004 and 2005, the cash ROCE % reduced from

30.6% to 29.9%. Operating cash flow for 2005 increased by only 19.5% over 2004, despite the fact that operating profit for 2005 increased by 22.2% over 2004.

Operating profit before depreciation (EBITDA) was £895,000 [£550,000 + £345,000] for 2005, which was an increase of 20.5% over 2004 [£450,000 + £293,000 = £743,000]. If pre-depreciation operating profit had been used to calculate ROCE, it would have been 28.6% for 2005 compared with 29.0% for 2004, a reduction of 0.4% and more in line with the picture shown by the cash ROCE.

The chairman of Flatco plc expects that ROCE will be improved in 2006 as a result of:

- increased profitability resulting from higher sales levels generated from the investments in new projects
- reduction in levels of working capital, with more efficient use of company resources.

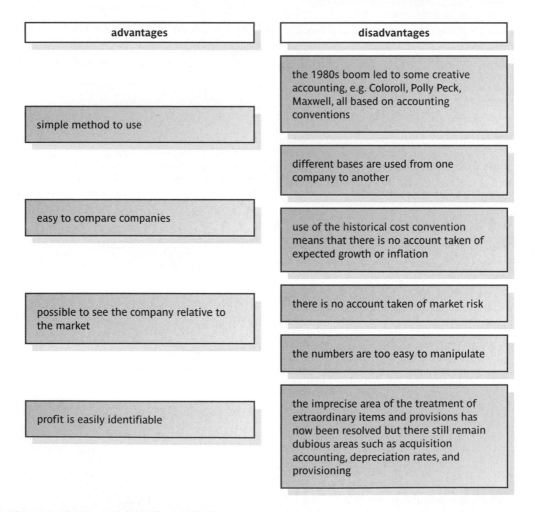

Figure 5.16 The advantages and disadvantages of using earnings per share (eps) as a measure of company performance

Cash flow has assumed increasing importance and has gained popularity as a measure of performance because the profit and loss account has become somewhat discredited due to the unacceptable degree of subjectivity involved in its preparation. Some of the financial ratios that we have already looked at may be considered in cash terms, for example:

$$\text{cash ROCE \%} = \frac{\text{net cash flow from operations}}{\text{average capital employed}}$$

and

$$\text{cash interest cover} = \frac{\text{net cash inflow from operations} + \text{interest received}}{\text{interest paid}}$$

which, in cash terms, calculates the number of times the interest payable is covered by cash available for such payments.

The increasing importance of cash flow as a measure of performance has led to new methods of measurement:

- the Rappaport method uses DCF looking 10 years ahead as a method of valuing a company
- the economic value added (EVA^{TM}) method, which we will discuss in Chapter 8 (p. 311)
- enterprise value, which is a very similar method to EVA, which excludes the peripheral activities of the company.

> **Progress check 5.8** What are the benefits of using cash flow instead of profit to measure financial performance? What are the disadvantages of using cash flow?

A profit-based measure of financial performance **EBITDA**, or earnings before interest, tax, depreciation, and amortisation, is now becoming widely used as an approximation to operational cash flow. Amortisation, in the same way as depreciation applies to tangible fixed assets, is the systematic write-off of the cost of an intangible asset. The way in which EBITDA may be used has been illustrated in the Flatco plc Worked Example 5.6.

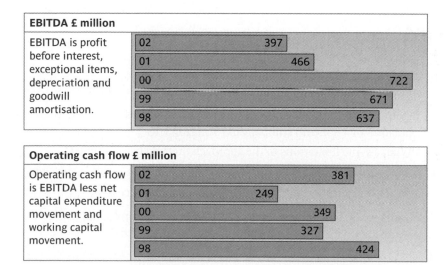

Figure 5.17 Tomkins plc EBITDA and operating cash flow for 1998 to 2002

Tomkins plc, in their 1999 annual report, commented on their use of EBITDA as a performance measure. 'Sophisticated investors increasingly employ a range of measures when assessing the financial health and value of a company, diversifying into cash-based yardsticks from a simplistic earnings per share test. EBITDA is becoming widely accepted as a reliable guide to operational cash flow.'

Graphs showing Tompkins plc's EBITDA and operating cash flows derived from EDITDA for the years 1998 to 2002, which were included in the group's annual report for the year 2002, are shown in Fig. 5.17.

We have seen that the method of performance measurement is not a clear-cut cash or profit choice. It is generally useful to use both. However, many analysts and the financial press in general continue to depend heavily on profit performance measures with a strong emphasis on earnings per share (eps) and the price/earnings ratio (P/E).

Summary of key points

- The main aims of a business performance review are to provide an understanding of the business and provide an interpretation of results.
- Care must be taken in reviewing business performance, primarily because of lack of consistency in definitions, and changes in economic conditions.
- An important area of business performance review is the use of ratio analysis looking at profitability, efficiency, liquidity, investment, and also growth and financial structure.
- Cash flow and cash ratios are becoming increasingly as important as profit and profitability ratios in the measurement of business performance.
- There is no best way of evaluating financial performance and there are advantages and disadvantages in using earnings per share or cash flow as the basis of measurement.
- Earnings before interest, tax, depreciation and amortisation – EBITDA – is now commonly used as a close approximation of a cash flow performance measure.

Questions

Q5.1   (i)   Who is likely to carry out a business performance review?

        (ii)   Describe what may be required from such reviews giving some examples from different industries and differing perspectives.

Q5.2   (i)   Outline how the business performance review process may be used to evaluate the position of a dot.com company like Amazon UK.

        (ii)   What are the limitations to the approach that you have outlined?

Q5.3   How is ratio analysis, in terms of profitability ratios, efficiency ratios, liquidity ratios, and investment ratios, used to support the business review process?

Q5.4   Why should we be so careful when we try to compare the profit and loss account of a limited company with a similar business in the same industry?

Q5.5 (i) Why does profit continue to be the preferred basis for evaluation of the financial performance of a business?

(ii) In what ways can cash flow provide a better basis for performance evaluation, and how may cash flow be approximated?

Discussion points

D5.1 In what ways may the performance review process be used to anticipate and react to change?

D5.2 'Lies, damned lies, and statistics.' In which of these categories do you think ratio analysis sits, if at all?

Exercises

Solutions are provided in Appendix 3 to all exercise numbers highlighted in colour.

Level I

E5.1 *Time allowed – 30 minutes*
The information below relates to Priory Products plc's actual results for 2004 and 2005 and their budget for the year 2006.

Figures in £000

	2004	2005	2006
Cash at bank	100	0	0
Overdraft	0	50	200
Loans	200	200	600
Ordinary shares	100	200	400
Profit and loss account	200	300	400

You are required to calculate the following financial ratios for Priory Products for 2004, 2005, and 2006:

(i) debt/equity ratio (net debt to equity)
(ii) gearing (long-term loans to equity and long-term loans).

E5.2 *Time allowed – 60 minutes*

From the financial statements of Freshco plc, a Lancashire-based grocery and general supplies chain supplying hotels and caterers, for the year ended 30 June 2005, prepare a report on performance using appropriate profitability ratios for comparison with the previous year.

Freshco plc
Balance sheet as at 30 June 2005

	2005	2004
	£m	£m
Fixed assets	146	149
Current assets		
Stocks	124	100
Debtors	70	80
Cash and bank	14	11
	208	191
Current liabilities (less than one year)		
Creditors	76	74
Dividends	20	13
Taxation	25	20
	121	107
Net current assets	87	84
Total assets less current liabilities	233	233
less		
Long-term liabilities (over one year)		
Debenture	20	67
Net assets	213	166
Capital and reserves		
Capital	111	100
General reserve	14	9
Profit and loss account	88	57
	213	166

Freshco plc
Profit and loss account for the year ended 30 June 2005

	2005 £m	2004 £m
Turnover	894	747
Cost of sales	(690)	(581)
Gross profit	204	166
Distribution and administrative costs	(101)	(79)
Operating profit	103	87
Other costs	(20)	(5)
Profit before interest and tax	83	82
Net interest	(2)	(8)
Profit before tax	81	74
Tax on profit on ordinary activities	(25)	(20)
Profit on ordinary activities after tax	56	54
Retained profit brought forward	57	16
	113	70
Dividends	(20)	(13)
	93	57
Transfer to general reserve	(5)	–
Retained profit for the financial year	88	57

Additional information:

(i)   Authorised and issued share capital 30 June 2005, £222m £0.50 ordinary shares (£200m, 2004).

(ii) Total assets less current liabilities 30 June 2003, £219m. Trade debtors 30 June 2003, £60m.

(iii) Market value of ordinary shares in Freshco plc 30 June 2005, £3.93 (£2.85, 2004).

(iv) Fixed assets depreciation provision 30 June 2005, £57m (£44m, 2004).

(v) Depreciation charge for the year to 30 June 2005, £13m (£10m, 2004).

Freshco plc
Cash flow statement for the year ended 30 June 2005

Reconciliation of operating profit to net cash flow from operating activities

	2005 £m	2004 £m
Operating profit	103	87
Depreciation charges	13	10
Increase in stocks	(24)	(4)
Increase in debtors	(10)	(20)
Increase in creditors	2	4
Net cash inflow from operating activities	84	77

Cash flow statement

	2005	2004
	£m	£m
Net cash inflow from operating activities	84	77
Returns on investments and servicing of finance	(2)	(8)
Taxation	(20)	(15)
Capital expenditure	(10)	(40)
	52	14
Equity dividends paid	(13)	(11)
	39	3
Management of liquid resources	–	–
Financing	(36)	7
Increase in cash	3	10

E5.3 *Time allowed – 60 minutes*

Using the financial statements of Freshco plc from Exercise E5.2, for the year ended 30 June 2005, prepare a report on performance using appropriate efficiency ratios for comparison with the previous year.

E5.4 *Time allowed – 60 minutes*

Using the financial statements of Freshco plc from Exercise E5.2, for the year ended 30 June 2005, prepare a report on performance using appropriate liquidity ratios for comparison with the previous year.

E5.5 *Time allowed – 60 minutes*

Using the financial statements of Freshco plc from Exercise E5.2, for the year ended 30 June 2005, prepare a report on performance using appropriate investment ratios for comparison with the previous year.

E5.6 *Time allowed – 60 minutes*

Using the financial statements of Freshco plc from Exercise E5.2, for the year ended 30 June 2005, prepare a report on performance using appropriate financial ratios for comparison with the previous year.

Level II

E5.7 *Time allowed – 60 minutes*

The summarised profit and loss account for the years ended 31 March 2003 and 2004 and balance sheets as at 31 March 2003 and 31 March 2004 for Boxer plc are shown below:

Boxer plc
Profit and loss account for the year ended 31 March

Figures in £000

	2003	2004
Turnover	5,200	5,600
Cost of sales	(3,200)	(3,400)
Gross profit	2,000	2,200
Expenses	(1,480)	(1,560)
Profit before tax	520	640

Boxer plc
Balance sheet as at 31 March

Figures in £000

	2003	2004
Fixed assets	4,520	5,840
Current assets		
Stocks	1,080	1,360
Trade debtors	640	880
Prepayments	40	80
Cash and bank	240	–
	2,000	2,320
Creditors due within one year		
Overdraft	–	160
Trade creditors	360	520
Tax payable	240	120
Dividend payable	280	384
	880	1,184
Net current assets	1,120	1,136
Total assets less current liabilities	5,640	6,976
less		
Creditors due in over one year		
Debentures	(1,200)	(1,200)
Net assets	4,440	5,776
Capital and reserves		
Ordinary share capital	4,000	5,200
Profit and loss account	440	576
	4,440	5,776

Case Study I

BUZZARD LTD

Buzzard Ltd is a first-tier supplier to major passenger car and commercial vehicle manufacturers. As a first-tier supplier Buzzard provides systems that fit directly into motor vehicles, which they have manufactured from materials and components acquired from second, third, fourth-tier, etc., suppliers. During the 1990s, through investment in R&D and technology, Buzzard became regarded as one of the world's leaders in design, manufacture and supply of innovative automotive systems.

In the mid-1990s Buzzard started business in one of the UK's many development areas. It was established through acquisition of the business of Firefly from the Stonehead Group. Firefly was a traditional, mass-production automotive component manufacturer, located on a brownfield site in Gentbridge, once a fairly prosperous mining area. Firefly had pursued short-term profit rather than longer-term development strategies, and had a poor image with both its customers and suppliers. This represented a challenge but also an opportunity for Buzzard to establish a World Class manufacturing facility.

A major part of Buzzard's strategic plan was the commitment to investing £30m to relocate from Gentbridge to a new, fully equipped 15,000 square metre purpose-built factory on a 20-acre greenfield site in Bramblecote, which was finally completed during the year 2004. At the same time, it introduced the changes required to transform its culture and implement the operating strategies required to achieve the highest level of industrial performance. By 2004 Buzzard Ltd had become an established supplier of high quality and was close to achieving its aim of being a World Class supplier of innovative automotive systems.

In December 2004 a seven-year bank loan was agreed with interest payable half-yearly at a fixed rate of 8% per annum. The loan was secured with a floating charge over the assets of Buzzard Ltd.

The financial statements of Buzzard Ltd, its accounting policies and extracts from its notes to the accounts, for the year ended 31 December 2004, are shown below, prior to the payment of any proposed dividend. It should be noted that Note 3 to the accounts – Profit on ordinary activities before taxation – reports on some of the key items included in the profit and loss account for the year and is not a complete analysis of the profit and loss account.

Required

(i) **Prepare a SWOT analysis for Buzzard Ltd based on the limited information available.**

(ii) **What do you consider to be the main risks faced by Buzzard Ltd, both internally and external to the business, based on your SWOT analysis and your own research about the automotive industry in the UK?**

(iii) **Prepare a report for shareholders that describes Buzzard's performance, supported by the appropriate profitability, efficiency, liquidity, and investment ratios required to present as complete a picture as possible from the information that has been provided.**

(iv) **The company has demonstrated its achievement of high levels of quality and customer satisfaction but would you, as a shareholder, be satisfied with the financial performance of Buzzard Ltd?**

Profit and loss account
for the year ended 31 December 2004

	Notes	2004 £000	2003 £000
Turnover	1	115,554	95,766
Cost of sales		(100,444)	(80,632)
Gross profit		15,110	15,134
Distribution costs		(724)	(324)
Administrative expenses		(12,348)	(10,894)
Operating profit		2,038	3,916
Net interest	2	(868)	(972)
Profit on ordinary activities before taxation	3	1,170	2,944
Taxation		–	–
Profit for the financial year		1,170	2,944

The company has no recognised gains and losses other than those included above, and therefore no separate statement of total recognised gains and losses has been presented.

Balance sheet
as at 31 December 2004

	Notes	2004 £000	2003 £000
Fixed assets			
Tangible assets	8	42,200	29,522
Current assets			
Stocks	9	5,702	4,144
Debtors	10	18,202	16,634
Cash at bank and in hand		4	12
		23,908	20,790
Creditors: amounts falling due within one year	11	(23,274)	(14,380)
Net current assets		634	6,410
Total assets less current liabilities		42,834	35,932
Creditors: amounts falling due after more than one year			
Borrowings and finance leases	12	(6,000)	–
Provisions for liabilities and charges	13	(1,356)	(1,508)
Accruals and deferred income	14	(1,264)	(1,380)
Net assets		34,214	33,044

Capital and reserves

Share capital	15	22,714	22,714
Profit and loss account		11,500	10,330
Shareholders' funds	16	34,214	33,044

Cash flow statement
for the year ended 31 December 2004

	2004	2003
	£000	**£000**
Net cash inflow from operating activities	12,962	3,622
Returns on investments and servicing of finance		
Interest received	268	76
Interest paid	(1,174)	(1,044)
Net cash outflow from returns on investments		
and servicing of finance	(906)	(968)
Capital expenditure		
Purchase of tangible fixed assets	(20,490)	(14,006)
Sale of tangible fixed assets	12	30
Government grants received	1,060	1,900
Net cash outflow from investing activities	(19,418)	(12,076)
Net cash inflow/(outflow) before financing	(7,362)	(9,422)
[Hint: 12,962 – 906 – 19,418]		
Financing		
Issue of ordinary share capital	–	8,000
Increase in borrowings	6,000	–
Net cash (outflow)/inflow from financing	6,000	8,000
Decrease in cash in the period	(1,362)	(1,422)

	2004	2003
	£000	**£000**
Note – reconciliation of net cash flows to the		
movement in net funds		
Decrease in cash in the period	(1,362)	(1,422)
Cash inflow from movement in borrowings	(6,000)	–
Opening net debt	(1,974)	(552)
Closing net debt	(9,336)	(1,974)

	2003 £000	Cash flow £000	2004 £000
Note – analysis of changes in net debt during the year			
Cash at bank and in hand	12	(8)	4
Overdraft	(1,986)	(1,354)	(3,340)
Borrowings due after one year	–	(6,000)	(6,000)
Net debt	(1,974)	(7,362)	(9,336)

Accounting policies
The financial statements have been prepared in accordance with applicable accounting standards. A summary of the more important accounting policies which have been applied consistently is set out below.

Basis of accounting   The accounts are prepared under the historical cost convention.

Research and development   Expenditure on research and development is written off as it is incurred.

Tangible fixed assets   Tangible fixed assets are stated at their purchase price together with any incidental costs of acquisition.

Depreciation is calculated so as to write off the cost of tangible fixed assets on a straight line basis over the expected useful economic lives of the assets concerned. The principal annual rates used for this purpose are:

Freehold buildings	20 years
Plant and machinery (including capitalised tooling)	4–8 years
Office equipment and fixtures and fittings	5–8 years
Motor vehicles	4 years

Freehold land is not depreciated.

Government grants   Grants received on qualifying expenditure or projects are credited to deferred income and amortised in the profit and loss account over the estimated useful lives of the qualifying assets or over the project life as appropriate.

Stocks and work in progress   Stocks and work in progress are stated at the lower of cost and net realisable value. In general, cost is determined on a first in first out basis; in the case of manufactured products cost includes all direct expenditure and production overheads based on the normal level of activity. Net realisable value is the price at which stocks can be sold in the normal course of business after allowing for the costs of realisation and, where appropriate, the cost of conversion from their existing state to a finished condition. Provision is made where necessary for obsolescent, slow-moving and defective stocks.

Foreign currencies   Assets, liabilities, revenues and costs denominated in foreign currencies are recorded at the rate of exchange ruling at the date of the transaction; monetary assets and liabilities at the balance sheet date are translated at the year-end rate of exchange or where there are related forward foreign exchange contracts, at contract rates. All exchange differences thus arising are reported as part of the results for the period.

Turnover   Turnover represents the invoiced value of goods supplied, excluding value added tax.

Warranties for products   Provision is made for the estimated liability arising on all known warranty claims. Provision is also made, using past experience, for potential warranty claims on all sales up to the balance sheet date.

Notes to the accounts

1 Segmental analysis

	Turnover		Profit on ordinary activities before taxation	
	2004	**2003**	**2004**	**2003**
	£000	**£000**	**£000**	**£000**
Class of business				
Automotive components	115,554	95,766	1,170	2,944
Geographical segment				
United Kingdom	109,566	92,020		
Rest of Europe	5,290	3,746		
Japan	698	–		
	115,554	95,766		

2 Net interest

	2004	**2003**
	£000	**£000**
Interest payable on bank loans and overdrafts	(1,182)	(1,048)
Interest receivable	314	76
	(868)	(972)

3 Profit on ordinary activities before taxation

	2004 £000	2003 £000
Profit on ordinary activities before taxation is stated after crediting:		
Amortisation of Government grant	1,176	796
(Loss)/profit on disposal of fixed assets	(18)	10
And after charging		
Depreciation charge for the year:		
Tangible owned fixed assets	7,782	4,742
Research and development expenditure	7,694	6,418
Auditors' remuneration for:		
Audit	58	58
Other services	40	52
Hire of plant and machinery – operating leases	376	346
Hire of other assets – operating leases	260	314
Foreign exchange losses	40	20

4 Directors and employees

The average weekly number of persons (including executive directors) employed during the year was:

	2004 number	2003 number
Production	298	303
Engineering, quality control and development	49	52
Sales and administration	56	45
	403	400

	2004 £000	2003 £000
Staff costs (for the above persons):		
Wages and salaries	6,632	5,837
Social security costs	562	483
Other pension costs	286	218
	7,480	6,538

8 Tangible fixed assets

	Freehold land and buildings	Motor vehicles	Plant, machinery and tooling	Office equipment, fixtures and fittings	Total
	£000	£000	£000	£000	£000
Cost					
At 1 January 2004	15,450	114	20,648	4,600	40,812
Additions	20	28	19,808	634	20,490
Disposals	–	–	(80)	(10)	(90)
At 31 December 2004	15,470	142	40,376	5,224	61,212
Depreciation					
At 1 January 2004	834	54	7,932	2,470	11,290
Charge for year	734	22	6,226	800	7,782
Eliminated in respect of disposals	–	–	(58)	(2)	(60)
At 31 December 2004	1,568	76	14,100	3,268	19,012
Net book value					
at 31 December 2004	13,902	66	26,276	1,956	42,200
Net book value at 31 December 2003	14,616	60	12,716	2,130	29,522

9 Stocks

	2004	2003
	£000	£000
Raw materials and consumables	4,572	3,274
Work in progress	528	360
Finished goods and goods for resale	602	510
	5,702	4,144

10 Debtors

	2004	2003
	£000	£000
Amounts falling due within one year		
Trade debtors	13,364	8,302
Other debtors	4,276	7,678
Prepayments and accrued income	562	654
	18,202	16,634

11 Creditors: amounts falling due within one year

	2004 £000	2003 £000
Overdraft	3,340	1,986
Trade creditors	13,806	8,646
Other taxation and social security payable	2,334	1,412
Other creditors	122	350
Accruals and deferred income	3,672	1,986
	23,274	14,380

12 Borrowings

	2004 £000	2003 £000
Bank and other loans repayable otherwise than by instalments		
Over five years	6,000	–

13 Provisions for liabilities and charges

	Pensions £000	Warranties for products £000	Total £000
At 1 January 2004	732	776	1,508
Expended in the year	(572)	(494)	(1,066)
Charge to profit and loss account	562	352	914
At 31 December 2004	722	634	1,356

14 Accruals and deferred income

	2004 £000	2003 £000
Government grants		
At 1 January 2004	1,380	2,176
Amount receivable	1,060	–
Amortisation in year	(1,176)	(796)
At 31 December 2004	1,264	1,380

15 Share capital

	2004 £000	2003 £000
Authorised		
28,000,000 (2003: 28,000,000) ordinary shares of £1 each	28,000	28,000
Issued and fully paid		
22,714,000 (2003: 22,714,000) ordinary shares of £1 each	22,714	22,714

16 Reconciliation of movement in shareholders' funds

	2004 £000	2003 £000
Opening shareholders' funds	33,044	22,100
Issue of ordinary share capital	–	8,000
Profit for the financial year	1,170	2,944
Closing shareholders' funds	34,214	33,044

17 Capital commitments

	2004 £000	2003 £000
Capital expenditure that has been contracted for but has not been provided for in the financial statements	1,506	162
Capital expenditure that has been authorised by the directors but has not yet been contracted for	6,768	5,404

18 Financial commitments

At 31 December 2004 the company had annual commitments under non-cancellable operating leases as follows:

	Land and Buildings 2004 £000	Other 2004 £000	Land and buildings 2003 £000	Other 2003 £000
Expiring within 1 year	–	96	112	210
Expiring within 2 to 5 years	–	254	–	360
Expiring after 5 years	–	120	–	90
	–	470	112	660

6

Published reports and accounts

Contents

Learning objectives

Completion of this chapter will enable you to:

- explain why annual reports and accounts of limited companies are filed and published
- recognise the key elements of the contents of the annual report and accounts of a typical public limited company
- evaluate the information disclosed within the annual report and accounts
- carry out a horizontal analysis of the profit and loss account and the balance sheet
- carry out a vertical analysis of the profit and loss account and the balance sheet
- interpret the information provided by segmental reporting
- critically evaluate the quality of corporate social responsibility (CSR) performance reporting within annual reports
- appreciate the impact of inflation on the financial performance of companies
- prepare and describe an alternative perception of the profit and loss account illustrated by the value added statement.

Introduction

This chapter builds on the business performance analysis techniques we introduced in Chapter 5. It is concerned with the type of information, both financial and non-financial, that is included in company annual reports and accounts. We will use the annual report and accounts of Johnson Matthey plc for the year 2004 to illustrate the financial statements of a large UK plc. We will not consider the whole of the Johnson Matthey plc annual report, a copy of which may be obtained from their head office in Trafalgar Square, London, UK. Further information about the company and copies of its report and accounts 2004 may be obtained from the Johnson Matthey website which is linked to the website accompanying this book at www.mcgraw-hill.co.uk/text-books/davies.

We will look at extracts from Johnson Matthey plc's report and accounts 2004, including the:

- chairman's statement
- chief executive's statement
- financial review
- accounting policies
- financial highlights
- financial statements
- segmental reporting
- **corporate social responsibility (CSR)** reporting
- directors' report.

The information disclosed in Johnson Matthey plc's report and accounts 2004 provides us with a broad picture of what sort of company Johnson Matthey is. The report and accounts include not only Johnson Matthey's historical financial performance, but also an indication of Johnson Matthey's prospects for the future. Included within the financial review is an example of how such a group manages risk.

In Chapter 5 we considered ratio analysis in our review of business performance. In this chapter we will look at some further tools of analysis. The first is horizontal analysis, or common size analysis, which provides a line-by-line comparison of the accounts of a company (profit and loss account and balance sheet) with those of the previous year. The second approach is the vertical analysis, where each item in the profit and loss account and balance sheet is expressed as a percentage of the total.

The reports and accounts of companies are now including more and more non-financial information, for example employee accident rates. Companies are also increasing generally their reporting on their corporate social responsibility performance. This includes areas such as health and safety, the environment, equal opportunities, employee development, and ethical issues. Johnson Matthey's report and accounts 2004 includes a comprehensive report on its corporate social responsibility performance, which is reproduced within this chapter.

The chapter closes with a look at the nature and purpose of the value added statement and its preparation. The value added statement is a variation on the profit and loss account and is concerned with measuring the value added by a business rather than the profit earned by the business.

An area of increasing importance now reported on in the annual reports and accounts of UK plcs is **corporate governance**. Corporate governance, including the role of auditors, will be covered in detail in Chapter 7.

Why are annual accounts filed and published?

After each year end, companies prepare their annual report and accounts, which include the financial statements and the auditors' report, for their shareholders. Copies of the annual report and accounts must be filed with the Registrar of Companies, and presented for approval by the shareholders at the company's annual general meeting (AGM). Further copies are usually made available to other interested parties such as financial institutions, major suppliers and other investors. The annual report and accounts of a plc usually takes the form of a glossy booklet which includes photographs of the directors, products and activities and other promotional material, and many non-financial performance measures, as well as the statutory legal and financial information. Large companies also issue half-yearly, or interim reports, which include the standard financial information, but the whole report is on a much smaller scale than the annual report.

The following press extract includes comments on the interim financial report published by Johnson Matthey plc for the first half of their financial year to 30 September 2003.

Johnson Matthey plc's pre-tax profits fell by 5% for the first six months of its financial year to 31 March 2004. Despite this, financial analysts lifted their share price forecasts because the results were better than they had expected, and because of the underlying strength of the company.

The publication of the annual report and accounts is of course always the time when such forecasts may be seen to have been justified or not. As it turned out, the figures were slightly below market expectations, and so the share price actually fell by 13% on announcement of the full year results to 31 March 2004. Johnson Matthey plc's report and accounts 2004 saw the profits of its pharmaceuticals division, which uses platinum products to create cancer drugs, increase by 16% over the previous year. Profits for the Johnson Matthey group as a whole rose 2.6% to £178m, while turnover increased

Interim financial reporting

Johnson Matthey, the precious metals and chemicals firm, said yesterday it is selling its ceramics business to concentrate on making catalytic converters.

The company said it expected a number of offers for its tiles and tableware businesses, which generate two-thirds of the profits at its colours and coatings arms.

Meanwhile, the company reported that total turnover had fallen 4pc to £2.17 billion in the first half.

Profits fell 5pc to £88.9m. It also raised its interim dividend 5pc to 8.2p.

The shares fell 3.3pc to £10.20 as investors digested that Johnson's renegotiated contract with producer Anglo Platinum would earn the company £1.5m less each year into the next decade.

It said the main reason for the loss was a 10pc drop in revenue from precious metals sales because of low palladium and rhodium prices. The weak US dollar also drove profits down by £2.8m.

Chief executive Chris Clark said: 'The new contract with Anglo Platinum is at a lesser rate than in previous years, but we expect the company's platinum output to increase considerably in coming years, which will more than outweigh the negative effects.'

The group said its catalytic converters arm, which nets just over half its earnings, was aided by buoyant car sales in Asia, offsetting disappointment in the West.

Pharmaceuticals, based on its platinum-based cancer drug, grew 8pc.

Johnson to sell ceramics side, by Edmund Conway

© *The Daily Telegraph*, 28 November 2003

by 3.9% to £4.5bn. The weakness of the US$, in which Johnson Matthey makes most of its sales, had a big impact on its 2004 results, and took £6.7m off the group's pre-tax profits.

Financial statements, whether to internal or external parties, are defined as summaries of accounts to provide information for interested parties. The key reports and statements within the published annual report and accounts are illustrated in Fig. 6.1.

In 1993 the Accounting Standards Board (ASB) issued a statement of good practice that supported the earlier suggestion made in the report of the **Cadbury Committee** (1992) that companies should include in their annual reports an operating and financial review (OFR) of the business. The reason for this suggestion was that businesses had become increasingly diversified and complex, and it had become increasingly difficult to understand information contained in financial reporting. Complex financial and organisational structures made it difficult to analyse and interpret financial information. It was felt that the OFR was needed to provide a greater insight into the affairs of the company, in addition to the information traditionally already provided by the chairman's statement and the directors' report.

The OFR was intended to cover the business as a whole for the year under review, and to include issues relevant to the assessment of future prospects. The OFR should include:

- brief reports that are easy to understand
- reports on each of the individual aspects of the business
- explanations of non-recurring aspects of the business
- discussion of matters that underpin the financial results for the period
- consideration of factors that might impact on the future performance of the business.

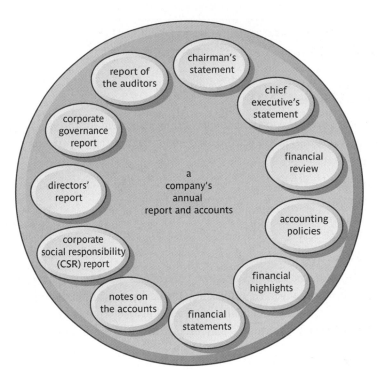

Figure 6.1 The key reports and statements within a company's annual report and accounts

The OFR includes two separate reports:

- an operating review, which includes:
  - new product development information
  - details of shareholders' returns
  - sensitivities of the financial results to specific accounting policies
  - risks and uncertainties
  - future investment
- a financial review, which includes:
  - current cash position
  - sources of funding
  - treasury policy
  - capital structure
  - confirmation that the business is a going concern
  - factors outside the balance sheet impacting on the value of the business
  - taxation.

We will look at each of the reports and statements included in Fig. 6.1 in this chapter, using the annual report and accounts 2004 of Johnson Matthey plc as an illustration, except for the last two reports, the corporate governance report and the report of the auditors, which will be discussed in Chapter 7. It should be noted that Johnson Matthey's operating review is included within the chief executive's statement. With regard to the notes on the accounts, in this chapter we will consider only Note 1 that relates to **segmental reporting**.

> **Progress check 6.1 Why are annual accounts filed and published?**

Chairman's statement

In addition to the profit and loss account and cash flow statement for the year and the balance sheet as at the year-end date, the annual report and accounts includes much more financial and non-financial information such as:

- company policies
- financial indicators
- directors' remuneration
- employee numbers
- business analysis.

The annual report and accounts includes the chairman's statement. This offers an opportunity for the chairman of the company to report in unquantified and unaudited terms on the performance of the company during the past financial period and on likely future developments. Let's take a look at the Johnson Matthey chairman's statement from its chairman, Michael Miles, OBE (see pp. 197–198).

The Johnson Matthey chairman's statement can be seen to include his general comments about the performance of the company over the past year, its current position, and its outlook for the future. A couple of paragraphs describe the strategy of the group. As with most chairmen's statements, Johnson Matthey's statement includes comments about the board of directors, investments in research and development and in people, and the achievements of the management team and other employees over the preceding year. The Johnson Matthey statement devotes a large section to the importance of the company's employees, their training and development. It also includes reference to the importance of the company's full commitment to its reporting on its corporate social responsibility performance, including environmental issues (which we shall deal with later in this chapter). Michael Miles' report concludes with a return to the company's goal of delivering superior shareholder value, and the importance of its employees and investment in research and development and manufacturing technology in achieving that goal.

> **Progress check 6.2 What is the purpose of a chairman's statement?**

Chief executive's statement

Chief executives' statements generally include detail on the performance of the business particularly relating to products, markets, technology and the various geographical areas of activity. These statements include brief comments on the financial highlights of the preceding year and the recommended dividend payable to shareholders. The chief executive's statement includes a review of operations, which outlines the main factors underlying the business and identifies any changes or expected future changes which may impact on the business. It normally concludes with an outlook on the future prospects of the business.

Chairman's Statement

"*The company's most important investment will always be the one it makes in its people. We place an absolute priority on the continuing development of our management talent and the skills of all our employees.*"

Michael Miles OBE
Chairman

I am pleased to report to shareholders that despite some quite strong headwinds, generated by the weak US dollar and the challenging conditions in some of our markets, Johnson Matthey made good progress in 2003/04.

The board's commitment to investment in research & development and manufacturing technology has enabled the company to remain at the forefront of the high technology industries that it serves and to continue its record of growth.

In 2003/04 we took a number of important steps in the strategic development of the group. The former Synetix businesses, which were acquired from ICI last year, have been successfully integrated into Johnson Matthey's Process Catalysts and Technologies business. These businesses have not only made a good contribution to the year but provide important opportunities for the group's future growth, especially in catalysts for the emerging gas to liquids market, an area where we have begun a significant programme of investment. The year also witnessed a further example of our strategy of making bolt-on acquisitions in core areas of activity with the acquisition of AMC in the United States which further enhances Catalysts Division's product portfolio.

The board is also committed to investment in growth markets around the world. Asia continues to be a major focus. In Shanghai, we are increasing capacity at our autocatalyst manufacturing facility to serve the rapidly growing Chinese vehicle market. In Japan, we achieved significant sales of retrofit heavy duty diesel catalysts. In India, we constructed a new platinum group metal catalyst manufacturing facility to serve the fast growing pharmaceutical and speciality chemical markets in that region.

The company's most important investment will always be the one it makes in its people. We place an absolute priority on the continuing development of our management talent and the skills of all our employees to enable them to perform to the highest standards to meet the challenges of the future. On behalf of the board I would like to thank all of our employees around the world for their hard work and dedication during the year.

I would like to welcome two new executive directors who joined the board in August 2003; Pelham Hawker, Executive Director, Environmental Catalysts and Technologies and Larry Pentz, Executive Director, Process Catalysts and Technologies. Both have made important contributions to recent developments in Johnson Matthey's Catalysts Division. Pelham has overseen a period of strong growth and technological change in our autocatalyst business and Larry has undertaken a leading role in the successful integration of the former Synetix businesses since their acquisition from ICI.

Johnson Matthey is very fortunate to have a strong group of independent directors who bring to the board many years of invaluable experience of international business from across a wide range of industrial sectors. I would also like to thank them for their valuable contribution during the year.

In July 2003 we announced that Chris Clark, our Chief Executive, will retire following this year's Annual General Meeting in July after 42 years with Johnson Matthey, the last six as Chief Executive. Chris has had a long and distinguished career with Johnson Matthey since joining the company in 1962. He has great experience of all of the group's operations and has run all of its major businesses. Chris has made an outstanding contribution to Johnson Matthey. As Chief Executive he has overseen the evolution of the group into a world leading speciality chemicals company. Through his strong leadership, Chris has steered the company through a successful period of strategic change and growth. As I said at the time of his appointment as Chief Executive in June 1998, I can think of no person better suited to have undertaken this task. On behalf of the whole board, and indeed all of us at Johnson Matthey, I would like to thank Chris for the key role that he has played in the development and success of the group and wish him all the best for a well deserved, long and very happy retirement.

As we also announced last July, Chris Clark will be succeeded as Chief Executive by Neil Carson, Executive Director, Catalysts and Precious Metals. Neil has 23 years of experience of working at Johnson Matthey and will be an excellent successor to Chris. The board is particularly pleased to have been able to appoint its new Chief Executive from within the company.

Your board is fully committed to reporting on Johnson Matthey's corporate social responsibility performance. Once again, this year's annual report features a review of the company's policies and performance in this important area. This is to be found on pages 24 to 28. Our comprehensive web based corporate social responsibility report was published last year for the first time. This report has been very well received and has generated a good deal of valuable feedback from shareholders. The 2004 edition of our corporate social responsibility report can be accessed on Johnson Matthey's corporate website at www.matthey.com.

I am very pleased that Johnson Matthey continues to make good progress towards our goal of delivering superior shareholder value. I remain confident that with our talented staff and our commitment to investment in research & development and world leading manufacturing technology, your company is well positioned to deliver continued growth in the years ahead.

Michael Miles

Michael Miles OBE
Chairman

Chief Executive's Statement

"Johnson Matthey made good progress in 2003/04. Operating profit before exceptional items and goodwill amortisation was 9% up on prior year despite the fall in the value of the US dollar."

Chris Clark
Chief Executive

Johnson Matthey made good progress in 2003/04. Operating profit before exceptional items and goodwill amortisation was 9% up on prior year despite the fall in the value of the US dollar. Both Catalysts and Pharmaceutical Materials divisions achieved 15% profit growth. We continue to see excellent prospects for both these divisions and we have increased our investment in research and development to take full advantage of anticipated market growth over the next few years.

Our Catalysts Division has leading positions in market segments which will expand rapidly in the next few years. These include catalysts for heavy duty diesel (HDD) emission control, where legislation is due to take full effect in 2007 in the USA and 2008 in Europe, and catalysts for the gas to liquids process which uses a series of different catalytic steps to convert stranded natural gas to sulphur free diesel fuel.

We are increasing our investment in R&D to support these opportunities, and are also selectively looking at possible acquisitions to expand our range of catalyst products. We are pleased to have concluded the acquisition of AMC in March 2004, which strengthens our position in the pharmaceutical and speciality chemicals catalyst markets.

As well as growing revenues we are also focusing on improving efficiency. In these results we have taken a £12.7 million exceptional provision to improve efficiency across the Catalysts Division. One element of this relates to restructuring our platinum group metal (pgm) refining business, which has been adversely affected by the downturn in the palladium market. In addition, we will be phasing out our older autocatalyst manufacturing process technology now that precision coating technology has been fully installed in all our worldwide autocatalyst manufacturing plants. We expect this rationalisation programme to reduce costs in the division by £8 million in 2005/06.

Diesel emission control continues to be a focus for environmentalists and regulators worldwide and remains a key priority for us. The market for diesel cars is mainly in Europe where we have increased our market share. Whilst oxidation catalysts remain the key current product, there is growing interest in the use of soot filter technology for particulate emission control and we have been nominated for several important customer programmes.

"In the next few years we should start to see significant benefits from Johnson Matthey's investment in new product areas."

Demand for platinum remained strong and the average price of the metal for Johnson Matthey's financial year 2003/04 was $744 per ounce, an increase of 27% over 2002/03. Purchases for use in autocatalysts increased robustly in response to further growth in diesel car sales in Europe. In addition, North American car companies stepped up their purchases of platinum having largely depleted inventories of the metal the year before. However, platinum demand from the Chinese jewellery market dropped after almost a decade of rapid growth, as the rise in the platinum price reduced profit margins throughout the industry.

In contrast with platinum, the average price of palladium was $200 per ounce, 34% below the average in 2002/03, and trading conditions remained subdued for most of the year. Physical demand for palladium began to recover from the fall in the previous year, with purchases by the auto and electronics industries increasing significantly. The surplus between supply and demand, however, widened considerably as Russian sales of palladium recovered and South African production was expanded.

The division's platinum fabrication businesses achieved further growth with good demand for both medical components and industrial products. Operating profit for the gold refining businesses was down on last year with the stronger gold price having little immediate impact on mine output.

Colours & Coatings Division's sales were very similar to last year at £254 million. Operating profit rose by 6% to £26.7 million with an improvement in margins.

The glass coatings business achieved good growth in sales and profits benefiting from new product introductions and market share gains. The Structural Ceramics sector, which sells largely to the tile industry, experienced weaker demand for most of the year and profits were down, but demand picked up in the final quarter and the outlook is now much stronger. Profits for Speciality Coatings were well up on prior year, benefiting from the rationalisation programme undertaken in 2002/03.

Pharmaceutical Materials Division's sales rose by 9% to £140 million despite the impact of the weaker US dollar. The division's operating profit increased by 15% to £42.3 million.

The division's US business at West Deptford, NJ achieved strong growth in the year, benefiting from an expanded range of platinum based anticancer compounds. One new product has recently been launched and another is in phase three clinical trials. The new opiate extraction facility was completed in the year and is now operational. Macfarlan Smith also achieved excellent growth in profits benefiting from increasing sales of high margin specialist opiates. Additional capacity is being installed to meet future growth. Pharm-Eco experienced the industry-wide drop in demand for contract research in the first quarter of the year but was able to respond by gaining new business and its performance in the second half of the year was much stronger.

Outlook In 2004/05 we expect to see further growth in Catalysts and Pharmaceutical Materials. However, exchange translation may be adverse if the US dollar remains at its current level.

In the next few years we should start to see significant benefits from Johnson Matthey's investment in new product areas, including heavy duty diesel catalysts which represents a major opportunity once legislation comes into force in 2007 and 2008. In Pharmaceutical Materials we have a strong worldwide position in the manufacture of controlled drugs and complex molecules, such as prostaglandins, where the generic market should see significant growth. Excellent progress is also being made in other long term growth markets, such as gas to liquids catalysts and fuel cells, where revenues are expected to grow in the years ahead.

Overall, supported by a strong balance sheet, the group is very well positioned to deliver good long term growth.

Chris Clark
Chief Executive

Financial Review

"Johnson Matthey's balance sheet remains strong with shareholders' funds rising by £74.9 million to £862.2 million and gearing of 45%."

John Sheldrick
Group Finance Director

Review of Results Total sales for the financial year ending 31st March 2004 rose by 4% to £4.5 billion. Sales excluding the value of precious metals rose by 6% to £1.2 billion.

Operating profit before exceptional items and goodwill amortisation increased by 9% to £206.0 million, despite the effects of adverse exchange translation. The group has adopted FRS 17, the new accounting standard for pensions, and last year's results have been restated accordingly. Divisional results are discussed in the Chief Executive's Statement on pages 4 to 7, and in the individual divisional reports on pages 16 to 23.

Interest also rose, partly reflecting higher average borrowings following the acquisition of Synetix, but also as a consequence of the change to FRS 17 and the reduction in pension fund surplus at 31st March 2003. Profit before tax, exceptional items and goodwill amortisation rose by 3% to £195.7 million.

Earnings per share before exceptional items and goodwill amortisation increased by 4% to 64.0 pence.

Exceptional items gave rise to a net credit of £2.1 million before tax, compared with a £2.7 million charge last year. Goodwill amortisation increased by £6.1 million to £19.8 million reflecting the full year's ownership of Synetix which was acquired in November 2002. After exceptional items and goodwill amortisation, profit before tax rose by 3% to £178.0 million. Earnings per share on the same basis increased by 1% to 56.0 pence.

The board is recommending to shareholders a final dividend of 18.2 pence, making a total dividend for the year of 26.4 pence, an increase of 4%. The proposed dividend would be covered 2.4 times by earnings before exceptional items and goodwill amortisation.

Sales and Margins Johnson Matthey's turnover is heavily impacted by the high value of precious metals sold by the group particularly in the Precious Metals Division (PMD). The total value of sales each year varies according to the mix of metals sold and level of trading activity. The value of the precious metals included in sales is generally separately invoiced and payment made within a few days. Consequently, although return on sales (operating profit / total external sales) for the precious metals businesses is low, return on investment is high.

To provide a more useful measure of return on sales, the adjacent table shows sales by division excluding the value of precious metals. Total sales excluding precious metals were £1,224 million which was 6% up on last year and return on these sales averaged 16.8% which was 0.5% up on 2002/03 (restated for FRS 17). The group's target for each of its divisions is to achieve a return on sales excluding precious metals in excess of 10%. All four divisions were ahead of that target in 2003/04.

Catalysts achieved 10% growth in sales excluding precious metals benefiting from a full year's ownership of former Synetix businesses. A significant proportion of the division's operations are located in the USA, and both sales and profits were adversely affected by exchange translation as a result of the decline in value of the US dollar. Margins improved, benefiting from sales of new, technologically advanced products.

PMD's sales excluding precious metals were down 9% reflecting subdued trading conditions for palladium and rhodium for most of the year and the impact of the renewed contracts with Anglo Platinum in the final quarter.

Colours & Coatings' sales were very similar to last year but margins improved as a result of good growth in our glass coatings business, which has higher margins than other parts of the division.

Pharmaceutical Materials achieved 8% growth in sales excluding precious metals, despite adverse exchange translation, with good growth in sales of platinum anticancer compounds and opiates. Margins improved at our Edinburgh based business, Macfarlan Smith, as a result of increased sales of high margin specialist opiates.

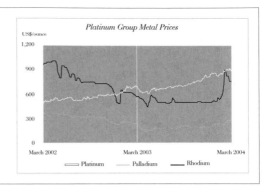

Platinum Group Metal Prices

Financial Risk Management The group uses financial instruments, in particular forward currency contracts and currency swaps, to manage the financial risks associated with the group's underlying business activities and the financing of those activities. The group does not undertake any trading activity in financial instruments. Our Treasury department is run as a service centre rather than a profit centre.

Interest Rate Risk At 31st March 2004 the group had net borrowings of £394.5 million. Some 35% of this debt is at fixed rates with an average interest rate of 5.6%. The remaining 65% of the group's net borrowings are funded on a floating rate basis. A 1% change in all interest rates would have a 1.4% impact on group profit before tax. This is within the range the board regards as acceptable.

Liquidity Policy The group's policy on funding capacity is to ensure that we always have sufficient long term funding and committed bank facilities in place to meet foreseeable peak borrowing requirements. The group has committed bank facilities of £280 million. Borrowings drawn under these facilities at 31st March 2004 amounted to £219.8 million. The group also has a number of uncommitted facilities and overdraft lines.

Foreign Currency Risk Johnson Matthey's operations are global in nature with the majority of the group's operating profits earned outside the UK. The group has operations in 34 countries with the largest single investment being in the USA. In order to protect the group's sterling balance sheet and reduce cash flow risk, the group finances most of its US investment by US dollar borrowings. Although most of this funding is obtained by directly borrowing US dollars, some is achieved by using currency swaps to reduce costs and credit exposure. The group also uses local currency borrowings to fund its operations in other countries (see page 59).

The group uses forward exchange contracts to hedge foreign exchange exposures arising on forecast receipts and payments in foreign currencies. Currency options are occasionally used to hedge foreign exchange exposures, usually when the forecast receipt or payment amounts are uncertain. Details of the contracts outstanding on 31st March 2004 are shown on page 61.

Precious Metal Prices Fluctuations in precious metal prices can have a significant impact on Johnson Matthey's financial results. Our policy for all our manufacturing businesses is to limit this exposure by hedging against future price changes where such hedging can be done at acceptable cost. The group does not take material exposures on metal trading.

All the group's stocks of gold and silver are fully hedged by leasing or forward sales. Currently the majority of the group's platinum stocks are unhedged because of the lack of liquidity in the platinum market.

John Sheldrick
Group Finance Director

The Johnson Matthey chief executive's statement for 2004, presented by Chris Clark (see pp. 199–202, provides details about developments in the various divisions of the company including acquisitions. The report provides a great deal of information of particular interest to current and potential new shareholders relating to future growth opportunities, planned major investments, the development of new and existing technologies, and new product development. This report includes some detail of the headline financial results, but its main focus is the operating review containing the sort of information referred to earlier, and an outlook for the business over the next few years.

Financial review

The financial review goes into further financial detail than the chief executive's statement and is normally prepared by the finance director. In the case of Johnson Matthey, the financial review has been prepared by its group finance director, John Sheldrick. The purpose of the financial review is to review the results for the past year and to provide an overview of financial policy. Let's look at the Johnson Matthey financial review, included in its annual report and accounts for the year 2004 (see pp. 203–6).

The Johnson Matthey financial review begins with a review of the results for the year to 31 March 2004, with an initial focus on sales, profit before tax, earnings per share and dividends. The review goes on to look in a little more detail at:

- sales and margins
- exceptional items and goodwill amortisation
- exchange rates
- cash flow
- financing
- return on investment
- interest rates
- taxation
- pensions
- financial risk management.

We can see that the review includes many of the financial performance measures we have discussed in Chapter 5. Examples are return on sales and return on investment, which are analysed by each area of business activity.

Johnson Matthey has commented with regard to the impacts of both the strength of the **euro**, and the weakness of the US$. The group benefited by £2.4m from the translation of profits of euro-zone companies made in euros, but the strength of the euro also had a negative impact on demand for products in the Colours & Coatings division. The group's pre-tax profit suffered from an 8% deterioration of the US$, with a large part of the group's operating income being derived from North America. The group's net cash flow was at around the same level as the previous year; operating cash flow increased, but there was reduced capital expenditure.

The first part of the financial review concludes with a comment on the refinancing of the group's acquisition of Synetix in 2002. The initial financing of the acquisition, using its existing bank facilities, was refinanced at the end of March 2003 with the proceeds of a long-term private placement bond issue amounting to £40m plus 230m US$.

The final part of the review is devoted to the group's policy on financial **risk management**. Risk management is a key strategic area for the type of business in which Johnson Matthey is involved. Policy is explained relating to interest rate, liquidity, and foreign currency **risk** and the **financial instruments** that are used by Johnson Matthey to manage financial risks.

Risk relating to precious metals prices is also outlined in terms of policy and the way in which that area of risk is managed. The group finance director indicated in an outline of its policy the extent to which the group is risk averse. The group hedges against future changes in precious metal prices, using leasing or forward sales, except for platinum because of the lack of liquidity in that market.

Johnson Matthey has not reported on its share price performance in its report and accounts for the year 2004. This information, available from Johnson Matthey plc, is illustrated in Fig. 6.2 for each 31 March from 1995 to 2004.

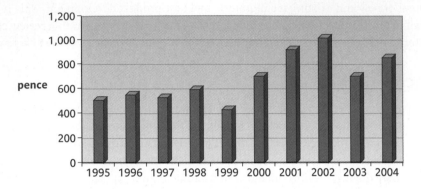

Figure 6.2 Johnson Matthey plc year-end 31 March share price 1995 to 2004

Accounting policies

The statement of accounting policies informs readers of the policies the company has pursued in preparation of the report and accounts, and of any deviation from the generally accepted fundamental accounting concepts and conventions. Johnson Matthey devotes a large part of its statement of accounting policies to the management of risk, (see pp. 210–11).

> **Progress check 6.3 What information does the chief executive's statement and the financial review provide and how do these reports differ?**

Financial highlights

The section headed financial highlights serves to focus on the headline numbers of sales, profit before tax, earnings per share, and dividends. Johnson Matthey's financial highlights are illustrated in both summary and graphical form on p. 212.

Worked Example 6.1

We can use the Johnson Matthey plc ten-year record, which you will find on pp. 241–2 in the **Exercises** section at the end of this chapter, to present earnings per share and dividends per share for 1995 to 2004:

(i)   in tabular form, and

(ii)   in one bar chart for comparison.

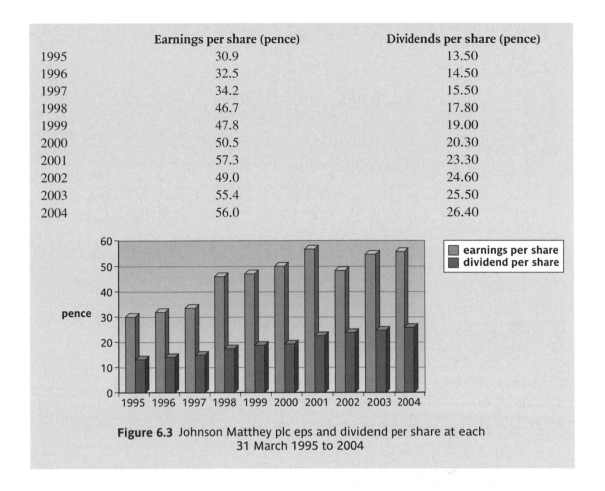

	Earnings per share (pence)	Dividends per share (pence)
1995	30.9	13.50
1996	32.5	14.50
1997	34.2	15.50
1998	46.7	17.80
1999	47.8	19.00
2000	50.5	20.30
2001	57.3	23.30
2002	49.0	24.60
2003	55.4	25.50
2004	56.0	26.40

Figure 6.3 Johnson Matthey plc eps and dividend per share at each 31 March 1995 to 2004

Profit and loss account, balance sheet, and cash flow statement

The three financial statements that are shown on pp. 213–15 illustrate Johnson Matthey plc's consolidated profit and loss account, and consolidated cash flow statement for the year to 31 March 2004, and its consolidated and parent company balance sheets as at 31 March 2004.

The profit and loss account is consolidated to include the results of all the companies within the group, which together with the parent company, Johnson Matthey plc, total 34. Profit is stated both before exceptional items and after exceptional items, and the consolidated profit and loss account also shows previous year comparative figures.

The balance sheet is presented in consolidated form, also showing previous year comparative figures, and includes a separate balance sheet for the parent company only.

The cash flow statement is consolidated to include the cash flows of all the companies within the group, and includes the parent company, Johnson Matthey plc.

We will look at the financial performance of Johnson Matthey in Worked Examples 6.2 and 6.3 using the two approaches to ratio analysis that were mentioned in the introduction to this chapter:

■ horizontal analysis, or common size analysis, which provides a line-by-line comparison of the profit and loss account (and balance sheet) with those of the previous year

Accounting Policies

for the year ended 31st March 2004

Accounting convention: The accounts are prepared in accordance with applicable accounting standards under the historical cost convention.

Basis of consolidation: The consolidated accounts comprise the accounts of the parent company and all its subsidiary undertakings and include the group's interest in associates.

The results of companies acquired or disposed of in the year are dealt with from or up to the effective date of acquisition or disposal respectively. The net assets of companies acquired are incorporated in the consolidated accounts at their fair values to the group at the date of acquisition.

The parent company has not presented its own profit and loss account as permitted by section 230 of the Companies Act 1985.

Turnover: Comprises all invoiced sales of goods and services exclusive of sales taxes.

Financial instruments: The group uses financial instruments, in particular forward currency contracts and currency swaps, to manage the financial risks associated with the group's underlying business activities and the financing of those activities. The group does not undertake any trading activity in financial instruments.

A discussion of how the group manages its financial risks is included in the Financial Review on page 11. Financial instruments are accounted for as follows:

> Forward exchange contracts are used to hedge foreign exchange exposures arising on forecast receipts and payments in foreign currencies. These forward contracts are revalued to the rates of exchange at the balance sheet date and any aggregate unrealised gains and losses arising on revaluation are included in other debtors / other creditors. At maturity, or when the contract ceases to be a hedge, gains and losses are taken to the profit and loss account.

> Currency options are occasionally used to hedge foreign exchange exposures, usually when the forecast receipt or payment amounts are uncertain. Option premia are recognised at their historic cost in the group balance sheet as prepayments or accruals and released to the profit and loss account, net of any realised gains, on a straight line basis over the remaining term of the option when the outcome becomes certain.

> Interest rate swaps are occasionally used to hedge the group's exposure to movements in interest rates. The interest payable or receivable on such swaps is accrued in the same way as interest arising on deposits or borrowings. Interest rate swaps are not revalued to fair value prior to maturity.

> Currency swaps are used to reduce costs and credit exposure where the group would otherwise have cash deposits and borrowings in different currencies. The difference between spot and forward rate for these contracts is recognised as part of the net interest payable over the period of the contract. These swaps are revalued to the rates of exchange at the balance sheet date and any aggregate unrealised gains or losses arising on revaluation are included in other debtors / other creditors. Realised gains and losses on these currency swaps are taken to reserves in the same way as for the foreign investments and borrowings to which the swaps relate.

The aggregate fair values at the balance sheet date of the hedging instruments described above are disclosed as a note on the accounts.

The group has taken advantage of the exemption available for short term debtors and creditors.

Foreign currencies: Profit and loss accounts in foreign currencies and cash flows included in the cash flow statement are translated into sterling at average exchange rates for the year. Foreign currency assets and liabilities are translated into sterling at the rates of exchange at the balance sheet date. Gains or losses arising on the translation of the net assets of overseas subsidiaries and associated undertakings are taken to reserves, less exchange differences arising on related foreign currency borrowings. Other exchange differences are taken to the profit and loss account.

Research and development expenditure: Charged against profits in the year incurred.

Goodwill: Goodwill arising on acquisitions made after 1st April 1998 is capitalised and amortised on a straight line basis over the estimated useful economic life, which is 20 years or less if it is considered appropriate. Goodwill previously eliminated against reserves has not been reinstated, but will be charged to the profit and loss account on subsequent disposal of the businesses to which it relates.

Depreciation: Freehold land and certain office buildings are not depreciated. The depreciation charge and accumulated depreciation of these properties would be immaterial and they are reviewed for impairment annually. Other fixed assets are depreciated on a straight line basis at annual rates which vary according to the class of asset, but are typically: leasehold property 3.33% (or at higher rates based on the life of the lease); freehold buildings 3.33%; and plant and equipment 10% to 33%.

Leases: The cost of assets held under finance leases is included under tangible fixed assets and the capital element of future lease payments is included in borrowings. Depreciation is provided in accordance with the group's accounting policy for the class of asset concerned. Lease payments are treated as consisting of capital and interest elements and the interest is charged to the profit and loss account using the annuity method. Rentals under operating leases are expensed as incurred.

Accounting Policies

for the year ended 31st March 2004

Grants in respect of capital expenditure: Grants received in respect of capital expenditure are included in creditors and released to the profit and loss account in equal instalments over the expected useful lives of the related assets.

Precious metal stocks: Stocks of gold, silver and platinum group metals are valued according to the source from which the metal is obtained. Metal which has been purchased and committed to future sales to customers or hedged in metal markets is valued at the price at which it is contractually committed or hedged, adjusted for unexpired contango or backwardation. Leased metal is valued at market prices at the balance sheet date. Other precious metal stocks owned by the group, which are unhedged, are valued at the lower of cost and net realisable value.

Other stocks: These are valued at the lower of cost, including attributable overheads, and net realisable value.

Deferred taxation: Provided on all timing differences that have originated but not reversed by the balance sheet date and which could give rise to an obligation to pay more or less tax in the future.

Pensions and other retirement benefits: The group operates a number of contributory and non-contributory schemes, mainly of the defined benefit type, which require contributions to be made to separately administered funds.

The cost of the defined contribution schemes is charged to the profit and loss account as incurred.

For defined benefit schemes, the group recognises the net assets or liabilities of the schemes in the balance sheet, net of any related deferred tax liability or asset. The changes in scheme assets and liabilities, based on actuarial advice, are recognised as follows:

> The current service cost, based on the most recent actuarial valuation, is deducted in arriving at operating profit.

> The interest cost, based on the present value of scheme liabilities and the discount rate at the beginning of the year and amended for changes in scheme liabilities during the year, is included as interest.

> The expected return on scheme assets, based on the fair value of scheme assets and expected rates of return at the beginning of the year and amended for changes in scheme assets during the year, is included as interest.

> Actuarial gains and losses, representing differences between the expected return and actual return on scheme assets, differences between the actuarial assumptions underlying the scheme liabilities and actual experience during the year, and changes in actuarial assumptions, are recognised in the statement of total recognised gains and losses.

> Past service costs are spread evenly over the period in which the increases in benefit vest and are deducted in arriving at operating profit. If an increase in benefits vests immediately, the cost is recognised immediately.

> Gains or losses arising from settlements or curtailments not covered by actuarial assumptions are included in operating profit.

Employee share ownership trusts (ESOTs) and long term incentive plan (LTIP): The cost of shares held by the ESOTs are deducted in arriving at shareholders' funds until they vest unconditionally in employees. The cost to the group of the LTIP is recognised on a straight line basis over the period to which the performance criteria relate, adjusted for changes in the probability of performance criteria being met or conditional awards lapsing. The creditor arising from the charge is deducted in arriving at shareholders' funds.

Changes in accounting policies: Under the provisions of Financial Reporting Standard (FRS) 17 – 'Retirement Benefits', which the group adopted on 1st April 2003, the group has restated its accounts to reflect the revised recognition of its retirement benefits schemes and the resultant changes to deferred tax and amounts recognised in the profit and loss account and statement of total recognised gains and losses. Consequently, the group has restated its comparatives for the year ended 31st March 2003. The effect is to decrease the profit after taxation by £1.8 million in the year ended 31st March 2003. The group's net assets at 31st March 2003 have decreased by £95.7 million. No calculation has been performed of the effect on the results for the year ended 31st March 2004 because it was not considered practicable.

Under the provisions of Urgent Issues Task Force (UITF) Abstract 38 – 'Accounting for ESOP Trusts', which the group adopted on 1st April 2003, the group has restated its accounts to recognise amounts related to the group's ESOTs and LTIP as a component of shareholders' funds. The effect is to decrease short term investments by £13.8 million and to decrease other creditors falling due within one year by £1.2 million, resulting in net assets decreasing by £12.6 million at 31st March 2003. There is no effect on the profit and loss account.

	2004	2003 restated [1]	% change
Turnover	£4,493m	£4,324m	+4
Sales excluding precious metals	£1,224m	£1,159m	+6
Operating profit	£188.3m	£167.9m	+12
Profit before tax	£178.0m	£173.5m	+3
Earnings per share	56.0p	55.4p	+1
Before Exceptional Items and Goodwill Amortisation:			
Operating profit	£206.0m	£189.2m	+9
Profit before tax	£195.7m	£189.9m	+3
Earnings per share	64.0p	61.8p	+4
Dividend per share	26.4p	25.5p	+4

[1] Restated for FRS 17

Financial
Highlights
2004

*Divisional
Operating Profit*

*Earnings Per Share Before
Exceptional Items and Goodwill
Amortisation*

Dividend Per Share

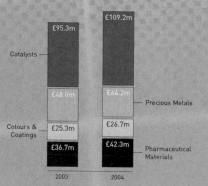

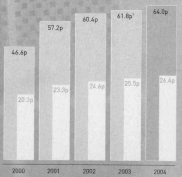

Consolidated Profit and Loss Account

for the year ended 31st March 2004

	Notes	2004 Before exceptional items and goodwill amortisation £ million	2004 Exceptional items and goodwill amortisation £ million	2004 Total £ million	2003 Before exceptional items and goodwill amortisation restated £ million	2003 Total restated £ million
Turnover	1	**4,492.9**	**–**	**4,492.9**	4,323.9	4,323.9
Operating profit	1					
Before goodwill amortisation		**205.3**	**–**	**205.3**	188.7	188.7
Goodwill amortisation		**–**	**(19.7)**	**(19.7)**	–	(13.7)
Before exceptional items		**205.3**	**(19.7)**	**185.6**	188.7	175.0
Exceptional items	2	**–**	**2.1**	**2.1**	–	(7.4)
Group operating profit	5	**205.3**	**(17.6)**	**187.7**	188.7	167.6
Share of profit in associates		**0.7**	**–**	**0.7**	0.5	0.5
Goodwill amortisation on associates		**–**	**(0.1)**	**(0.1)**	–	–
Share of exceptional items in associates	2	**–**	**–**	**–**	–	(0.2)
Total operating profit		**206.0**	**(17.7)**	**188.3**	189.2	167.9
Profit on sale of continuing operations						
Sale of an interest in Johnson Matthey Fuel Cells Limited		**–**	**–**	**–**	–	10.9
Exchange of Australian gold operations for share of AGR Matthey		**–**	**–**	**–**	–	(6.0)
Profit on ordinary activities before interest		**206.0**	**(17.7)**	**188.3**	189.2	172.8
Net interest	3	**(16.3)**	**–**	**(16.3)**	(13.2)	(13.2)
Net return on retirement benefits assets and liabilities	4	**6.0**	**–**	**6.0**	13.9	13.9
Profit on ordinary activities before taxation	6	**195.7**	**(17.7)**	**178.0**	189.9	173.5
Taxation	8	**(58.3)**	**0.4**	**(57.9)**	(56.4)	(53.7)
Profit after taxation		**137.4**	**(17.3)**	**120.1**	133.5	119.8
Minority interests	26	**1.7**	**–**	**1.7**	0.4	0.4
Profit attributable to shareholders		**139.1**	**(17.3)**	**121.8**	133.9	120.2
Dividends	9	**(57.4)**	**–**	**(57.4)**	(55.5)	(55.5)
Retained profit for the year	27	**81.7**	**(17.3)**	**64.4**	78.4	64.7

	Notes	pence		pence	restated pence	restated pence
Earnings per ordinary share						
Basic	10	**64.0**		**56.0**	61.8	55.4
Diluted	10	**63.7**		**55.8**	61.4	55.1
Dividend per ordinary share	9	**26.4**		**26.4**	25.5	25.5

The notes on pages 46 to 69 form an integral part of the accounts.

Consolidated and Parent Company Balance Sheets

as at 31st March 2004

	Notes	Group 2004 £ million	2003 restated £ million	Parent company 2004 £ million	2003 restated £ million
Fixed assets					
Goodwill	12	377.1	373.4	106.6	110.0
Tangible fixed assets	13	608.1	601.1	200.2	196.1
Investments	14	5.5	6.4	462.0	463.4
		990.7	980.9	768.8	769.5
Current assets					
Stocks	16	417.3	438.4	268.8	232.8
Debtors: due within one year	17	387.4	365.7	556.9	599.3
Debtors: due after more than one year	17	–	–	320.9	344.5
Short term investments	18	1.6	1.5	–	–
Cash at bank and in hand	19	106.5	100.4	2.7	33.4
		912.8	906.0	1,149.3	1,210.0
Creditors: amounts falling due within one year					
Borrowings and finance leases	19	(46.5)	(46.5)	(16.4)	(27.5)
Precious metal leases	21	(127.4)	(128.0)	(142.5)	(107.9)
Other creditors	22	(358.9)	(382.6)	(750.3)	(757.4)
Net current assets		380.0	348.9	240.1	317.2
Total assets less current liabilities		1,370.7	1,329.8	1,008.9	1,086.7
Creditors: amounts falling due after more than one year					
Borrowings and finance leases	19	(454.5)	(456.4)	(448.4)	(450.3)
Other creditors	22	(0.7)	(0.6)	(103.4)	(153.0)
Provisions for liabilities and charges	23	(47.4)	(49.3)	(18.9)	(13.8)
Net assets excluding retirement benefits assets and liabilities		868.1	823.5	438.2	469.6
Retirement benefits net assets	11	31.5	1.5	–	–
Retirement benefits net liabilities	11	(28.0)	(26.9)	(9.3)	(7.0)
Net assets including retirement benefits assets and liabilities		871.6	798.1	428.9	462.6
Capital and reserves					
Called up share capital	25	220.6	219.5	220.6	219.5
Share premium account	27	137.1	131.8	137.1	131.8
Capital redemption reserve	27	4.9	4.9	4.9	4.9
Shares held in employee share ownership trusts	27	(28.8)	(14.8)	(28.4)	(14.4)
Associates' reserves	27	(0.5)	0.1	–	–
Profit and loss account	27	528.9	445.8	94.7	120.8
Shareholders' funds		862.2	787.3	428.9	462.6
Minority interests	26	9.4	10.8	–	–
		871.6	798.1	428.9	462.6

The accounts were approved by the Board of Directors on 1st June 2004 and signed on its behalf by:

C R N Clark

J N Sheldrick   Directors

The notes on pages 46 to 69 form an integral part of the accounts.

Consolidated Cash Flow Statement

for the year ended 31st March 2004

	Notes	2004 £ million	2003 restated £ million
Reconciliation of operating profit to net cash inflow from operating activities			
Operating profit		187.7	167.6
Depreciation, amortisation and net loss on disposal of fixed assets and investments		83.5	68.6
Net retirement benefit charge less contributions		1.0	(6.7)
Decrease / (increase) in owned stocks		17.3	(7.7)
(Increase) / decrease in debtors		(41.7)	13.9
Increase / (decrease) in creditors and provisions		11.9	(5.8)
Net cash inflow from operating activities		259.7	229.9

Cash Flow Statement

	Notes	2004 £ million	2003 restated £ million
Net cash inflow from operating activities		259.7	229.9
Dividends received from associates		0.5	0.1
Returns on investments and servicing of finance	28	(16.4)	(13.4)
Taxation		(43.1)	(42.4)
Capital expenditure and financial investment	28	(114.4)	(124.7)
Acquisitions and disposals			
Acquisitions	28	(18.4)	(271.2)
Disposals	28	–	22.4
Net cash outflow for acquisitions and disposals		(18.4)	(248.8)
Equity dividends paid		(56.4)	(54.0)
Net cash flow before use of liquid resources and financing		11.5	(253.3)
Management of liquid resources	28	1.1	1.0
Financing			
Issue and purchase of share capital	28	(8.5)	2.8
Increase in borrowings and finance leases	28	6.3	259.7
Net cash (outflow) / inflow from financing		(2.2)	262.5
Increase in cash in the period		10.4	10.2

	Notes	2004 £ million	2003 restated £ million
Reconciliation of net cash flow to movement in net debt			
Increase in cash in the period		10.4	10.2
Cash inflow from movement in borrowings and finance leases	29	(6.3)	(259.7)
Cash inflow from term deposits included in liquid resources		(1.1)	(1.0)
Change in net debt resulting from cash flows		3.0	(250.5)
Borrowings acquired with subsidiaries		–	(0.4)
Loan notes (issued) / cancelled to acquire subsidiaries	29	(1.1)	(6.8)
Translation difference	29	6.1	14.2
Movement in net debt in year		8.0	(243.5)
Net debt at beginning of year	29	(402.5)	(159.0)
Net debt at end of year	29	(394.5)	(402.5)

The notes on pages 46 to 69 form an integral part of the accounts.

- vertical analysis, where each item in the profit and loss account (and balance sheet) is expressed as a percentage of the total sales (total assets).

Horizontal analysis

We introduced the technique of horizontal analysis in Chapter 5. The following example illustrates the technique applied to a summary of the Johnson Matthey plc profit and loss account for the years to 31 March 2004 and 31 March 2003.

Worked Example 6.2

We can prepare a horizontal analysis using a summary of the profit and loss account results for Johnson Matthey plc for 2003 and 2004, using 2003 as the base year.

(You may note that a part of the profit and loss account refers to profit on sale of continuing operations. **Continuing operations**, as distinct from **discontinued operations**, are defined in the glossary at the end of this book.)

Johnson Matthey plc
Summary consolidated profit and loss account for the year ended 31 March 2004

Figures in £m

		2004		2003
Turnover		4,492.9		4,323.9
Operating profit				
Before goodwill amortisation	205.3		188.7	
Goodwill amortisation	(19.7)		(13.7)	
Before exceptional items	185.6		175.0	
Exceptional items	2.1		(7.4)	
Group operating profit	187.7		167.6	
Share of profit in associates	0.7		0.5	
Goodwill amortisation on associates	(0.1)		(0.0)	
Share of exceptional items in associates	(0.0)		(0.2)	
Total operating profit		188.3		167.9
Profit on sale of continuing operations				
Sale of interest in Fuel Cells Ltd		–		10.9
Exchange of Australian gold operations for share of AGR Matthey		–		(6.0)
Profit on ordinary activities before interest		188.3		172.8
Net interest		(16.3)		(13.2)
Net return on retirement benefits assets and liabilities		6.0		13.9
Profit on ordinary activities before taxation		178.0		173.5
Taxation		(57.9)		(53.7)

Profit after tax	120.1	
Minority interests	1.7	
Profit attributable to shareholders	121.8	120.2
Dividends	(57.4)	(55.5)
Retained profit for the year	64.4	64.7

Johnson Matthey plc
Consolidated profit and loss account for the year ended 31 March 2004

Horizontal analysis	2003	2004
Turnover	100.0	103.9
Operating profit		
Before goodwill amortisation	100.0	108.8
Goodwill amortisation	100.0	143.8
Before exceptional items	100.0	106.1
Exceptional items	100.0	(28.4)
Group operating profit	100.0	112.0
Share of profit in associates	100.0	140.0
Goodwill amortisation on associates	100.0	–
Share of exceptional items in associates	100.0	–
Total operating profit	100.0	112.2
Profit on sale of continuing operations		
Sale of interest in Fuel Cells Ltd	100.0	–
Exchange of Australian gold operations for share of AGR Matthey	100.0	–
Profit on ordinary activities before interest	100.0	109.0
Net interest	100.0	123.5
Net return on retirement benefits assets and liabilities	100.0	43.2
Profit on ordinary activities before taxation	100.0	102.6
Taxation	100.0	107.8
Profit after tax	100.0	100.3
Minority interests	100.0	–
Profit attributable to shareholders	100.0	101.3
Dividends	100.0	103.4
Retained profit for the year	100.0	99.5

'ed only two years, and has used 2003 as the base year 100. This

'.9m = 100

$$m = \frac{£4,492.9m \times 100}{£4,323.9m} = 103.9$$

...ed with 2003 as base 100, using the same sort of calculation.

...cularly useful to make a line-by-line comparison of a company's accounts
...g period over say five or ten years, using the first year as the base year. When we
...ot accounts we may by observation automatically carry out this process of assessing per-
...ge changes in performance over time. However, presentation of the information in tabular
rorm, for a number of years, gives a very clear picture of trends in performance in each area of activity
and may provide the basis for further analysis.

We can see from the above horizontal analysis how the net profit for the year has been derived
compared with that for 2003. Despite an increase of 3.9% in sales, operating profit before tax was
increased by only 2.6%. Higher average corporation tax levels incurred by the company meant that
Johnson Matthey was able to increase the level of profit attributable to shareholders by only 1.3%
compared with the previous year.

> **Progress check 6.4** What can a horizontal analysis of the information contained in the financial statements of a company add to that provided from ratio analysis?

Vertical analysis

Worked Example 6.3 uses total turnover as the basis for calculation. The following analysis confirms
the conclusions drawn from the horizontal analysis.

Worked Example 6.3

We can prepare a vertical analysis using a summary of the consolidated profit and loss account
results for Johnson Matthey plc for 2003 and 2004.

Johnson Matthey plc
Consolidated profit and loss account for the year ended 31 March 2004

Vertical analysis	2004	2003
Turnover	100.0	100.0
Operating profit		
Before goodwill amortisation	4.6	4.3
Goodwill amortisation	(0.4)	(0.3)
Before exceptional items	4.2	4.0
Exceptional items	(0.0)	(0.1)

Group operating profit	4.2	3.9
Share of profit in associates	0.0	0.0
Goodwill amortisation on associates	(0.0)	0.0
Share of exceptional items in associates	0.0	0.0
Total operating profit	4.2	3.9
Profit on sale of continuing operations		
Sale of interest in Fuel Cells Ltd	0.0	0.2
Exchange of Australian gold operations for share of AGR Matthey	(0.0)	(0.1)
Profit on ordinary activities before interest	4.2	4.0
Net interest	(0.3)	(0.3)
Net return on retirement benefits assets and liabilities	0.1	0.3
Profit on ordinary activities before taxation	4.0	4.0
Taxation	(1.3)	(1.2)
Profit after tax	2.7	2.8
Minority interests	0.0	0.0
Profit attributable to shareholders	2.7	2.8
Dividends	(1.3)	(1.3)
Retained profit for the year	1.4	1.5

Profit on ordinary activities before interest was increased from 4.0% in 2003 to 4.2% in 2004. Net interest charges and other financial items were higher than the previous year, and so profit before tax was the same for both years at 4% of sales. An increase in the percentage burden of taxation reduced the profit attributable to shareholders from 2.8% in 2003 to 2.7% in 2004. Dividends were 1.3% of sales for both years, giving a retained profit for the year of 1.4% (2003 1.5%).

> **Progress check 6.5** What can a vertical analysis of the information contained in the financial statements of a company add to the information provided from a horizontal analysis and a ratio analysis?

Notes on the accounts

The section headed 'Notes on the Accounts' in the annual report and accounts contains information that must be reported additional to, and in support of, the financial statements. This may be used to comment on financial performance. Generally, the information disclosed in notes to the accounts includes:

ital information – analysis by
ss and geographical area relating to
ver, operating profit and net assets
- otional items
- operating profit
- net interest
- net return on retirement benefits assets and liabilities
- profit before taxation
- fees paid to auditors
- taxation
- earnings per share
- dividends
- employees/directors information – employee numbers, costs, and retirement benefits
- fixed assets

- stocks
- debtors
- investments
- borrowings
- derivatives and financial instruments
- creditors
- finance leases
- provisions for liabilities and charges
- deferred taxation
- share capital
- minority interests
- reserves
- cash flows
- analysis of net debt
- commitments and **contingent liabilities**
- acquisitions and disposals
- **post balance sheet events.**

Segmental reporting

The first note in the Notes on the Accounts in Johnson Matthey's report and accounts for 2004 is headed segmental information. Accounting standard SSAP 25, Segmental Reporting, requires large companies to disclose segmental information by each class of business, and by geographical region, unless the directors feel that by doing so they may seriously damage the competitive position of the company. This analysis is required in order that users of financial information may carry out more meaningful financial analysis.

Most large companies are usually comprised of diverse businesses supplying different products and services, rather than being engaged in a single type of business. Each type of business activity may have:

- a different structure
- different levels of profitability
- different levels of growth potential
- different levels of risk exposure.

The financial statements of such diversified companies are consolidated to include all business activities, which is a potential problem for the users of financial information. For analysis and interpretation of financial performance, aggregate figures are not particularly useful for the following reasons:

- difficulties in evaluation of performance of a business which has interests that are diverse from the aggregated financial information
- difficulties of comparison of trends over time and comparison between companies because the various activities undertaken by the company are likely to differ in size and range in comparison with other businesses
- differences in conditions between different geographical markets, in terms of levels of risk, profitability and growth

- differences in conditions between different geographical markets, in terms of political and social factors, environmental factors, currencies and **inflation** rates.

Segmental reporting analysis enables:

- the further analysis of segmental performance to determine more accurately the likely growth prospects for the business as a whole
- evaluation of the impact on the company of changes in conditions relating to particular activities
- improvements in internal management performance, because it may be monitored through disclosure of segmental information to shareholders
- evaluation of the acquisition and disposal performance of the company.

Worked Example 6.4

The information in the table below relates to global sales by Guinness plc for the years 2000 and 1999.

Figures in £m

	2000	1999
Global Sales	4,730	4,681
Asia/Pacific – B	349	324
Asia/Pacific – S	454	426
North America – B	166	151
North America – S	491	551
Rest of Europe – B	1,025	954
Rest of Europe – S	723	741
Rest of the World – B	203	198
Rest of the World – S	402	384
UK – B	519	495
UK – S	398	457

S = spirits B = beer

(i)   Using the information provided we may prepare a simple table that compares the sales for 1999 with the sales for the year 2000.

(ii) We can also consider how a simple sales analysis can provide an investor with information that is more useful than just global sales for the year.

(i)

	2000	2000 versus 1999	2000	2000 versus 1999	2000	2000 versus 1999	1999	1999	1999
	£m	%	£m	%	£m	%	£m	£m	£m
Global sales	Spirits		Beers		Total		Spirits	Beers	Total
UK	398	−12.9	519	+4.8	917	−3.7	457	495	952
Rest of Europe	723	−2.4	1,025	+7.4	1,748	+3.1	741	954	1,695
North America	491	−10.9	166	+9.9	657	−6.4	551	151	702
Asia/Pacific	454	+6.6	349	+7.7	803	+7.1	426	324	750
Rest of the World	402	+4.7	203	+2.5	605	+3.9	384	198	582
Total global sales					4,730	+1.0			4,681

(ii)

Numbers that are blandly presented in a global format do not usually reveal trends. Analysis of information by area, for example, may reveal trends and may illustrate the impact of new policies or the changes in specific economic environments. The analysis of the Guinness sales for two years shows:

- in which geographical area sales have increased or decreased
- for which products sales have increased or decreased.

Analysis of the results over several years is usually needed to provide meaningful trend information as a basis for investigation into the reasons for increases and decreases.

Class of business is a part of the overall business, which can be identified as providing a separate product or service, or group of related products or services. A geographical segment may comprise an individual country or a group of countries in which the business operates.

If a company operates in two or more classes of business activity or two or more geographical segments, there should normally be separate disclosure of information for each segment, which should include:

- sales to external customers and sales to other segments within the business, according to origin, and also by destinations of the goods and services if they are substantially different from the geographical region from which they were supplied
- operating profit before accounting for finance charges, taxation, minority interests and extraordinary items
- net assets.

Let's take a look at Johnson Matthey's segmental reporting, (see pp. 223–4). This may be used to provide even more useful information through horizontal and vertical analysis of the numbers. Such an analysis over a 5 or 10-year period would be particularly useful to identify trends in performance,

Notes on the Accounts

for the year ended 31st March 2004

1   Segmental information

	Turnover		Operating profit		Net operating assets	
	2004	2003	2004	2003 restated	2004	2003 restated
	£ million	£ million	£ million	£ million	£ million	£ million
Activity analysis						
Catalysts	**1,142.7**	1,083.4	**109.2**	95.3	**819.7**	747.2
Precious Metals	**2,956.4**	2,857.1	**44.2**	48.0	**19.0**	48.4
Colours & Coatings	**254.1**	255.7	**26.7**	25.3	**204.7**	210.3
Pharmaceutical Materials	**139.7**	127.7	**42.3**	36.7	**281.4**	281.3
Corporate	**–**	–	**(16.4)**	(16.1)	**(62.2)**	(61.2)
	4,492.9	4,323.9	**206.0**	189.2	**1,262.6**	1,226.0
Goodwill amortisation (note 12)			**(19.7)**	(13.7)		
Goodwill amortisation on associates			**(0.1)**	–		
Exceptional items included in operating profit (note 2)			**2.1**	(7.6)		
			188.3	167.9	**1,262.6**	1,226.0
Profit on sale of continuing operations			**–**	4.9		
Net interest			**(16.3)**	(13.2)		
Net return on retirement benefits assets and liabilities			**6.0**	13.9		
Profit on ordinary activities before taxation			**178.0**	173.5		
Net borrowings and finance leases					**(394.5)**	(402.5)
Net assets excluding retirement benefits assets and liabilities					**868.1**	823.5
Retirement benefits net assets / (liabilities)					**3.5**	(25.4)
Net assets including retirement benefits assets and liabilities					**871.6**	798.1

	Turnover		Operating profit		Net operating assets	
	2004	2003	2004	2003 restated	2004	2003 restated
	£ million	£ million	£ million	£ million	£ million	£ million
Geographical analysis by origin						
Europe	**3,235.1**	2,964.7	**81.0**	59.3	**916.6**	871.9
North America	**965.7**	1,082.2	**72.3**	87.3	**229.4**	234.4
Asia	**838.1**	844.7	**19.3**	12.4	**55.4**	74.6
Rest of the World	**277.6**	234.2	**33.4**	30.2	**61.2**	45.1
	5,316.5	5,125.8	**206.0**	189.2	**1,262.6**	1,226.0
Less inter-segment sales	**(823.6)**	(801.9)				
Total turnover	**4,492.9**	4,323.9				
Goodwill amortisation (note 12)			**(19.7)**	(13.7)		
Goodwill amortisation on associates			**(0.1)**	–		
Exceptional items included in operating profit (note 2)			**2.1**	(7.6)		
			188.3	167.9	**1,262.6**	1,226.0
Profit on sale of continuing operations			**–**	4.9		
Net interest			**(16.3)**	(13.2)		
Net return on retirement benefits assets and liabilities			**6.0**	13.9		
Profit on ordinary activities before taxation			**178.0**	173.5		
Net borrowings and finance leases					**(394.5)**	(402.5)
Net assets excluding retirement benefits assets and liabilities					**868.1**	823.5
Retirement benefits net assets / (liabilities)					**3.5**	(25.4)
Net assets including retirement benefits assets and liabilities					**871.6**	798.1

Notes on the Accounts

for the year ended 31st March 2004

1   *Segmental information* (*continued*)

	2004 £ million	2003 £ million
External turnover by geographical destination		
Europe	**2,011.4**	1,800.2
North America	**1,144.8**	1,228.7
Asia	**1,020.0**	1,023.0
Rest of the World	**316.7**	272.0
Total turnover	**4,492.9**	4,323.9

Turnover by destination relating to the United Kingdom amounted to £1,255.4 million (2003 £1,050.3 million).

2   *Exceptional items*

An exceptional credit of £2.1 million (2003 charge of £7.6 million) has been included in operating profit. This comprises:

	2004 £ million	2003 £ million
Litigation settlement (Pharmaceutical Materials)	**14.8**	–
Cost of integrating Synetix	**–**	(6.5)
Other Catalysts' rationalisation costs	**(12.7)**	(4.8)
Profit on sale of unhedged palladium	**–**	5.1
Cost of rationalising Australian operations following the set up of AGR Matthey	**–**	(1.2)
Exceptional items in group operating profit	**2.1**	(7.4)
Share of exceptional items in associates – AGR Matthey	**–**	(0.2)
Exceptional items in total operating profit	**2.1**	(7.6)

These charges arise in Europe (£10.5 million, 2003 £4.8 million), North America (credit £13.7 million, 2003 charge £1.4 million), Asia (£0.2 million, 2003 £ nil) and Rest of the World (£0.9 million, 2003 £1.4 million).

3   *Net interest*

	2004 £ million	2003 £ million
Interest payable on bank loans and overdrafts	**(9.0)**	(8.5)
Interest payable on other loans	**(17.2)**	(13.6)
	(26.2)	(22.1)
Interest receivable from associates	**–**	0.2
Other interest receivable	**10.2**	9.0
Net interest – group	**(16.0)**	(12.9)
Share of interest payable by associates – payable to group	**–**	(0.2)
Share of interest payable by associates – other	**(0.3)**	(0.1)
Net interest	**(16.3)**	(13.2)

4   *Net return on retirement benefits assets and liabilities*

	2004 £ million	2003 restated £ million
Expected return on scheme assets	**37.5**	46.4
Interest on scheme liabilities	**(31.5)**	(32.5)
Net return on retirement benefits assets and liabilities	**6.0**	13.9

and changes that may have taken place in the activities of the business and the areas of the world in which the company has operated.

There are many problems relating to the principle of disclosure of segmental information, some of which we have already identified:

- directors may be reluctant to disclose information that may damage the competitive position of the company – foreign competitors may not have to disclose similar data
- segmental information may not be useful since the total company results are what should be relevant to shareholders
- some users of information may not be sufficiently financially expert to avoid being confused by the segmental information
- conglomerates may choose not to disclose segmental information, whereas a single activity company by definition is unable to hide anything.

There are, in addition, some accounting problems concerned with the preparation of segmental reports:

- identification of business class and geographical segments is not defined in SSAP 25, but is left to the judgement of the directors of the company
- lack of definition of segments results in difficulty in comparison of companies
- difficulties in analysis and apportionment of costs that are common between activities and geographical regions
- difficulties in the treatment of costs of transfers of goods and services between segments.

Progress check 6.6 Describe what is meant by segmental reporting and to whom it is useful.

Worked Example 6.5

If we refer to Note 1 in the Johnson Matthey plc Notes on the Accounts in their annual report and accounts 2004 we can identify activity – turnover for 2004 and 2003. This will enable us to present the data in both pie chart and bar chart format, and more clearly explain JM's sales results for 2004 and 2003.

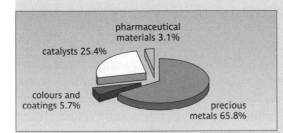

Figure 6.4 Johnson Matthey plc turnover 2004

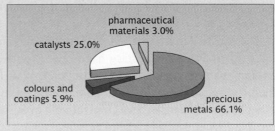

Figure 6.5 Johnson Matthey plc turnover 2003

The pie charts give a broad indication of turnover by type of business, and show that for both years precious metals provide just below two thirds of the turnover, catalysts provide around one quarter of the turnover. Colours and coatings, and pharmaceutical materials are small sectors that provide the balance. The bar chart is probably more useful in showing more clearly that turnover from the two largest sectors has increased in 2004 over 2003 but the two small sectors have remained at around the same volume.

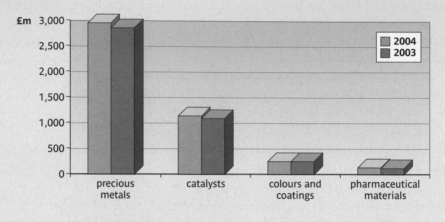

Figure 6.6 Johnson Matthey plc turnover 2004 and 2003

Corporate social responsibility (CSR) reporting

An inspection of Johnson Matthey's report and accounts 2004 will reveal that environmental issues and the health and safety of its employees, customers, and the community, rank highly amongst the company's priorities. This is demonstrated in the coverage given to such issues in the chairman's statement and in the separate five-page section devoted to these issues (see pp. 228–32).

Throughout the past 10 years or so companies have started to show greater interest in their position with regard to environmental and social issues. General corporate awareness has increased as to how the adoption of particular policies may have adverse social and environmental effects. Environmental issues naturally focus on our inability to sustain our use of non-renewable resources, the disappearance of the ozone layer and forestation, pollution and waste treatment. Social issues may include problems associated with race, gender, disability, sexual orientation, and age, and the way that companies manage bullying, the incidence of accidents, employee welfare, training and development.

The increase in awareness of environmental and social issues has followed the concern that the focus of traditional reporting has been weighted too heavily towards the requirements of shareholders, with too little regard for the other stakeholders. This has led to an over-emphasis on the financial performance, particularly the profitability, of the business. The accountancy profession and other interested parties have given thought to the widening of the annual report and accounts to meet the requirements of all stakeholders, and not just the shareholders of the business.

In March 2000, the UK Government appointed a Minister for Corporate Social Responsibility. The Government's first report on CSR was published in March 2001, which has been followed by subsequent reports, all of which can be accessed from its website devoted to CSR, www.CSR.gov.uk. The

Government sees CSR as the business contribution to sustainable development goals. They regard CSR as essentially about how business takes account of its economic, social and environmental impacts in the way it operates – maximising the benefits and minimising the downsides. CSR is about companies moving beyond a base of legal compliance to integrating socially responsible behaviour into their core values, in recognition of the sound business benefits in doing so. In principle, CSR applies to SMEs as well as to large companies.

There is currently no consensus of 'best practice' in the area of social and **environmental reporting**. Nor is there a compulsory requirement for companies to include such statements in their annual reports and accounts. The Government's approach is to encourage the adoption and reporting of CSR through best practice guidance, including development of its Corporate Responsibility Index and, where appropriate, intelligent regulation and fiscal incentives. Most large companies have reacted positively to the need for such reporting, although the quality, style and content, and the motives for inclusion, may vary. Motives may range from a genuine wish to contribute to the goal of sustainable development to simple reassurance, or attempts to mould and change opinion, and political lobbying.

Companies that include CSR reporting in their annual reports and accounts are now endeavouring to go beyond a simple outline of their environmental and social policies. Many companies include reports expanding on these policies in qualitative terms, which explain the performance of the business in its compliance with national and international standards. Some companies have taken the next step to provide detailed quantitative reports of targets, and performance and the financial impact of social and environmental issues.

CSR performance reporting is still in its infancy. The current UK Government is actively supporting the creation of a shift in the UK enterprise culture. It has emphasised how companies engaged in CSR are reporting benefits to their reputation and their bottom line. It seems likely that as the focus on standardisation of targets, indicators and audit of social and environmental performance increases, then the pressure for wider reporting will increase, and be supported by a CSR performance reporting standard.

> **Progress check 6.7 What is CSR performance reporting and why is it becoming increasingly important to companies and the UK Government?**

Directors' report

The directors' report includes financial and non-financial information, and it is a statutory requirement for a copy of this report, along with the accounts of the business, to be sent to shareholders. The directors' report includes a great deal of detail, for example:

- details of the principal activities of the business
- information about directors and their share ownership
- details about auditors
- company employment policy
- proposed dividends payable to shareholders
- major fixed assets acquisitions and disposals, and changes in valuation
- changes to share capital
- charitable and political donations made by the company.

Corporate Social Responsibility (continued)

Environment, Health and Safety Policy Statement

Johnson Matthey is firmly committed to managing its activities throughout the group so as to provide the highest level of protection to the environment and to safeguard the health and safety of its employees, customers and the community.

The company's Environment, Health and Safety policies have been widely disseminated and provide the guiding principles necessary to ensure that high standards are achieved at all sites around the world. They also afford a means of promoting continuous improvement based on careful risk assessment and comprehensive EHS management systems, against which all sites are audited.

This policy and its associated procedures are designed to achieve the following corporate objectives:
> That all locations meet legal and group environment, health and safety requirements.
> That the design, manufacture and supply of products is undertaken so as to satisfy the highest standards of health, safety, environmental protection and resource efficiency.
> That management systems are effective in maintaining standards and fulfilling the challenge of securing continuous improvement in environmental, health and safety performance.

In order to achieve these objectives we will:
> Provide leadership and commitment as an expression of the importance that the board and the senior management team places on EHS issues.
> Ensure accountability by holding corporate management and senior executives within each operating division and business unit responsible for EHS performance.
> Provide the financial and human resources to allow EHS issues to be given an appropriate level of priority.
> Provide good communication internally and externally and encourage employee involvement and cooperation at all levels in the organisation in meeting EHS objectives.

> Ensure competence on EHS matters through education, training and awareness at all levels in the organisation, including creating an understanding of individual responsibilities for health and safety and the environment.
> Undertake assessments to identify the risks to health, safety and the environment from company operations and ensure that appropriate control measures are implemented.
> Ensure that new investments are designed and operated to the latest standards so as to eliminate or minimise risks to health, safety and the environment.
> Investigate incidents to identify the root cause and take action to prevent recurrence.
> Promote programmes to achieve energy and resource efficiency.
> Set key corporate objectives and performance targets that can be measured and assessed, reporting results in a meaningful and transparent way both internally and externally.
> Undertake regular EHS inspections and internal audits of operations, and review performance to ensure continuous improvement in EHS management.

The group EHS management system will be reviewed regularly to ensure that it reflects international best practice and our growing understanding of the practical application of sustainable development.

Employment Policies and Business Integrity and Ethics Policy Statement

Employment Policies

Equal Opportunities It is the policy of the group to recruit, train and manage employees who meet the requirements of the job, regardless of gender, ethnic origin, age or religion. Employees who become disabled and disabled people are offered employment consistent with their capabilities.

Training and Development of People Johnson Matthey recognises the importance of recruiting the very highest calibre of employees, training them to achieve challenging standards in the performance of their jobs, and developing them to their maximum potential.

Our policy requires careful review of organisation structure, succession and the development of high potential people to meet our business goals. The Management Development and Remuneration Committee of the board takes a special interest in ensuring compliance with the Training and Development of People Policy.

Training and Development of People Policy
> Ensure highest standards in the recruitment of staff.
> Assess training needs in the light of job requirements.
> Ensure relevance of training and link with business goals.
> Employ and evaluate effective and efficient training methods.
> Promote from within, from high potential pools of talent.
> Understand employees' aspirations.
> Provide development opportunities to meet employees' potential and aspirations.

Employee Relations and Communication Johnson Matthey recognises the importance of effective employee communications. Information and comment is exchanged with employees through the company's in house magazine, regular news bulletins, presentations to staff and team briefings.

Business Integrity and Ethics Policy Statement

A reputation for integrity has been a cornerstone of Johnson Matthey's business since it was founded by Percival Norton Johnson in 1817. It gives customers the confidence that the company's products meet the standards claimed for them and that they may safely entrust their own precious metals to Johnson Matthey for processing and safe keeping. Employees at all levels are required to protect Johnson Matthey's reputation for integrity.

The company strives to maintain the highest standards of ethical conduct and corporate responsibility worldwide through the application of the following principles:
> Compliance with national and international laws and regulations is required as a minimum standard.
> Reputable business practices must be applied worldwide.
> Conflicts of interest must be declared and appropriate arrangements made to ensure those with a material interest are not involved in the decision making process.
> Improper payments of any kind are prohibited, similarly no gift whose value is material and which may be interpreted as a form of inducement should be accepted or offered by Johnson Matthey employees.
> Reporting of business performance should be undertaken in such a way that senior management is fully and properly informed concerning the business' true performance, risks and opportunities in a timely manner.
> Ethical issues must be dealt with in an efficient and transparent manner.
> A positive contribution to society as a whole, and specifically the communities in which we operate, must be ensured.
> We must seek to influence our suppliers to operate to similar high standards as ourselves.

We support the principles set out within the United Nations Universal Declaration of Human Rights and International Labour Organisation Core Conventions.

All employees have a duty to follow the principles set out in this policy statement. It is the responsibility of directors and senior management to ensure that all employees who directly or indirectly report to them are fully aware of Johnson Matthey's policies and values in the conduct of the company's businesses. It is also the responsibility of directors and senior management to lead by example and to demonstrate the highest standards of integrity in carrying out their duties on behalf of the company. These issues are further safeguarded through corporate governance processes and monitoring by the board and sub-committees to the board.

Corporate Social Responsibility *(continued)*

Celebrating 30 years
of Johnson Matthey autocatalysts

When the first car to be fitted with a catalytic converter rolled off a production line in the USA in 1974, it was a huge landmark for both the platinum group metals markets and the global auto industry. In 2004 Johnson Matthey celebrates 30 years in the development of autocatalysts.

1950s…
Automotive exhaust emissions are proved to be a major source of photochemical smog in Los Angeles.

1960s…
The first federal emission standards to control pollution from automobiles are set in the US in 1965. These targets are met without catalysts.

1970s…
> In 1970, US Congress substantially lowers vehicle emissions limits and lead is phased out in gasoline in the USA from 1972 onwards.
> Johnson Matthey files a patent in 1971 covering the use of a rhodium promoted platinum catalyst to control NOx and gaseous organic compounds.
> In 1972, Johnson Matthey proves to the Environmental Protection Agency that the US emissions regulations can be met using rhodium-platinum catalysts.
> The first cars fitted with oxidation catalysts reach showrooms in the USA in 1975; unleaded gasoline is widely available.
> Japanese vehicle emissions standards to control HC, CO and NOx come into effect in 1976.
> US Clean Air Act amendments made in 1977 agree to tighten emissions standards further from 1981 onwards.
> Increased substrate surface area helps to improve pollution conversion efficiency of catalysts.

1980s…
> More sophisticated 'three-way' catalytic converters are introduced in 1981 to meet strict NOx limits.
> Performance of three-way catalytic converters significantly enhanced by use of improved oxygen storage materials (based on cerium dioxide) in catalyst washcoats.
> Vehicle emissions regulations introduced in Australia, incentives introduced in Germany.

1990s…
> In 1990, Johnson Matthey files a patent covering the use of NO_2 to reduce the combustion temperature of diesel particulate matter in a filter, a system subsequently commercialised as the Continuously Regenerating Trap (CRT®).
> New legislation introduced in Japan in 1991 sets much more stringent vehicle NOx emissions limits.
> European Union emissions regulations that necessitate the use of catalytic converters (Euro 1) come into effect from 1993.
> In 1996, European Union emissions regulations tighten as Euro 2 standards are applied. Californian Low Emission Vehicle (LEV) standards come into force, emphasising the cold-start control of pollutants; palladium based catalysts found to be particularly suited to controlling HC emissions on engine start-up.
> Further improvements made in substrate surface area of catalysts.
> National Low Emissions Vehicle (NLEV) emissions standards take effect in the USA from 1999, requiring very substantial reductions in NOx.

2000 Onwards
> EU emissions standards for all road vehicles become more stringent with introduction of Euro 3 regulations in 2000.
> A substantial retrofit programme is created by the Tokyo Metropolitan Government in a move to improve particulate pollution from diesel trucks and buses in the city.
> Diesel car sales in Europe surpass six million vehicles for the first time.
> Phase in of US Tier II emissions standards begins in 2004. These mandate further large reductions in NOx and particulate matter emissions. Tier II compliant vehicles are up to 99% cleaner than vehicles sold in the 1960s.
> Regulations will be introduced in the EU and USA between 2005 and 2010 which will create a significant new original equipment market for exhaust aftertreatment products.

Directors' Report

The directors submit to shareholders their one hundred and thirteenth annual report, together with the audited accounts of the group for the year ended 31st March 2004. Pages 1 to 38 are an integral part of the report.

Principal Activities
The group's principal activities are summarised on page 15.

Dividends
The interim dividend of 8.2 pence per share, up 0.4 pence, was paid in February 2004. A final dividend, which will be paid as an ordinary dividend, of 18.2 pence per share, up 0.5 pence, is being proposed to shareholders as Resolution 3 at the Annual General Meeting (AGM), making a total for the year of 26.4 pence, an increase of 4% over last year. Dividends for the year total £57.4 million.

A low cost Dividend Reinvestment Plan is in place for the benefit of shareholders. This allows them to purchase additional shares in Johnson Matthey with their dividend payment. Further information and a mandate can be obtained from the Company Secretary at the company's registered office.

Share Capital
Allotments of ordinary shares of £1 each of the company were made during the year as set out in note 25 on page 63.

The board will again seek shareholders' approval to renew the annual authority for the company to make purchases of its own ordinary shares through the market. No shares were purchased under this authority during the year ended 31st March 2004.

Employee Share Schemes
4,636 current and former employees, representing approximately 63% of employees worldwide as at 31st March 2004, are shareholders in Johnson Matthey through the group's employee share schemes, which held 3,507,288 shares (1.59% of ordinary share capital) at 31st March 2004. A total of 834 current and former executives hold options over 6,183,642 shares through the company's executive share option schemes.

Directors
Details of the directors of the company are shown on pages 12 and 13. Dr P N Hawker and Mr L C Pentz, both appointed to the board on 1st August 2003, offer themselves for election at the forthcoming AGM. In accordance with the company's Articles of Association, Mr M B Dearden, Mr C D Mackay, Mr J N Sheldrick and Mr I C Strachan retire by rotation and, being eligible, offer themselves for re-election at the AGM.

Directors' Material Interests in Contracts
Other than service contracts, no director had any interest in any material contract with any group company at any time during the year.

Substantial Shareholdings
The company has been advised of the following interest in its ordinary share capital as at 28th May 2004:

Schroder Investment Management Ltd	7.66%	Legal & General Assurance Society Ltd	4.38%
Merrill Lynch Investment Managers	7.61%	Deutsche Asset Management	3.74%
Scottish Widows Investment Partnership Ltd	4.96%	AXA Investment Managers UK Ltd	3.05%

Auditors
In accordance with section 384 of the Companies Act 1985, a resolution is to be proposed at the forthcoming AGM for the reappointment of KPMG Audit Plc as auditors of the company.

Policy on Payment of Commercial Debts
The group's policy in relation to the payment of all suppliers (set out in its Group Control Manual, which is distributed to all group operations) is that payment should be made within the credit terms agreed with the supplier. At 31st March 2004, the company's aggregate level of 'creditor days' amounted to 5 days. Creditor days are calculated by dividing the aggregate of the amounts which were owed to trade creditors at the end of the year by the aggregate of the amounts the company was invoiced by suppliers during the year and multiplying by 365 to express the ratio as a number of days.

Donations
During the year the group donated £313,000 (2003 £323,000) to charitable organisations, of which £279,000 (2003 £299,000) was in the UK. There were no political donations made in the year (2003 £ nil).

Going Concern
The directors have a reasonable expectation that the group has sufficient resources to continue in operational existence for the foreseeable future and have, therefore, adopted the going concern basis in preparing the accounts.

This report was approved by the directors on 1st June 2004 and is signed on their behalf by:

S. Farrant

Simon Farrant
Company Secretary

The Johnson Matthey plc directors' report (see p. 233), includes a section on each of the headings we have outlined above. In addition, it includes a section on directors' (lack of) material interests in contracts, and the group policy on payment of commercial debts. The inclusion of the company's 'creditor days' performance is important. There has been general pressure for companies to rely less on funding from extended credit from suppliers, over and above agreed terms.

Following the publication of the Cadbury Committee report in 1992, the directors' report now includes a section on corporate governance (see Chapter 7), and includes details about the company's system of internal control, and its various committees, for example the remuneration committee. Johnson Matthey has reported on the many committees it has in place, and their functions:

- chief executive's committee: strategy, planning and executive management
- audit committee: financial reporting, corporate control, internal and external audit
- nomination committee: appointment of executive and non-executive directors
- management development and remuneration committee: senior management remuneration.

> **Progress check 6.8** What purpose does the directors' report serve and what information does it usually include?

Inflation and reporting

Inflation is a general increase in the price level over time. We will consider the impact of inflation on the financial statements prepared under the traditional, historical cost convention. In this book we will not cover in detail the alternative approaches to reporting the effect of inflation, other than to highlight the level of awareness of the problem. The accountancy profession has, over the years, considered many proposals of methods to try and deal with inflation-related problems requiring financial reports to reflect the effects of inflation. The proposals relating to the treatment of inflation in financial reporting have revolved around two schools of thought:

- the purchasing power approach, using a price index like the Retail Price Index, to adjust the historical costs of transactions
- the current cost accounting approach, which requires fixed assets and stocks to be included in the accounts at their current value rather than their historical cost.

We have previously discussed the reasons for using money as the unit of measurement, which include its properties as a medium of exchange and a store of value. Its use implies some stability in its value, which in the real world is patently not the case. One £ held today does not have the same value as one £ held in a year's time; it will purchase less in a year's time despite the relatively low levels of inflation prevailing in the UK over recent years – but note how in the mid-1970s the inflation level reached nearly 25% per annum!

The basic problem of inflation in financial reporting is that it tends to overstate profit calculated using traditional historical costs. In periods of inflation the impact on profit is seen in four key areas:

- borrowing and extended credit received are worth less in real terms when settled compared to when the borrowing took place or the credit was received, which is a gain for the business
- financial investments made and extended credit allowed are worth less in real terms when settled compared to when the investments took place or the credit was granted, which is a loss for the business
- depreciation of fixed assets is understated, being based on fixed assets' historical costs and so

when assets eventually have to be replaced the replacement cost will be higher, for which the company may have provided insufficient cash resources

- closing stocks will be more likely to have higher values, on a like-for-like basis, compared with opening stocks and so profit may be overstated, but the pressure on cash resources will be felt when stocks have been sold and then need to be replaced at higher prices.

It is important for the non-accounting specialist to be aware that the published financial statements of UK limited companies have not been adjusted to allow for the effects of inflation. Over extended periods there is therefore significant distortion in the accounting information that has been presented based on historical costs. However, the non-specialist may be assured that the accountancy profession continues to grapple with the problem of inflation in financial reporting.

> **Progress check 6.9** Why should users of financial information be aware of the effects of inflation on financial reporting?

Value added statements

Value added is a measure of the wealth created by a company through its activities. It is the difference between the value of its sales and the cost of the materials and services that it has bought in.

The **value added statement** is effectively a rearrangement of the profit and loss account. It shows how value added is distributed among the relevant parties:

- employees
- lenders
- shareholders
- Government

and the amount to provide maintenance and expansion of the business.

The value added statement has often been compared with a cake or a pie (see Fig. 6.7 and Fig. 6.8), with interested parties asking 'are we getting our fair share of the cake?' This question is often the basis of trade union employee wage negotiations with companies.

The Accounting Standards Committee in 1975 published *The Corporate Report*, which described the value added statement as 'the simplest and most immediate way of putting profit into a proper perspective *vis à vis* the whole enterprise as a collective effort of capital, management and employees'. The value added statement has certain advantages as a business performance measure:

- is simple to calculate
- enables comparison between companies with different activities
- improves relationships between shareholders, managers and employees
- cannot be manipulated to the same extent as accounting profit
- enables further analysis for example vertical analysis against turnover
- lends itself to integration with employee incentive schemes.

The value added statement for Johnson Matthey plc shown in Worked Example 6.6 illustrates how value added has been derived and how it has been applied in absolute terms for the years 2003 and 2004. A vertical analysis of the numbers would perhaps provide a better basis for comparison, which is illustrated in Worked Example 6.7.

- some difficulty encountered in measurement and reporting
- classification of items – for example taxation, which normally excludes employee tax and National Insurance, and business rates
- unstandardised format with varying treatment of items in the value added statement
- current lack of popularity among companies, despite the inclusion of a value added statement by a large percentage of large companies up to the early 1980s in their annual reports and accounts.

The value added statement seems unlikely to replace the conventional profit and loss account, or cash flow statement as a decision-making tool or as a measure of business performance. However, it may continue to be useful for internal communication of company financial performance to employees, and in support of employee incentive schemes.

> **Progress check 6.10** What is a value added statement and what does it tell us?

Summary of key points

- Limited companies prepare their annual reports and accounts to keep shareholders informed about financial performance and the financial position of the business.
- The annual report and accounts of a public limited company now requires disclosure of a great deal of both financial and non-financial information in addition to the financial statements.
- The annual report and accounts allows evaluation of a public limited company in a wider context than was possible from the sort of financial information traditionally required by the shareholders.
- Horizontal analysis of the profit and loss account (which may also be applied to the balance sheet) for two or more years starts with a base year 100 and shows each item, line-by-line, indexed against the base year, and is particularly useful in looking at performance trends over a number of years.
- Vertical analysis of the profit and loss account (which may also be applied to the balance sheet) shows every item as a percentage of turnover (balance sheet – total assets), and is also particularly useful in looking at performance trends over a number of years.
- Segmental reporting provides a further dimension to the financial statements through analysis of turnover, operating profit and net assets, by business class and geographical segments.
- The quality and depth of corporate social responsibility (CSR) performance reporting, in both qualitative and quantitative terms, is becoming increasingly important as annual reports and accounts are required to meet the needs of all stakeholders, not just the shareholders.
- Although the financial statements of limited companies are not adjusted for the effects of inflation, the impact of inflation is a factor that must be considered in evaluation of business performance.
- The value added statement, which is an alternative presentation of the traditional profit and loss statement, measures wealth as the value added by the business rather than the profit earned by the business.

Questions

Q6.1   **(i)**   Why, and for whom, do the annual reports and accounts of limited companies have to be prepared?

       (ii)   Where do they have to be filed?

       (iii)   Who are the main users of the information contained in the annual report and accounts?

       (iv)   How do they use the information?

Q6.2   **(i)**   Why do you think that the chairman, chief executive, and finance director of a plc each need to provide a statement or report for inclusion in the annual report and accounts?

       (ii)   What purpose do these reports serve and in what ways do they differ?

Q6.3   **(i)**   Describe the key elements of Johnson Matthey's financial review that are included in their report and accounts for 2004, and what these indicate about the performance of the business.

       (ii)   Why do you think that a third of this report is devoted to financial risk management?

       (iii)   What does risk management mean?

       (iv)   What are the financial risks faced by Johnson Matthey?

Q6.4   Describe the technique of horizontal analysis and how it may be used to evaluate, explain and compare company performance.

Q6.5   Describe the technique of vertical analysis and how it may be used to evaluate, explain and compare company performance.

Q6.6   **(i)**   What were the inadequacies in financial statement reporting that SSAP 25, Segmental Reporting, sought to address and how did it do this?

       (ii)   What are the practical problems that companies face associated with their compliance with SSAP 25?

Q6.7   **(i)**   Why do you think that corporate social responsibility (CSR) reporting has become increasingly important in terms of corporate awareness, and with regard to the awareness of the non-business community?

       (ii)   Examine the annual reports and accounts of a number of large UK plcs to critically evaluate and compare their CSR reporting with that provided by Johnson Matthey in its 2004 report and accounts.

Q6.8   **(i)**   How does inflation distort accounting information that has been prepared under the historical cost convention?

       (ii)   In what ways has the accountancy profession considered some alternative approaches to try and deal with the problem of inflation?

Q6.9   **(i)**   Explain what is meant by a value added statement.

       (ii)   In what ways may a value added statement be used to measure financial performance?

       (iii)   What are the disadvantages in using value added statements?

       (iv)   Why do you think the levels of popularity they enjoyed in the 1980s have not been maintained?

Ten Year Record

2000 £ million	2001 £ million	2002 £ million	2003 £ million	**2004 £ million**
3,866.0	5,903.7	4,830.1	4,323.9	**4,492.9**
–	–	–	–	**–**
3,866.0	5,903.7	4,830.1	4,323.9	**4,492.9**
146.2	175.0	193.3	189.2	**206.0**
(0.2)	(0.3)	(6.8)	(13.7)	**(19.8)**
(9.8)	(0.6)	(18.1)	(7.6)	**2.1**
136.2	174.1	168.4	167.9	**188.3**
23.4	1.1	(5.6)	4.9	**–**
159.6	175.2	162.8	172.8	**188.3**
(2.4)	5.3	(6.1)	(13.2)	**(16.3)**
–	–	–	13.9	**6.0**
157.2	180.5	156.7	173.5	**178.0**
(47.3)	(54.2)	(50.2)	(53.7)	**(57.9)**
109.9	126.3	106.5	119.8	**120.1**
(0.2)	(0.6)	0.3	0.4	**1.7**
109.7	125.7	106.8	120.2	**121.8**
(44.3)	(51.3)	(53.2)	(55.5)	**(57.4)**
65.4	74.4	53.6	64.7	**64.4**
50.5p	57.3p	49.0p	55.4p	**56.0p**
46.6p	57.2p	60.4p	61.8p	**64.0p**
20.3p	23.3p	24.6p	25.5p	**26.4p**
5.1	8.6	182.6	373.4	**377.1**
311.3	386.8	495.1	601.1	**608.1**
1.0	1.0	2.7	6.4	**5.5**
253.2	278.8	414.3	438.4	**417.3**
434.7	522.9	456.0	367.2	**389.0**
(452.5)	(534.7)	(584.4)	(560.5)	**(534.4)**
–	–	–	(25.4)	**3.5**
552.8	663.4	966.3	1,200.6	**1,266.1**
(165.8)	(139.9)	159.0	402.5	**394.5**
389.2	465.9	466.4	445.9	**528.4**
324.9	332.8	337.0	341.4	**333.8**
4.5	4.6	3.9	10.8	**9.4**
552.8	663.4	966.3	1,200.6	**1,266.1**
46.0	46.0	46.0	40.6	**40.6**
19.3%	26.8%	22.5%	16.8%	**16.2%**

1. Earnings Per Share Before Exceptional Items and Goodwill Amortisation

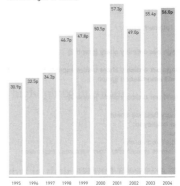

2. Earnings Per Share

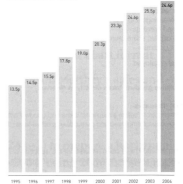

3. Dividend Per Share

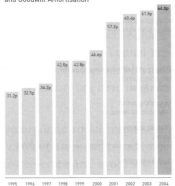

E6.3 *Time allowed – 60 minutes*

(i) Use the 10-year record of Johnson Matthey (see pp. 241–2) to prepare a horizontal analysis of the balance sheet for the 5 years years 2000 to 2004, using 2000 as the base year.

(ii) What does this analysis tell us about Johnson Matthey's financial position over that period?

Level II

E6.4 *Time allowed – 60 minutes*

(i) Use the 10-year record of Johnson Matthey (see pp. 241–2) to prepare a vertical analysis of the profit and loss account for the 5 years years 2000 to 2004.

(ii) What does this analysis tell us about Johnson Matthey's financial performance over that period?

E6.5 *Time allowed – 60 minutes*

Note 1 to the report and accounts of Johnson Matthey provides segmental analysis for the years 2004 and 2003.

Prepare a horizontal analysis from this information, with 2003 as the base year, and use it to explain the appropriate elements of financial performance and the changes in the financial position of the business.

E6.6 *Time allowed – 60 minutes*

Refer to the financial statements included in Johnson Matthey's report and accounts 2004 to calculate the appropriate ratios for comparison with the previous year, and include them in a report on the profitability of the group (see Chapter 5).

E6.7 *Time allowed – 60 minutes*

Refer to the financial statements included in Johnson Matthey's report and accounts 2004 to calculate the appropriate ratios for comparison with the previous year, and to give your assessment of the company's sources and uses of cash, and include them in a report on the group's cash position (see Chapter 5).

E6.8 *Time allowed – 60 minutes*

Refer to the financial statements included in Johnson Matthey's report and accounts 2004 to calculate the appropriate ratios for comparison with the previous year, and include them in a report on the working capital of the group (see Chapter 5).

E6.9 *Time allowed – 60 minutes*

Refer to the financial statements included in Johnson Matthey's report and accounts 2004 to calculate the appropriate ratios for comparison with the previous year, and include them in a report on the investment performance of the group (see Chapter 5).

E6.10 *Time allowed – 60 minutes*

Refer to the financial statements included in Johnson Matthey's report and accounts 2004 to calculate the appropriate ratios for comparison with the previous year, and include them in a report on the financial structure of the group (see Chapter 5).

E6.11 *Time allowed – 90 minutes*

The notes and five-year profit and loss account extracts from the financial statements of Guinness plc are shown below.

You are required to use these to carry out an appropriate analysis and provide a report on the likely explanations of differences in performance over the five years.

Notes:

- The group sells alcohol-based products to consumers and operates in nearly every major country throughout the world.
- Local and global competition is intense in many markets.
- Brands have been sold during the five years.
- New products are invariably variants on the group's basic products of beers, wines and spirits.
- The group share price had been relatively static due to the maturity of the market and the pattern of profits.
- Other investment income shown in the five-year analysis related to an investment in a French luxury goods group.
- Soon after year 6 the group merged with another international food and drinks business, which also had an extensive portfolio of own and purchased brands.
- After the merger several brands were sold to competitors.
- After the merger many of the directors left the group's management team.
- Exchange rates over the five-year period in several of the group's markets were quite volatile.
- The group had £1.4 billion of brands in its balance sheet.

Guinness plc five-year profit and loss account

Figures in £m

	Year 5	Year 4	Year 3	Year 2	Year 1
Turnover	4,730	4,681	4,690	4,663	4,363
Gross profit	961	943	956	938	1,023
Other investment income	113	47	89	(48)	(24)
Profit before interest and tax (operating profit)	1,074	990	1,045	890	999
Net interest	(99)	(114)	(130)	(188)	(204)
Profit before tax	975	876	915	702	795
Tax on profit on ordinary activities	(259)	(251)	(243)	(247)	(242)
Profit on ordinary activities after tax	716	625	672	455	553
Minority interests	(31)	(30)	(31)	(22)	(29)
Profit for financial year	685	595	641	433	524
Dividends	(295)	(302)	(279)	(258)	(237)
Retained profit	390	293	362	175	287
Earnings per share	35.1p	29.4p	31.8p	22.9p	28.1p
Interest cover	10.8	8.7	8.0	4.7	4.9
Dividend cover	2.2	2.0	2.3	1.8	2.3

E6.12 *Time allowed – 90 minutes*
The BOC Group is a company in the chemical industry, in the same industrial sector as Johnson Matthey. Locate the website for BOC Group plc on the Internet. Carry out a review of their most recent annual report and accounts and prepare a report that compares it with Johnson Matthey's report and accounts for the same year. Your report should include comments that relate to specific items that have been covered in Chapter 6, and also the differences and the similarities between the two companies.

7

Corporate governance

Contents

Learning objectives

Completion of this chapter will enable you to:

- describe how the framework for establishing good corporate governance and accountability has been established in a Combined Code of Practice, developed from the work of the Cadbury, Greenbury, Hampel, and Turnbull Committees
- explain the statutory requirement for the audit of limited companies, the election by shareholders of suitably qualified, independent auditors, and the role of the auditors
- outline directors' specific responsibility to shareholders, and responsibilities to society in general, for the management and conduct of companies
- recognise the fiduciary duties that directors have to the company, and their duty of care to all stakeholders and to the community at large, particularly with regard to the Companies Act 1985/1989, Health and Safety at Work Act 1974, and Financial Services Act 1986
- explain the implications for companies and their directors that may arise from the UK Government's promised legislation on the issue of corporate manslaughter
- appreciate the importance of directors' duties regarding insolvency, the Insolvency Act 1986, and the Enterprise Act 2002
- consider the implications for directors of wrongful trading, and recognise the difference between this and the offence of fraudulent trading, and the possibility of criminal penalties
- outline the implication for directors of the Company Directors Disqualification Act 1986, and the Enterprise Act 2002
- explain the actions that directors of companies should take to ensure compliance with their obligations and responsibilities, and to protect themselves against possible non-compliance.

Introduction

In Chapter 6 we saw that a large part of Johnson Matthey plc's report and accounts 2004 was devoted to the subject of corporate governance, the systems by which companies are directed and controlled. This chapter turns to the statutory and non-statutory rules that surround the accounting for limited companies.

In earlier chapters we discussed the way in which the limited company exists in perpetuity as a legal entity, separate from the lives of those individuals who both own and manage it. The limited company has many rights, responsibilities, and liabilities in the same way as individual people. As a separate legal entity the company is responsible for its own liabilities. These are not the obligations of the shareholders who have paid for their shares, being the limit of their obligations to the company.

The directors of a limited company are appointed by, and are responsible to, the shareholders for the management of the company, maintained through their regular reporting on the activities of the business. The responsibilities of directors, however, are wider than to just the shareholders. They are also responsible for acting correctly towards their employees, suppliers, customers, and the public at large.

The annual audit of the accounts is a statutory requirement for all limited companies, excluding smaller limited companies. As with directors, the auditors of a limited company are also appointed by, and are responsible to, the shareholders. Their primary responsibility is to make an objective report to shareholders and others as to whether, in their opinion, the financial statements show a true and fair view, and compliance with statutory, regulatory and accounting standard requirements. Therefore, the management and regulation of a company as a separate legal entity lies with the directors and the auditors. The directors are within, and part of, the company, and the auditors are external to, and not part of, the company.

This chapter will look at roles and responsibilities of directors and auditors. It will also consider the obligations of directors, particularly with regard to the corporate governance Combined Code of Practice, and the many Acts that are now in place to regulate the behaviour of directors of limited companies. The chapter closes with a look at some of the steps that directors may take to protect themselves against possible non-compliance.

Corporate governance code of practice

Concerns about financial reporting and accountability, and the impact on the business community (see Fig. 7.1), grew during the 1980s following increasing numbers of company failures and financial scandals.

During the 1980s and 1990s there was huge concern within the business community following the financial scandals surrounding BCCI, Polly Peck and Robert Maxwell's companies. The concerns increased as we saw even larger scandals involving companies such as Enron and WorldCom, and particularly the involvement of the consulting arms of firms like Arthur Andersen. These concerns were seen in a lack of confidence in financial reporting, and in shareholders and others being unable

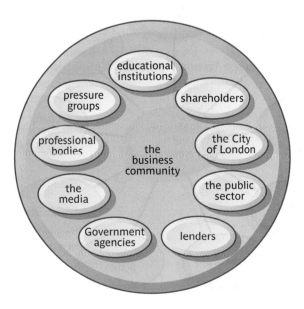

Figure 7.1 The business community

- internal financial control
- incentive compensation
- directors' pensions
- corporate strategy.

This may not be a complete list but it gives a broad indication of the areas of compliance under the Combined Code of Practice. This compliance can be seen as set out in the annual reports and accounts of UK plcs.

Accountability

Accountability of boards of directors to their shareholders requires the commitment from both to make the accountability effective. Boards of directors must play their part by ensuring the quality of information that is provided to shareholders. Shareholders must exercise their responsibilities as owners of the business. The major investing institutions (for example, pension funds and insurance companies) are in regular contact with the directors of UK plcs to discuss past, current, and future performance.

Subsequent to 1998, further reviews of various aspects of corporate governance were set up:

- *Review of the role and effectiveness of non-executive directors*, by Derek Higgs and published January 2003
- *Audit Committees Combined Code guidance*, by a group led by Sir Robert Smith and published January 2003.

The above reviews were undertaken during a period in which investor confidence had been badly shaken both by lapses in corporate governance and by the high-profile failure of some corporate strategies, the latter two being very much in response to these events. The reviews were reflected in a revision to the 1998 Combined Code of Practice, which was published by the Financial Reporting Council (FRC) in July 2003 – the Revised Code on Corporate Governance.

Companies listed on the Stock Exchange are requested to comply with the Code, but other companies may also benefit from compliance. It is not compulsory for any company, but rather a target of best practice to aim for. The revised Code continued to include the 'comply or explain' approach that was introduced by Cadbury. This means that companies listed on the Stock Exchange are required to include in their annual report and accounts a statement to confirm that they have complied with the Code's provisions throughout the accounting period, or to provide an explanation if that is not the case.

> **Progress check 7.1** What is corporate governance and how is it implemented?

Let's take a look at the Johnson Matthey section on corporate governance, included in pages 30 to 38 of their report and accounts 2004, and reproduced on pages 251–9 of this book. This section includes the corporate governance report itself, and the audit committee report, remuneration committee report, remuneration of the directors, and the responsibility of directors report. The company states that 'The group was in compliance with the provisions of the Code throughout the year'.

A number of the headings required as part of corporate governance reporting are not included within Johnson Matthey plc's main corporate governance report, but are shown elsewhere in the report and accounts. For example, the composition and functions of the board, and directors'

Corporate Governance

Statement of Compliance with the Combined Code

The company has applied all of the principles set out in section 1 of the Combined Code on Corporate Governance (the Code) relating to the structure and composition of the board, the remuneration of the directors, relations with shareholders and procedures for financial reporting, internal control and audit. This statement describes how the principles of the Code have been applied. The group was in compliance with the provisions of the Code throughout the year.

Directors and the Board

The board is responsible to the company's shareholders for the group's system of corporate governance, its strategic objectives and the stewardship of the company's resources and is ultimately responsible for social, environmental and ethical matters. The board met eight times in the year and delegated specific responsibilities to board committees, as described below. The board reviews the key activities of the business and receives papers and presentations to enable it to do so effectively. The Company Secretary is responsible to the board, and is available to individual directors, in respect of board procedures.

The board comprises the Chairman, the Chief Executive, five other executive directors and five independent non-executive directors. Following the retirement of Mr C R N Clark at the company's Annual General Meeting (AGM) to be held on 20th July 2004, half of the board, excluding the Chairman, will comprise independent non-executive directors. The Chairman's other commitments are disclosed on page 12. The roles of Chairman and Chief Executive are separate. The Chairman leads the board, ensuring that each director, particularly the independent non-executive directors, is able to make an effective contribution. He monitors, with assistance from the Company Secretary, the information distributed to the board to ensure that it is sufficient, accurate, timely and clear. The Chief Executive maintains day-to-day management responsibility for the company's operations, implementing group strategies and policies agreed by the board.

Mr C D Mackay was appointed Senior Independent Director upon the retirement of Mr H R Jenkins on 16th July 2003. The role of non-executive directors is to enhance the independence and objectivity of the board's deliberations and decisions. All non-executive directors are independent of management and free from any business or other relationship which could materially interfere with the exercise of their independent judgment. The executive directors have specific responsibilities, which are detailed on pages 12 and 13, and have direct responsibility for all operations and activities.

All directors submit themselves for re-election at least once every three years. The board composition allows for changes to be made with minimum disruption. The board annually reviews the senior managers and their succession and development plans.

Committees of the Board

The **Chief Executive's Committee** is responsible for the recommendation to the board of strategic and operating plans and on decisions reserved to the board where appropriate. It is also responsible for the executive management of the group's business. The Committee is chaired by the Chief Executive and meets at least monthly. It comprises the executive directors and four senior executives of the company.

The **Audit Committee** is a sub-committee of the board whose purpose is to assist the board in the effective discharge of its responsibilities for financial reporting and corporate control. The Committee meets quarterly and, since the retirement of Mr H R Jenkins on 16th July 2003, is chaired by Mr A M Thomson. It comprises all the independent non-executive directors with the Chairman, the Chief Executive, the Group Finance Director and the external and internal auditors attending by invitation. A report from the Committee on its activities is given on page 32.

The **Nomination Committee** is a sub-committee of the board responsible for advising the board and making recommendations on the appointment of new directors. The Committee is chaired by Mr H M P Miles and comprises the Chairman and all the independent non-executive directors.

The **Management Development and Remuneration Committee** (MDRC) is a sub-committee of the board, which determines on behalf of the board the remuneration of the executive directors. The Committee is chaired by Mr C D Mackay and comprises all the independent non-executive directors. The Committee meets at least four times per year. The Chairman attends by invitation. The Chief Executive also attends by invitation except when his own performance and remuneration are discussed.

Attendance at board and board committee meetings in 2003/04 was as follows:

Director	Full Board Eligible to attend	Full Board Attended	MDRC Eligible to attend	MDRC Attended	Nomination Committee Eligible to attend	Nomination Committee Attended	Audit Committee Eligible to attend	Audit Committee Attended
H M P Miles	8	8	5[1]	6[3]	1	1	2[1]	4[3]
C R N Clark	8	8	–	6[3]	–	1[3]	–	4[3]
N A P Garson	8	8	–	3[3]	–	–	–	–
M B Dearden	8	8	7	7	1	1	1	3
P N Hawker	5	4	–	–	–	–	–	–
H R Jenkins[2]	3	3	3	3	1	1	1	1
C D Mackay	8	8	7	7	1	1	4	3
D W Morgan	8	8	–	–	–	–	–	–
L C Pentz	5	5	–	–	–	–	–	–
J N Sheldrick	8	8	–	–	–	–	–	4[3]
I C Strachan	8	7	7	6	1	1	4	4
A M Thomson	8	7	7	7	1	1	4	4
R J W Walvis	8	8	7	7	1	1	4	3

[1] Mr Miles ceased to be a member of the Audit Committee and the MDRC on 25th November 2003.
[2] Retired July 2003.
[3] Includes meetings attended by invitation for all or part of meeting.

Corporate Governance

Directors' Remuneration

The Remuneration Report on pages 33 to 38 includes details of remuneration policies and of the remuneration of the directors.

Relations with Shareholders

The board considers effective communication with shareholders, whether institutional investors, private or employee shareholders, to be extremely important.

The company reports formally to shareholders twice a year, when its half year and full year results are announced and an interim report and a full report are issued to shareholders. These reports are posted on Johnson Matthey's website (www.matthey.com). At the same time, executive directors give presentations on the results to institutional investors, analysts and the media in London and other international centres. Copies of major presentations are also posted on the company's website.

The company's Annual General Meeting takes place in London and formal notification is sent to shareholders with the annual report at least 20 working days in advance of the meeting. The directors are available, formally during the AGM and informally afterwards, for questions. Details of the 2004 AGM are set out in the notice of the meeting enclosed with this annual report.

There is a programme of regular dialogue with major institutional shareholders and fund managers. The Chairman and the Senior Independent Director are always available to shareholders on all matters relating to governance.

Accountability, Audit and Control

The statement of directors' responsibilities in relation to the accounts is set out on page 38.

In its reporting to shareholders, the board aims to present a balanced and understandable assessment of the group's financial position and prospects.

The group's organisational structure is focused on its four divisions. These entities are all separately managed, but report to the board through a board director. The executive management team receives monthly summaries of financial results from each division through a standardised reporting process.

The group has in place a comprehensive annual budgeting process including forecasts for the next two years. Variances from budget are closely monitored.

The board has overall responsibility for the group's system of internal controls and for reviewing its effectiveness. The internal control systems are designed to meet the group's needs and address the risks to which it is exposed. Such a system can provide reasonable but not absolute assurance against material misstatement or loss.

There is a continuous process for identifying, evaluating and managing the significant risks faced by the company which has been in place during the year under review and up to the date of approval of the annual report and accounts. The board regularly reviews this process.

The assessment of group and strategic risks is reviewed by the board and updated on an annual basis. At the business level the processes to identify and manage the key risks are an integral part of the control environment. Key risks and internal controls are the subject of regular reporting to the Chief Executive's Committee.

The Group Control Manual, which is distributed to all group operations, clearly sets out the composition, responsibilities and authority limits of the various board and executive committees and also specifies what may be decided without central approval. It is supplemented by other specialist policy and procedures manuals issued by the group, divisions and individual business units or departments. The high intrinsic value of many of the metals with which the group is associated necessitates stringent physical controls over precious metals held at the group's sites.

The internal audit function is responsible for monitoring the group's systems of internal financial controls and the control of the integrity of the financial information reported to the board. The Audit Committee approves the plans for internal audit reviews and receives the reports produced by the internal audit function on a regular basis. Actions are agreed with management in response to the internal audit reports produced.

In addition, significant business units provide assurance on the maintenance of financial and non-financial controls and compliance with group policies. These assessments are summarised by the internal audit function and a report is made annually to the Audit Committee.

The directors confirm that the system of internal control for the year ended 31st March 2004 and the period up to 31st May 2004 has been established in accordance with the Turnbull Guidance included with the Code and that they have reviewed the effectiveness of the system of internal control.

Corporate Social Responsibility

Measures to ensure responsible business conduct and the identification and assessment of risks associated with social, ethical and environmental matters are managed in conjunction with all other business risks and reviewed at regular meetings of the board and Chief Executive's Committee.

A summary report on the group's policies and targets for corporate social responsibility is set out on pages 24 to 28. A full version of the report is available on the company's website.

The identification, assessment and management of environment, health and safety (EHS) risks are standing items at the Chief Executive's Committee. Performance is monitored using monthly statistics and detailed site audit reports. An annual review of EHS performance is undertaken by the board.

Risks from employment and people issues are identified and assessed by the Chief Executive's Committee and reported through to the board.

Employment contracts, handbooks and policies specify acceptable business practices and the group's position on ethical issues. The Group Control Manual and security manuals provide further operational guidelines to reinforce these.

The Audit Committee reviews risks associated with corporate social responsibility on an annual basis and monitors performance through the annual control self-assessment process conducted by the internal audit function.

Audit Committee Report

Role of the Audit Committee

The Audit Committee is a sub-committee of the board whose responsibilities include:

> Reviewing the interim and full year accounts and results announcements of the company and any other formal announcements relating to the company's financial performance and recommending them to the board for approval;

> Reviewing the group's systems for internal financial control and risk management;

> Monitoring and reviewing the effectiveness of the company's internal audit function and considering regular reports from Internal Audit on internal financial controls and risk management;

> Considering the appointment of the external auditors; overseeing the process for their selection; and making recommendations to the board in relation to their appointment (to be put to shareholders for approval at a general meeting);

> Monitoring and reviewing the effectiveness and independence of the external auditors, agreeing the nature and scope of their audit, their remuneration, and considering their reports on the company's accounts and systems of internal financial control and risk management.

The full terms of reference of the Audit Committee are provided on our website at www.matthey.com.

Composition of the Audit Committee

The Audit Committee comprises all the independent non-executive directors. Biographical details of the independent directors are set out on pages 12 and 13. Their remuneration is set out on page 34. The Chairman of the Audit Committee is Mr A M Thomson who took over from Mr H R Jenkins following his retirement from the board at the Annual General Meeting on 16th July 2003. The group Chairman, Mr H M P Miles, stepped down as a member of the Audit Committee on 25th November 2003 and now attends by invitation. The Chief Executive, Group Finance Director, Head of Internal Audit and external auditors (KPMG Audit Plc) attend Audit Committee meetings by invitation. The Committee also meets separately with the Head of Internal Audit and with the external auditors without management being present. The Company Secretary, Mr S Farrant, is secretary to the Audit Committee.

Main Activities of the Audit Committee

The Audit Committee met four times during the financial year ended 31st March 2004. At its meeting on 29th May 2003 the Committee reviewed the company's preliminary announcement of the results for the financial year ended 31st March 2003, and the draft report and accounts for that year. The Committee received reports from the internal auditors on control matters and the external auditors on the conduct of their audit, their review of the accounts, including accounting policies and areas of judgment, and their comments on risk management and control matters. The Committee also reviewed the group's corporate social responsibility (CSR) review which is available on our website at www.matthey.com.

The Audit Committee met on 31st July 2003 to receive a presentation by the external auditors setting out their audit approach and procedures, including matters relating to scope, auditor independence and audit fees. Following this presentation, and further discussion and review, the Committee recommended to the board that KPMG Audit Plc should be re-appointed as the company's external auditors.

At its meeting on 25th November 2003 the Audit Committee reviewed the company's interim results, the half year report and the external auditors' review.

At its meeting on 25th February 2004 the Audit Committee reviewed management's and internal audit's reports on the effectiveness of the company's systems for internal financial control and risk management. In addition the Committee reviewed and approved revised policies on whistleblowing and ethics.

Independence of External Auditors

Both the board and the external auditors have for many years had safeguards to avoid the possibility that the auditors' objectivity and independence could be compromised. Our policy in respect of services provided by the external auditors is as follows:

> Audit related services – the external auditors are invited to provide services which, in their position as auditors, they must or are best placed to undertake. It includes formalities relating to borrowings, shareholders' and other circulars, various other regulatory reports and work in respect of acquisitions and disposals.

> Tax consulting – in cases where they are best suited, we use the external auditors. All other significant tax consulting work is put out to tender.

> General consulting – in recognition of public concern over the effect of consulting services on auditors' independence, our policy is that the external auditors are not invited to tender for general consulting work.

Internal Audit

During the year the Audit Committee reviewed the performance of the internal audit function, the findings of the audits completed during the year, the department's resource requirements and also approved the internal audit plan for the year ending 31st March 2005.

A M Thomson
Chairman of the Audit Committee

Remuneration Report

Remuneration Report to Shareholders

Management Development and Remuneration Committee and its Terms of Reference

The Management Development and Remuneration Committee of the board comprises all the non-executive directors of the company, other than the group Chairman, as set out on pages 12 and 13. Mr Jenkins retired from the Committee on 16th July 2003 and Mr Miles stepped down from the Committee on 25th November 2003.

The Committee's terms of reference are to determine on behalf of the board competitive remuneration for the executive directors, which recognises their individual contributions to the company's overall performance. The Committee believes strongly that remuneration policy should be completely aligned with shareholder interests. In addition the Committee assists the board in ensuring that the senior management of the group are recruited, developed and remunerated in an appropriate fashion.

The remuneration of the non-executive directors is determined by the board, within the limits prescribed by the company's Articles of Association.

Executive Remuneration Policy

The Committee recognises that, in order to maximise shareholder value, it is necessary to have a competitive pay and benefits structure. The Committee also recognises that there is a highly competitive market for successful executives and that the provision of appropriate rewards for superior performance is vital to the continued growth of the business. To assist with this the Committee appoints and receives advice from independent remuneration consultants on the pay and incentive arrangements prevailing in comparably sized industrial companies in each country in which Johnson Matthey has operations. During the year such advice was received from The Hay Group, which also provided advice on job evaluation, and the Monks Partnership. Watson Wyatt provided actuarial services. The Committee also receives recommendations from the Chief Executive on the remuneration of those reporting to him as well as advice from the Director of Human Resources. Total potential rewards are earned through the achievement of demanding performance targets based on measures that represent the best interests of shareholders.

The remuneration policy was reviewed by the Committee in 2002 and consists of basic salary, annual bonus, a long term incentive plan, share options and other benefits as detailed below. Salaries are based on median market rates with incentives providing the opportunity for upper quartile total remuneration, but only for achieving outstanding performance. Following a further comprehensive review by the Committee in 2003/04, which included advice from independent consultants, changes are proposed to the annual bonus, long term incentive plan and share options. These require shareholder approval and are the subject of a separate circular.

Executive directors' remuneration consists of the following:

Basic Salary – which is in line with the median market salary for each director's responsibilities as determined by independent surveys. Basic salary is normally reviewed on 1st August each year and the Committee takes into account individual performance and promotion during the year. Where an internal promotion takes place, the median salary relative to the market would usually be reached over a period of a few years, which can give rise to higher than normal salary increases while this is being achieved.

Annual Bonus – which is paid as a percentage of basic salary under the terms of the company's Executive Compensation Plan (which also applies to the group's 150 or so most senior executives). The executive directors' bonus award is based on consolidated profit before tax, exceptional items and goodwill amortisation (PBT) compared with the annual budget. The board of directors rigorously reviews the annual budget to ensure that the budgeted PBT is sufficiently stretching. An annual bonus payment of 30% of basic salary (prevailing at 31st March) is paid if the group meets the annual budget. This bonus may rise to 50% of basic salary if the group achieves PBT of 107.5% of budget. There is a provision that a maximum 105% of basic salary may be paid to the Chief Executive and 85% to other executive directors if 125% of budgeted PBT is achieved. PBT must reach 95% of budget for a minimum bonus to be payable. The Committee has discretion to vary the awards made. The bonus awarded to executive directors in 2003/04 was 42.5% of salary at 31st March 2004.

Long Term Incentive Plan (LTIP) – which was introduced in August 1998, is designed to achieve above average performance and growth. Shares are allocated to directors and key executives subject to performance conditions. For shares allocated in the years 1998, 1999 and 2000 the number of shares released to the individual was dependent upon growth in Johnson Matthey's relative total shareholder return (TSR) compared with the FTSE 250 over a three year performance period. 100% of the allocated shares will be released to the individual if the company's relative TSR is in the 75th percentile or above. Between 35% and 100% of the allocated shares will be released pro rata between the 50th and the 75th percentiles. No shares will be released at or below 50th percentile performance. Earnings per share (EPS) is used as a second performance measure and requires an increase in EPS to be at least equal to the increase in UK RPI plus 2% p.a. over the performance period before any release is made.

In 2001 shareholder approval was obtained for certain changes to the LTIP. The LTIP will continue to provide for the release of half of the allocated shares based on the company's relative TSR and EPS measures, as described above. The other half of the allocation will be released subject to the achievement of absolute TSR growth over a three year period. Under this test no shares will be released should the absolute TSR growth be less than 30%. 100% of the allocated shares will be released should the absolute TSR growth be 45% or more. Pro rata allocations will be made for absolute TSR growth between 30% and 45%.

On 12th June 2002 Johnson Matthey moved into the FTSE 100, and as a consequence of this the Committee decided that a comparator group of those companies ranked 51 – 150 in the FTSE index would be more appropriate than the FTSE 250 previously used. Hence the August 2002 and 2003 allocations will be tested against this revised comparator group for that half of the allocation subject to the relative TSR test.

Remuneration Report

Executive Remuneration Policy (continued)

Share Options – option grants were not made to executive directors in the years 1998, 1999 and 2000. Previously, options were granted to executive directors under the 1985 scheme (under which the final grant was made in November 1994) and the 1995 schemes with the latter having a performance target of EPS growth of UK RPI plus 2% over a three year period. Options under all the schemes were granted in annual tranches, up to the maximum permitted of four times earnings.

Following the review by independent remuneration consultants, the Committee obtained shareholder approval in 2001 for the introduction of a new employee share option scheme, known as the Johnson Matthey 2001 Share Option Scheme. The executive directors and approximately 800 employees are awarded an annual grant of share options under the terms of this scheme. For executive directors the Committee will award options each year up to a maximum value equal to basic annual salary. The options will only be exercisable upon the achievement of appropriate performance targets. The performance target is EPS growth of UK RPI plus 4% p.a. over any three year period. The Committee has discretion to alter the performance targets for future options, but not so as to make the targets less challenging, and would only do so after consultation with institutional investors.

Pensions – all the executive directors are members of the Johnson Matthey Employees Pension Scheme in the UK, with the exception of Mr Pentz who is a member of the Johnson Matthey Inc. Salaried Employees Pension Plan in the US. Under the UK scheme, members are entitled to a pension based on their service and final pensionable salary subject to Inland Revenue limits. The scheme also provides life assurance cover of four times annual salary. The normal pension age for directors is 60. None of the non-executive directors are members of the schemes. Details of the individual arrangements for executive directors are given on page 37.

Other Benefits – available to the executive directors are private medical insurance, a company car and membership of the group's employee share incentive plans which are open to all employees in the countries in which the group operates such schemes.

Service Contracts – Mr Clark was appointed to the board on 1st March 1990, Mr Sheldrick on 1st September 1990, Messrs Carson and Morgan on 1st August 1999 and Dr Hawker and Mr Pentz on 1st August 2003. All are employed on contracts subject to one year's notice at any time. On early termination of their contracts the directors would normally be entitled to 12 months' salary and benefits.

Non-executive directors' remuneration consists of fees, which are set following advice taken from independent consultants. They are reviewed at three year intervals.

Remuneration

Directors' Emoluments 2003/04

	Fees £'000	Salary £'000	Annual bonus £'000	Benefits £'000	Total excluding pension £'000	Total prior year excluding pension[10] £'000
Executive						
C R N Clark[8]	–	603	264	30	897	819
N A P Carson[9]	–	283	128	23	434	366
P N Hawker[1]	–	127	54	10	191	–
D W Morgan	–	233	102	25	360	320
L C Pentz[1] [2]	–	146	52	53	251	–
J N Sheldrick	–	317	138	12	467	426
Total	–	1,709	738	153	2,600	1,931
Non-Executive[3]						
H M P Miles (Chairman)	180			20	200	198
M B Dearden	33			–	33	33
H R Jenkins[4]	12			–	12	37
C D Mackay	37[5]			–	37	33
I C Strachan	33			–	33	33
A M Thomson	36[6]			–	36	17[7]
R J W Walvis	33			–	33	17[7]
Total	364			20	384	368

Notes:

[1] Appointed August 2003.

[2] Mr Pentz's emoluments are based on US basic salary adjusted for the cost of living differential in the UK including UK taxation. He will be provided, for two years only, with an expatriation package commensurate with the company's policy on international assignments, including accommodation costs, education expenses and relocation expenses. One-off costs associated with Mr Pentz's move to the UK were £24,316. These costs are not included in the above table.

[3] Non-executive fees were last reviewed on 1st April 2001 for all non-executives and on 1st October 2001 for the Chairman.

[4] Retired July 2003. Includes £4,000 per annum for chairmanship of the Audit Committee.

[5] Includes £4,000 per annum for chairmanship of the Management Development and Remuneration Committee.

[6] Includes £4,000 per annum for chairmanship of the Audit Committee. Appointed July 2003.

[7] Appointed September 2002.

[8] Mr Clark is a non-executive director of Rexam PLC and FKI plc. His annual fees are £90,000 from Rexam PLC and £35,000 from FKI plc. These amounts are excluded from the table above and retained by him.

[9] Mr Carson is a non-executive director of Avon Rubber plc. His annual fee is £25,000. This amount is excluded from the table above and retained by him.

[10] Excludes emoluments of £281,000 for directors who retired in the year ended 31st March 2003.

Remuneration Report

Pensions

Pensions and life assurance benefits for UK executive directors are provided through the company's final salary occupational pension scheme for UK employees – the Johnson Matthey Employees Pension Scheme (JMEPS) – which is constituted under a separate Trust Deed. JMEPS is an exempt approved scheme under Chapter I of Part XIV of the Income & Corporation Taxes Act 1988 and its members are contracted out of the State Earnings Related Pension Scheme and the State Second Pension. With the agreement of the scheme actuary, the company paid contributions to JMEPS of 10% of basic salaries during the year.

In previous years' accounts, disclosure of directors' pension benefits has been made under the requirement of the Financial Services Authority Listing Rules. These rules are still in place, but it is now also necessary to make disclosures in accordance with the Directors' Remuneration Report Regulations 2002. The information below sets out the disclosures under the two sets of requirements.

a.　Financial Services Authority Listing Rules

	Age at 31st March 2004	Years of service at 31st March 2004	Director's contributions to JMEPS during the year[1] £'000	Increase in accrued pension during the year (net of inflation)[2] £'000 pa	Total accrued pension at 31st March 2004[3] £'000 pa	Total accrued pension at 31st March 2003[4] £'000 pa	Transfer value of increase (less director's contributions)[4] £'000	FURBS contribution in the year[5] £'000	FURBS related tax payments[5] £'000
C R N Clark	62	41	–	26	433	396	460	–	–
N A P Carson	46	23	11	24	129	103	184	–	–
P N Hawker[6]	50	17	5	18	80	61	180	–	–
D W Morgan	46	15	4	2	32	29	14	55	37
J N Sheldrick	54	13	4	2	38	34	27	76	51
L C Pentz[6] [7]	48	19	–	(2)	35	37	(8)	–	–

b.　Directors' Remuneration Report Regulations 2002

	Years of service at 31st March 2004	Director's contributions to JMEPS during the year[1] £'000	Increase in accrued pension during the year £'000 pa	Total accrued pension at 31st March 2004[3] £'000 pa	Transfer value of accrued pension at 31st March 2004[4] £'000	Transfer value of accrued pension at 31st March 2003[4] £'000	Increase in transfer value (less director's contributions) £'000	FURBS contribution for the year[5] £'000	FURBS related tax payment[5] £'000
C R N Clark	41	–	37	433	7,625	6,968	657	–	–
N A P Carson	23	11	26	129	1,065	654	400	–	–
P N Hawker[6]	17	5	19	80	810	545	260	–	–
D W Morgan	15	4	3	32	252	176	72	55	37
J N Sheldrick	13	4	4	38	475	356	115	76	51
L C Pentz[6] [7]	19	–	(2)	35	118	112	6	–	–

Notes:

[1]　Members' contributions are at the general scheme rate of 4% of pensionable pay, i.e. basic salary excluding bonuses. In accordance with the JMEPS' rules, Mr Clark ceased contributing to the scheme on attaining his normal retirement date at age 60.

[2]　The increase in accrued pension during the year excludes any increase for inflation from 31st March 2003.

[3]　The entitlement shown under "Total accrued pension at 31st March 2004" is the pension which would be paid annually on retirement, based on pensionable service to 31st March 2004. The pension would, however, be subject to an actuarial reduction of 0.3% per month for each month that retirement precedes age 60.

[4]　The transfer values have been calculated on the basis of actuarial advice in accordance with Actuarial Guidance Note 11, less directors' contributions. No allowance has been made in the transfer values for any discretionary benefits that have been or may be awarded under JMEPS. The transfer values in the Directors' Remuneration Report Regulations 2002 have been calculated at the start and the end of the year and, therefore, take into account market movements.

[5]　The JMEPS' benefits and contributions for Messrs Morgan and Sheldrick are restricted by reference to the 'earnings cap' imposed by the Finance Act No. 2, 1989. Contributions have therefore been paid to Funded Unapproved Retirement Benefit Schemes (FURBS) established by the company, independently of JMEPS, with effect from 1st April 2000. The purpose of each FURBS is to provide retirement and death benefits in relation to basic salary in excess of the earnings cap. Because FURBS are not exempt approved under Chapter I of Part XIV of the Income & Corporation Taxes Act 1988, payments have been made to meet the tax liabilities in respect of these contributions.

[6]　Dr Hawker and Mr Pentz were appointed to the board with effect from 1st August 2003. Pensions shown are the amounts accrued since appointment. The contributions are those that have been paid since appointment.

[7]　Mr Pentz is a US citizen and is not a member of the UK pension scheme. Instead, he is a member of the US salaried pension plan, which is a non-contributory defined benefit arrangement. The entitlements shown in the tables are those arising out of his membership of this arrangement converted into sterling by reference to the exchange rates on 31st July 2003 and 31st March 2004. The reduction in accrued pension is the result of exchange rate differences. Mr Pentz is also a member of a savings plan (401k), to which the company contributed $8,000 between 1st August 2003 and 31st March 2004. This is not included in the tables above but is included in his benefits in the table on page 34.

Remuneration Report

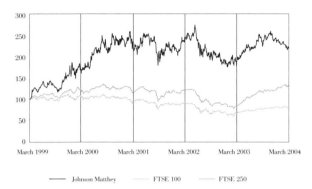

Johnson Matthey Total Shareholder Return, FTSE 100 and FTSE 250 rebased to 100
(31st March 1999 to 31st March 2004)

——— Johnson Matthey   ——— FTSE 100   ——— FTSE 250

C D Mackay
Chairman of the Management Development and Remuneration Committee

Responsibility of Directors

for the preparation of the accounts

Company law requires the directors to prepare accounts for each financial year which give a true and fair view of the state of affairs of the company and group and of the profit or loss for that period. In preparing those accounts, the directors are required to:

>   select suitable accounting policies and apply them consistently;

>   make judgments and estimates that are reasonable and prudent;

>   state whether applicable accounting standards have been followed, subject to any material departures disclosed and explained in the accounts;

>   prepare the accounts on the going concern basis unless it is inappropriate to presume that the group will continue in business.

The directors are responsible for keeping proper accounting records which disclose with reasonable accuracy at any time the financial position of the company and enable them to ensure that the accounts comply with the Companies Act 1985. They have general responsibility for taking such steps as are reasonably open to them to safeguard the assets of the group and to prevent and detect fraud and other irregularities.

(i)   Why should the external auditors of a plc report direct to the shareholders and not to the chairman of the company?

(ii)   Why should the internal auditors of a plc report to the audit committee and not to the finance director?

(iii) In what ways may the independence of a company's audit committee be demonstrated?

The answers to these questions are:

(i)   The external auditors are appointed by and are responsible to the shareholders. The annual general meeting (AGM) is the formal meeting of directors, shareholders and auditors. Conceivably, the chairman could shelve the report, with shareholders unaware of the contents. The law is quite strict on auditors' access to the shareholders.

(ii)   The finance director is responsible for the system of recording transactions. The finance director could prevent vital information from the internal auditors being distributed to others in the organisation.

(iii) The audit committee may request the non-executive directors to review specific areas, for example, the output from the internal auditors. The audit committee meets many times during the year and it offers a degree of objectivity. The careers of its members do not depend on the continuance of their directorship.

The directors of a company may not be accountants and they very rarely have any hands-on involvement with the actual putting-together of a set of accounts for the company. However, directors of companies must make it their business to be fully conversant with the content of the accounts of their companies. Directors are responsible for ensuring that proper accounting records are maintained, and for ensuring reasonably accurate reporting of the financial position of their company, and ensuring their compliance with the Companies Act 1985/1989. Johnson Matthey plc's report and accounts 2004 includes a section headed 'Responsibility of Directors (for the preparation of the accounts)' that follows the remuneration committee report on page 259, which details the responsibilities of its directors in the preparation of its accounts.

We will now consider the role of directors and their responsibilities in more detail, and with regard to the corporate governance Combined Code of Practice. We will also look at some of the circumstances in which directors of limited companies are particularly vulnerable, and how these may lead to disqualification of directors.

The fact that a corporate governance Code of Practice exists or even that the appropriate corporate governance committees have been established is not necessarily a guarantee of effective corporate governance. There have been many examples of companies that have had corporate governance committees in place relating to directors and their remuneration, relations with shareholders, accountability and audit. Nevertheless, these companies have given cause for great concern from shareholders following much-publicised revelations about financial scandals and apparent loosely-adhered-to corporate governance practices.

Such examples have been by no means confined to the UK, as the press extract on pp. 265–6 illustrates. Dennis Kozlowski was the head of the conglomerate Tyco International from 1992 to 2002, which enjoyed phenomenal growth from the acquisition of hundreds of companies involved in

Another huge fraud case in the

...as Jack
...etically
...lar guy

...e Tyco
...oversaw
...big and
...34bn), in
...uipment,
...systems.
...as a leg-
...ll Street

...n 200,000
...osidiaries
...revenues,
...wo-storey
...ampshire,

...wski once
...executive

...adging it a
...Kozlowski
...k Swartz,
...ey Robert
...ers while
...ly referred
...Executive

...rgues that
...d the tiny
...s in the till
...y bank' for
...Koz, 57, and
...llegedly pil-

...ged $170m
...d abuses of
...and netted
...o shares by
...bout Tyco's

results and then dumping their holdings.

Compared with the 'Marthathon', the lengthy and complex Tyco proceedings haven't received heaps of attention. (There is one odd similarity, however: both Koz and Stewart – her maiden name is Koystra – hailed from working-class Polish families in New Jersey.)

But Koz may be ready for his close-up now that the trial is wrapped up: the jury could deliver its verdict as soon as this week.

In fact, Stewart's obstruction of justice doesn't even register compared with the epic scale of the charges against Kozlowski. It is the first real attempt by a criminal court to hold accountable corporate executives for the alleged fraudulent pumping of their stocks during the bull market.

Indeed, as 'nothing exceeds like excess' scandals go, Koz's ordeal offered something for everyone. Toys? Check. Koz has plenty, including three Harley-Davidson motorcycles, a classic sailing yacht and a private plane to whisk him between his grand homes in New York, New Hampshire, Nantucket and Florida.

Furnishings and antiques – including the now legendary $6,000 wastebasket and $15,000 umbrella stand – were charged to the company account.

Ladies? Check. The trial featured testimony from former Koz paramours and the disclosure of his divorce agreement with former wife Angie, who was entitled to $30m in cash plus two New York apartments and homes in Connecticut, New Hampshire and Florida – not to mention a new Mercedes every three years. These obligations were depicted by prosecutors as the potential motivation for a successful executive making millions a year to carry on looting his company for much more.

Parties? Check. There was of course the infamous 40th birthday party held for his wife Karen in Sardinia in 2001, half of its $2m cost – including a vodka-peeing ice sculpture and Jimmy Buffett performance – on the Tyco tab.

Interesting pals? Check. Probably the most fascinating tale to emerge during the testimony was Koz's closeness to Phua Young, an analyst hired to cover Tyco for Merrill Lynch after Koz complained to Merrill's CEO about his company's coverage in 1999.

In addition to being unfailingly bullish on Tyco stock – Young once described himself as being 'indirectly paid by Tyco' – the analyst also fell in love during those heady times with a woman he met in Singapore. Young then did what any person in that situation would do: he asked Tyco for assistance in hiring a private detective to investigate her, which Kozlowski agreed to do at a cost of some $20,000.

Fortunately, the woman checked out, and she and the analyst were married. Unfortunately, Young was fired by Merrill in

2002 for improper conduct and has been charged by securities regulators with publishing misleading research on Tyco.

'Greed is greed, and sometimes when you have a lot you want more,' Ann Donnelly, the assistant district attorney, said of Kozlowski and Swartz. 'They have an extravagant lifestyle and there is nothing wrong with that. But you have to pay for it. Don't these guys have credit cards? Don't they have chequebooks? Why does Tyco have to buy a house for every place they travel to?'

For their closing arguments last week, Donnelly and her colleagues displayed a large chart outlining for the jury the 32 counts against Koz and Swartz, just as they did when the case opened. The charges include grand larceny, conspiracy, falsifying business records and violating state business laws.

The grand larceny charge alone is punishable by up to 25 years in prison. (Earlier this month the judge did throw out a charge of 'enterprise corruption', a statute normally applied to mob figures.)

It all seems very sensational, but the reality is that the proceedings have been convoluted and tiring. Kozlowski's lawyer, Stephen Kaufman, argued to the jury that his client might be culpable in a civil court for misusing shareholder funds but he is no criminal.

And he played a bit of a post-Martha card when he urged the jury not to view his client's case as a chance to 'win one for the little guy'. He pointed out that 'we're not WorldCom, we're not Adelphia, we're not Enron'.

Indeed, those three companies, whose former CEOs are being prosecuted for fraud, are all now bankrupt. Tyco stock isn't the high flier it was in Koz's day, but it's still plugging along.

In his two hours of instruction to the jury, Judge Michael Obus told them that their purpose is a 'narrow one' and that they should not 'evaluate any other cases you might have heard about' or be 'judges of corporate governance'.

Indeed, the only question is whether Kozlowski, the man who 'doesn't believe in perks', was legally entitled to an obscenely super-sized helping of them.

Time for Kozlowski to pick up the tab?, by Richard Sykes

© *Daily Telegraph*, 21 March 2004

widely diverse industries. Kozlowski once told a reporter: 'We don't believe in perks, not even executive parking spots.' In the USA, during an extremely long and complicated case against Kozlowski for fraud, it appears that he in fact received an inordinate portion of perks himself, either legally or illegally.

The case against Mr Kozlowski and the former chief financial officer of Tyco, Mark Swartz, collapsed in a mistrial in April 2004 when a juror began receiving threats. However, a retrial was expected.

Directors' responsibilities

The responsibilities of directors, in terms of the Combined Code of Practice, can be seen to be important and far-reaching. It has been said that being a director is easy, but being a responsible director is not. It is important for all directors to develop an understanding and awareness of their ever-increasing legal obligations and responsibilities to avoid the potential personal liabilities, and even disqualification, which are imposed if those obligations are ignored.

It can be seen that the aims of most of the codes of practice and legislation have been to promote better standards of management in companies. This has also meant penalising irresponsible directors, the effect of which has been to create an increasingly heavy burden on directors regardless of the size or nature of the business they manage. The Government is actively banning offending directors.

Directors' duties are mainly embodied in the:

- Companies Act 1985/1989
- Insolvency Act 1986 (as amended by the Enterprise Act 2002)
- Company Directors Disqualification Act 1986 (as amended by the Enterprise Act 2002)
- Enterprise Act 2002
- Health and Safety at Work Act 1974
- Financial Services Act 1986

and there is

- potential for legal action on corporate manslaughter.

In addition, it should be noted that further statutory provisions giving rise to vicarious liability of directors for corporate offences are included in Acts of Parliament, which currently number well over 200! Directors can be:

- forced to pay a company's losses
- fined
- prevented from running businesses
- imprisoned.

The Directors' Remuneration Report Regulations 2002 (Statutory Instrument 2002 No. 1986) are now in force and require the directors of a company to prepare a remuneration report that is clear, transparent and understandable to shareholders. Many smaller companies without continuous legal advice are unaware about how much the rules have tightened. It is usually not until there is wide publicity surrounding high-profile business problems that boards of directors are alerted to the demands and penalties to which they may be subjected if things go wrong.

It was not only the 1980s and early 1990s that saw corporate scandals and irregularities (for example, Polly Peck, and the Maxwell companies). At the end of 1999, accounting irregularities caused trading in engineering company TransTec shares to be suspended, with Arthur Andersen called in as administrative receiver. The case was fuelled by the revelation by former TransTec chief accountant Max Ayris that nearly £500,000 of a total of £1.3m in grants from the Department of Trade and Industry was obtained fraudulently. TransTec, founded by former Government minister Geoffrey Robinson, collapsed in December 1999, after the accounting irregularities were discovered, with debts of more than £70m. Following the collapse of the company the role of the auditors to the company, PricewaterhouseCoopers, was also to be examined by the Joint Disciplinary Scheme, the accountancy professions' senior watchdog.

Also during 1999, the trade finance group Versailles discovered that there had been some double counting of transactions, which prompted the Department of Trade and Industry to take a close interest in its affairs. Actual and apparent corporate misdemeanours continued, on an even larger scale, through the late 1990s and on into the twenty-first century (note the Barings debacle, Enron, WorldCom, and Tyco).

Non-executive directors are legally expected to know as much as executive directors about what is going on in the company. Ignorance is not a defence. Directors must be aware of what is going on and have knowledge of the law relating to their duties and responsibilities. Fundamentally, directors must:

- use their common sense
- be careful in what they do

Solicitors representing the injured and families of the victims welcomed news of prosecutions, as did rail safety groups. Carol Bell, co-chairman of the Safe Trains Action Group, said: 'It is going to be really important for the families because it gives them a chance to put some kind of closure on it. If they decide to go to court it will be difficult but they will be glad that someone is taking responsibility for it'. Mrs Bell is a survivor of the 1997 Southall rail crash. But Balfour Beatty criticised the decision and defended its safety record.

In a statement, the company said: 'The charge of manslaughter against our maintenance business will be firmly defended as we see no plausible basis for it in law or on the evidence. The individuals charged will have the company's fullest support in their defence of the charges against them'. Network Rail also pledged to defend itself and its employees against the charges. 'As the company stated last week, we believe that our employees conduct their duties to the best of their abilities with the sole intention of delivering a safe, reliable and efficient railway network. It is now a matter for the courts and it would be inappropriate to comment further,' a statement said.

Andrew Faiers, a Crown Prosecutor, said that the decision to press charges was based on 'substantial evidence'. More than 1,500 witnesses gave evidence during the two-and-a-half year long probe. The police seized more than one million pages of documentary evidence.

The families of those who died at Hatfield have campaigned for a corporate manslaughter prosecution, as have relatives of victims of other rail accidents. It is difficult to obtain a conviction on such a charge, however. Great Western Trains was acquitted of the charge on a point of law when it was prosecuted for the 1997 Southall rail crash, but it was fined £1.5 million under health and safety legislation. Labour promised to update corporate manslaughter law in its 1997 manifesto and the Home Secretary has said that he intends to introduce a draft law in October to make it easier to prosecute companies, but that would not target individual directors. Under present corporate manslaughter law, a company can be convicted only if a person is identified as its 'controlling mind' and is found responsible for someone's death. If he or she is found not guilty, the company is cleared as well.

If a junior member of staff is responsible for safety, he or she is not regarded as a controlling mind and again the company escapes prosecution. In the Southall case, the CPS did not charge any individual with manslaughter, so the case against the company failed. Only small companies, where it is easy to establish the lines of responsibility, have been convicted of corporate manslaughter.

In 1994 Peter Kite, managing director of an activity centre responsible for a canoeing disaster that killed four children, was jailed for three years after his company became the first in the country to be convicted of manslaughter. It was fined £60,000. P&O European Ferries was prosecuted after the 1987 Zeebrugge disaster, but the case collapsed half-way through the trial.

Rail chiefs on Hatfield manslaughter charges, by PA News and Angela Jameson

© *The Times*, 9 July 2003

---

relatively easy to discover the 'controlling mind'; the risks to which pupils were exposed were serious and obvious and, critically, they were not technical or esoteric in any way. Moreover, very unusually, the directors could not claim ignorance of the risks because of a damning letter they had received from former instructors telling them to improve safety at the centre.

Great Western Trains was fined £1.5m over the Southall (1997) rail crash in which seven people were killed, following a Health and Safety Executive (HSE) prosecution. But no individual within the company was charged with manslaughter.

The Paddington (1999) rail crash case, again brought by the HSE, resulted in 31 people killed and over 400 injured. The company, Thames Trains, was fined £2m in April 2004, but even though the HSE said its enquiries had revealed 'serious failing in management', there was no prosecution for corporate manslaughter.

A few years ago the legal profession considered that the promised review of the Law Commission's recommendation for an Involuntary Homicide Act 'could result in company directors being made personally responsible for safety and therefore potentially liable in cases of avoidable accidents'. The current Government has promised to legislate on the issue of corporate manslaughter. In its consultation document in 2000 it considered a proposed offence of corporate killing, allowing easier prosecution of any employing organisation for a death that results from a serious management failure. In May 2003 the Government said that it would issue a draft Bill on corporate manslaughter, and that it would target the companies themselves and not the criminal liability of individual directors, and would not set up a system of standards in parallel to existing health and safety standards. In November 2004 the Government included the issue of corporate manslaughter in the Queen's Speech, and placed it on their legislative agenda for 2005.

Other responsibilities

Directors do not owe a direct duty to shareholders, but to the company itself. Directors have no contractual or fiduciary duty to outsiders and are generally not liable unless they have acted in breach of their authority. Directors must have regard to the interests of employees but this is enforceable against directors only by the company and not by the employees.

> **Progress check 7.4 What is meant by a duty of care and fiduciary duty with regard to company directors?**

Insolvency

Insolvency, or when a company becomes insolvent, is when the company is unable to pay creditors' debts in full after realisation of all the assets of the business. The penalties imposed on directors of companies continuing to trade while insolvent may be disqualification and personal liability. Many directors have lost their houses (as well as their businesses) as a result of being successfully pursued by the receivers appointed to their insolvent companies.

The Insolvency Act 1986 (as amended by the Enterprise Act 2002) provides guidance on matters to be considered by liquidators and receivers in the reports, which they are required to prepare on the conduct of directors. These matters include:

- breaches of fiduciary and other duties to the company
- misapplication or retention of monies or other property of the company
- causing the company to enter into transactions which defrauded the creditors
- failure to keep proper accounting and statutory records
- failure to make annual returns to the Registrar of Companies and prepare and file annual accounts.

If a company is insolvent, the courts assess the directors' responsibility for:

- the cause of the company becoming insolvent
- the company's failure to supply goods or services which had been paid for
- the company entering into fraudulent transactions or giving preference to particular creditors

■ failure of the company to adhere to the rules regarding creditors' meetings in a creditors' **voluntary winding-up**

■ failure to provide a **statement of affairs** or to deliver up any proper books or information regarding the company.

> **Progress check 7.5 How does insolvency impact on directors and what are their responsibilities in this regard?**

Wrongful trading

A major innovation of the Insolvency Act 1986 was to create the statutory tort (civil wrong) of **wrongful trading**. It occurs where a director knows or ought to have known before the commencement of winding up that there was no reasonable prospect of the company avoiding insolvency and he/she does not take every step to minimise loss to creditors. If the court is satisfied of this it may:

■ order the director to contribute to the assets of the business, and

■ disqualify him/her from further involvement in corporate management for a specified period.

A director will not be liable for wrongful trading if he/she can show that from the relevant time he/she 'took every step with a view to minimising the potential loss to the company's creditors as (assuming him/her to have known that there was no reasonable prospect that the company would avoid going into insolvent liquidation) he/she ought to have taken'. A company goes into insolvent liquidation, for this purpose, if it does so at a time when its assets are insufficient for the payment of its debts and other liabilities and the expenses of winding-up.

Both subjective tests and objective tests are made with regard to directors. A director who is responsible, for example, for manufacturing, quality, purchasing, or human resources, is likely to have less skill and knowledge regarding the financial affairs of the company than the **finance director**, unless otherwise fully briefed. Directors with financial or legal experience will certainly be expected to bear a greater responsibility than other directors because of their specialist knowledge.

Fraudulent trading

Fraudulent trading is an offence committed by persons who are knowingly party to the continuance of a company trading in circumstances where creditors are defrauded, or for other fraudulent purposes. Generally, this means that the company incurs more debts at a time when it is known that those debts will not be met. Persons responsible for acting in this way are personally liable without limitation for the debts of the company. The offence also carries criminal penalties.

The offence of fraudulent trading may apply at any time, not just in or after a winding-up. If a company is wound up and fraudulent trading has taken place, an additional civil liability arises in respect of any person who was knowingly a party to it.

> **Progress check 7.6 Are there any differences between wrongful trading and fraudulent trading? If so, what are they?**

Disqualification of directors

Worked Example 7.3

A director of a Hampshire building and double-glazing contractor was disqualified for six years after his company collapsed owing creditors £364,000. Ronald Norris, director of the Aldershot-based Berg Group, which was wound up on 6 January 1999, was found guilty of trading while insolvent since 3 December 1997. Norris from West Sussex, stood before Reading County Court on 8 January 1999. The other grounds for his disqualification were the transfer of a pension fund, of which Norris was a beneficiary on a property owned by Berg, failing to ensure that VAT was collected as due, and failing to ensure that monies due to Berg from connected companies were collected.

There are some fundamental reasons why it is necessary for society to ban certain individuals from becoming directors of limited companies.

The limited liability company is a very efficient means of conducting business, but if used by unscrupulous persons then innocent people can lose money, through no fault of their own.

The limited liability company can offer a financial shield to protect employees and investors if things go wrong and the company ceases trading, unable to pays its creditors.

UK law is now quite strict and will attack an obviously unscrupulous person taking advantage of the limited liability company and leaving various creditors out of pocket.

In recent times the UK Government has been banning an increasing number of persons from becoming directors, as well as publishing their names in the public domain (for example, on the Internet). Almost certainly the recently introduced regime is showing its teeth and punishing guilty directors in a most practical manner.

Disqualification means that a person cannot be, for a specified period of time, a director or manager of any company without the permission of the courts. Disqualification is governed under the Company Directors (Disqualification) Act 1986, and may result from breaches under:

- the Companies Act 1985/1989
  - from cases of fraud or other breaches of duty by a director
- the Insolvency Act 1986 (as amended by the Enterprise Act 2002)
  - if the courts consider that the conduct of a director makes him/her unfit to be concerned in the future management of a company.

Whilst there are serious implications for directors of companies under the Company Directors (Disqualification) Act 1986, it should be noted that the Act is not restricted to company directors. Over one half of the liabilities fall on 'any persons' as well as company directors. 'Any persons' in this context potentially includes any employee within the organisation.

The following offences, and their penalties, under the Act relate to any persons:

- being convicted of an indictable offence – disqualification from company directorships for up to five years, and possibly for up to 15 years
- fraud in a winding up – disqualification from company directorships for up to 15 years
- participation in fraudulent or wrongful trading – disqualification from company directorships for up to 15 years

- acting as a director while an undischarged bankrupt, and failure to make payments under a county court administration order – imprisonment for up to two years, or a fine, or both
- personal liability for a company's debts where the person acts while disqualified – civil personal liability.

The following offences, and their penalties, under the Act relate to directors (but in some instances include other managers or officers of the company):

- persistent breaches of company legislation – disqualification from company directorships for up to five years
- convictions for not less than three default orders in respect of a failure to comply with any provisions of companies' legislation requiring a return, account or other document to be filed, delivered, sent, etc., to the Registrar of Companies (whether or not it is a failure of the company or the director) – disqualification from company directorships for up to five years
- finding of unfitness to run a company in the event of the company's insolvency – disqualification from company directorships for a period of between two years and 15 years
- if after investigation of a company the conduct of a director makes him unfit to manage a company – disqualification from company directorships for up to 15 years
- attribution of offences by the company to others if such persons consent, connive or are negligent – imprisonment for up to two years, or a fine, or both, or possibly imprisonment for not more than six months, or a fine.

In some circumstances directors may be disqualified automatically. Automatic disqualification occurs in the case of an individual who revokes a county court administration order, and in the case of an undischarged bankrupt unless **leave of the court** is obtained. In all other situations the right to act as a director may be withdrawn only by an order of the court, unless a company through its Articles of Association provides for specific circumstances in which a director's appointment may be terminated. The City of London has seen a major toughening of the regime where persons have found themselves unemployable (for example, the fallout from the Baring Bank debacle in the mid-1990s).

> Progress check 7.7 In what circumstances may a director be disqualified?

Summary of directors' obligations and responsibilities

In summary, the following may serve as a useful checklist of directors' obligations and responsibilities:

- both executive and non-executive directors must act with care, look after the finances and act within their powers, and look after employees
- directors are responsible for keeping proper books of account and presenting shareholders with accounts, and failure to do so can result in disqualification
- directors should understand the accounts and be able to interpret them
- the board of directors is responsible for filing accounts with the Registrar of Companies and must also notify changes to the board of directors and changes to the registered address
- shareholders must appoint auditors
- the directors are responsible for calling and holding annual general meetings, and ensuring minutes of all meetings are appropriately recorded

- directors are responsible for ensuring that the company complies with its memorandum and articles of association
- if a company continues to trade while technically insolvent and goes into receivership a director may be forced to contribute personally to repaying creditors
- a director trading fraudulently is liable to be called on for money
- any director who knew or ought to have known that insolvency was unavoidable without minimising loss to the creditors becomes liable
- directors can be disqualified for paying themselves too much
- inadequate attention paid to the financial affairs of the company can result in disqualification
- directors are required to prepare a remuneration report.

We have seen the onerous burden of responsibility placed on directors of limited companies in terms of compliance with guidelines and legislation. The obligations of directors continue to grow with the increase in Government regulation and legislation. Sixteen new directives were introduced during the two years to 2001, relating to such issues as employee working conditions, health and safety and, for example, administration of a minimum wage policy.

How can directors make sure that they comply and cover themselves in the event of things going wrong?

Actions to ensure compliance

Directors of companies need to be aware of the dividing line between the commission of a criminal offence and the commission of technical offences of the Companies Act. Directors should take the necessary actions to ensure compliance with their obligations and responsibilities, and to protect themselves against possible non-compliance:

- directors may delegate their responsibilities within or outside the company and in such circumstances they must ensure that the work is being done by competent, able and honest people
- directors of small companies in particular should get professional help to ensure compliance with statutory responsibilities
- directors must ensure that they are kept fully informed about the affairs of the company by having regular meetings and recording minutes and material decisions
- directors should ensure they have service contracts that cover the company's duties, rights, obligations, and directors' benefits
- directors must ensure that detailed, timely management accounts are prepared, and, if necessary, professional help sought to provide, for example, monthly reporting systems and assistance with interpretation of information produced and actions required.

It is essential that directors carefully watch for warning signs of any decline in the company's position, for example:

- falling sales/market share
- overdependence on one product/customer/supplier
- overtrading
- pressure on bank borrowings
- increases in trade creditors
- requirements for cash paid in advance

E7.2 *Time allowed – 30 minutes*
Outline the basic reasons why there should be openness regarding directors' benefits and 'perks'.

E7.3 *Time allowed – 30 minutes*
Can you think of any reasons why directors of UK plcs found that their contracts were no longer to be open-ended under the new regime of corporate governance?

E7.4 *Time allowed – 60 minutes*
William Mason is the managing director of Classical Gas plc, a recently formed manufacturing company in the chemical industry, and he has asked you as finance director to prepare a report that covers the topics, together with a brief explanation, to be included in a section on corporate governance in their forthcoming annual report and accounts.

Level II

E7.5 *Time allowed – 60 minutes*
After the birth of her twins Vimla Shah decided to take a couple of years away from her career as a company lawyer. During one of her coffee mornings with Joan Turnbull, Joan confided in her that although she was delighted at her husband Ronnie's promotion to commercial director of his company, which was a large UK plc in the food industry, she had heard many horror stories about problems that company directors had encountered, seemingly through no fault of their own. She was worried about the implications of these obligations and responsibilities (whatever they were) that Ronnie had taken on. Vimla said she would write some notes about what being a director of a plc meant, and provide some guidelines as to the type of things that Ronnie should be aware of, and to include some ways in which Ronnie might protect himself, that may all offer some reassurance to Joan.

Prepare a draft of what you think Vimla's notes for Joan may have included.

E7.6 *Time allowed – 60 minutes*
Li Nan has recently been appointed managing director of Pingers plc, which is a company that supplies table tennis equipment to clubs and individuals throughout the UK and Europe. Lin Nan is surprised at the high figure that appeared in last year's accounts under audit fees.

Li Nan is not completely familiar with UK business practices and has requested you to prepare a detailed report on what the audit fees cover, and to include the general responsibilities of directors in respect of the external audit.

E7.7 *Time allowed – 60 minutes*
Use the following information, extracted from Tomkins plc report and accounts for 2000, as a basis for discussing the users of financial information's need for information on directors' remuneration.

	Basic salary	Benefits in kind	Bonuses
G Hutchings, executive director	£975,000	£45,000	£443,000
G Gates (USA), non-executive director	nil, but has a 250,000 US$ consultancy agreement		
R Holland, non-executive director	£23,000	Nil	nil

E7.8 *Time allowed – 60 minutes*
Explain what is meant by insolvency and outline the responsibilities of receivers appointed to insolvent companies.

Case Study II

BUZZARD (1) LTD

Buzzard Ltd is a first-tier supplier to major passenger car and commercial vehicle manufacturers. As a first-tier supplier Buzzard provides systems that fit directly into motor vehicles, which they have manufactured from materials and components acquired from second, third, fourth, etc., -tier suppliers. During the 1990s, through investment in R&D and technology, Buzzard became regarded as one of the world's leaders in design, manufacture and supply of innovative automotive systems.

In the mid-1990s Buzzard started business in one of the UK's many development areas. It was established through acquisition of the business of Firefly from the Stonehead Group. Firefly was a traditional, mass production automotive component manufacturer, located on a brownfield site in Gentbridge, once a fairly prosperous mining area. Firefly had pursued short-term profit rather than longer-term development strategies, and had a poor image with both its customers and suppliers. This represented a challenge but also an opportunity for Buzzard to establish a World Class manufacturing facility.

A major part of Buzzard's strategic plan was the commitment to investing £30m to relocate from Gentbridge to a new fully-equipped 15,000 square metre purpose-built factory on a 20-acre greenfield site in Bramblecote, which was finally completed during the year 2004. At the same time, it introduced the changes required to transform its culture and implement the operating strategies required to achieve the highest level of industrial performance. By 2004 Buzzard Ltd had become an established supplier of high quality and was close to achieving its aim of being a World Class supplier of innovative automotive systems.

In December 2004 a seven-year bank loan was agreed with interest payable half-yearly at a fixed rate of 8% per annum. The loan was secured with a floating charge over the assets of Buzzard Ltd.

The financial statements of Buzzard Ltd, its accounting policies and extracts from its notes to the accounts, for the year ended 31 December 2004 are shown below, prior to the payment of any proposed dividend. It should be noted that Note 3 to the accounts – Profit on ordinary activities before taxation – reports on some of the key items included in the profit and loss account for the year and is not a complete analysis of the profit and loss account.

Required

(i)   Prepare a vertical analysis of the profit and loss account and balance sheet of Buzzard Ltd based on turnover and net assets respectively, for 2003 and 2004.

(ii)   Prepare an horizontal analysis of the profit and loss account, balance sheet, and the segmental analysis from Note 1 to the Accounts, using 2003 as base 100.

(iii) Prepare a value added statement for the profit and loss account for 2003 and 2004 and a vertical analysis of the value added statement for both years.

(iv)   Prepare a report on the financial performance and the financial position of Buzzard Ltd that makes extensive use of the analyses that have been prepared in (i), (ii), and (iii) above.

	2003 £000	Cash flow £000	2004 £000
Note – analysis of changes in net debt during the year			
Cash at bank and in hand	12	(8)	4
Overdraft	(1,986)	(1,354)	(3,340)
Borrowings due after one year	–	(6,000)	(6,000)
Net debt	(1,974)	(7,362)	(9,336)

Accounting policies

The financial statements have been prepared in accordance with applicable accounting standards. A summary of the more important accounting policies which have been applied consistently is set out below.

Basis of accounting   The accounts are prepared under the historical cost convention.

Research and development   Expenditure on research and development is written off as it is incurred.

Tangible fixed assets   Tangible fixed assets are stated at their purchase price together with any incidental costs of acquisition.

Depreciation is calculated so as to write off the cost of tangible fixed assets on a straight line basis over the expected useful economic lives of the assets concerned. The principal annual rates used for this purpose are:

Freehold buildings	20 years
Plant and machinery (including capitalised tooling)	4–8 years
Office equipment and fixtures and fittings	5–8 years
Motor vehicles	4 years

Freehold land is not depreciated.

Government grants   Grants received on qualifying expenditure or projects are credited to deferred income and amortised in the profit and loss account over the estimated useful lives of the qualifying assets or over the project life as appropriate.

Stocks and work in progress   Stocks and work in progress are stated at the lower of cost and net realisable value. In general, cost is determined on a first in first out basis; in the case of manufactured products cost includes all direct expenditure and production overheads based on the normal level of activity. Net realisable value is the price at which stocks can be sold in the normal course of business after allowing for the costs of realisation and, where appropriate, the cost of conversion from their existing state to a finished condition. Provision is made where necessary for obsolescent, slow-moving and defective stocks.

Foreign currencies Assets, liabilities, revenues and costs denominated in foreign currencies are recorded at the rate of exchange ruling at the date of the transaction; monetary assets and liabilities at the balance sheet date are translated at the year-end rate of exchange or where there are related forward foreign exchange contracts, at contract rates. All exchange differences thus arising are reported as part of the results for the period.

Turnover Turnover represents the invoiced value of goods supplied, excluding value added tax.

Warranties for products Provision is made for the estimated liability arising on all known warranty claims. Provision is also made, using past experience, for potential warranty claims on all sales up to the balance sheet date.

Notes to the accounts

1 Segmental analysis

	Turnover		Profit on ordinary activities before taxation	
	2004	2003	2004	2003
	£000	£000	£000	£000
Class of business				
Automotive components	115,554	95,766	1,170	2,944
Geographical segment				
United Kingdom	109,566	92,020		
Rest of Europe	5,290	3,746		
Japan	698	–		
	115,554	95,766		

2 Net interest

	2004	2003
	£000	£000
Interest payable on bank loans and overdrafts	(1,182)	(1,048)
Interest receivable	314	76
	(868)	(972)

3 Profit on ordinary activities before taxation

	2004 £000	2003 £000
Profit on ordinary activities before taxation is stated after crediting:		
Amortisation of Government grant	1,176	796
(Loss)/profit on disposal of fixed assets	(18)	10
And after charging		
Depreciation charge for the year:		
Tangible owned fixed assets	7,782	4,742
Research and development expenditure	7,694	6,418
Auditors' remuneration for:		
Audit	58	58
Other services	40	52
Hire of plant and machinery – operating leases	376	346
Hire of other assets – operating leases	260	314
Foreign exchange losses	40	20

4 Directors and employees
The average weekly number of persons (including executive directors) employed during the year was:

	2004 number	2003 number
Production	298	303
Engineering, quality control and development	49	52
Sales and administration	56	45
	403	400

	2004 £000	2003 £000
Staff costs (for the above persons):		
Wages and salaries	6,632	5,837
Social security costs	562	483
Other pension costs	286	218
	7,480	6,538

8 Tangible fixed assets

	Freehold land and buildings	Motor vehicles	Plant, machinery and tooling	Office equipment, fixtures and fittings	Total
	£000	£000	£000	£000	£000
Cost					
At 1 January 2004	15,450	114	20,648	4,600	40,812
Additions	20	28	19,808	634	20,490
Disposals	–	–	(80)	(10)	(90)
At 31 December 2004	15,470	142	40,376	5,224	61,212
Depreciation					
At 1 January 2004	834	54	7,932	2,470	11,290
Charge for year	734	22	6,226	800	7,782
Eliminated in respect of disposals	–	–	(58)	(2)	(60)
At 31 December 2004	1,568	76	14,100	3,268	19,012
Net book value					
at 31 December 2004	13,902	66	26,276	1,956	42,200
Net book value at 31 December 2003	14,616	60	12,716	2,130	29,522

9 Stocks

	2004 £000	2003 £000
Raw materials and consumables	4,572	3,274
Work in progress	528	360
Finished goods and goods for resale	602	510
	5,702	4,144

10 Debtors

	2004 £000	2003 £000
Amounts falling due within one year		
Trade debtors	13,364	8,302
Other debtors	4,276	7,678
Prepayments and accrued income	562	654
	18,202	16,634

11 Creditors: amounts falling due within one year

	2004	2003
	£000	£000
Overdraft	3,340	1,986
Trade creditors	13,806	8,646
Other taxation and social security payable	2,334	1,412
Other creditors	122	350
Accruals and deferred income	3,672	1,986
	23,274	14,380

12 Borrowings

	2004	2003
	£000	£000
Bank and other loans repayable otherwise than by instalments		
Over five years	6,000	–

13 Provisions for liabilities and charges

	Pensions	Warranties for products	Total
	£000	£000	£000
At 1 January 2004	732	776	1,508
Expended in the year	(572)	(494)	(1,066)
Charge to profit and loss account	562	352	914
At 31 December 2004	722	634	1,356

14 Accruals and deferred income

	2004	2003
	£000	£000
Government grants		
At 1 January 2004	1,380	2,176
Amount receivable	1,060	–
Amortisation in year	(1,176)	(796)
At 31 December 2004	1,264	1,380

15 Share capital

	2004 £000	2003 £000
Authorised		
28,000,000 (2003: 28,000,000) ordinary shares of £1 each	28,000	28,000
Issued and fully paid		
22,714,000 (2003: 22,714,000) ordinary shares of £1 each	22,714	22,714

16 Reconciliation of movement in shareholders' funds

	2004 £000	2003 £000
Opening shareholders' funds	33,044	22,100
Issue of ordinary share capital	–	8,000
Profit for the financial year	1,170	2,944
Closing shareholders' funds	34,214	33,044

17 Capital commitments

	2004 £000	2003 £000
Capital expenditure that has been contracted for but has not been provided for in the financial statements	1,506	162
Capital expenditure that has been authorised by the directors but has not yet been contracted for	6,768	5,404

18 Financial commitments

At 31 December 2004 the company had annual commitments under non-cancellable operating leases as follows:

	Land and Buildings 2004 £000	Other 2004 £000	Land and buildings 2003 £000	Other 2003 £000
Expiring within 1 year	–	96	112	210
Expiring within 2 to 5 years	–	254	–	360
Expiring after 5 years	–	120	–	90
	–	470	112	660

Sources of finance

In Chapter 2 we considered some of the various types of business finance when we looked at the balance sheet. Organisations require finance for both short- and medium- to long-term requirements and the financing is usually matched with the funding requirement. Longer-term finance (longer than one year) is usually used to fund capital investment in fixed assets and other longer-term projects. Short-term finance (shorter than one year) is usually used to fund the organisation's requirement for working capital.

Both short- and long-term finance may be either internal or external to the organisation.

Internal finance may be provided from:

■ retained earnings
■ trade credit
■ cash improvements gained from the more effective management of working capital.

Retained earnings

Retained earnings are the funds generated that are surplus to:

■ the costs of adding to or replacing fixed assets
■ the operational costs of running the business
■ net interest charges
■ tax charges
■ dividend payments.

There is statistical evidence, which shows that through the 1990s the majority of capital funding of UK companies continued to be derived from internal sources of finance. However, this is not free. The profit or net earnings generated from the operations of the company belongs to the shareholders of the company. There is a cost, an opportunity cost, which is the best alternative return that shareholders could obtain on these funds elsewhere in the financial markets.

It is the shareholders who decide at the annual general meeting (AGM) how much of those earnings are distributed to shareholders as dividends, the balance being held and reinvested in the business. The retained earnings of the company are increased by net profit less any dividends payable; they are part of the shareholders' funds and therefore appear within the equity of the company. Similarly any losses will reduce the retained earnings of the company. The cost of shareholders' equity is reflected in the level of dividends paid to shareholders, which is usually dependent on how well the company has performed during the year.

The main source of external short-term funding is short-term debt.

Short-term debt

Short-term financial debts are the elements of overdrafts, loans and leases that are repayable within one year of the balance sheet date. Short-term finance tends to be less expensive and more flexible than long-term debt. Short-term debt is therefore normally matched to finance the fluctuations in levels of the company's net current assets, its working capital.

Such short-term finance represents a higher risk for the borrower. Interest rates can be volatile, and an overdraft, for example, is technically repayable on demand. The company may finance its operations by taking on further short-term debt, as levels of working capital increase. Because of the higher risk associated with short-term debt, many companies adopting a conservative funding policy may accept a reduction in profitability and use long-term debt to finance not only fixed assets, but also a proportion of the company's working capital. Less risk-averse companies may use short-term debt to finance both working capital and fixed assets; such debt provides increased profitability because of its lower cost.

We will discuss each of the other sources of external finance, which are primarily long-term, and include:

- **ordinary shares** (or equity shares)
- **preference shares**
- **loan capital** (financial debt that includes bank loans, debentures, and other loans)
- **hybrid finance** (for example, convertible loans)
- leasing
- UK Government funding
- European funding.

The two main primary sources of long-term finance available to a company, which are both external, are broadly:

- equity share capital (ordinary shares)
- debt (long-term loans and debentures).

Both types of financing have a unique set of characteristics and rights. The main ones are shown in the table in Fig. 8.1.

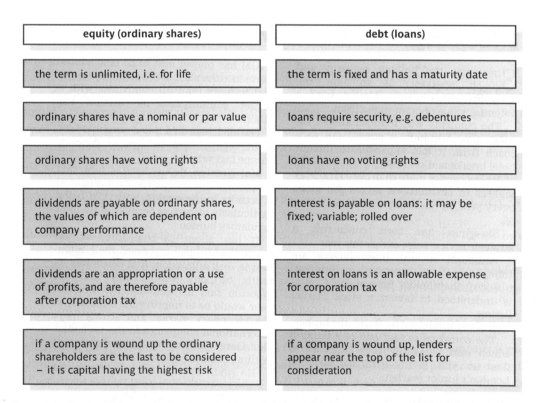

equity (ordinary shares)	debt (loans)
the term is unlimited, i.e. for life	the term is fixed and has a maturity date
ordinary shares have a nominal or par value	loans require security, e.g. debentures
ordinary shares have voting rights	loans have no voting rights
dividends are payable on ordinary shares, the values of which are dependent on company performance	interest is payable on loans: it may be fixed; variable; rolled over
dividends are an appropriation or a use of profits, and are therefore payable after corporation tax	interest on loans is an allowable expense for corporation tax
if a company is wound up the ordinary shareholders are the last to be considered – it is capital having the highest risk	if a company is wound up, lenders appear near the top of the list for consideration

Figure 8.1 Some of the main characteristics and rights of equity capital compared with debt capital

Worked Example 8.1

A company that achieves a profit after tax of 20% on capital employed has the following capital structure:

400,000 ordinary shares of £1	£400,000
Retained earnings	£200,000

In order to invest in some new profitable projects the company wishes to raise £252,000 from a rights issue. The company's current ordinary share price is £1.80.

The company would like to know the number of shares that must be issued if the rights price is: £1.60; £1.50; £1.40; £1.20.

Capital employed is £600,000 [£400,000 + £200,000]

Current earnings are 20% of £600,000 = £120,000

$$\text{Therefore, earnings per share (eps)} \quad = \frac{£120,000}{400,000} = 30p$$

After the rights issue earnings will be 20% of £852,000 [£400,000 + £200,000 + £252,000], which equals £170,400.

Rights price £	Number of new shares £252,000/ rights price £	Total shares after rights issue £	Eps £170,400/ total shares pence
1.60	157,500	557,500	30.6
1.50	168,000	568,000	30.0
1.40	180,000	580,000	29.4
1.20	210,000	610,000	27.9

We can see that at a high rights issue share price the earnings per share are increased. At lower issue prices eps are diluted. The 'break-even point', with no dilution, is where the rights price equals the capital employed per share £600,000/400,000 = £1.50.

Worked Example 8.2

A company has 1,000,000 £1 ordinary shares in issue with a market price of £2.10 on 1 June. The company wished to raise new equity capital by a 1 for 4 share rights issue at a price of £1.50. Immediately the company announced the rights issue the price fell to £1.95 on 2 June. Just before the issue was due to be made the share price had recovered to £2 per share, the cum rights price.

The company may calculate the theoretical ex-rights price, the new market price as a consequence of an adjustment to allow for the discount price of the new issue.

The market price will theoretically fall after the issue

1,000,000 shares × the cum rights price of £2	£2,000,000
250,000 shares × the issue price of £1.50	£375,000
Theoretical value of 1,250,000 shares	£2,375,000

Therefore, the theoretical ex-rights price is $\dfrac{£2,375,000}{1,250,000} = £1.90$ per share

Or to put it another way

Four shares at the cum rights value of £2	£8.00
One new share issued at £1.50	£1.50
	£9.50

Therefore, the theoretical ex-rights price is $\dfrac{£9.50}{5} = £1.90$ per share

Long-term debt

Generally, companies try and match their financing with what it is required for, and the type of assets requiring to be financed:

- fixed assets
- long-term projects.

Long-term debt is usually more expensive and less flexible, but has less risk, than short-term debt. Long-term debt is therefore normally matched to finance the acquisition of fixed assets, which are long-term assets from which the company expects to derive benefits over several periods.

Long-term financial debts are the elements of loans and leases that are payable after one year of the balance sheet date. Debt capital may take many forms: loans, debentures, Eurobonds, mortgages, etc. We will look at debentures, but we will not delve into the particular attributes of every type of debt capital. Suffice to say, each involves interest payment, and capital repayment and security for the loan is usually required. Loan interest is a fixed commitment, which is usually payable once or twice a year. But although debt capital is burdened with a fixed commitment of interest payable, it is a tax-efficient method of financing.

Debentures

Debentures and long-term loans are both debt, which are often taken to mean the same thing. However, loans may be either unsecured, or secured on some or all of the assets of the company. Lenders to a company receive interest, payable yearly or half-yearly, the rate of which may vary with market conditions. A debenture more specifically refers to the written acknowledgement of a debt by a company, usually given under its seal, and is secured on some or all of the assets of the company or its subsidiaries. A debenture agreement normally contains provisions as to payment of interest and the terms of repayment of principal. Other long-term loans are usually unsecured.

Security for a debenture may be by way of a floating charge, without attachment to specific assets, on the whole of the business's assets. If the company is not able to meet its obligations the floating charge will crystallise on specific assets like debtors or stocks. Security may alternatively, at the outset, take the form of a fixed charge on specific assets like land and buildings.

Debentures are a tax-efficient method of corporate financing, which means that interest payable on such loans is an allowable deduction in the computation of taxable profit. For example, if corporation tax were at 30%, a 10% debenture would actually cost the company 7%, that is $\{10\% - (10\% \times 30\%)\}$.

Debentures, and other loans, may be redeemable in which case the principal, the original sum borrowed, will need to be repaid on a specific date.

Hybrid finance

Loans may sometimes be required by companies as they move through their growth phase, and for them to finance specific asset acquisitions or projects. Disadvantages of loans are:

- the financial risk resulting from a reduction in the amount of equity compared with debt
- the commitment to fixed interest payments over a number of years
- the requirement of a build up of cash with which to repay the loan on maturity.

Alternatively, if an increase in equity is used for this type of funding, eps (earnings per share) may be immediately 'diluted'. However, some financing is neither totally debt nor equity, but has the characteristics of both. Such hybrid finance, as it is called, includes financial instruments like convertible loans. A **convertible loan** is a 'two stage' financial instrument. It may be a fixed interest debt or preference shares, which can be converted into ordinary shares of the company at the option of the lender. Eps will therefore not be diluted until a later date. The right to convert may usually be exercised each year at a predetermined conversion rate up until a specified date, at which time the loan must be redeemed if it has not been converted. The conversion rate may be stated as:

- a conversion price (the amount of the loan that can be converted into one ordinary share), or
- a conversion ratio (the number of ordinary shares that can be converted from one unit of the loan).

The conversion price or ratio will be specified at the outset and may change during the term of the loan. Convertibles tend to pay a lower rate of interest than straight loans, which is effectively charging lenders for the right to convert to ordinary shares. They therefore provide an additional benefit to company cash flow and cost of financing.

> **Progress check 8.1** What makes convertible loans attractive to both investors and companies?

Leasing

Leases are contracts between a lessor and lessee for the hire of a specific asset. Why then is leasing seen as a source of long-term financing? There are two types of leases, **operating leases** and **finance leases**, and the answer to the question lies in the accounting treatment of the latter.

Under both types of leasing contract the lessor has ownership of the asset but gives the lessee the right to use the asset over an agreed period in return for rental payments.

An operating lease is a rental agreement for an asset, which may be leased by one lessee for a period, and then another lessee for a period, and so on. The lease period is normally less than the economic life of the asset, and the lease rentals are charged as a cost in the profit and loss account as they occur. The leased asset does not appear in the lessee's balance sheet. The lessor is responsible for maintenance and regular service for assets like photocopiers, cars, and PCs. The lessor therefore retains most of the risk and reward of ownership.

A finance lease relates to an asset where the present value of the lease rentals payable amounts to at least 90% of its fair market value at the start of the lease. Under a finance lease the legal title to the asset remains with the lessor, but the difference in accounting treatment, as defined by SSAP 21, Accounting for Leases and Hire Purchase Contracts, is that a finance lease is capitalised in the balance sheet of the lessee. A value of the finance lease is shown under fixed assets, based on a calculation of the present value of the capital part (excluding finance charges) of the future lease rentals payable. The future lease rentals are also shown as long- and short-term creditors in the balance sheet. The lessee, although not the legal owner, therefore takes on the risks and rewards of ownership.

The leasing evaluation process involves appraisal of the investment in the asset itself, its outright purchase or lease, and an evaluation of leasing as the method of financing. These two decisions may be made separately in either order or they may form a combined decision, and take account of a number of factors:

- asset purchase price and residual value
- the lease rental amounts and the timing of their payments
- service and maintenance payments
- tax
    - capital allowances for purchased fixed assets
    - tax allowable expenses of lease rentals
- VAT (relating to the asset purchase and the lease rentals)
- interest rates (the general level of rates of competing financing options).

Apart from this outline of the process, the evaluation of leasing as a source of finance is beyond the scope of this book.

UK Government and European funding

Businesses involved in certain industries or located in specific geographical areas of the UK may from time to time be eligible for assistance with financing. This may be by way of grants, loan guarantees, and subsidised consultancy. Funding may be on a national or a regional basis from various UK Government or European Union sources.

By their very nature, such financing initiatives are continually changing in format and their areas of focus. For example, funding assistance has been available in one form or another for SMEs, the agriculture industry, tourism, former coal and steel producing areas, and parts of Wales.

This type of funding may include support for the following:

- business start-ups
- new factories
- new plant and machinery

- research and development
- IT development.

There are many examples of funding schemes that operate currently. For example, the Government, via the DTI (Department of Trade and Industry), can provide guarantees for loans from banks and other financial institutions for small businesses that may be unable to provide the security for conventional loans. Via the various regional development agencies, they may also provide discretionary selective financial assistance, in the form of grants or loans, for businesses that are willing to invest in 'assisted areas'. The DTI and Government Business Link websites, www.dti.gov.uk and www.businesslink.gov.uk, provide up-to-date information of all current funding initiatives.

The Welsh Assembly's use of European Structural Funds (ESFs) assists businesses in regenerating Welsh communities. For example, through a scheme called match funding, depending on the type of business activity and its location, ESFs can contribute up to 50% of a project's funding. The balance of the funding is provided from the business's own resources or other public or private sector funding. Websites like the Welsh European Funding Office website, www.wefo.wales.gov.uk, provide information on this type of funding initiative.

> **Progress check 8.2** Describe what is meant by debt and equity and give some examples of each. What are the other sources of long-term, external finance available to a company?

Gearing

In Chapter 5 when we looked at financial ratios we introduced gearing, the relationship between debt and equity capital that represents the financial structure of an organisation. We will now take a look at the application of gearing and then consider worked examples that compare the use of debt capital compared with ordinary share capital.

The relationship between the two sources of finance, loans and ordinary shares, or debt and equity gives a measure of the gearing of the company. A company with a high proportion of debt capital to share capital is highly geared, and low geared if the reverse situation applies. Gearing (leverage, or debt/equity) has important implications for the long-term stability of a company because of, as we have seen, its impact on financial risk.

Companies closely monitor their gearing ratios to ensure that their capital structure aligns with their financial strategy. Various alternative actions may be taken by companies, as necessary, to adjust their capital structures by increasing/decreasing their respective levels of debt and equity. An example of one of the ways in which this may be achieved is to return cash to shareholders. In May 2004 Marshalls plc, the paving stone specialist that supplied the flagstones for the newly-pedestrianised Trafalgar Square in London, announced that they were planning to return £75m to shareholders through a capital reorganisation. The reason the company gave for this was that it expected a more efficient capital structure as a result. The company was geared at only 6%, and had generated £5.3m cash in its previous financial year, after dividends and £40m capital expenditure, which its chairman said had reflected its success in growing shareholder value and generating cash.

The extent to which the debt/equity is high or low geared has an effect on the earnings per share (eps) of the company:

- if profits are increasing, then higher gearing is preferable
- if profits are decreasing, then lower gearing or no gearing is preferred.

Similarly, the argument applies to the riskiness attached to capital repayments. If a company goes into liquidation, lenders have priority over shareholders with regard to capital repayment. So, the more highly geared the company the less chance there is of ordinary shareholders being repaid in full.

The many types of short- and long-term capital available to companies leads to complexity, but also the expectation that overall financial risks may be reduced through improved matching of funding with operational needs. The gearing position of the company may be considered in many ways depending on whether the long-term capital structure or the overall financial structure is being analysed. It may also be analysed by concentrating on the income position rather than purely on the capital structure.

Financial gearing relates to the relationship between a company's borrowings, which includes debt, and its share capital and reserves. Concerning capital structure, gearing calculations may be based on a number of different capital values. All UK plcs disclose their net debt to equity ratio in their annual reports and accounts.

The two financial ratios that follow are the two most commonly used (see also Chapter 5). Both ratios relate to financial gearing, which is the relationship between a company's borrowings, which includes both prior charge capital and long-term debt, and shareholders' funds (share capital plus reserves).

$$\text{gearing} = \frac{\text{long-term debt}}{\text{equity} + \text{long-term debt}}$$

$$\text{debt equity ratio, or leverage} = \frac{\text{long-term debt}}{\text{equity}}$$

Worked Example 8.3 illustrates the calculation of both ratios.

Worked Example 8.3

Two companies have different gearing. Company A is financed totally by 20,000 £1 ordinary shares, whilst company B is financed partly by 10,000 £1 ordinary shares and a £10,000 10% loan. In all other respects the companies are the same. They both have assets of £20,000 and both make the same profit before interest and tax (PBIT).

	A	B
	£	£
Assets	20,000	20,000
less 10% loan	–	(10,000)
	20,000	10,000
Ordinary shares	20,000	10,000
$\text{Gearing} = \dfrac{\text{long-term debt}}{\text{equity} + \text{long-term debt}}$	$\dfrac{0}{20,000 + 0} = 0\%$	$\dfrac{10,000}{10,000 + 10,000} = 50\%$
$\text{Debt equity ratio} = \dfrac{\text{long-term debt}}{\text{equity}}$	$\dfrac{0}{20,000} = 0\%$	$\dfrac{10,000}{10,000} = 100\%$

Company B must make a profit before interest of at least £1,000 to cover the cost of the 10% loan. Company A does not have any PBIT requirement because it has no debt.

Company A is lower geared and considered less risky in terms of profitability than company B which is a more highly geared company. This is because PBIT of a lower geared company is more likely to be sufficiently high to cover interest charges and make a profit for equity shareholders.

As we have seen, gearing calculations can be made in a number of ways, and may also be based on earnings/interest relationships in addition to capital values. For example:

$$\text{dividend cover (times)} = \frac{\text{earnings per share (eps)}}{\text{dividend per share}}$$

This ratio indicates the number of times the profits attributable to the equity shareholders covers the actual dividends paid and payable for the period. Financial analysts usually adjust their calculations for any exceptional or extraordinary items of which they may be aware.

$$\text{interest cover (times)} = \frac{\text{profit before interest and tax}}{\text{interest payable}}$$

This ratio calculates the number of times the interest payable is covered by profits available for such payments. It is particularly important for lenders to determine the vulnerability of interest payments to a drop in profit. The following ratio determines the same vulnerability in cash terms.

$$\text{cash interest cover} = \frac{\text{net cash inflow from operations + interest received}}{\text{interest paid}}$$

> **Progress check 8.3** What is gearing? Outline some of the ways in which it may be calculated.

Worked Example 8.4

Swell Guys plc is a growing company that manufactures equipment for fitting out small cruiser boats. Its planned expansion involves investing in a new factory project costing £4m. Chief Executive, Guy Rope, expects the 12-year project to add £0.5m to profit before interest and tax each year. Next year's operating profit is forecast at £5m, and dividends per share are forecast at the same level as last year. Tax is not expected to be payable over the next few years due to tax losses that have been carried forward.

Swell Guys last two years' results are as follows:

	Last year £m	Previous year £m
Profit and loss account for the year ended 31 December		
Sales	18	15
Operating costs	16	11
Operating profit	2	4
Interest payable	1	1
Profit before tax	1	3
Tax on ordinary activities	0	0
Profit after tax	1	3
Dividends	1	1
Retained profit	0	2

Balance sheet as at 31 December

Fixed assets		8	9
Current assets			
Stocks		7	4
Debtors		4	3
Cash		1	2
		12	9
Creditors due within one year			
Bank overdraft		4	2
Trade creditors		5	5
		9	7
Net current assets		3	2
Total assets less current liabilities		11	11
less			
Long-term loans		6	6
Net assets		5	5
Capital and reserves			
Share capital (25p ordinary shares)		2	2
Profit and loss account		3	3
		5	5

Swell Guys is considering two options:

(a) Issue of £4m 15% loan stock repayable in five years' time

(b) Rights issue of 4m 25p ordinary shares at £1 per share after expenses
For each of the options the directors would like to see:
(i) how the retained profit (derived from operating profit) will look for next year
(ii) how earnings per share will look for next year
(iii) how the capital and reserves will look at the end of next year
(iv) how long-term loans will look at the end of next year
(v) how gearing will look at the end of next year.

(i) Swell Guys plc forecast profit and loss account for next year ended 31 December

Operating profit £5m + £0.5m from the new project

		New debt £m	New equity £m
Operating profit		5.5	5.5
Interest payable	[1.0 + 0.6]	1.6	1.0
Profit before tax		3.9	4.5
Tax on ordinary activities		0.0	0.0

Profit after tax		3.9	4.5
Dividends		1.0	1.5
Retained profit		2.9	3.0

(ii) Earnings per share

$$\frac{\text{Profit available for ordinary shareholders}}{\text{Number of ordinary shares}} \qquad \frac{£3.9m}{8m}=48.75p \qquad \frac{£4.5m}{12m}=37.5p$$

(iii) Capital and reserves

	As at 31 December		
	New debt		**New equity**
	£m		**£m**
Share capital (25p ordinary shares)	2.0	(8m shares)	3.0 (12m shares)
Share premium account	0.0		3.0
Profit and loss account	5.9		6.0
	7.9		12.0

(iv) Long-term loans	[6 + 4]	10.0	6.0

(v) Gearing

$$\frac{\text{long-term debt}}{\text{equity} + \text{long-term debt}} \qquad \frac{£6m + £4m}{£7.9m + £6m + £4m}=55.9\% \qquad \frac{£6m}{£12m + £6m}=33.3\%$$

> **Progress check 8.4 Explain how a high interest cover ratio can reassure a prospective lender.**

The weighted average cost of capital (WACC)

The weighted average cost of capital (WACC) may be defined as the average cost of the total financial resources of a company, i.e. the shareholders' equity and the net financial debt.

If we represent shareholders equity as E and net financial debt as D then the relative proportions of equity and debt in the total financing are:

$$\frac{E}{E+D} \quad \text{and} \quad \frac{D}{E+D}$$

The cost of equity is the expected return on equity, the return the shareholders expect from their investment. If we represent the return on shareholders' equity as e and the return on financial debt as d, and t is the rate of corporation tax, then we can provide a formula to calculate WACC. The return on shareholder equity comprises both cash flows from dividends and increases in the share price. We will return to how the cost of equity may be derived in a later section in this chapter.

Interest on debt capital is an allowable deduction for purposes of corporate taxation and so the cost of share capital and the cost of debt capital are not properly comparable costs. Therefore this tax relief on debt interest ought to be recognised in any discounted cash flow calculations. One way would be to include the tax savings due to interest payments in the cash flows of every project. A simpler method, and the one normally used, is to allow for the tax relief in computing the cost of debt capital, to arrive at an after-tax cost of debt. Therefore the weighted average cost of capital is calculated from:

$$\text{WACC} = \left\{\frac{E}{(E+D)} \times \boldsymbol{e}\right\} + \left\{\frac{D}{(E+D)} \times \boldsymbol{d}(1-\boldsymbol{t})\right\}$$

The market value of a company may be determined by its WACC. The lower the WACC then the higher the net present values of its future cash flows and therefore the higher its market value. The determination of the optimum D/E ratio is one of the most difficult tasks facing the finance director.

Worked Example 8.5

Fleet Ltd has the following financial structure:

$e =$	15%	return on equity (this may be taken as given for the purpose of this example)
$d =$	10%	lower risk, so lower than the return on equity
$t =$	30%	rate of corporation tax
$\dfrac{E}{E+D} =$	60%	equity to debt plus equity ratio
$\dfrac{D}{E+D} =$	40%	debt to debt plus equity ratio

We can calculate the WACC for Fleet Ltd, and evaluate the impact on WACC of a change in capital structure to equity 40% and debt 60%.

Calculation of WACC for Fleet Ltd with the current financial structure:

$$\text{WACC} = \left\{\frac{E}{(E+D)} \times e\right\} + \left\{\frac{D}{(E+D)} \times d(1-t)\right\}$$

$$\text{WACC} = (60\% \times 15\%) + \{40\% \times 10\% \, (1-30\%)\} = 11.8\%$$

If the company decides to change its financial structure so that equity is 40% and debt is 60% of total financing, then WACC becomes:

$$(40\% \times 15\%) + \{60\% \times 10\% \, (1-30\%)\} = 10.2\%$$

So it appears that the company has reduced its WACC by increasing the relative weight from 40% to 60% of the cheapest financial resource, debt, in its total financing. However, this is not true because as the debt/equity ratio of the company increased from 0.67 (40/60) to 1.50 (60/40) the company's risk has also increased. Therefore the providers of the financial resources will require a higher return on their investment. There is a well-established correlation between risk and return. So, it is not correct to calculate the WACC using the same returns on equity and debt, as both will have increased.

One of the consequences of this is the problem of calculating an accurate WACC for a company, which is based on its relative proportions and costs of debt and equity capital.

The risks and costs associated with debt capital and equity capital are different and subject to continual change, and may vary from industry to industry and between different types of business. Measurement of the D/E ratio may therefore not be a straightforward task, particularly for diversified groups of companies. Companies in different markets and indeed diversified companies that have trading divisions operating within different markets and producing different products face different levels of risk. If division A operates with a higher risk than division B then the required rate of return of A's investments should be higher than the hurdle rate of return of B's investments. The difference is 'paying' for the difference in risk. This is an important principle but very difficult to implement in practice.

In a later section, we will look at ways in which both the cost of equity and the cost of debt to the company may be determined.

There are many arguments for and against the use of WACC for investment appraisal. Its use is argued on the basis that:

- new investments must be financed by new sources of funds – retained earnings, new share issues, new loans, and so on
- the cost of capital to be applied to new project evaluation must reflect the cost of new capital
- the WACC reflects the company's long-term future capital structure, and capital costs; if this were not so, the current WACC would become irrelevant because eventually it would not relate to any actual cost of capital.

It is argued that the current WACC should be used to evaluate projects, because a company's capital structure changes only very slowly over time; therefore, the marginal cost of new capital should be roughly equal to the WACC. If this view is correct, then by undertaking investments which offer a return in excess of the WACC, a company will increase the market value of its ordinary shares in the long run. This is because the excess returns would provide surplus profits and dividends for the shareholders.

The arguments against the use of WACC are based on the criticisms of the assumptions made that justify the use of WACC:

- new investments have different risk characteristics from the company's existing operations therefore the return required by investors may go up or down if the investments are made, because their business risk is perceived to be higher or lower
- finance raised to fund a new investment
  - may substantially change the capital structure and perceived risk of investing in the company
  - may determine whether debt or equity used to finance the project will change the perceived risk of the entire company, which
  - must be taken into account in the investment appraisal
- many companies raise floating rate debt capital as well as fixed rate debt capital, having a variable rate that changes every few months in line with current market rates; this is difficult to include in a WACC calculation, the best compromise being to substitute an 'equivalent' fixed debt rate in place of the floating rate.

Progress check 8.5 What is WACC and why is it so important?

Cost of debt and equity capital

We have introduced the concept of risk and its correlation with returns on investments. The relationship between risk and return is also one of the key concepts relating to determination of the cost of debt and equity capital. It is an important concept and so we will briefly explore risk a little further, with regard to investments in companies. We shall discuss the cost of debt based on future income flows, that is, interest. We shall similarly discuss the cost of equity based on future income flows, that is, dividends. This will also provide an introduction to the **beta factor** and the **capital asset pricing model (CAPM)**.

The cost of servicing debt capital, as we have discussed, is the yearly or half yearly interest payment, which is an allowable expense for tax. The cost of repayment of a loan, or debt, depends on the type of loan. Loan capital, a debenture for example, may be irredeemable and traded, with a market value. The cost of capital for a redeemable loan may be calculated using a quite complicated formula.

For our purposes, to demonstrate the principle, we can look at the cost of irredeemable loan capital to a company that may be calculated as follows:

$$d = \frac{i \times (1 - t)}{L}$$

where

d = cost of debt capital
i = annual loan interest rate
L = the current market value of the loan
t = the rate of corporation tax.

By rearranging the formula it can be seen that market value of the debt is dependent on the level of future returns, the interest rate paid, which is determined by the level of risk associated with the investment, and the rate of corporation tax:

$$L = \frac{i \times (1 - t)}{d}$$

Worked Example 8.6

Owen Cash plc pays 12% interest (i) per annum on an irredeemable debt of £1m, with a nominal value of £100. The corporation tax rate (t) is currently 50%. The market value of the debt (L) is currently £90.

What is Owen Cash plc's cost of debt?

$$d = \text{cost of debt capital}$$

$$d = \frac{i \times (1 - t)}{L} = \frac{12\% \times (1 - 50\%)}{90}$$

$$d = \frac{12\% \times 50\%}{90} = 6.7\%$$

In a similar way, the cost of equity to a company may be determined by looking at future income flows. In the case of equity or ordinary shares this future income is dividends. A difference between this method and the method applied to debt is that there is no tax relief for dividend payments.

The value of an ordinary share may be simply expressed as the present value of its expected future dividend flows.

$$S = v_1/(1 + e) + v_2/(1 + e)^2 + v_3/(1 + e)^3 \dots v_n/(1 + e)^n$$

where

e = cost of equity capital
v = expected future dividends for n years
S = the current market value of the share

If dividends are expected to remain level over a period of time the formula may be simplified to:

$$S = \frac{v}{e}$$

Therefore, the cost of equity to the company would be:

$$e = \frac{v}{S}$$

Dividends payable on a particular share rarely stay constant from year to year. However, they may grow at a regular rate. This so-called dividend growth model approach to the cost of equity may then be used with the above formula revised as:

$$S = v/(e - G)$$

where G = the expected future dividend growth rate.

The cost of equity may then be stated as:

$$e = \frac{v}{S} + G$$

Worked Example 8.7

Cher Alike plc has 3m ordinary shares in issue that currently have a market price (S) of £2.71. The board have already recommended next year's dividend (v) at 17p per share. The chairman, Sonny Daze, is forecasting that dividends will continue to grow (G) at 4.2% per annum for the foreseeable future.

What is Cher Alike plc's cost of equity?

$$e = \text{cost of equity capital}$$
$$e = \frac{v}{S} + G = \frac{0.17}{2.71} + 4.2\%$$
$$e = 0.063 + 0.042 = 10.5\%$$

The interest rate paid on a loan is known almost with certainty. Even if the debt carries a variable interest rate it is far easier to estimate than expected dividend flows on ordinary shares.

The cost of equity to a company may alternatively be derived using the capital asset pricing model (CAPM). We will look at this approach to risk, and at how some risk may be diversified away by using a spread (or portfolio) of investments.

> **Progress check 8.6 In broad terms how are the costs of debt and equity determined?**

Cost of equity and risk, CAPM and the β factor

Whenever any investment is made there will be some risk involved. The actual return on investment in ordinary shares (equity capital) may be better or worse than hoped for. Unless the investor settles for risk-free securities a certain element of risk is unavoidable.

However, investors in companies or in projects can diversify their investments in a suitably wide portfolio. Some investments may do better and some worse than expected. In this way, average returns should turn out much as expected. Risk that can be diversified away is referred to as **unsystematic risk.**

Some investments are by their very nature more risky than others. This is nothing to do with chance variations in actual compared with expected returns, it is inherent risk that cannot be diversified away. This type of risk is referred to as **systematic risk** or market risk. The investor must therefore accept this risk, unless he/she invests entirely in risk-free investments. In return for accepting systematic risk an investor will expect to earn a return which is higher than the return on a risk-free investment.

The amount of systematic risk depends, for example, on the industry or the type of project. If an investor has a balanced portfolio of shares he/she will incur exactly the same systematic risk as the average systematic risk of the stock market as a whole. The capital asset pricing model (CAPM) is mainly concerned with how systematic risk is measured and how systematic risk affects required returns and share prices. It was first formulated for investments in shares on the stock exchange, but is now also used for company investments in capital projects.

Systematic risk is measured using what are known as beta factors. A beta factor β is the measure of the volatility of a share in terms of market risk. The CAPM is a statement of the principles outlined above. An investor can use the beta factor β in such a way that a high factor will automatically suggest a share is to be avoided because of considerable high risk in the past. Consider the impact in January 2001 on the beta factor of Iceland plc caused by the resignation from the board of the major shareholder together with the issue of a profits warning by the company.

The CAPM model can be stated as follows:

the expected return from a security = the risk-free rate of return, plus a premium for market risk adjusted by a measure of the volatility of the security

If

Rs	is the expected return from an individual security
β	is the beta factor for the individual security
Rf	is the risk-free rate of return
Rm	is the return from the market as a whole
(Rm – Rf)	is the market risk premium

$$Rs = Rf + \{\beta \times (Rm - Rf)\}$$

There are many analysts that specialise in the charting of the volatility of shares and markets, and their findings may regularly be found in the UK financial press.

A variation of the above β relationship may be used to establish an equity cost of capital to use in project appraisal. The cost of equity e equates to the expected return from an individual security Rs, and the beta value for the company's equity capital βe equates to beta factor for the individual security β.

So

| the return expected by ordinary shareholders, or the cost of equity to the company | = | the risk-free rate of return plus a premium for market risk adjusted by a measure of the volatility of the ordinary shares of the company |

$$e = \mathbf{Rf} + \{\beta e \times (\mathbf{Rm} - \mathbf{Rf})\}$$

Worked Example 8.8

Bittaboth plc has ordinary shares in issue with a market value four times the value of its debt capital. The debt is considered to be risk free and pays 11% (Rf) before tax. The beta value of Bittaboth's equity capital has been estimated at 0.9 (βe) and the average market return on equity capital is 17% (Rm). Corporation tax is at 50% (t).

We can calculate Bittaboth plc's WACC.

e = cost of equity capital
$e = \mathbf{Rf} + \{\beta e \times (\mathbf{Rm} - \mathbf{Rf})\} = 11\% + \{0.9 \times (17\% - 11\%)\}$
$e = 0.11 + (0.9 \times 0.06) = 0.164 = 16.4\%$
d = cost of debt capital
which after tax is $i \times (1 - t)$ or $11\% \times 50\% = 5.5\%$

Any capital projects that Bittaboth may wish to consider may be evaluated using its WACC, which may be calculated as:

{equity/(debt + equity) ratio × return on equity} + {debt/(debt + equity) ratio × after tax cost of debt}
$(4/5 \times 16.4\%) + (1/5 \times 5.5\%) = 14.2\%$
14.2% is Bittaboth's weighted average cost of capital (WACC).

It should be remembered that the CAPM considers systematic risk only, and is based on an assumption of market equilibrium.

β factors may be calculated using market and individual companies' information. β values are also obtainable from a variety of sources and are published quarterly by the London Business School.

> **Progress check 8.7** Describe what is meant by systematic risk and unsystematic risk.

Return on equity and financial structure

The important formula that follows shows the return on equity (ROE) as a function of return on investment (ROI) and the financial structure, leverage or gearing of the company, where:

D = debt capital
E = equity capital
t = corporation tax rate
i = interest rate on debt
ROI = return on investment

$$\text{ROS} = \text{return on sales} = \frac{\text{profit after tax}}{\text{total investment}}$$

ROE = {ROI × (1 − *t*)} + {(ROI − *i*) × (1 − *t*) × D/E}

Worked Example 8.9 illustrates the use of this relationship and also gives a general rule derived from it.

Worked Example 8.9

A hospital equipment manufacturing company, Nilby Mouth plc, makes an operating profit (PBIT) of £10m on sales of £100m and with a total investment of £60m. The investment is financed by equity (E) of £40m and debt (D) of £20m with an interest rate (i) of 10%. Assume the corporation tax rate (t) is 50%.

We will calculate:

(i)   the current return on equity (ROE)
(ii)   the ROE if financing were changed so that debt was £40m and equity was £20m
(iii)   the current ROE if operating profit were reduced to £4m
(iv)   the ROE if operating profit were reduced to £4m and if financing were changed so that debt was £40m and equity was £20m.

Figures in £m

(i) Calculation of return on equity (ROE)
Profit before interest and tax, or operating profit PBIT = 10
Profit before tax PBT = 10 − (20 × 10%) = 8
Profit after tax PAT = 8 × (1 − 50%) = 4
Return on sales ROS = 4/100 = 4%
Return on investment ROI (pre interest and tax) = 10/60 = 16.7%
Debt/equity ratio D/E = 20/40 = 50%
ROE = ROI × (1 − t) + {(ROI − i) × (1 − t) × D/E}
Return on equity ROE = {16.7% × (1 − 50%)} + {(16.7% − 10%) × (1 − 50%) × 50%}
                     = 0.10025 or 10%

(ii) Calculation of ROE if financing is changed so that debt is £40m and equity is £20m
PBIT = 10   PBT = 10 − (40 × 10%) = 6   PAT = 6 × (1 − 50%) = 3
ROS = 3/100 = 3%

ROI (pre interest and tax) = 10/60 = 16.7%

D/E = 40/20 = 200%

ROE = {16.7% × (1 − 50%)} + {(16.7% − 10%) × (1 − 50%) × 200%}

     = 0.15050 or 15.1%

Return on sales has reduced, whereas return on equity has increased.

(iii) Calculation of ROE if the operating profit were reduced to £4m

PBIT = 4   PBT = 4 − (20 × 10%) = 2   PAT = 2 × (1 − 50%) = 1

ROS = 1/100 = 1%

ROI (pre interest and tax) = 4/60 = 6.7%

D/E = 20/40 = 50%

ROE = {6.7% × (1 − 50%)} + {(6.7% − 10%) × (1 − 50%) × 50%} = 0.02525 or 2.53%

(iv) Calculation of ROE if financing is changed so that debt is £40m and equity is £20m

PBIT = 4   PBT = 4 − (40 × 10%) = 0   PAT = 0 × (1 − 50%) = 0

ROS = 0/100 = 0%

ROI (pre interest and tax) = 4/60 = 6.7%

D/E = 40/20 = 200%

ROE = {6.7% × (1 − 50%)} + {(6.7% − 10%) × (1 − 50%) × 200%} = 0.00050 or 0.05%

Return on sales has reduced and return on equity has also reduced.

The general rule apparent from the relationships outlined in Worked Example 14.10 is:

- when ROI is greater than i   the higher the D/E, the higher the ROE
- when ROI is less than i   the higher the D/E, the lower the ROE.

However, even if the ROI is greater than the debt interest the company's bankers may not automatically allow the D/E to increase indefinitely. The company's risk increases as the D/E or leverage increases, in terms of its commitment to high levels of interest payments, and bankers will not tolerate too high a level of risk; they will also be inclined to increase the debt interest rate as D/E increases. Shareholders will have the same reaction – they are happy with an increase in ROE but realise that they also have to face a higher risk.

For a high growth company, to limit the shareholders' investment, the company will have a tendency to increase D/E and therefore ROE, but also the financial risk. The press (for example Questor in the *Daily Telegraph*) usually comments when a plc is seen to embark on a policy of increased borrowings and increasing its gearing ratio, which alerts the reader to 'increased financial risk'. Plcs are usually prepared and ready for such comments in order to respond with their 'defence' of such a policy.

> **Progress check 8.8 Discuss why bankers may refuse additional lending to a company as its debt/equity ratio increases.**

Growth of a company may be looked at using profit and loss account horizontal analyses. Use of this technique, which was covered in Chapter 6, presents all numbers in the profit and loss account as a percentage using a base year, which is 100, for year-on-year comparison. Financial commentators usually begin articles on the performance of plcs by comparing the current year performance with the previous year, and then attempt a forecast of future performance. This is an example of a basic horizontal analysis that focuses on turnover and profits. Only a few companies actually succeed in growing year on year, over an extended period (for example, 10 years).

Economic value added (EVA™) and market value added (MVA)

Maximisation of shareholder wealth continues to be the prime objective with which managers of companies are charged. The measurement of managers' financial performance may be considered in various ways. The extent to which success in particular performance measures aligns with shareholder wealth is particularly relevant. Equally important are the ways in which managers are motivated to maximise shareholder wealth. In most organisations managerial remuneration provides the link between the measures of financial performance and shareholder value.

Financial performance measures such as a company's share price are commonly used to indicate how well the company is doing. However, it may be questioned as to how directly the share price reflects decisions that have been taken by management. In the context of managers' performance against budget targets, and the company's overall financial performance, we have previously discussed the merits and otherwise of other performance measures such as profit after tax, earnings per share, dividends, return on capital employed, and cash flow, etc. Each has its limitations, but cash flow based measures are now becoming accepted as perhaps better indicators than profit related measures.

During the mid-1980s, Rappaport developed shareholder value analysis, from which the American firm Stern Stewart Management Services evolved concepts known as economic value added (EVA), and **market value added (MVA)**. Through EVA, Stern Stewart attempted to reconcile the need for a performance measure correlated with shareholder wealth, and a performance measure which was also responsive to actions taken by managers. By the mid-1990s over 200 global companies had been in discussion with Stern Stewart with regard to adoption of EVA; Lucas Varity in the UK and Coca Cola in the USA were already successful users of EVA.

If we assume that the organisation's objective is to maximise shareholder wealth then this will be achieved if new projects are taken on and existing projects are allowed to continue only if they create value. **Investment** in capital projects may be made only on the basis of choosing those with a positive **net present value (NPV)**. However, NPV cannot be applied to remuneration schemes because it is a summary measure based on projected cash flows and not realised performance.

Companies usually turn to company earnings and cash flow (which are termed flow measures) for management remuneration schemes. EVA supports the same sort of recommendations that NPV provides at the project level, but also provides a better measure of management performance because it rewards for earnings generated, whilst also including charges for the amount of capital employed to create those earnings.

If profit after tax = PAT
Weighted average cost of capital = WACC
Net assets = adjusted book value of net capital = NA
Then we may define EVA as:

$$EVA = PAT - (WACC \times NA)$$

Worked Example 8.10 will illustrate the calculation of EVA and its relationship with NPV.

Worked Example 8.10

A manager has to choose between three mutually exclusive projects. The company may invest:

£50,000 in project A, or
£110,000 in project B, or
£240,000 in project C

Project A is expected to generate incremental profits after tax (PAT) of £50,000 in year one, £40,000 in year two (total £90,000), after which the project is terminated.

Project B is expected to generate incremental PATs of £45,000 in year one, £70,000 in year two, £70,000 in year three (total £185,000), after which the project is terminated.

Project C is expected to generate incremental PATs of £55,000 in year one, £75,000 in year two, £80,000 in year three (total £210,000), after which the project is terminated.

The company's WACC is 10% per annum. Capital levels may be assumed to be maintained throughout the life of each project. That is, each year's new capital investment equals depreciation in that year.

Capital items are sold at their book value in the final year of each project, so free cash flow (operating cash flow less capital expenditure) will be equal to PAT each year except the final years when the capital costs are recovered.

We will assess which project the manager will choose if:

(i)   his/her remuneration is tied to the NPV of the project
(ii)   his/her remuneration is based on IRR
(iii) his/her remuneration is based on project earnings
(iv)   his/her remuneration is based on EVA.

Using a discount rate of WACC at 10% per annum, we first calculate the NPVs of each project.

Year	Cash outflows	Cash inflows		Net cash flow at 10%	Discount factor	Present values
	£000	**£000**		**£000**		**£000**
Project A						
0	−50			−50	1.00	−50.0
1		50		50	0.91	45.5
2		90	[40 + 50]	90	0.83	74.7
3		0		0	0.75	0.0
Total	−50	140		90		+70.2
Project B						
0	−110			−110	1.00	−110.0
1		45		45	0.91	40.9
2		70		70	0.83	58.1
3		180	[70 + 110]	180	0.75	135.0
Total	−110	295		185		+124.0

Project C						
0	−240			−240	1.00	−240.0
1		55		55	0.91	50.0
2		75		75	0.83	62.3
3		320	[80 + 240]	320	0.75	240.0
Total	−240	450		210		+112.3

The IRR is the rate of return that would give an NPV of zero.

The **internal rate of return (IRR)** of each project may be derived using the appropriate IRR Excel spreadsheet function or by using the interpolation technique (which is not covered in this book).

For project C, if we assume a discount rate of 30%, we may calculate a revised NPV as follows:

Year	Cash outflows	Cash inflows	Net cash flow	Discount factor at 30%	Present values
	£000	£000	£000		£000
0	−240		−240	1.00	−240.0
1		55	55	0.77	42.4
2		75	75	0.59	44.3
3		320	320	0.46	147.2
Total	−240	450	210		−6.1

We have already calculated the positive NPV for project C of £112,300 using a cost of capital of 10%. The IRR of project C must be at some point between 30% and 10% (difference 20%).

An interpolation technique calculation gives IRR at a value of x below 30%:

$$\frac{£6,100}{x} = \frac{£112,300}{(20-x)}$$

$(£6,100 \times 20) − £6,100x = £112,300x$

$£122,000 = £118,400x$

$$x = \frac{£122,000}{£118,400}$$

$x = 1.03$

Therefore, interpolation gives us an IRR of 30% less 1.03%, which equals 28.97% and may be rounded to 29%.

The IRRs of projects A and B may be calculated in the same way.

The cash flows, NPVs and IRRs of the three projects may be summarised as:

Project	PAT			Cash out	Cash in			Total cash flow	IRR	NPV
	Year 1	Year 2	Year 3		Year 1	Year 2	Year 3			
	£000	£000	£000	£000	£000	£000	£000	£000	%	£000
A	50	40		−50	50	90 [40 + 50]		90	93	70.2
B	45	70	70	−110	45	70	180 [70 + 110]	185	53	124.0
C	55	75	80	−240	55	75	320 [80 + 240]	210	29	112.3

(i)   Based on the highest NPV, project B at £124,000 is best for the company shareholders.

(ii) But if the manager's remuneration is based on IRR then he/she will choose project A at 93%.

(iii) If the manager is remunerated on total project earnings then he/she will choose project C at £210,000.

(iv) We can calculate the EVA for each project, which equals profit after tax for each period, less capital employed at the start of each period multiplied by the weighted average cost of capital.

Year	Project A		Project B		Project C	
		EVA		EVA		EVA
	£000	£000	£000	£000	£000	£000
1	$50 - (50 \times 10\%)$	45	$45 - (110 \times 10\%)$	34	$55 - (240 \times 10\%)$	31
2	$40 - (50 \times 10\%)$	35	$70 - (110 \times 10\%)$	59	$75 - (240 \times 10\%)$	51
3			$70 - (110 \times 10\%)$	59	$80 - (240 \times 10\%)$	56
Total		80		152		138

We may also calculate the NPV of the EVAs of each project, the present values of the EVAs:

Year		Project A		Project B		Project C	
	Discount factor at 10%	Cash flow £000	NPV £000	Cash flow £000	NPV £000	Cash flow £000	NPV £000
1	0.91	45	41.0	34	30.9	31	28.2
2	0.83	35	29.1	59	48.9	51	42.3
3	0.75			59	44.2	56	42.0
Total		80	+70.1	152	+124.0	138	+112.5

This illustrates that EVAs actually equate to cash flows because their present values are the same as the NPV of each project. The small differences between the totals calculated for Project A and Project C are as a result of rounding differences.

We have seen from Worked Example 8.10 that earnings-based remuneration schemes may result in over-investment of capital whereas return on net assets will result in under-investment of capital. Use of EVA as a basis for management remuneration takes account of the fact that the use of capital is charged for by using WACC; additionally, at the project level, the present value of the EVAs gives the same result as NPVs derived from free cash flows. Compare the results in the project NPV tables with the NPVs of the EVAs of each project in Worked Example 8.10.

➡   Although the free cash flow NPVs give the same result as the **present values** of the EVAs, EVA is more appropriate for remuneration schemes because, as well as being fundamentally related to shareholder value, it is a flow measure of performance. The reason is that flow measures of performance are needed for periodic remuneration because remuneration is designed to provide a flow of rewards. The other flow measure is cash flow. EVA is a better measure than that because it takes into account the cost of capital invested in the project.

Worked Example 8.11

We will compute the EVA for 2002, 2003 and 2004 for a major plc from the following information.

Group cost of capital		5%
		£m
Adjusted net assets	2004	750
	2003	715
	2002	631
Profit after tax	2004	550
	2003	526
	2002	498
Equity	2004	100
	2003	48
	2002	115
Net debt	2004	800
	2003	802
	2002	546

Year	Profit after tax	Adjusted net assets	5% cost of capital × net assets	EVA	EVA % of net profit
	£m	£m	£m	£m	
2004	550	750	37.50	512.50	93%
2003	526	715	35.75	490.25	93%
2002	498	631	31.55	466.45	94%

Note how the profits are being earned using borrowed funds to finance the group. The plc can earn a very high EVA by using borrowed funds.

We have talked about EVA in respect of projects, and that the present value of future EVAs equals the NPV derived from future free cash flows. At a company level, the present value of EVAs equals the market value added (MVA) of a business. This is defined as the difference between the market value of the company and the adjusted book values of its assets.

EVA is a good financial performance measure because it answers the question of how well has the company performed in generating profits over a period, given the amount of capital tied up to generate those profits. However, the capital base is a difficult element to estimate in calculating EVA. The total net assets value on a balance sheet is not an accurate representation of either the liquidation value or the replacement cost value of the business. Stern Stewart consider more than 250 possible

Worked Example 8.12

We will compute the MVA for 2003 and 2004 from the following extracts from the annual report and accounts of a major plc, using the unadjusted value of net assets.

	2004	**2003**
Number of shares (5p)	950.2m	948.9m
Share price	278p	268p
Net assets	£1,097m	£1,437m

	2004	**2003**
Net assets	£1,097m	£1,437m
Market value	£2,641m	£2,543m
MVA	£1,544m	£1,106m

accounting adjustments to a balance sheet to arrive at a valuation of the company's assets. In practice most organisations find that no more than a dozen or so adjustments are truly significant, for example stocks, depreciation, goodwill, deferred tax, and closure costs.

Progress check 8.9 **What is economic value added (EVA) and what is it used for?**

EVA probably does not change or add anything to the conclusions reached on the basis of conventional cash flow based valuation analysis. EVA is primarily a behavioural tool that corrects possible distortions. However, along with most other financial measures, it fails to measure on an *ex post* basis. EVA is undoubtedly a very useful concept for measuring and evaluating management and company performance. It is not a cure for poor management and poor investment decisions but it raises the profile and the awareness of the costs of capital involved in undertaking projects and in running the business.

Summary of key points

- Sources of finance internal to a company are its retained earnings, extended credit from suppliers, and the benefits gained from the more effective management of its working capital.
- Short-term, external sources of finance include overdrafts and short-term loans.
- The two main sources of long-term, external finance available to a company are equity (ordinary shares), preference shares and debt (loans and debentures).
- Other sources of long-term, external finance available to UK companies include hybrid finance, leasing, and UK Government and European funding.
- Gearing, or the debt/equity ratio, is the relationship between the two sources of finance,

loans and ordinary shares – a company having more debt capital than share capital is highly geared, and a company having more share capital than debt capital is low geared.

■ The weighted average cost of capital (WACC) is the average cost of the total financial resources of a company, i.e. the shareholders' equity and the net financial debt, that may be used as the discount rate to evaluate investment projects, and as a measure of company performance.

■ Both the cost of debt and the cost of equity are based on future income flows, and the risk associated with such returns.

■ A certain element of risk is unavoidable whenever any investment is made, and unless a market investor settles for risk-free securities, the actual return on investment in equity (or debt) capital may be better or worse than hoped for.

■ Systematic risk may be measured using the capital asset pricing model (CAPM), and the β factor, in terms of its effect on required returns and share prices.

■ The return on equity may be considered as a function of the gearing, or financial structure of the company.

■ The recently developed techniques of economic value added (EVA) and market value added (MVA) are widely becoming used in business performance measurement and as value creation incentives.

Questions

Q8.1   **(i)**   What are the main sources of long-term, external finance available to an organisation?

       (ii)   What are their advantages and disadvantages?

Q8.2   What are the advantages and disadvantages of convertible loans?

Q8.3   Why may leasing be considered as a long-term source of finance?

Q8.4   What are the implications for a company of different levels of gearing?

Q8.5   What are the advantages and disadvantages for a company in using WACC as a discount factor to evaluate capital projects?

Q8.6   Describe the ways in which the costs of debt and equity capital may be ascertained.

Q8.7   How does risk impact on the cost of debt and equity?

Q8.8   What is the β factor, and how may it be related to WACC?

Q8.9   How may a company's return on equity (ROE) be related to its financial structure?

Q8.10   In what way is company growth of such interest to shareholders?

Q8.11   Business performance may be evaluated to determine ways in which it can be improved upon. If managers are capable of delivering improved performance how can EVA be used to support this?

Discussion points

D8.1 The ex-owner/manager of a private limited company recently acquired by a large plc, of which he is now a board member, said: 'This company has grown very quickly over the past few years so that our turnover is now over £20m per annum. Even though we expect our turnover to grow further and double in the next two years I cannot see why we need to change our existing financing arrangements. I know we need to make some large investments in new machinery over the next two years but in the past we've always operated successfully using our existing overdraft facility, which has been increased as required, particularly when we've needed new equipment. I don't really see the need for all this talk about additional share capital and long-term loans'. Discuss.

D8.2 The marketing manager of a large UK subsidiary of a multinational plc: 'Surely the interest rate that we should use to discount cash flows in our appraisal of new capital investment projects should be our bank overdraft interest rate. I don't really see the relevance of the weighted average cost of capital (WACC) to this type of exercise.' Discuss.

D8.3 In the long run does it really matter whether a company is financed predominantly by ordinary shares or predominantly by loans? What's the difference?

D8.4 'Economic value added (EVA) is nothing more than just flavour of the month.' Discuss.

Exercises

Solutions are provided in Appendix 3 to all exercise numbers highlighted in colour.

Level I

E8.1 *Time allowed – 30 minutes*

A critically important factor required by a company to make financial decisions, for example the evaluation of investment proposals and the financing of new projects, is its cost of capital. One of the elements included in the calculation of a company's cost of capital is the cost of equity.

(i) **Explain in simple terms what is meant by the 'cost of equity capital' for a company.**

The relevant data for Normal plc and the market in general is given below.

Normal plc

Current price per share on the London Stock Exchange	£1.20
Current annual dividend per share	£0.10
Expected average annual growth rate of dividends	7%
β beta coefficient for Normal plc's shares	0.5

The market

Expected rate of return on risk-free securities	8%
Expected return on the market portfolio	12%

(ii) **Calculate the cost of equity capital for Normal plc, using two alternative methods:**
   (a) the Capital Asset Pricing Model (CAPM)
   (b) a dividend growth model of your choice.

E8.2 *Time allowed – 30 minutes*

Normal plc pays £20,000 a year interest on an irredeemable debenture, which has a nominal value of £200,000 and a market value of £160,000. The rate of corporation tax is 30%.

You are required to:

(i) calculate the cost of the debt for Normal plc

(ii) calculate the weighted average cost of capital for Normal plc using the cost of equity calculated in Exercise E8.1 (ii) if Normal plc has only ordinary capital of £300,000

(iii) comment on the impact on a company's cost of capital of changes in the rate of corporation tax

(iv) calculate Normal plc's WACC if the rate of corporation tax were increased to 50%.

Level II

E8.3 *Time allowed – 30 minutes*

Lucky Jim plc has the opportunity to manufacture a particular type of self-tapping screw, for a client company, that would become indispensable in a particular niche market in the engineering field.

Development of the product requires an initial investment of £200,000 in the project. It has been estimated that the project will yield cash returns before interest of £35,000 per annum in perpetuity.

Lucky Jim plc is financed by equity and loans, which are always maintained as two thirds and one third of the total capital respectively. The cost of equity is 18% and the pre-tax cost of debt is 9%. The corporation tax rate is 40%.

If Lucky Jim plc's WACC is used as the cost of capital to appraise the project, should the project be undertaken?

E8.4 *Time allowed – 30 minutes*

You are required to compute the MVA for 2002, 2003 and 2004 from the estimated information for a large supermarket group.

	2004	2003	2002
Number of shares	6.823m	6.823m	6.770m
Share price	261p	169p	77p
Adjusted net assets	£5,000m	£4,769m	£4,377m

E8.5 *Time allowed – 60 minutes*

Yor plc is a fast growing, hi-tech business. Its profit and loss account for the year ended 30 September 2004 and its balance sheet as at 30 September 2004 are shown below. The company has the opportunity to take on a major project that will significantly improve its profitability in the forthcoming year and for the foreseeable future. The cost of the project is £10m, which will result in large increases in sales, which will increase profit before interest and tax by £4m per annum. The directors of Yor plc have two alternative options of financing the project:

The issue of £10m of 4% debentures at par, or a rights issue of 4m ordinary shares at a premium of £1.50 per share (after expenses).

Regardless of how the new project is financed, the directors will recommend a 10% increase in the dividend for 2004/2005. You may assume that the effective corporation tax rate is the same for 2004/2005 as for 2003/2004.

Yor plc
Profit and loss account for the year ended 30 September 2004

Figures in £m

PBIT	11.6
Interest payable	(1.2)
Profit before tax	10.4
Tax on profit on ordinary activities	(2.6)
Profit on ordinary activities after tax	7.8
Retained profit 1 October 2003	5.8
	13.6
Dividends	(3.0)
Retained profit 30 September 2004	10.6

Yor plc
Balance sheet as at 30 September 2004

Figures in £m

Fixed assets	
Tangible	28.8
Current assets	
Stocks	11.2
Debtors	13.8
Cash and bank	0.7
	25.7
Current liabilities (less than one year)	
Creditors	9.7
Dividends	1.6
Taxation	2.6
	13.9
Net current assets	11.8
Total assets less current liabilities	40.6
less	
Long-term liabilities (over one year)	
6% loan	20.0
Net assets	20.6
Capital and reserves	
Share capital (£1 ordinary shares)	10.0
Profit and loss account	10.6
	20.6

The directors of Yor plc would like to see your estimated profit and loss account for 2004/2005, and a summary of share capital and reserves at 30 September 2005, assuming:

(i) the new project is financed by an issue of the debentures
(ii) the new project is financed by the issue of new ordinary shares

To assist in clarification of the figures, you should show your calculations of:

(iii)   eps for 2003/2004
(iv)   eps for 2004/2005, reflecting both methods of financing the new project
(v)   dividend per share for 2003/2004
(vi)   dividend per share for 2004/2005, reflecting both methods of financing the new project

Use the information you have provided in (i) and (ii) above to:

(vii)   calculate Yor plc's gearing, reflecting both methods of financing the new project, and compare with its gearing at 30 September 2004
(viii)   summarise the results for 2004/2005, recommend which method of financing Yor plc should adopt, and explain the implications of both on its financial structure.

E8.6 *Time allowed – 90 minutes*

Sparks plc is a large electronics company that produces components for CD and iPod players. It is close to the current year end and Sparks is forecasting profits after tax at £60m. The following two years' post-tax profits are each expected to increase by another £15m, and years four and five by another £10m each.

The forecast balance sheet for Sparks plc as at 31 December is as follows:

	£m
Fixed assets	500
Current assets	
Stocks	120
Debtors	160
	280
Creditors due within one year	
Trade creditors	75
Overdraft	75
	150
Net current assets	130
Long-term loans	150
	480
Capital and reserves	
Share capital (£1 ordinary shares)	220
Share premium	10
Profit and loss account	250
	480

Sparks plc has a large overdraft of £75m on which it pays a high rate of interest at 15%. The board would like to pay off the overdraft and obtain cheaper financing. Sparks also has loan capital of £150m on which it pays interest at 9% per annum. Despite its high level of debt Sparks is a profitable organisation. However, the board is currently planning a number of new projects for the next year, which will cost £75m. These projects are expected to produce profits after tax of £8m in the first year and £15m a year ongoing for future years.

The board has discussed a number of financing options and settled on two of them for further consideration:

1. a 1 for 4 rights issue at £3.00 a share to raise £150m from the issue of 50m £1 shares
2. a convertible £150m debenture issue at 12% (pre tax) that may be converted into 45m ordinary shares in two years' time.

The equity share index has risen over the past year from 4,600 to the current 5,500, having reached 6,250. Sparks plc's ordinary shares are currently at a market price of £3.37. Gearing of companies in the same industry as Sparks plc ranges between 25% and 45%. In two years' time it is expected that all Sparks debenture holders will convert to shares or none will convert.

The rate of corporation tax is 50%. Repayment of the overdraft will save interest of £5.625m a year after tax.

The board requires some analysis of the numbers to compare against the current position:

(i)   **if they make the rights issue**
(ii)   **if they issue debentures**
(iii)   **if the debentures are converted.**

The analysis should show:

(a)   **the impact on the balance sheet**
(b)   **the impact on the profit after tax**
(c)   **earnings per share**
(d)   **gearing**
(e)   **which option should be recommended to the board and why.**

9

Information technology and accounting, and e-business

Contents

Learning objectives

Completion of this chapter will enable you to:

- outline the ways in which information technology (IT) has been used to change and improve the ways in which accounting and financial data is recorded, processed, stored, retrieved, and reported
- explain the ways in which IT has impacted on traditional payroll and accounting systems
- describe the ways in which computer systems have been developed to include all the operational areas of a business, for example manufacturing, distribution and quality management
- explain how businesses have been able to achieve the full integration of their applications software through the implementation of enterprise resource planning (ERP) systems
- illustrate the ways in which spreadsheets have taken the place of the traditional accountants' analysis pad and simplified and speeded up the most complicated and sophisticated financial calculations and analyses
- describe the use of databases for the storage, retrieval and reporting of wide ranges of related data
- explain how graphics tools and groupware have enhanced and improved the ways in which accounting information, ideas, and concepts may be shared and presented using computer projections and the Internet
- discuss the range of additional accounting-related software systems that have been developed for personal and business use
- outline the key data protection principles contained in the Data Protection Act 1998
- outline some of the changes in accounting following the emergence of the 'new economy' through the latter part of the twentieth century and the start of the twenty-first century
- explain the broad concept of e-business and its various elements, for example e-commerce, email and websites, and their impact on accounting systems.

Introduction

This chapter considers the important impact that computers increasingly continue to have not only on virtually every aspect of modern life, but on business organisations in particular. The development of the use of computers specifically and information technology (IT) in general has a huge influence on how organisations operate and on changes in the way accounting and financial management is able to support them.

The development of IT has been fuelled not only by the tremendous increase in the pace of technological change but also to a great extent by the vast increase in the range of products and services available to us all, increasing globalisation, and breadth of competition. Increasing competition is a fact of life within any industry, public or private, and whatever product or service is being offered to customers in the marketplace. Globalisation has brought increased pressures of competition. Pressures on a company's profit margins inevitably follow from the increasing pace of technological change, which results in shorter life cycles of products as completely new models are being developed at a much quicker rate. Thus, the obsolescence of capital equipment is accelerated. This all means that the basis of competition has changed.

The effects on businesses are significant (and those that do not respond successfully may fail, or be acquired by other companies):

- costs such as development costs and costs of capital equipment must be recovered over a shorter time period
- the phases within the product life cycle must be managed more effectively and efficiently
- the faster pace of business and the need for quick decisions and action mean that effective computerised information systems are required to provide relevant and timely information.

This has all resulted in the requirement for speedier and more accurate communication of information and data, delivery of products and services, and processing of transactions.

Business processes and IT

The use of computers by business organisations began with payroll applications and was developed to cover a wide range of general accounting applications. The early days, from the 1940s up until the 1970s, saw a growth in the use of large mainframe computers for payroll, sales ledger, purchase ledger, general ledger, and financial reporting systems (see the example in Fig. 9.1). As the technology advanced the size of mainframes decreased as their capacity and memories increased.

However, the early mainframe systems required:

- manual preparation of batches of large amounts of data for subsequent input to the computer system
- validation of data entry, and
- recording and processing of the data.

Figure 9.1 One of the earliest mainframe computer systems installed by HSBC (formerly Midland Bank) in 1962 at its West End Computer Centre in London

The whole process was very tedious and time-consuming and involved long delays between the recording of data and the provision of reports based on that data.

In the early 1980s the emergence of personal computers (PCs) – starting with computers like the Sinclair ZX81, Apple and BBC Acorn, through to IBM, Compaq and Hewlett Packard – provided the springboard for the revolution in ways that data could be recorded, analysed and reported on. Personal computers also opened up the paths along which many other applications could proceed. However, PCs did not make mainframe computers obsolete.

Mainframe computer systems increasingly continue to be used for the processing of extremely high volumes of transactions such as, for example, large payrolls, automated payment systems, and pay as you earn (PAYE) taxation. Mainframe software like PeopleSoft and SAP is also still used by some large organisations for their accounting, ordering and invoicing, purchasing, manufacturing, and distribution systems. These systems may or may not be linked with the PC systems used in such organisations. Since the 1990s there has been a move by the larger businesses to smaller computers. This has resulted in the development of what are called **client-server** computer systems, which are cheaper in terms of their initial cost, and maintenance, and require lower levels of staffing. **Small to medium sized enterprises (SMEs)** use either standalone or networked PCs, and client-servers for applications similar to those run on the larger mainframe systems.

Application software includes accounting software, which is used to record, process, store, retrieve and report on transactions and produce financial statements and other reports. Decision support software (DSS) is used in the decision-making process to analyse data and predict the outcome of decisions in order to assist in choosing between alternatives. Executive information systems (EIS) provide internal and external information to managers, usually at a consolidated and summarised level but with a facility to drill down to transaction level.

This chapter will look at examples of the accounting software that is run on PC systems. It will also look at some of the other associated applications that have been developed over the past 20 years or so, for example:

- **computer-aided design** and **computer-aided manufacturing (CAD/CAM)**
- **computer-aided engineering (CAE)**
- **computer-integrated manufacturing (CIM)**
- just in time (JIT) and *kanban*
- materials requirements planning (MRP)
- manufacturing resource planning (MRPII)
- quality management
- **enterprise resource planning (ERP)**
- **spreadsheets** and modelling
- **database management systems (DBMS)**
- communication and presentation of information
- VAT audits
- year-end statutory accounts audits
- risk management
- **knowledge management**.

The chapter will conclude with an introduction to the emergence of **new economy** businesses, **e-business**, and how businesses are increasingly using **website** resources, electronic mail (or **email**) and **e-commerce** in the further development of their organisations, and their accounting systems.

It is important to appreciate that there may be many advantages to be gained from the close involvement of accounting in each of the areas discussed above, some of which at first glance seem completely unrelated, like CAD/CAM. Note, for example, the article in the June 2004 of *Financial Management*, 'Draft Excluders', where it was observed that 'When management accountants get closely involved in the process of designing new products and services, the results tend to be highly beneficial. But this message doesn't seem to have got through to many designers.'

The development of computerised accounting systems

Up until the 1970s many businesses continued to use manual, paper-based systems for maintaining accounting records and reporting financial information. Traditionally, batches of source accounting data were prepared by entering details of transactions on analysis sheets for sales invoices, purchase invoices, cash receipts, and cash payments. These data were then entered either in detail or summary into the sales and purchase ledgers, to maintain records of amounts owed by/to customers/suppliers; the general ledger, to maintain records of sales and costs; the cash book, to maintain records of the cash position. Various other books of account, or ledgers, were in the same way maintained manually relating to information on product costs, special projects, fixed assets, etc.

Throughout the 1970s increasing numbers of organisations began to take their first steps along the computerisation path. The first main use of computers in the finance function was the recording and processing of payroll information. This enabled details of gross pay and deductions (pay as you earn tax (PAYE), national insurance (NI) contributions, pension contributions, etc.) to be held for individual employees and the total for the whole organisation. Payroll systems are used to print individual pay slips in support of net pay paid to each employee, and to provide reports for the organisation relating to employee costs, and amounts payable to their pension schemes, and payable to the Inland Revenue for PAYE and NI. Computerised payroll systems were either run for organisations by external agencies or run within and by the organisations themselves.

Computerised payroll applications were quickly followed by the development of computerised accounting ledger systems. These systems used batches of transactions similar to those used in the manual systems. The batches were prepared so that they could be uniquely identified and have the data verified and validated. The data were then input by computer department staff dedicated to transferring the data onto punched cards for each transaction. In the earliest punched card systems the punched cards were read by a card reader and then sorted appropriately for specific reports to be produced on a printer. The next development was the use of punched cards, which were similarly read by a card reader, from which information was processed by the computer system and the records held on magnetic tape. The data on the tapes could then subsequently be used to provide printed reports. Tape was soon replaced as the storage medium by computer discs, but back-ups were still maintained on tape for some time, until disc technology had advanced to a stage that made tapes obsolete.

Punched card systems were subsequently replaced with screen-based systems, which enabled individual transactions to be keyed directly into the computer system. The transition to screen-based input by individuals led to the demise of the large data processing departments that had grown within companies as their use of computerisation increased. Instead, transaction data could be input directly by user departments, primarily the accounting and finance departments. Initially, the reporting from these systems for the user departments continued to be relatively slow, with delays between data input and the reporting of information, and remained under the control of the data processing, or IT, department. Driven by user requirements for faster reporting of information, systems were soon developed that allowed complete control of data input and output reporting of information by user departments, and with much faster response times in terms of data entry and reporting.

Payroll and human resources management (HRM) software

As we have already seen, application software to run payrolls either within the organisation by its own staff, or by using specialist agencies, was the first area of computerisation of an 'accounting' process. The basics of these systems were not substantially different from the manual payroll processes. As with manual payrolls, very tight authorisation and control procedures are essential in support of computerised payroll systems to ensure absolute accuracy and dependability, and to prevent fraud.

A payroll system maintains details of all employees with regard to name and address, PAYE tax coding, gross pay, payment frequency, payment method, pension, and other additions and deductions. This is to ensure that employees are always paid the correct net pay, on the right date, and in the right place. It also ensures that employers account appropriately for income tax, NI contributions, pension contributions, and any other deductions. In addition, payroll systems maintain employee details relating to their department, cost centre, and/or project codes so that total employee costs of gross pay, employer's NI, employer's pension contributions, and any other costs are properly accounted for and charged to the appropriate expense codes and departments.

Payrolls were traditionally the responsibility of the accounting or finance departments in most organisations. As payroll systems were developed and enhanced to encompass personnel or human resources processes, the responsibility became blurred as to whether these systems should be controlled by the finance department or the human resources department. An important issue arises here relating to the adequacy of internal control within the organisation. Should the department responsible for authorisation of additions and changes to the payroll/human resource management system (the personnel or human resources department) also have responsibility for the processing of the data and the generation of the payments from the system? Segregation of responsibilities is required to provide an adequate level of internal control. This control is provided when the payroll processing/payments functions are carried out by a department (i.e. the finance department) separate from the department responsible for authorisation of additions/changes to the system (i.e. the personnel or the human resources department).

A fully-integrated HRM (human resources management) system provides the fundamental payroll processes and the links with the accounting and planning systems. It also provides much more. It maintains data relating to departmental budgets in terms of numbers of employees in particular roles and grades. A complete HRM system maintains individual employee details about age, sex, ethnic origin, skills, qualifications, experience, training, promotion progression, retirement and pension details, grievance and disciplinary issues, and the results of staff appraisals. This data provides the basis for the information required for HR planning and succession planning, implementation of HR policy, and control and evaluation of performance. HRM software continues to be developed to assist in the effective management of the entire range of human resources available to an organisation.

Currently, the most recent development in HRM systems is 'employee self-service'. This is a term that is used to describe the way in which employees may have direct access to their organisation's HRM system to input their hours worked (if they are paid on an hours worked basis) and also their expenses claims for travel, hotel accommodation, etc. The results of employees' input is then routed to their managers for approval and acceptance by the system for electronic payment into their bank accounts, and automatic recording of the costs in the accounting system.

> **Progress check 9.1** In what ways has the computerisation of payrolls improved the recording of accounting information?

Accounting software

A variety of operating systems have been developed on which to run application software. Operating system software is a group of computer programs that manage the basic operations of the computer by communicating with and instructing the hardware components of the computer. Operating software tells the computer how to execute application programs and manage the storage of data.

Mainframe operating systems were developed like the IBM S/390 and the VSE/VM, and used in very large organisations with huge volumes of transactions. Currently the market leaders include companies like SAP, PeopleSoft, JD Edwards, and Oracle. PC-based operating systems were developed in parallel with their mainframe brothers and included, for example, various versions of MS DOS that ran software like Pegasus, Sun, and Sage accounting software. As an alternative, many organisations chose to write their own accounting software using business systems programming languages like Cobol.

The development of the Windows operating system saw the emergence of other software that may have been developed using MS DOS and then modified to run on the Windows operating system. Such accounting software, of which Sage is currently the market leader, runs on PC standalone or networked systems, primarily for use by smaller and medium sized companies with a relatively small volume of transactions (although these volumes are also actually very large). The use of graphics technology enabled users to use a mouse or a pointer to click on icons rather than using a keyboard for inputting text instructions. The use of **GUI (graphic user interfaces)** has made IT much more accessible and easy to operate.

As we have already discussed, the use of mainframe computers for accounting packages has gradually been replaced by smaller centralised systems on large **server** PCs. These servers are linked to desktop PCs, which are then called clients, and which gives the systems their name of client-servers. As the use of mainframes diminished the accounting packages that were run on them were modified to run on client-server systems.

PCs may be used standalone or may be linked into networks. They may be linked in a **local area network (LAN)** to allow common use of hard disc drives, printers, scanners, **modems**, etc. Modems may be telephone modems, which transmit at 56 **kilobytes** per second, and which are usually used for computer connections for transmission via telephone lines; they may also be **cable modems**, which transmit data at much higher speeds (from 1 to 3 or megabytes or more) and may additionally provide television access to the **Internet**. **Wide area networks (WANs)** allow geographically more diverse network links between users on a worldwide basis. Accounting and other data may then be collected from such diverse locations and communicated to other sites for maintenance and analysis.

Operating system software is used to drive application programs like accounting systems software. The early computerised accounting systems based on traditional methodology may be criticised because of their narrow focus and their inability to extend across all other business functions. At the centre of such systems was the general ledger or nominal ledger. As its name implies, this held summary totals of transactions under each account heading, which does not facilitate detailed reporting. Additionally, these systems did not record and process data in real time; there were usually considerable time gaps between when transactions took place and when they were recorded, when they were processed, and when they could be reported on. Many systems were developed in parallel with general ledger systems like sales ordering, purchase ordering, fixed assets records, stocks management, personnel records, and so on. However, these were largely run as separate and independent systems with little integration.

General ledger, sales ledger and purchase ledger

The general ledger (GL) or nominal ledger was one of the first accounting software applications to be developed. Manual maintenance of GLs was very time-consuming and costly in terms of the staff required to carry out this function. GL software automates most of the features of the traditional manual bookkeeping approach and makes the process more efficient and reliable; it reduces the time spent in collecting transaction data and preparing financial statements.

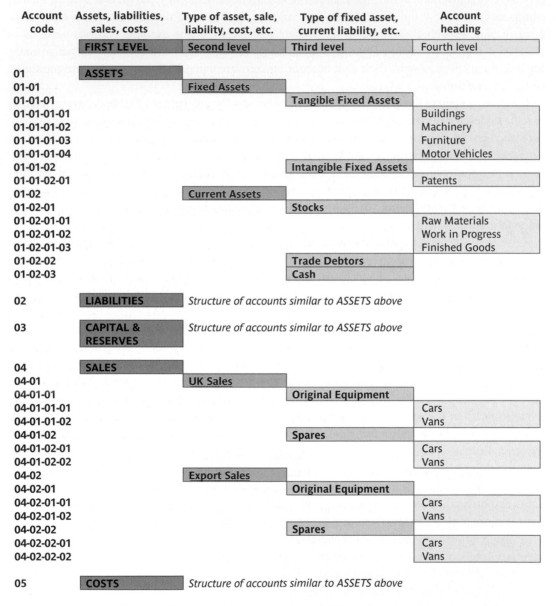

Account code	Assets, liabilities, sales, costs	Type of asset, sale, liability, cost, etc.	Type of fixed asset, current liability, etc.	Account heading
	FIRST LEVEL	Second level	Third level	Fourth level
01	ASSETS			
01-01		Fixed Assets		
01-01-01			Tangible Fixed Assets	
01-01-01-01				Buildings
01-01-01-02				Machinery
01-01-01-03				Furniture
01-01-01-04				Motor Vehicles
01-01-02			Intangible Fixed Assets	
01-01-02-01				Patents
01-02		Current Assets		
01-02-01			Stocks	
01-02-01-01				Raw Materials
01-02-01-02				Work in Progress
01-02-01-03				Finished Goods
01-02-02			Trade Debtors	
01-02-03			Cash	
02	LIABILITIES	*Structure of accounts similar to ASSETS above*		
03	CAPITAL & RESERVES	*Structure of accounts similar to ASSETS above*		
04	SALES			
04-01		UK Sales		
04-01-01			Original Equipment	
04-01-01-01				Cars
04-01-01-02				Vans
04-01-02			Spares	
04-01-02-01				Cars
04-01-02-02				Vans
04-02		Export Sales		
04-02-01			Original Equipment	
04-02-01-01				Cars
04-02-01-02				Vans
04-02-02			Spares	
04-02-02-01				Cars
04-02-02-02				Vans
05	COSTS	*Structure of accounts similar to ASSETS above*		

Figure 9.2 Extract of an example of a GL chart of accounts

A computerised GL requires the development of a chart of accounts, which is a coding scheme that uses numbers or letters to represent an account. For example, a range of numbers may be used for assets, liabilities, capital and reserves, sales and costs. A further range of numbers may relate to the different categories of assets, liabilities, etc., for example fixed assets, and current liabilities. A further range of numbers may relate to different types of fixed assets, current liabilities, etc., for example tangible fixed assets, and intangible fixed assets. A further range of numbers may relate to the different headings within tangible assets, and intangible assets, etc., for example land and buildings, and patents.

An example of this type of chart of accounts may, at the highest level, define assets as 01, liabilities as 02, capital and reserves as 03, sales as 04, and costs as 05. The further codings may then be cascaded down through the second, third, and fourth levels (and possibly more) of the chart of accounts, as shown in Fig. 9.2. The hierarchical coding structure enables ease of analysis.

Cash transactions, receipts and payments, were usually recorded in one or two accounts in the GL that were created for a bank account or overdraft. The details of these accounts showing the opening and closing balances, at the start and end of each accounting period, and the receipts and payments within each period were also recorded in a separate book of account, the cash book. On a regular basis it was necessary to manually reconcile each of the cash book balances with the balances on the accounts that represented them in the GL to ensure that there were no differences.

Alongside the general ledger, most of the early accounting software suites included subsidiary ledgers: sales ledgers (SL), which recorded all sales transactions with, and cash received from, customers; and purchase ledgers (PL), which recorded all purchase transactions with, and cash paid to, suppliers. These early SL and PL systems were not integrated with the GL but maintained separately (see Fig. 9.3). In the same way as with the cash book, this meant that their total balances at any one time required manual reconciliation with their respective control accounts in the GL. Within the sales and purchase ledgers, codings were required to uniquely identify customers and suppliers. For example, SL or AR may denote the sales ledger (or accounts receivable) and similarly PL or AP may denote the purchase ledger (or accounts payable). Therefore, for example, AR001, AR002, AR003 may define customers Abbott, Adams, and Alan, and PL001, PL002, PL003, for example, may define suppliers Abrahams, Appleby, and Ascot, and so on.

Fully integrated GL, SL and PL systems were soon developed which facilitated the recording of each transaction in the SL or PL, but at the same time simultaneously recording each sale, purchase and cash receipt and payment transaction in summary or in detail within the GL. This eliminated the need for the manual reconciliation of control account balances with the total balances of the subsidiary ledgers (SL and PL). Such fully-integrated accounting systems also included many other ledgers and books of account (see Fig. 9.4). An example of a fully-integrated computerised accounting system is Sage Sterling, which is distributed by the Sage Group plc.

Sage accounting software provides input forms for each module in the system, which are all screen-based, and which are completed using the computer mouse. The Sage modules also provide a screen-based numeric pad that enables simple calculations to be made at the appropriate points in the entry of transactions. At its basic level the Sage accounting software includes the following fully-integrated modules:

- sales ledger
- purchase ledger
- general ledger
- cash book
- stock control
- sales order processing and invoicing
- purchase order processing

- supplier invoice matching
- fixed assets register.

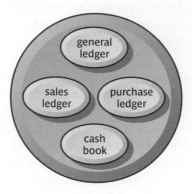

Figure 9.3 Traditional standalone computerised accounting systems

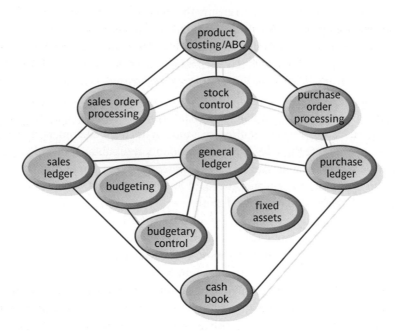

Figure 9.4 An integrated computerised accounting system

In addition, Sage Sterling provides audit trail reports and standard transaction and balance reports from each of the modules, as well as VAT reports, financial statement reporting of the profit and loss account and balance sheet, and a budgeting facility.

Stock control and distribution software

A stock control system is another subsidiary ledger like the sales ledger. Stock control software deals with the acquisition, storage, control, and movement of stocks:

- materials and components
- work in progress
- finished goods.

As with the SL and PL, such systems began as standalone systems that were not integrated with the GL, but were soon developed to allow the simultaneous recording of each transaction in stock control at the same time as recording each transaction in summary or in detail within the GL.

Many businesses have implemented even more sophisticated stock control systems that are also integrated with purchasing and manufacturing systems. This is to provide a higher level of control with the aim of ensuring that precise quantities of stocks are available in the right place at the right time without allowing any build up of unnecessary stocks. Such systems may, for example, involve the use of just in time (JIT), materials requirement planning (MRP), and manufacturing resource planning systems (MRPII), which are discussed later.

Warehousing and distribution systems have been developed to include much more than the recording of items in and out of warehouses. Bar coding systems allow individual stock items to be stamped with individual codings. The codings may be used to check items into the warehouse using fixed or remote scanners, and facilitate the checking of quantities of items held in various locations at any point in time. Bar coding systems may also be used to enable tracking systems to follow the movement of stocks out of one location and throughout their journey to their final destination.

Bar codings are also now widely used in the retail business. They may be used to check items into each store and also to record sales more efficiently and reliably by scanning items out as they are purchased by customers. In this way, these **electronic point of sale (EPOS)** systems as they are called, support the stock control systems but also provide important sales data that enable the business to develop a valuable information resource database. EPOS systems:

- provide the immediate updating of stock records so that stock-outs are avoided
- enable trends in sales of products to be identified, which is an extremely useful marketing tool
- enable consumer profiles and buying activities to be identified linking types of items sold with types of customer through links with customer store loyalty cards – another extremely useful marketing tool.

> **Progress check 9.2 What are the main aims of computerised stock control systems?**

Sales order processing and invoicing software

Sales order processing (SOP) software is used to process customer orders. Such systems are linked to the stock control system to provide details on numbers of stock items held and their availability. SOP systems are also supported by lists of the complete product range supplied by the business together with their selling prices, and customer account information, so that invoices may be produced for goods supplied and allowing for any special discounts given to specific customers. SOP systems are also linked with SL systems to enable sales invoices that have been produced from sales orders to be recorded within the relevant customer accounts and for the sales and VAT values of invoices to be recorded within the GL, via the SL. The SOP link with the stock control system ensures that sales of an item simultaneously reduce the stock numbers of that item.

Purchase order processing and supplier invoice matching software

Purchase order processing (POP) software is used to create and process orders for goods and services from suppliers. Such systems are linked to the stock control system to provide details on numbers of items already held and possibly their requirement in the foreseeable future. POP systems are also supported by lists of the complete range of items purchased by the business together with their contracted purchase prices, allowing for any trade discounts. When goods are received by the business they are booked into stock and their quantities checked against purchase orders. Invoice matching systems are used to match invoices with goods received and to check that correct prices have been charged by suppliers. These systems are also used to register suppliers' invoices and record them on the PL in the appropriate suppliers account, and for the costs of stock (and non-stock) items and VAT values of invoices to be recorded within the GL, via the PL. The POP link with the stock control system ensures that purchases of an item simultaneously increase the stock numbers of that item.

> **Progress check 9.3** With which other parts of an integrated accounting system should the sales order processing and purchase order processing software be linked and why?

Product costing systems software

Generally, product costs may be assembled to meet the following three requirements:

- stock valuation and internal and external profit measurement, by allocating costs between products sold and fully and partly completed products that are unsold
- provision of relevant information to help managers make better decisions, for example profitability analysis, product pricing, make or buy (or outsourcing), product mix and discontinuation
- provision of information for planning, control and performance measurement, for example long-term planning and short-term planning (budgeting), periodic performance reports for feedback control, and performance reports which are widely used to evaluate managerial performance.

Product costing software is used to maintain data relating to the complete range of finished and partly-completed products or services created and/or sold by the business, using a hierarchical coding system for materials, components, work-in-progress and finished products. Such systems may be linked to the SOP and POP systems and the stock control system to provide a valuation of these items of stock at any time in terms of cost or sales value. They may be linked to budgeting systems and systems used for the reporting of actual versus budget performance, and also to modelling and decision-making systems used for product sales pricing and other decision-making.

Activity based costing (ABC) software

➡ **ABC** software systems require the identification of the major processes or activities that take place in the organisation. The activities chosen should be at a reasonable level of aggregation based on cost/benefit criteria. The choice of activities is influenced by the total cost of the activity centre and the ability of a single cost driver to provide a satisfactory determinant of the cost of the activity. Costs are assigned to cost pools/cost centres for each activity. Costs assigned to activity cost pools include direct and indirect costs.

In the same way as traditional product costing, ABC software is used to maintain data relating to the complete range of finished and partly-completed products or services created and/or sold by the business. Such systems may be linked to budgeting systems and systems used for the reporting of actual versus budget performance, and also to modelling and decision-making systems used for product sales pricing and other decision-making. ABC may also be linked to the stock control system to provide a valuation of stock items.

> **Progress check 9.4 Discuss the benefits of a computerised ABC system compared with a traditional product costing system.**

Fixed assets register software

The fixed assets register is effectively another subsidiary ledger like the sales ledger. In the same way as the GL, SL, PL, and product costing/stock control systems, fixed assets software requires a coding system to define each category of asset, type of asset within categories and a unique code to identify each individual asset. The category and type codes may be linked to similar codes used within the GL. Fixed assets registers record the acquisition and disposal of fixed assets. They provide the facility to calculate depreciation values for each month and year of the asset's life (using whichever depreciation method may be appropriate) and calculate profits or losses arising when fixed assets are disposed of. As with the SL and PL, fixed assets register systems began as standalone systems that were not integrated with the GL, but were soon developed to allow the simultaneous recording of each transaction in the fixed asset register (acquisition, proceeds of disposal, depreciation, profit/loss on disposal) at the same time as recording each transaction in summary or in detail within the GL.

> **Progress check 9.5 Discuss the main features of a computerised fixed assets register and its many advantages over a manually prepared register.**

Budgeting and budgetary control software

Most software packages have a budgeting facility that is linked to the GL or a part of the GL, using the same coding structures as the GL and providing the same sort of reporting including the financial statements. Some budgeting packages allow budget data to be input for the budget period at the level of individual elements of cost, sale, asset, and liability, for each department of the business, and possibly for a number of companies within a group. Alternatively, departmental managers may use spreadsheets (see later) to prepare their individual, detailed sales and cost budgets, and details of their planned fixed asset additions/disposals and possibly their working capital requirements for the budget period.

The preparation of a master budget for the business, which provides a budgeted profit and loss account, balance sheet and cash flow statement for the budget period, may then be produced from the budgeting software either directly from input of budget data or from input or downloads of departmental spreadsheets.

After the budgeting process has been completed it is necessary to compare actual performance against the plan and a basis for comparison is usually established through the setting of predetermined cost estimates, for example using standard costing. Budgetary control software calculates and reports differences, or variances, between a planned, budgeted or standard cost or sale and the actual cost or sale, whose timely reporting should maximise the opportunity for managerial action. Variance analysis is the evaluation of performance by means of variances, which are either favourable variances (F) or adverse variances (A), and neither will occur if the standard is correct and actual performance is as expected.

The use of computers in the budget preparation process has made it much easier to manage. The resulting shorter budget preparation timeframes has also required much greater accuracy in estimating the data going into the **budget**. Many companies have developed dynamic budgeting models, using packaged IT solutions that may link both financial and non-financial performance measures.

> **Progress check 9.6** What have been the main advantages and disadvantages for businesses from the computerisation of budget preparation and budgetary control systems?

Consolidation software

Software packages have been developed to provide reporting at the highest level on a budget and actual basis for businesses that are comprised of a very large number of departments, divisions, or companies. Such software is rarely used for reporting totals below the departmental total level. Consolidation packages like Hyperion are primarily used in this way to consolidate, or accumulate, the financial results of a number of companies within a large group for specified accounting periods. Such software can make the consolidation adjustments that are necessary when combining the financial results of two or more companies within a group. This software is particularly useful for consolidating the results of companies, whose financial statements are denominated in a variety of different currencies, into the one common currency adopted for group reporting.

> **Progress check 9.7** What is consolidation software and how is it used by businesses?

Accounting software, and GL systems in particular, has been criticised for a number of reasons:

- the lack of real-time processing of data
- the narrow focus on financial data to the exclusion of important non-financial data
- the emphasis only on specific areas of the business's processes
- the summarisation of data
- the exclusion of much of the data surrounding a transaction (focusing primarily on dates and values)
- the focus primarily on one stakeholder perspective, namely the shareholder.

As a result, GL systems continue to be developed as organisations search for new methods for recording and reporting transaction data. Consequently, GL software is becoming a smaller percentage of the total of software applications. Very often, data from computerised manufacturing systems and other processes' systems are interfaced with GL packages.

Manufacturing and other processes

The development of accounting software over recent years has been extended to include the operational areas of design and development, engineering, manufacturing, and quality management. This area of IT has had a significant impact on organisations in the area of production management. Production processes may be evaluated and planned using production management system software.

These may also assist organisations in their design and implementation of more effective operational processes. The extensive use of IT assists organisations involved in such diverse industries as food, automotive manufacture, construction, and publishing, in their aim of minimising manufacturing costs whilst maintaining the highest levels of quality. IT now provides decision-makers with greater volumes of higher quality information with which to better manage such processes.

Organisational productivity tools are available which may be used to enhance processes and improve productivity. An example is the use of **workflow software**, which graphically represents, documents, and defines business processes. The software may then be used to analyse and automate business processes. Other examples of software development relating to operational processes, which have accounting implications, are:

- computer-aided design and manufacturing (CAD/CAM)
- computer-integrated manufacturing (CIM)
- computer-aided engineering (CAE)
- just in time (JIT)
- materials requirement planning (MRP)
- manufacturing resource planning (MRPII)
- quality management.

These areas of software development are important to the accounting function for a number of reasons, for example:

- appraisal of investments in manufacturing systems software requires an appreciation of their true costs and the benefits that may be derived
- an understanding of how such systems operate is necessary to develop the appropriate links with accounting and other systems
- appropriate performance measurement systems must be installed to evaluate the economic and managerial performance of such tools.

> **Progress check 9.8 Why do you think that the use of IT has been extended to include manufacturing and other operational processes?**

Computer-aided design and manufacturing (CAD/CAM) software

Computer-aided design (CAD) is a general term referring to software applications and the method used in art, architecture, engineering and manufacturing to design and provide precision drawings for objects such as buildings, machinery, components and other items, using a computer. Computer-aided manufacturing (CAM) is the use of computers for managing manufacturing processes. The standardisation of CAD/CAM systems now enables the interchange of design and manufacturing information between organisations, for example suppliers and customers.

Worked Example 9.1

It is possible for a designer and manufacturer of a seating system for a car manufactured by General Motors to ensure that it provides compatibility and a perfect fit for the vehicle in which it is intended.

The seating system supplier may exchange a three-dimensional CAD/CAM file that contains the detailed drawing of a seat with GM, who are then able to integrate it with their CAD/CAM system relating to the entire vehicle. Both GM and the seating system supplier may then ensure complete compatibility and fit with the intended vehicle. Both supplier and customer may then use this technology to ensure compliance with the original specification or to discuss and implement agreed deviations from it. The benefits from improved project management and the cost savings derived from the use of CAD/CAM systems are immense.

Computer-aided engineering (CAE) software

Computer-aided engineering (CAE) is the broad term used by the electronic design automation (EDA) industry for the use of computers to design, analyse, and manufacture products and processes, and includes computer-aided design (CAD – the use of a computer for drafting and modelling designs) and computer-aided manufacturing (CAM).

Computer-integrated manufacturing (CIM) software

Computer-integrated manufacturing (CIM) is the use of computers to give instructions that automatically set up and run manufacturing equipment. The costs involved in the setting up of a production process and the calibration of equipment have traditionally been very high. Reduction in set-up times is a key objective in most manufacturing organisations that can result in significant ongoing cost savings. Additionally, the use of robotic plant and equipment provides computer software to monitor the manufactured product and directly control processes, which ensures high quality manufacturing output that is defect-free.

There is extensive use of robotics in the automotive industry, the result of which has been to significantly reduce the amount of labour employed in manufacturing. Apart from the design and support of the software systems, manufacturing labour becomes increasingly focused on the areas of manufacturing engineering and maintenance of plant and equipment.

Just in time (JIT) software

Another key objective of most manufacturing businesses these days is to significantly reduce the amount of stocks required to be held in their warehouses and so reduce their operating costs. Coordination of shipments of goods to and from internal and external suppliers and customers can ensure that stocks are produced and/or delivered no sooner and no later than exactly when they are needed in exactly the right quantities required. The necessary level of coordination requires the use of sophisticated IT systems.

Just in time (JIT) software systems are sometimes referred to merely as stock reduction or zero stock systems. JIT is actually a management philosophy that has been developed in response to two key factors:

- the reduction in product life cycles
- the increase in levels of quality required from demanding customers.

Materials requirement planning (MRP), and its development into manufacturing resource planning (MRPII), are sometimes seen as alternatives to JIT, but in fact can be used to complement JIT systems.

Materials requirement planning (MRP) software

MRP software converts a production schedule into a listing of the materials and components required to meet that schedule, so that adequate stock levels are maintained and items are available when needed. MRP is a set of techniques, which uses the bill of materials (BOM), stock data and the master production schedule to calculate future requirements for materials. The master production schedule is a computerised time-phased statement of how many items are to be produced in a given period (like a giant timetable), based on customer orders and demand forecasts.

MRP software essentially makes recommendations to release material to the production system. MRP is a 'push' down approach that starts with forecasts of customer demand and then calculates and reconciles using basic mathematics. MRP relies on accurate BOMs and scheduling algorithms, EOQ (economic order quantity) analyses and allowances for wastage and shrinkage.

In a later section of this chapter on electronic data interchange (EDI) we will discuss how suppliers and customers may communicate using Internet technology. Increasing numbers of businesses now allow suppliers and customers to link into their systems via the Internet. For example, supply chain software modules enable companies to run their MRP systems in such a way that they may create purchase orders in the order processing systems of their suppliers.

Manufacturing resource planning (MRPII) software

MRPII software is effectively an expansion of material requirements planning (MRP) to give a broader approach than MRP to the planning and scheduling of resources, embracing areas of the business such as finance, logistics, engineering and marketing.

Quality management software

The most effective way of achieving the highest levels of quality is to design this into the products, through the use of CAD/CAM and techniques like **FMEA (failure mode and effect analysis)**. FMEA may be used in the design and development stage of a product to examine the various ways in which a product or service may fail and what the effect of each mode of failure will be. This technique leads to the identification of the most important possible modes of failure so that action may be taken to reduce the risks of those occurrences. FMEA is a Pareto analysis technique that focuses on the 'vital few' failure modes that relate to the majority of failures.

If it has not been possible to design total quality into the product then the safety net is the implementation of quality measurement systems that enable problems to be prevented or if they cannot be prevented then detected, or identified, and rectified so that they do not recur. In the area of manufacturing, computerised systems that use **SPC (statistical process control)** software aim at achieving the highest quality during manufacture through prevention rather than detection. SPC is used to control the processes used in making products. SPC computer software provides charts on which the performance of the process is plotted. If the process goes out of control then it can be stopped before many (if any) defective products are produced.

Cost of quality (COQ) is used to measure the difference between the actual costs incurred within each of the processes of manufacture and/or supply of goods, and services, and the equivalent costs if there were no failures within each of those processes. Standalone software systems may be used to analyse cost of quality, or these systems may be linked to the traditional costing systems so that costs may be linked to their appropriate COQ categories:

- costs of achieving quality – prevention costs and appraisal costs

- costs of not achieving quality – internal failure costs and external failure costs
- cost of exceeding requirements
- cost of lost opportunities.

> **Progress check 9.9** Explain how a computerised COQ system may help to achieve a large increase in the profitability of a business.

Enterprise resource planning (ERP) systems software

We have discussed the ways in which standalone accounting software systems such as the general ledger and sales ledger have been integrated, and then further integrated with for example sales order processing, sales invoicing and stock control.

We have also seen how software has been developed to encompass the whole range of organisational processes beyond payroll and accounting to include for example design, manufacturing, and quality management. Software is now available that provides full integration of an organisation's systems. Full integration of an organisation's systems may be achieved through the installation and implementation of enterprise resource planning (ERP) software. ERP systems provide software that is focused on processes spanning across functional boundaries, which are totally integrated, but at the same completely flexible. These processes include all of the software systems that we have discussed above.

The earliest ERP systems began with implementation by only the largest companies, but ERP packages are now also being installed by an increasing number of SMEs. These ERP packages comprise a number of individual modules, supporting a range of processes internal to the organisation including:

- supply chain management
- stocks management
- logistics
- human resource management
- finance
- accounting
- manufacturing planning
- sales
- distribution.

➡ ERP systems can facilitate the use of Internet and **intranet** resources, and also support processes external to the organisation that may facilitate information flows and global operations between the organisation and its trading partners, suppliers, and customers. ERP systems are provided by software providers like, for example, PeopleSoft, SAP, Oracle, and JD Edwards.

Unfortunately, due to the complexity of ERP systems it is often necessary for organisations to adapt the way in which they operate to meet the system requirements rather than receive a system that is tailored to their needs. This may provide benefits to the organisation from changing its business processes in line with 'best practice' rather than continuing with organisational methods that may be out of date and no longer appropriate. Another advantage of this is the lower cost of the software and its implementation.

From the outset, computerised accounting systems have provided great benefits from the fact that data are only required to be entered, or input once and then used in many ways. The verification and validation checks provided by the systems mean that there are fewer errors and corrections made, and greater accuracy in the recorded data. This compares with the manual systems in which data may have been entered many times into their various sub-systems, and with a high likelihood of error.

A further benefit of computerised accounting systems is achieved from the facility to 'close the books' if not at the end of the last day of an accounting period then very soon afterwards. Most ERP systems are real time systems and so monthly, weekly, and even daily reporting is possible, which is a great aid to decision-making and provides a further justification for the cost of ERP implementation and development.

> **Progress check 9.10 What are the benefits of ERP systems, which may be weighed against their costs of implementation and support?**

Spreadsheets

At the start of the 1980s PC technology really took off because of the interest of home users in computer games and the interest of business users in word processing and spreadsheets. The spreadsheet replicated the accountant's paper analysis pad of rows and columns, which was used for numbers and text. The computerised spreadsheet additionally has a calendar, and a calculator and a host of accounting, mathematical, statistical and scientific functions used for quite complex calculations and to enable ease of handling and manipulation of data.

The ground-breaking Sinclair Spectrum computer even had a very simple spreadsheet application. But it was the spreadsheet called VisiCalc that ran on the Apple II computer, which paved the way for the future development of spreadsheet technology. VisiCalc, which was created and developed by Mitch Kapor at VisiCorp, really captured the imagination of the business world by showing how simple 'what-if' scenarios could be provided by changing one or more variables within the spreadsheet. Mitch Kapor soon left VisiCorp to set up the Lotus Development Corporation which then released Lotus 123™ to be run on the newly developed IBM PCs.

The success of Lotus 123™ was astronomical and led the way for yet further development of spreadsheet technology. By the late 1980s Microsoft Excel, which included all the features of Lotus and more, became extremely popular and has long since eclipsed the early success of Lotus 123™. Microsoft Excel has now replaced Lotus 123™ as the leading spreadsheet software and is used in a wide variety of ways for analysis and support for decision-making.

The additional features that have taken spreadsheets on to a level that is far higher than that of the first computerised spreadsheets include:

- the use of graphics for enhancement of analytical presentations
- the vast range of mathematical, statistical and financial functions for increasingly complex calculations
- macros to enable automation of many calculation processes
- the ability to link and 'layer' spreadsheets, making them effectively three-dimensional
- the ability to link spreadsheets and embed spreadsheets in other application software like word processing and presentations.

The Excel spreadsheet software is now currently so successful that most modern ERP systems include automatic downloads of any report into Excel. Some ERP packages actually have Excel embedded within their systems to take care of their reporting requirements.

In the area of accounting and finance, the spreadsheet is now used in so many useful ways that makes it an indispensable tool. Indeed, it is easy to forget a world without spreadsheets and how tedious were the tasks, which could only be carried out manually.

Some of the key areas of use of spreadsheets in accounting and finance are:

- depreciation, including for example
  - straight line depreciation
  - reducing balance depreciation
- break-even analysis, including for example
  - break-even sales volume calculations
  - break-even sales value calculations
  - margin of safety calculations
  - sensitivity analysis, for example the impact on the break-even point of changes in selling price, changes in variable costs, changes in volumes, changes in fixed costs
- budgeting, including for example
  - extensions of selling prices and sales volumes to produce a sales budget
  - extensions of product costs and production volumes to produce a production budget
  - preparation of a company profit and loss account budget from detailed departmental budgets of sales and costs
  - budgeted balance sheet using data from the budgeted profit and loss account, capital expenditure, financing, and working capital relationships
  - sensitivity analysis, for example the impact on profit of changes in sales prices or demand volumes
  - three-dimensional spreadsheets for modelling, and consolidation of multi-company organisations into group budgets
  - flexed budgets
  - variance analysis
- financing, including for example
  - interest calculations
  - lease amortisations
- capital investment appraisal, including for example
  - net present values (NPV)
  - internal rate of return (IRR)
  - sensitivity analysis, for example the impact on NPV on changes in investment values and lives, discount rates, and cash flows.

> **Progress check 9.11** Explain, giving examples, in what ways spreadsheet technology has been developed over the past 30 years to provide the indispensable accountants' tool it has now become.

You may find it useful to re-visit some of the Worked Examples in earlier chapters of this book to see how the solutions may be simplified through use of the appropriate spreadsheet features. The following Worked Example 9.2 illustrates the use of Excel spreadsheets in depreciation calculations.

Worked Example 9.2

Please refer to Chapter 3 Depreciation, Worked Example 3.6.

Castle Ltd purchases an item of equipment for £16,000 and estimates its residual value, at the end of its useful economic life of five years, at £1,000. At the start of year one the net book value (NBV) is the acquisition cost of the asset £16,000.

The different net book values may be calculated from using the appropriate spreadsheet functions (see Fig. 9.5) for each of the alternative depreciation methods of:

- straight line
- reducing balance.

	A	B	C	D	E	F	G
1	**straight line depreciation**						
2	@SLN(cost, residual value, useful life of asset)						
3	cost		£16,000				
4	useful life of asset		5	years			
5	residual value		£1,000				
6							
7	depreciation per year	=	@SLN(+C3, +C5, +C4)				
8		=	@SLN(16000, 1000,5)		=	£3,000	per month
9	total depreciation	=	+F8*C4	+3000*5	=	£15,000	

	A	B	C	D	E	F	G
1	**reducing balance depreciation**						
2	@DB(cost, residual value, useful life of asset, year, months in first year)						
3	cost		£16,000				
4	useful life of asset		5	years			
5	residual value		£1,000				
6	months in first year		12				
7							
8	depreciation 1st year	=	@DB(+C3, +C5, +C4, 1, +C6)				
9		=	@DB(16000, 1000,5, 1, 12)		=	£6,816.00	
10	depreciation 2nd year	=	@DB(+C3, +C5, +C4, 2, +C6)				
11		=	@DB(16000, 1000,5, 2, 12)		=	£3,912.38	
12	depreciation 3rd year	=	@DB(+C3, +C5, +C4, 3, +C6)				
13		=	@DB(16000, 1000,5, 3, 12)		=	£2,245.71	
14	depreciation 4th year	=	@DB(+C3, +C5, +C4, 4, +C6)				
15		=	@DB(16000, 1000,5, 4, 12)		=	£1,289.04	
16	depreciation 5th year	=	@DB(+C3, +C5, +C4, 5, +C6)				
17		=	@DB(16000, 1000,5, 5, 12)		=	£739.91	
18	total depreciation	=	+F9+F11+F13+F15+F17		=	£15,003.04	
19				or approximately		£15,000	

Figure 9.5 Castle Ltd straight line and reducing balance depreciation Excel model

The spreadsheet solution to Worked Example 9.2 may be downloaded from the OLC that supports this book (www.mcgraw-hill.co.uk/textbooks/davies).

Databases

Relational database management systems (DBMS) have been developed to set up relationships between different kinds of data. A DBMS system like Microsoft Access enables different types of data to be linked from which reports may be generated.

Relational databases organise and store data in two-dimensional tables of rows and columns. The rows are called records, which may contain a number of columns or fields. Each row is divided into cells that contain a single piece of data. Fields separate the different types of data. When a table is created, the fields are required to be named and with a designation of what type of data they contain. The type of data establishes the amount of storage reserved for the field content and specifies the types of formatting and mathematical or logical operations that can be performed on the data.

Data may be text, numbers, dates, times, or currency. For example:

- a sales invoicing table may list
  - invoice numbers
  - invoice dates
  - customer names
- a customer table may list
  - customer names
  - telephone numbers
- a product table may list
  - product codes
  - product descriptions
  - unit selling prices
- a product sales table may list
  - invoice numbers
  - product codes
  - numbers of products sold.

Each of the above examples is shown in tabular format in Fig. 9.6.

A database may be individually updated and used to provide reports. It may also be linked with many other different external databases. A relational DBMS is very powerful because it can maintain several tables of related information that can be accessed by several different users in several different ways. The data items from the various tables shown in Fig. 9.6 can be used to provide reports like the examples shown in Figs. 9.7 and 9.8.

It can be seen from the reports in Figs. 9.7 and 9.8 that data has been linked from each of the tables to produce the reports, and additional data created by using database instructions or functions. In the examples, the multiplication and addition functions have been used to create calculated columns for total balance, and total sales, and the report totals in both reports.

A disadvantage of a relational DBMS is that its *ad hoc* search ability uses a large amount of the computer's resources. This may result in an increasing loss of computer efficiency as the number of data tables increases.

Customer	
Name	**Phone Number**
Bloggs	01564239989
Rabbit	02453548990

Sales Invoicing		
Invoice Number	**Invoice Date**	**Customer Name**
1234	01Apr2004	Bloggs
2345	05Apr2004	Rabbit

Product		
Product Code	**Product Description**	**Unit Selling Price**
AGR	fridge	£200
GMK	oven	£250

Product Sales		
Invoice Number	**Product Code**	**Numbers Sold**
1234	AGR	12
2345	GMK	10

Figure 9.6 Example of relational DBMS tables

Customer Total Balances at 30 April 2004		
Customer Name	**Phone Number**	**Total Balance**
Bloggs	01564239989	£2,400
Rabbit	02453548990	£2,500
Total		**£4,900**

Figure 9.7 Example of a customer total balance report

Customer Sales During April 2004						
Customer Name	**Product Code**	**Product Description**	**Unit Selling Price**	**Number Sold**	**Total Sales**	**Invoice Number**
Bloggs	AGR	fridge	£200	12	£2,400	1234
Rabbit	GMK	oven	£250	10	£2,500	2345
Total					**£4,900**	

Figure 9.8 Example of a sales report by customer

> **Progress check 9.12 What is a database? Discuss how a database may be used effectively by an organisation and the circumstances when it may cease to be an effective tool.**

Communicating and presenting information

IT can be seen to have made a tremendous contribution to the recording, processing and analysis of accounting and financial data. IT has simplified accounting tasks and provided greater accuracy and speed in the processing and reporting of information. In parallel with the development of accounting and operations software, databases, and spreadsheets, there has been an increasing additional requirement to communicate accounting and financial information to people through speeches, presentations, lectures, seminars, workshops, etc. Powerful graphics tools have been developed to present ideas and concepts to people either directly using computer projections or via websites. These tools have made accounting information easier to understand and more accessible to a much wider audience, in areas like employee communication, training, and education.

An example of a presentation graphics program is Microsoft PowerPoint, which enables the creation of computerised slide shows that include text, numbers, pictures, and sound effects, using a range of designs, layouts and formats. Graphics programs like PowerPoint may also be enhanced though the integration of multimedia effects including music, clip art, and video. Wider audiences may be reached using broadcasting to an intranet either live or for later viewing. Even wider audiences may be reached through the delivery of web-based presentations.

Software developers like Lotus and Microsoft have enhanced and adapted some of their products to provide what is called **groupware** such as Lotus Notes and Microsoft Exchange, which enables organisational tasks to be worked on and completed using a team approach. Such software may be adopted by users who work individually, or in groups or teams, to coordinate efforts and collaborate on various tasks and projects, and may support collaborative decision-making. Groupware activities may also incorporate interactive group meetings and videoconferencing.

Other applications

There are a number of further areas in accounting and finance on which IT has an impact.

Personal income tax

Since self-assessment was introduced for personal income taxation by the Inland Revenue a few years ago there has been an increasing endeavour to persuade individuals to complete and process their self-assessment returns **online**.

Value added tax (VAT)

Businesses which are registered for VAT complete VAT returns either monthly or quarterly and either pay/receive the balance on their VAT account to/from HMCE (Her Majesty's Customs and Excise) depending on whether their input VAT is less than or greater than their output VAT for the period. HMCE inspectors visit VAT registered businesses periodically to carry out audits of their VAT records and accounts. HMCE are now able to access most organisations' computer systems directly to read the appropriate files and provide an audit and analysis of transactions using their own VAT audit software.

Annual accounts audit

An annual audit of their accounts is a statutory requirement for all limited companies, except for those currently having an annual turnover of less than £5.6 million and a balance sheet total of less than £2.8 million. For firms of accountants that are appointed by the shareholders of companies to carry out the annual audits this was traditionally a very labour intensive and time-consuming task. Their task was particularly onerous before accounting software was introduced by companies to replace their manual accounting systems. However, since accounting systems began to be computerised the focus of the audit has changed. Traditionally, the audit involved the testing of large samples of accounting transactions to verify their accuracy and authenticity and the ticking of transactions against their entries in the ledgers and books of account.

The introduction of computerised accounting systems has resulted instead in audit firms auditing the computer systems to ensure they provide accurate processing and adequate controls, together with reviews of much smaller samples of transactions to verify their accuracy and correct processing. In addition, audit firms have developed their own audit system software that is able to access companies computer systems directly to read the appropriate files and provide an audit of a company's computer systems and analyses of transaction samples.

Risk management

In an increasingly uncertain world the management of risk is becoming a very high profile responsibility with which company accountants and finance directors are particularly concerned. Consultancy firms that specialise in risk assessment and risk management use software that enables them, for example, to analyse areas of risk in terms of their likelihood or probability of occurrence and the significance or the impact of their occurrence on the business. Risk analysis may then identify the appropriate actions a business may implement to minimise its exposure.

Knowledge management

We have seen how accounting systems software (and other personal and business software with which it is associated) that were initially developed as standalone have increasingly become integrated – note ERP systems and groupware. At the same time, the unprecedented growth in IT in the areas of computerisation and communications has overwhelmed both individuals and organisations with the volume of data and information available from seemingly limitless sources. This presents a new challenge in how to ensure that useful information is easily accessible and how effectively it may be used. Effective use of useful information increasingly becomes more important than simply producing more information. To this end what is termed knowledge management software has become very important.

Knowledge management emerged as a discipline in the mid-1990s primarily as a response to the destruction by business process engineering (BPR) of accumulated knowledge and experience, informal networks and rules of thumb that enable organisations to function effectively. Its focus has now moved to include human capital as well as intellectual capital. The aim of knowledge management systems software is to identify and locate the useful knowledge that may be gleaned from the mass of information that individuals and organisations are now able to produce. Knowledge management promises better access to the knowledge and experience of individuals leading to greater innovation and protection against the risk of loss of vital business information. Knowledge management fails if there is a breakdown in information-sharing and interpretation, and if there is information overload.

> **Progress check 9.13 Discuss the benefits that may be achieved both by their clients and from audit firms as a result of their implementation of computerised audit systems.**

The new economy

Accountants and accounting systems have needed to change as technological development has created the basis for the emergence of the 'new economy'. Any new economy occurs when the normal progress of the economy is disturbed to the extent that there is a fundamental change in its structure. We have seen this in the past in the invention of the wheel, the industrial revolution, and the development of steam power and of electricity. The current 'new economy' has emerged throughout the latter part of the twentieth century and the start of the twenty-first century from the advances in IT, particularly in the development of the computer chip, telecommunications, and the Internet, and their impact on the economic environment in which organisations operate.

E-business

E-business (electronic business) is generally considered to relate to the ways in which the Internet impacts on organisations. It is normally used to broadly describe the ways in which technology has changed the economic environment and the ways in which businesses operate. The impact of the development of IT in e-business is seen in communication, new product development, sales and marketing, manufacturing, quality management, customer service, and the various service functions that support the operations of the organisation.

The use of e-business requires new skills to be acquired by managers of organisations. Accounting and financial techniques have in the past traditionally focused on the internal aspects of the organisation. E-business requires a shift of emphasis to include the external relationships between the organisation and its customers and suppliers, and other business partners.

E-commerce

Organisations may provide internal networks, or intranets, that use Internet technologies so that their users, for example employees, may find, use and share documents and webpages. They may also use **extranets** in a similar way to communicate both privately and selectively with their customers. An extranet is really a part of the organisation's intranet that is extended to users outside the organisation.

E-commerce (electronic commerce) is a term that is normally used with regard to the parts of e-business that are concerned with the use of IT for business-to-business transactions (as distinct from business-to-customer transactions) between an organisation and its suppliers and customers. E-commerce includes the sharing and transfer of information between the organisation and its suppliers and customers, for example details, specifications and prices about products and services. E-commerce includes the use of IT in the commercial transactions of selling and buying products and services. The major advantages of e-commerce can be seen in the way that it enables:

- information, goods and service transactions to be made 24 hours a day, 365 days a year
- expansion of the scope of business to encompass global markets.

E-commerce transactions include much business-sensitive and confidential information. It is therefore of paramount importance that all parties to e-commerce transactions are confident that they are properly controlled in terms of security, accuracy and reliability. It is essential that the **Internet service providers** (ISPs) that facilitate e-commerce transactions ensure its availability with acceptable response times on a 24/7 basis.

The key tools of e-commerce are websites, **electronic data interchange (EDI)**, **electronic funds transfer (EFT)** and electronic mail (email).

Websites

A website is a related collection of World Wide Web (www) computer files with a unique reference address or **url (uniform resource locator)**. Organisations have created and developed their websites with increasing creativity. This has enabled them to present and advertise themselves and the products and services they can offer in ways that are informative and attention-grabbing.

In the early days of website development, their success was seen in the number of 'hits' or visits to the website by individuals or organisations using the Internet. This measure gave an indication of the level of awareness about the organisation and the level of potential interest in what it had to offer. Websites remain a rich source of information. Examples include the very useful government information websites like www.ukonlineforbusiness.gov.uk and www.dti.gov.uk, professional websites like www.cimaglobal.com and www.icaew.co.uk, and news information and journals websites like www.businessweek.com and www.reuters.com.

Websites are also a valuable marketing tool for advertising and promotion and facilitate communication to markets on both a national and a global level. In addition, and increasingly, websites have become the vehicle for consumer-to-business transactions. One of the first uses was sale of books (e.g. Amazon on www.amazon.com). Online book sales was quickly followed by other businesses, for example the banking industry, which introduced online banking (e.g. the HSBC bank on www.hsbc.co.uk) and the tourism industry for online accommodation bookings (e.g. the Wales Tourist Board www.wtbonline.gov.uk).

There were initial problems in the early days of selling online by dot.com businesses, mainly due to the enthusiasm and eagerness to be first in the marketplace. Many dot.com businesses had the front ends of their systems developed by web designers as standalone applications. This meant that potential customers saw what looked like fully-integrated web-linked order, invoice, delivery and payment systems, but in fact they were front-end systems only, which were supported by armies of clerks employed to re-key data into the support systems. The heavy staffing requirements probably contributed in some way to the many dot.com failures in the late 1990s and the early part of the twenty-first century.

Videoconferencing

Videoconferencing has been a business communications tool that has been in use since the early 1980s. Its increase in sophistication and ease of use has been matched by its greatly reduced cost to now make it a viable alternative to the high cost of air travel and accommodation and the logistical problems of arranging meetings, for example, to resolve problems or to present financial or other information.

The early days of videoconferencing involved the use of dedicated videoconference suites, very expensive hardware and dedicated communications lines. It is now possible to obtain very cheap kit that uses standard telecommunications connections to provide high quality videoconference facilities almost anywhere and at any time. The accounting implications, particularly for large multinational companies, include the huge cost savings achieved from fewer face-to-face meetings. They also include the vast savings in time and cost in situations, for example, where technical staff who are based in many different locations may all be working on a major project; design and engineering problems can be speedily resolved so that project costs are reduced and the project lead times cut to an absolute minimum.

Electronic data interchange (EDI)

Electronic data interchange (EDI) is a form of e-commerce that is used to improve the relationships between sellers and buyers. EDI enables transmission of data between or within organisations in structured formats that allow it to be retrieved by their computer systems and may be used for sales order processing and invoicing, purchase order processing, cash payments, and cash receipts. It is different from fax or simple text email messages, which are not in structured formats. EDI data is usually presented in batches for transmission between businesses compared with the interactive customer/business transactions that currently take place via websites.

A key feature of EDI systems is the disappearance of the need for paper trails for sales and purchase order, invoice, delivery, and receipt transactions, and the need for EDI-specific computer hardware and software. The structured transmission formats comply with standards like, for example, EDIFACT (Electronic Data Interchange for Administration, Commerce, and Transport), which therefore allow the transmission and receipt of data between different configurations of hardware and software within the user organisations. The application software of the user organisations then enables EDI data to be input and processed by the appropriate systems. EDI users may communicate directly or via third party providers that enable connectivity between the various users.

EDI appears to rely on complicated behind-the-scenes activities, but the development of Internet processes has simplified EDI usage and its implementation. This has resulted in a number of major advantages gained from the use of EDI from:

- reduction in errors
- reduction in the use of paper documentation
- reduction in mail and telephone costs
- considerable reduction in costs of transactions.

As well as large corporations, EDI may be used to advantage by even the smallest businesses with a minimum investment. The major benefits of EDI can be classified as business benefits and also supply chain benefits. Business benefits include:

- more efficient purchasing, production scheduling, stock control and order fulfillment resulting in reduced ordering costs, labour costs and stockholding costs and increased customer satisfaction
- increased competitiveness from better product availability and pricing information, reduced lead times, more reliable and accurate delivery, and the passing on of internal savings to customers, and a reduction in out-of-stock items
- reduction of human error since there is no re-keying of data
- time saved from automation of routine tasks such as ordering time for ordering staff to be engaged in other functions
- a reduction in the operating cycle from production to final cash inflow, resulting in lower costs and improved cash flow.

Supply chain benefits include:

- expansion of potential markets through global trading 24 hours a day, 365 days a year
- increased trust between partners in the supply chain built from a commitment to share information and to work collaboratively through the EDI links
- greater speed and accuracy enabling EDI to support the implementation of just in time (JIT) systems

- a broadening of the trading base through links with existing supply chains that are already using EDI, and may insist on it as a requirement for doing business with them.

A note of caution should be mentioned with regard to the implementation of EDI systems. The risks arising out of the EDI systems' ability to guarantee the transmission of complete and accurate data together with its verification of their authenticity, must be considered by the system designers. It is crucial that user organisations also put in place appropriate procedures for limiting authorised access to the EDI systems and for error detection and correction.

Electronic funds transfer (EFT)

Electronic funds transfer (EFT) is a system used by banks for the movement of funds between accounts and for the provision of services to the customer. EFT uses a different set of standards for the control of transmission of financial data. The **bankers automated clearing services (BACS)** system was one of the earliest EFT systems to be developed in the UK. It is an electronic bulk clearing system used by banks and building societies for low value and/or repetitive items such as standing orders, direct debits and automated payments such as salary and suppliers payments made by their customers.

EFT methods have the same risks as EDI but with the additional risk of possible fraudulent transfers of funds. However, EFT transfers do reduce human involvement with cash if customers pay directly into the selling organisation's bank account, and if the organisation pays directly into a supplier or employee bank account.

Electronic mail (email)

Electronic mail, or email, enables any person with Internet access to send and receive written messages, together with attached files of text and numeric data and both still and moving images, to and from any other person with Internet access, anywhere in the world, and almost instantaneously.

Over recent years, there has been a massive increase in the volume of electronic exchanges involving commercial and legal transactions, documents, funds, and the whole range of text and numeric data. This has necessitated a requirement for greater emphasis on security of information against unauthorised access, **hackers** (malicious intruders) and the receipt of **spam** or unwanted emails.

Information security is critical to business organisations (as well as home users) and so security software packages are now an essential element in the management and control of this area of risk. The different types of information security devices include, for example, physical controls, **encryption**, **intrusion detection software**, **firewalls**, and anti-virus software.

Computer security

Unauthorised access to computers is a serious, major problem, from which even the largest organisations and most sophisticated systems are not immune. The mighty Microsoft Corporation, for example, has had its computer security attacked (see the press extract below which shows that even Bill Gates has protection problems).

Microsoft security protection problems

IN OCTOBER 2000 MICROSOFT called in the FBI to investigate one of the most embarrassing breaches of computer security in corporate history. Hackers were reported to have copied the source code blueprints of the latest versions of its flagship Windows and Office products, which are installed on 90 per cent of the world's personal computers.

The break-in was discovered when security employees detected passwords being sent to an email account in St Petersburg while electronic footprints showed that the passwords had been used to transfer source code outside Microsoft's campus at Redmond, near Seattle.

The company had been frequently castigated for the security of its own products, so the news came as little surprise within the computer industry, but the feeling remains that if the world's largest software company can be breached, then it must be easy to get into smaller businesses.

The area of security has remained a hot topic since, despite it being shrouded in secrecy with most companies trying to hush up any breaches. But essentially the aims remain the same: to protect against internal and external threats.

According to Paul King, a senior consultant at Cisco, securing a business begins not with technology, but by setting out the ground rules. 'A security policy is where it starts,' says Mr King. 'If you haven't got one it all breaks down.'

For example, a company may provide its staff with Internet access. But does it allow uncensored use or does it control the sites its employees visit? 'The bigger problem is not just having a policy, but making sure your employees know about it,' adds Mr King.

'If you're a small 30-user software development company in California you may allow unrestricted access to do what they like. But you could be a big law firm and there might be legal risks to that stance. You might say 'our policy is that we allow access to the Internet but don't go to non-business sites'.

Everyone understands that. On top of the policy you might have URL logging where you say you'll record the sites people are visiting and go through the logs, or you could block sites and hope the software is good enough.'

Another policy might outline how staff access the internal network. If they are sitting inside the company, most staff will probably be allowed access without using encryption, a code which only allows those authorised to unscramble the message.

However, if someone is working from home, say, the policy most companies will have is that the employee can only access the network through an encrypted virtual private network (VPN), more of which later.

It is on top of these basic rules that the rest of the security system is based and it takes on many levels. This process is known as 'defence in depth' which sounds like a catchphrase that George Graham might once have used but Tom Scholtz, an analyst with technology researcher the Meta Group, explains: 'It is best practice [within large companies] to develop a policy and then implement different layers of security technology. But in the case of small companies, defence in depth is often more than they need.'

The level of security a company requires depends on how much confidential information it holds and the value of the transactions it conducts online, Mr Scholtz says. Because smaller companies often will not have security experts internally they will typically buy products as part of a bundle from their existing network supplier. 'Small businesses need to make sure they understand what this entails because otherwise they end up with inappropriate products being pushed on them,' he adds. 'Too many products and it will cost too much. Nothing comes for free.'

Still, most smaller companies will begin with perimeter security which is generally seen as the first line of defence. One of the most common technologies used is the firewall – which is essentially a fence which sits between the internal and external network and prevents and detects any security attacks.

On top of that, anti-virus software on PCs will detect intrusions from trojans (a piece of code which appears to be harmless but allows an outsider to access a network or PC). This is the most common way hackers penetrate systems and was the method successfully employed by the Microsoft hackers.

But despite the front page news when a system is broken, it is estimated that up to 80% of crimes are committed by insiders. The same principle of layered security applies within a company.

Employees will have different requirements depending on their status. For example, only the human resources department should be able to alter salary details, but a manager may need to see the details before an appraisal.

Most commonly a company makes sure the right people have access through a username and a password, but this method has its weaknesses as users can easily forget them or they can be intercepted.

The next level identifies users not only by what they know (username and password) but also by what they have, for example a key fob which generates a one-off pin number each time they log on.

If that method is not secure enough, companies can employ an even more sophisticated method called biometrics, which includes eye and fingerprint scanning. However, this is currently far too costly for most businesses.

For added security information is often encrypted as it is sent and received. This is particularly true for access to the system from outside the company and, with the current trend towards employees working from outside the office, the most common solution is to set up a VPN.

A VPN is essentially a private network that uses the Internet, thereby avoiding the costs of leasing a private line. To maintain privacy VPNs use access control and encryption, so they can exchange information privately.

The final security layer usually contains monitoring software, which checks the network for faults and reports on any breaches. However, these products need interpreting and therefore can be costly for smaller companies to deploy.

Still, cost should not be an inhibitor to securing a small business. According to a recent white paper by technology researcher Ovum, throwing lots of money at security is no answer. 'The key to successful security is planning and assessment,' it states. 'Many of the most effective steps you can take do not require expensive products, although some will be needed within a comprehensive strategy.'

Safety begins with rules, not technology, by Simon Goodley

© *Daily Telegraph*, 13 January 2004

Security covers many aspects of computer hardware, software and communications. It relates to the physical security of the computer hardware itself, and the risk of it being easily stolen or damaged. Security relates to ensuring that regular back-ups of data are regularly and frequently carried out and securely stored away from the premises where the business normally operates. Security relates to control of the ways in which confidential information may be copied on to removable disks and CDs, or downloaded on to laptops, all of which may easily be stolen. Encryption technology may be used to secure data in the case of physical theft.

Encryption is one of the best ways to protect highly confidential and sensitive information from being stolen. Encryption is a process, which is used to encode data that is entered into a system, and storing or transmitting the data in coded form, and then decoding the data when it arrives at its destination. Encryption therefore provides security through preventing unauthorised access to data while it is being stored or transmitted and before it reaches its required destination.

Public key encryption is widely used to ensure privacy and protect data in the e-business environment. The users who are communicating each have a key, one of which is publicly known and the other of which is private. The relationship between the keys is such that if one key locks data then the other key must be used to unlock it. Encryption may be used for securing files of data and also for data handled via the Internet.

Physical information security controls relate to how a company or an individual's computer system is accessed. Such controls are concerned with access to computer resources. It is essential that only those people who are authorised to do so have access to, and are able to communicate via, the computers and servers that hold sensitive information. Access may be controlled using unique user IDs and **passwords** at a number of levels:

- computer rooms housing the computers and peripheral equipment
- computer hardware
- operating software
- application software
- e-business resources, such as email, EFT and EDI software.

Passwords are most effective if they contain a random set of alphanumeric characters, and not names, places or dates of birth, although these may not be so easy for users to remember. Passwords should be changed on a regular basis and never disclosed by one user to another.

Intrusion detection software packages are designed to detect intrusion of entrance to systems. They monitor the entire computer system continuously and notify users if the system has been entered without authorisation or if the system is being used inappropriately. In a business environment pre-defined levels of management may be alerted if the systems for which they are responsible, for example, have received many unsuccessful attempts at access, or have had orders processed with zero or non-standard selling prices. Intrusion detection software may also be reactive in limiting the access of a possible intruder to the system and by the immediate locking of the system. The system is then only unlocked after the problem has been resolved by the network administrator.

Firewall software applications are designed to block unauthorised access to files, directories and networks. Firewalls are a must for e-business users and are used extensively in both the business and home use environment. Firewalls are extremely effective but may only provide security if they are correctly configured; many businesses that use firewalls may still be exposed to unauthorised access. Firewalls are also vulnerable to hackers (malicious intruders to computer systems). Hackers may find a way into a system that may be password deficient in just one area, and then gain entry to try and access and transfer funds or change numbers or text in accounts, email or other electronic transactions. The firewall itself then becomes completely ineffective.

Computer **viruses** are software programs that may infect computer files in a number of ways. Viruses may infect the system that boots up the computer system and runs its operating software; they may also infect the files of the operating software itself. Both types of virus may create virus files by changing file extensions like .exe or .com and making new files with the same names but different file extensions. Computer viruses are designed to replicate themselves and to spread from one location to another without the knowledge of the users; they may spread within a standalone computer system, or throughout a network or from one system to many external systems via the Internet. Virus-infected files are used to instruct computer systems to change, reformat, or delete important programs or data. Computer **worms** are the same as computer viruses except that they do not replicate themselves. Worms are created to change or delete data within a system.

It is essential for both commercial and home use of electronic communications and e-business to protect themselves by installing anti-virus and anti-worm software, and/or intrusion detection software. However, there are tens of thousands of computer viruses or worms currently in existence and the number is always increasing with new viruses and worms being discovered each day. Consequently, computer users are never one 100% protected from all viruses and worms, and therefore protection software must be frequently and regularly updated. A number of software companies provide such software updates that may be freely downloaded from their websites. Examples are Grisoft Incs AVG anti-virus software and McAfee Stinger software, which detects and removes specific viruses that may exist within a computer system.

Data protection

The use of data and information has been discussed in various parts of this book, particularly with regard to decision-making. Some information relates to data about individuals. The Data Protection Act 1998, effective from 1 March 2000, is designed to protect personal information held about individuals who are alive, and is used to regulate the processing of that data.

This Act implements part of the European Convention on Human Rights. It applies only to data and information about an individual (called a data subject) that all companies and organisations may record and store, either manually or electronically, for example name; address; personal reference number. The Act applies to personal details about employees, clients, customers and other third parties, but does not apply to non-personal data, such as data and information relating to other businesses.

There are eight principles within the Data Protection Act 1998, which are based on three key concepts:

- data held only for a clear purpose
- fairness
- transparency.

The principles state that personal data must:

1. be processed fairly and lawfully
2. be obtained only for one or more specified and lawful purposes
3. be adequate, relevant and not excessive
4. be accurate and kept up-to-date where necessary
5. not be kept for longer than necessary
6. be processed in accordance with the rights of data subjects under the Act, for example right of access, and the right to prevent processing for the purposes of direct marketing
7. be protected by appropriate measures against unauthorised or unlawful processing, accidental loss, destruction, or damage
8. not be transferred outside the European Economic Area unless the rights and freedoms of data subjects are maintained.

The rights of individuals are probably the most significant parts of the Data Protection Act 1998. It is important that companies are aware of the potential of individuals to seek compensation through the courts for any breach.

The impact of IT and e-business on accounting

Traditional accounting systems, as we have already seen, were totally supported by paper transactions and records. These provided a paper trail, which enabled transactions to be followed through from their inception to their recording and subsequent reporting. Such audit trails, as they are called, provided the fundamental basis on which their authenticity and accuracy could be verified.

As accounting systems became increasingly computerised, accounting records enhanced and to a large extent replicated the manual recording systems. Transactions were still supported by paper trails and their verification continued as with traditional systems, but they were increasingly supported by the use of audit software.

As yet, e-commerce systems like EDI have not impacted greatly on accountants and accounting recording systems within the organisations, which are engaged in the buying and selling transactions. This is because sales and purchase order, invoice, delivery, and receipt transactions, whether provided manually or totally electronically, nevertheless provide transaction records within the relevant computer accounting systems together with their appropriate cost and revenue analysis codings. However, in terms of provision of information for decision-making, computerised accounting systems supporting e-commerce are able to provide much more detailed and informative reporting faster and more reliably than traditional systems.

Verification of the authenticity and accuracy of transactions and records is an area of great concern with regard to internal and external auditors. E-commerce transactions are likely to be supported by little or no paper trails. The focus of verification or audit of such transactions therefore necessarily moves away from the method of checking samples of transactions to assurance that the e-commerce systems are properly controlled in terms of their operation and their security and that they ensure that transactions are created and recorded accurately and reliably and that the data are complete.

> **Progress check 9.14 Discuss the major impacts of e-commerce on accounting systems.**

The decisions that businesses have to make with regard to investment in IT require the use of the appropriate appraisal techniques in the same way as any other capital project. However, the justifications for IT investment are usually more far reaching than those of other investments since they normally impact on the whole organisation and its trading partners for a very long time into the future. Nevertheless, the costs must generally be more than offset by the overall benefits to the business and as with any other project an investment in IT should not be made unless it is expected to add value to the business for its shareholders.

As with the majority of technological developments, over the past few years the costs of computer hardware and software have reduced significantly. This has resulted from the huge increases in demand, and technological development of more effective ways of providing increasingly sophisticated systems with enhanced functionality. The standardisation of the technology used to connect the various PC systems particularly via the Internet has also resulted in reduced costs, and ease of communication of data between a variety of different computer configurations that may have been installed to meet the specific local needs of the users. Information on the Internet is accessed or navigated through the use of **browsers**, programs which present text and numeric data, still and moving images, sound and other information.

Further cost savings are being achieved through the development of faster and cheaper communication systems. **Integrated services digital networks (ISDN)** provide digital data services over traditional analogue telephone lines enabling both data and voice transmission over the same lines. However, the use of ISDN has been matched by the development of the **asymmetric digital subscriber line (ADSL)**, which is potentially 40 times faster than a 56 kilobyte modem (see glossary for the definition of kilobytes, **megabytes**, **gigabytes**, **bytes** and **bits**), and has enabled **broadband** transmission on existing telephone networks. Broadband systems provide much faster ways of connecting computers to the Internet than conventional dial-up systems.

One of the aims of this chapter has been to provide an insight into the extent of the use of computers in business organisations. It has also aimed to provide a practical context for many of the accounting and finance topics covered in this book, and how they are inextricably linked to all other business disciplines, for example manufacturing, human resources management, and distribution. The role of the accountant can be seen to have changed as IT systems have eliminated the need for tasks such as the verification of data and the reconciliation of control account balances. Accountants are now more involved with analysis and evaluation of information, and the use of techniques in support of business decision-making. However, it should be borne in mind that the subject of IT soon becomes out of date; by its very nature IT continues to change the ways in which things are done, and continues to develop at an ever-increasing pace.

Summary of key points

- Information technology (IT) over the past 20 or 30 years has been used to vastly change and improve the ways in which accounting and financial data is recorded, processed, stored, retrieved, and reported.
- IT has had a significant impact on traditional payroll and accounting systems.
- Computer systems have been developed in a number of ways to include all the operational areas of a business, for example manufacturing, distribution and quality management.
- Businesses are now able to achieve the full integration of their applications software through the implementation of enterprise resource planning (ERP) systems.
- Spreadsheets have revolutionised accounting and financial analysis, having taken the place of the traditional accountant's analysis pad and simplified and speeded up the most complicated and sophisticated financial calculations and analyses.
- Databases are now extensively used for the storage, retrieval and reporting of wide ranges of related data.
- Graphics tools and groupware have enhanced and improved the ways in which accounting information, ideas, and concepts may be shared and presented using computer projections and the Internet.
- There is a wide range of additional accounting-related software systems that have been developed for personal and business use.
- In the same way as its predecessors the invention of the wheel, and the industrial revolution, the IT-based new economy has emerged through the latter part of the twentieth century and the start of the twenty-first century.
- The broad concept of e-business and its various elements, such as e-commerce, email and websites, have had a significant impact on accounting systems.
- There are eight principles contained in the Data Protection Act 1998, aimed to protect the rights of individuals with regard to their personal data that is stored by organisations.

Questions

Q9.1 Explain how IT has improved the running of payroll systems and outline the enhancements that have resulted from the development of payroll processing software into fully-integrated HRM systems. What are the internal control implications of these developments?

Q9.2 Explain the ways in which integrated accounting software packages have overcome some of the criticisms of earlier computerised accounting systems.

Q9.3 Why were enterprise resource planning (ERP) systems developed and what have they achieved?

Q9.4   Spreadsheet and database packages were developed primarily for dealing with accounting and financial information. In what ways have they also become indispensable tools for the non-accountant?

Q9.5   Describe the 'new economy' and how it has changed the ways in which organisations conduct their business.

Q9.6   What is e-business and how has it impacted on manufacturing and service functions that support the operations of an organisation?

Q9.7   Outline some of the problems faced by computerised accounting and e-commerce systems and how these are being addressed.

Discussion points

D9.1 'As the use of IT in businesses has increased so has the number of accounting scandals.' Discuss.

D9.2 'The accountants' analysis pad provided everything and more than a spreadsheet such as Excel.' Discuss.

D9.3 'Traditional annual audits of companies were very labour intensive, but more effective than the current computerised audits.' Discuss.

Exercises

The following exercises appear in other chapters of this book (see cross-references to the original exercises), or in the Additional Exercises section of the book's accompanying website. Excel model solutions to each exercise are provided in the OLC accompanying this book (www.mcgraw-hill.co.uk/textbooks/davies).

Level I

E9.1 *Time allowed – 30 minutes (E5.1)*
The information below relates to Priory Products plc's actual results for 2004 and 2005 and their budget for the year 2006.

Figures in £000

	2004	2005	2006
Cash at bank	100	0	0
Overdraft	0	50	200
Loans	200	200	600
Ordinary shares	100	200	400
Profit and loss account	200	300	400

Use a spreadsheet to calculate the following financial ratios for Priory Products for 2004, 2005, and 2006:

(i)   **debt/equity ratio (net debt to equity)**

(ii) **gearing (long-term loans to equity and long-term loans).**

E9.2 *Time allowed – 45 minutes (E2.4)*

The following information relates to Major plc at 31 December 2005, and the comparative numbers at 31 December 2004.

	2004 £000	2005 £000
Accruals	800	1,000
Bank overdraft		16,200
Cash at bank	600	
Plant and machinery at cost	17,600	23,900
Debentures (interest at 15% per annum)	600	750
Plant and machinery depreciation	9,500	10,750
Proposed dividends	3,000	6,000
Ordinary share capital	5,000	5,000
Preference share capital	1,000	1,000
Prepayments	300	400
Profit and loss account	3,000	10,100
Stocks	5,000	15,000
Taxation	3,200	5,200
Trade creditors	6,000	10,000
Trade debtors	8,600	26,700

Use a spreadsheet to prepare a balance sheet in the format adopted by most of the leading UK plcs showing the previous year comparative figures.

E9.3 *Time allowed – 45 minutes (E3.5)*

Tartantrips Ltd, a company in Scotland, operates several ferries and has a policy of holding several in reserve, due to the weather patterns and conditions of various contracts with local authorities. A ferry costs £5 million and has an estimated useful life of 10 years, at which time its realisable value is expected to be £1 million.

Use the appropriate spreadsheet functions to calculate three methods of depreciation available to the company:

(i)   **sum of the digits**

(ii)   **straight line**

(iii) **reducing balance.**

E9.4 *Time allowed – 60 minutes (E3.6)*

From the following profit and loss information that has been provided by Lazydays Ltd, for the year ended 31 March 2005 (and the corresponding figures for the year to 31 March 2004), use a spreadsheet to construct a profit and loss account, using the format adopted by the majority of UK plcs, including comparative figures.

	2005	**2004**
	£	**£**
Administrative expenses	22,000	20,000
Depreciation	5,000	5,000
Closing stock	17,000	15,000
Distribution costs	33,000	30,000
Dividends paid	32,000	30,000
Dividends received from non-related companies	5,000	5,000
Interest paid	10,000	10,000
Interest received	3,000	3,000
Opening stock	15,000	10,000
Purchases	99,000	90,000
Redundancy costs	5,000	
Sales	230,000	200,000
Taxation	25,000	24,000

(a)   Depreciation is to be included in the administrative expenses

(b)   Redundancy costs are to be regarded as an exceptional item

E9.5 *Time allowed – 60 minutes (E4.3)*

Jaffrey Packaging plc have used the following information in the preparation of their financial statements for the year ended 31 March 2005:

	£000
Dividends paid	25
Issue of a debenture	200
Reduction in stocks	32
Corporation tax paid	73
Interest paid	28
Operating profit for the year	450
Bank and cash balance 31 March 2005	376
Purchase of factory equipment	302
Dividends payable at 31 March 2005	25
Interest received	5
Depreciation charge for the year	195
Purchase of a new large computer system	204
Sale of a patent (intangible fixed asset)	29
Increase in trade debtors	43
Reduction in short-term creditors	62
Bank and cash balance 1 April 2004	202

You are required to use spreadsheets to prepare a cash flow statement in compliance with the provisions of FRS 1, together with the appropriate supporting schedules and reconciliations.

Level II

E9.6 *Time allowed – 60 minutes (E3.8)*

From the trial balance of Retepmal Ltd at 31 March 2004 use spreadsheets to prepare a profit and loss account for the year to 31 March 2004 and a balance sheet as at 31 March 2004 using the vertical formats used by most UK companies.

	£
Premises (net book value)	95,000
Trade debtors	75,000
Purchases of stocks	150,000
Retained earnings at 31 March 2003	130,000
Stocks at 31 March 2003	15,000
Furniture and fixtures	30,000
Sales	266,000
Distribution costs and administrative expenses	90,000
Trade creditors	54,000
Motor vehicles (net book value)	40,000
Cash and bank	35,000
Share capital	80,000

Additional information:

(a) Stocks at 31 March 2004 were £25,000.

(b) Dividend proposed for 2004 was £7,000.

(c) An accrual for expenses of £3,000 was required at 31 March 2004.

(d) A prepayment of expenses of £5,000 was required at 31 March 2004.

(e) Corporation tax estimated to be payable on 2003/2004 profits was £19,000.

(f) Annual depreciation charges on premises and motor vehicles for the year to 31 March 2004 are included in administrative expenses and distribution costs respectively, and in the cumulative depreciation provisions used to calculate the net book values of £95,000 and £40,000, shown in the trial balance at 31 March 2004.

The furniture and fixtures balance of £30,000 relates to purchases of assets during the year to 31 March 2004. The depreciation charge to administrative expenses and the corresponding depreciation provision are not included in the trial balance at 31 March 2004. They are required to be calculated for a full year to 31 March 2004, based on a useful economic life of eight years and an estimated residual value of £6,000.

Case Study III

DESIGN PIERRE LTD

Design Pierre Ltd is a designer and manufacturer of gift and presentation packaging, aimed particularly at the mass market, via jewellery shops and large retail chains, and mail order companies. The company was founded many years ago by Pierre Girault, who was the managing director and was involved in the sales and marketing side of the business.

Towards the end of 2001 when Pierre was due to retire, Marie Girault, Pierre's daughter, joined the company as managing director, along with Erik Olsen as marketing director. Marie had worked as a senior manager with Saturn Gifts plc, a large UK designer and manufacturer of giftware, of which Erik had been a director. Marie and Erik capitalised on their experience with Saturn to present some very innovative ideas for developing a new product range for Design Pierre. However, Marie and Erik's ideas for expanding the business required additional investment, the majority of which was spent during the financial year just ended on 31 March 2004.

The share capital of Design Pierre Ltd, 800,000 £1 ordinary shares, had all been owned by Pierre himself. On retirement he decided to transfer 390,000 of his shares to his daughter Marie, and to sell 390,000 shares to Erik Olsen (to help fund his pension). Pierre gifted his remaining 20,000 shares to Nigel Finch, who was the production director and had given the company many years of loyal service. Although Marie had received her share in the company from her father, Erik had used a large part of his personal savings and had taken out an additional mortgage on his house to help finance his investment in the business. This was, of course, paid to Pierre Girault and did not provide any additional capital for the business.

In order to raise additional share capital, Marie and Erik asked Pierre's advice about friends, family and business contacts who may be approached. Pierre suggested approaching a venture capital company, Fishtale Ltd, which was run by a friend of his, Paul Fish. Fishtale already had a wide portfolio of investments in dot.com and service businesses, and Paul was interested in investing in this type of growing manufacturing business. He had known Pierre and the Girault family for many years, and was confident that Marie and Erik would make a success of the new ideas that they presented for the business. Additional capital was therefore provided from the issue of 800,000 new £1 shares at par to Fishtale Ltd, to become the largest shareholder of Design Pierre Ltd. Design Pierre Ltd also had a bank loan, which it increased during 2003/04, and a bank overdraft facility.

The directors of the newly structured Design Pierre Ltd and its shareholders were as follows:

Marie Girault	Managing director	390,000 shares
Erik Olsen	Marketing director	390,000 shares
Nigel Finch	Production director	20,000 shares
Paul Fish	Non-executive director	
Fishtale Ltd		800,000 shares

As a non-executive director of Design Pierre Ltd, Paul Fish attended the annual general meetings, and review meetings that were held every 6 months. He did not have any involvement with the day-to-day management of the business.

The new range at Design Pierre did quite well and the company also began to export in a small way to the USA and Canada. Marie and Erik were pleased by the way in which the sales of the business had grown, and in the growth of their customer base. They had just received a large order from Norbox, a Swedish company, which was regarded as an important inroad into the Scandinavian market. If Norbox became a regular customer, the sales of the company were likely to increase rapidly over the next few years and would establish Design Pierre as a major player in the market.

In the first week of May 2004, the day that Design Pierre received the order from Norbox, Marie also received a letter from the bank manager. The bank manager requested that Design Pierre Ltd immediately and considerably reduce their overdraft, which he felt was running at a level which exposed the bank and the company to a higher level of risk than he was prepared to accept. Marie Girault was very angry and felt very frustrated. Marie, Erik, and Nigel agreed that since they had just had such a good year's trading and the current year looked even better, the reduction in the overdraft facility was going to seriously jeopardise their ability to meet the commitments they had to supply their customers.

When they joined the company, Marie and Erik decided that Design Pierre, which had always been production led, would become a design and marketing led business. Therefore, a great deal of the strategic planning was concerned with integrating the product design and development with the sales and marketing operations of the business. Over the past three years Marie and Erik had invested in employing and training a young design team to help continue to develop the Design Pierre brand. The marketing team led by Erik had ensured that the enthusiasm of their key customers was converted into new firm orders, and that new orders were received from customers like Norbox. The order book grew until it had now reached the highest level ever for the company.

In addition to his role as production director, Nigel had always tended to look after the books and any financial matters. Nigel was not an accountant and he had not had any formal financial training. But, as he said, he had a small and experienced accounts team who dealt with the day-to-day transactions; if ever there had been a problem, they would ask Design Pierre's auditors for some advice.

As soon as she received the letter from the bank, Marie called the bank manager to try and persuade him to continue to support the overdraft facility at the current level, but with no success. Marie also convened an urgent meeting of the directors, including Paul Fish, to talk about the letter and the draft accounts of the business for the year ended 31 March 2004. The letter from the bank was distributed to all the directors before the meeting.

Erik Olsen was very worried about his investment in the company. He admitted that his accounting knowledge was fairly limited. He thought that the company was doing very well, and said that the draft accounts for the year to 31 March 2004 seemed to confirm their success. Profit before tax was more than double the profit for 2003. He could not understand why the cash flow was so bad. He appreciated that they had spent a great deal of money on the additional plant and equipment, but they had already had a bank loan to help with that. He thought that the cash situation should really be even better than the profit because the expenses included £1.5m for depreciation, which does not involve any cash at all.

Marie Girault still appeared very angry at the lack of support being given by the bank. She outlined the impact that the overdraft reduction would have on their ability to meet their commitments over the next year. She said that the bank's demand to cut their overdraft by 50% over the next 3 months put them in an impossible position with regard to being able to meet customer orders. Design Pierre Ltd could not find an alternative source of such a large amount of money in such a short time.

Erik, Marie, and Nigel had, before the meeting, hoped that Paul Fish would be prepared to help out by purchasing further additional new shares in the company or by making a loan to the company. However, it was soon made clear by Paul that further investment was not a possible option. Fishtale Ltd had made a couple of new investments over the past few months and so did not have the money to invest further in Design Pierre. As a venture capitalist, Fishtale had actually been discussing the possible exit from Design Pierre by selling and trying to realise a profit on the shares. Finding a prospective buyer for their shares, or floating Design Pierre on the alternative investment market (AIM), did not currently appear to be a realistic option.

Paul Fish had been so much involved in running his own business, Fishtale Ltd, that he had neglected to monitor the financial position of Design Pierre Ltd as often and as closely as he should have done. At the directors' meeting he realised that he should have been much more attentive and there was now a possibility that Design Pierre would not provide the returns his company expected, unless things could be drastically improved.

The accounts of Design Pierre Ltd for the past two years are shown below.

Profit and loss account for the year ended 31 March

	2003 £000	2004 £000
Turnover	7,000	11,500
Cost of sales	3,700	5,800
Gross profit	3,300	5,700
Operating expenses	2,200	3,100
Operating profit	1,100	2,600
Interest payable	200	500
Profit before taxation	900	2,100
Taxation	200	400
Profit after taxation	700	1,700
Dividend	200	300
Retained profit for the year	500	1,400
Retained profit brought forward	1,100	1,600
Retained profit carried forward	1,600	3,000

Balance sheet as at 31 March

	2003		2004	
	£000	£000	£000	£000
Fixed assets		4,300		7,200
Current assets				
Stocks	1,200		2,900	
Trade debtors	800		1,900	
Other debtors	100		200	
Cash at bank and in hand	100		–	
	2,200		5,000	
Creditors: Amounts falling due within one year				
Trade creditors	600		1,300	
Other creditors	100		200	
Taxation	200		400	
Dividends	200		300	
Bank overdraft	–		2,100	
	1,100		4,300	
Net current assets		1,100		700
		5,400		7,900
Creditors: Amounts falling due after more than one year				
Loan		2,200		3,300
		3,200		4,600
Capital and reserves				
Ordinary shares (£1)		1,600		1,600
Retained profit		1,600		3,000
		3,200		4,600

The directors of Design Pierre Ltd were unable to agree on a way of dealing with the financial problem faced by the company. Marie thought it best that she continue to try and negotiate with the bank manager, and believed that she could change the bank managers mind if she:

- presented him with the accounts for 31 March 2004, which showed such good results, and
- made him fully aware of the implications of the reduction in the overdraft facility on the future of Design Pierre.

However, Erik and Nigel said that they were aware that Design Pierre Ltd had exceeded its agreed overdraft limit a few times over the past two years and so they were not confident that Marie could persuade the bank to change its mind. They suggested that they should try and find another investor prepared to provide additional funds for the business, to keep the business going. They really believed that the year-end accounts showed how successful Design Pierre had been over the past 2 years and that their track record was sufficient to attract a potential new investor in the business. Paul did not agree. He felt that this would not be a practical solution. More importantly, Fishtale did not want to have another large shareholder in the company because it would dilute its shareholding, and also reduce its influence over the future direction of the business. However, Paul agreed that immediate and radical action needed to be taken by the company.

After hours of argument and discussion, it became apparent that the problem would not be resolved at the meeting. Therefore, it was agreed by all present that expertise from outside the company should be sought to help the company find an acceptable and viable solution to the problem. The directors decided to approach Lucis Consulting, which specialises in helping businesses with financial problems, and to ask them to produce a plan of action for their consideration.

Required

As a member of the Lucis team, prepare a report for the board of directors of Design Pierre Ltd which analyses the problems faced by the company and which sets out a detailed plan of action for dealing with its financing problem.

Your report should be supported by the appropriate analyses, and a full cash flow statement for the year ended 31 March 2004.

Appendices

Contents

Outline of Appendices

Appendix 1 is about the system used to record accounting transactions and accounting data and provides the fundamental basis for the further analysis and reporting of financial information. It provides an introduction to double-entry bookkeeping. Bookkeeping is a process that records accounting data in such a way that allows subsequent preparation of financial reports in appropriate formats which inform shareholders and others about the financial position and the financial performance of the business. The topics covered may or may not be required by you in order to use the rest of this book. Alternatively, this appendix may be used as a learning aid in support of study of the topics covered in Chapters 1 to 9.

Appendix 2 includes schedules of all Statements of Standard Accounting Practice (SSAPs) and Financial Reporting Standards (FRSs) currently in use in the UK. It also includes schedules of current International Accounting Standards (IASs) and International Financial Reporting Standards (IFRSs), for which with effect from 1 January 2005 there is mandatory application for all listed companies in the European Union. Additions, changes and withdrawals to these standards may be found on the book's accompanying website, which is regularly updated.

Appendix 3 contains solutions to around one half of the chapter-end exercises, which include a mix of both Level I and Level II exercises. They refer to the chapter-end exercise numbers which are highlighted in colour. This allows you to attempt the exercises at the end of each chapter and then check on your understanding of the key points and how well you have been able to apply the various learning topics and techniques. Further exercises are included on the book's accompanying website.

Appendix 1

Double-entry – the basics

Contents

Learning objectives

Completion of this appendix will enable you to:

- explain the convention of double-entry bookkeeping
- describe what is meant by 'debit' and 'credit'
- enter business transactions into accounts
- account for closing stocks and other accounting adjustments
- explain the balancing of accounts
- extract a trial balance from a company's accounts
- prepare a profit and loss account, balance sheet and cash flow statement from a trial balance
- appreciate the concepts of accrual accounting and cash accounting
- explain and account for payments in advance (prepayments) and charges not yet received (accruals)
- appreciate the importance of accounting periods.

Introduction

This appendix begins by explaining what is sometimes referred to as the dual aspect rule. This rule recognises that for all transactions there is a two-sided effect within the entity. A manager in a non-accounting role may not be expected to carry out the recording of transactions in this way, but an appreciation of how accounting data has been recorded will be extremely helpful in the interpretation of financial information. We will go on to describe the processes that deal with the two sides of each transaction, the 'debits' and 'credits' of double-entry bookkeeping.

Don't worry if at first these topics seem a little difficult and confusing. They will become clearer as we follow through some transactions step-by-step into the accounts of a business and show how these accounts are kept in balance.

The appendix continues with an introduction to the way in which each of the accounts are held in what are termed the books of account and ledgers of the business. The balances on all the accounts in an entity are summarised in what is called a trial balance. The trial balance may be adjusted to allow for payments in advance, charges not yet received, and other adjusting entries. From this information we will show how to prepare a simple profit and loss account, balance sheet, and cash flow report.

This appendix refers to some of the accounting concepts introduced in Chapter 1. In that context we will look at the time period chosen by a business, to which the financial reporting relates – the accounting period.

Theory and practice of double-entry bookkeeping

Double-entry bookkeeping has a long history, having been created by the father of modern accounting, the Franciscan monk Luca Pacioli in Italy in the late fifteenth century. His publication, *Summa de Arithmetica, Geometria, Proportioni et Proportionalita* (Everything About Arithmetic, Geometry and

Proportion), published in 1494, was the first printed work dealing with algebra and also contained the first text on **bookkeeping**, entitled *De Computis et Scripturis*. Bookkeeping then spread throughout the world by a series of plagiarisms and imitations of Pacioli's work.

It is important to remember that the idea of double-entry is a convention. There are two main objectives of bookkeeping: to have a permanent record of transactions; to show the effect of each transaction and the combined effect of all the transactions on the financial position of the entity.

The fundamental idea of double-entry bookkeeping is that all business transactions of a business entity, for example, cash and invoices, should be recorded twice in the entity's business records. It is based on the principle that every financial transaction involves the simultaneous receiving and giving of value, and is therefore recorded twice. Transactions of course involve both services and goods. We shall find out later in this appendix that there are other accounting entries which do not result directly from invoice or cash transactions but which also result in double-entry records being created. These **accounting adjustment** entries relate, for example, to accounting for **depreciation**, **bad debts**, and **doubtful debts**.

The convention of double-entry assumes that in all business transactions equal and opposite values are exchanged. For example, if a company purchases materials for £1,000 for cash it adds to its stock of materials to the value of £1,000, but reduces its cash balance also to the value of £1,000. The convention uses two terms for convenience to describe the two aspects of each transaction. These terms are debit and credit.

There is sometimes confusion in the use of the terms of debit and credit used in bookkeeping when they are compared with the same terms used on bank statements. Bank statements traditionally refer to receipt of cash as a credit, whereas receipt of cash in bookkeeping terms is referred to as a debit. The reason for this is that customer accounts are presented from the bank's point of view; as far as the bank is concerned, account holders are creditors, to whom the bank will eventually have to repay any money deposited by them.

Debits and credits

The explanation of debits and credits in terms of value received and value given respectively is not perhaps one that provides the clearest understanding. Neither is the explanation that debits are in the left-hand column and credits are in the right-hand column, or debits are on the side of the room closest to the window!

Debits and credits do represent certain types of account, as we will see later, in both the **balance sheet: assets** and **liabilities**, and the **profit and loss account: costs** and **sales**. However, for the purpose of clarity of explanation we shall propose a couple of basic assumptions with which to work from as we go through some elementary accounting entries.

If we initially consider all business transactions as either goods or services then it is reasonable to assume (unless we are in a barter society) that all these transactions will ultimately end up with cash (or cash equivalents, such as cheques, bank transfers, etc.) changing hands. We can also assume that all these transactions will involve a document being raised, as a record of the transaction and an indication of the amount of cash that will change hands, namely an invoice. A **purchase invoice** records a purchase from a third party and so it represents an account to be payable at some time. A **sales invoice** records a sale to a third party and so it represents an account to be receivable at some time.

Business entities themselves have a separate identity from the owners of the business. When we consider double-entry we will now assume that all the entries we are discussing relate to those of the business entity, in whatever form the entity takes: sole trader; partnership; limited company; public limited company (see Chapter 1).

For the business entity, we shall define the following business transactions:

Transaction		Accounting entries	
CASH RECEIPT	=	DEBIT CASH	and credit something else
CASH PAYMENT	=	CREDIT CASH	and debit something else
PURCHASE INVOICE	=	CREDIT PAYABLES	and debit something else
SALES INVOICE	=	DEBIT RECEIVABLES	and credit something else

These are definitions within the convention of double-entry bookkeeping, which may be usefully remembered as a basis for establishing whether all further subsequent transactions are either debits or credits. It is suggested that the above four statements are kept filed in permanent memory, as a useful aid towards the understanding of further accounting entries.

> **Progress check A1.1 Outline what is meant by double-entry bookkeeping.**

An elementary method of representing and clarifying double-entry is known as the T account. We shall use this method to demonstrate double-entry in action using a simple example. (Note that in the UK there are many computerised accounting packages that automate the double-entry for a business, for example Sage. The purpose of this extensive worked example is to illustrate how such transactions take place).

Worked Example A1.1

Mr Bean decides to set up a wholesale business, Ayco, on 1 January 2005. He has his own cash resources available for the purpose of setting it up and has estimated that an initial £50,000 would be required for this purpose. During the first month in business, January 2005, **Ayco** (as distinct from Mr Bean) will enter into the following transactions:

	£
Receipt of cheque from Mr Bean	50,000
Purchase for cash the freehold of a shop	30,000
Purchase for cash the shop fittings	5,000
Cash expenses on printing and stationery	200
Purchases of stock, from Beeco, of Aymen toys, payable two months later (12,000 toys at £1 each)	12,000
Sales of Aymen toys to Ceeco for cash (1,000 toys at £2 each)	2,000
Sales of Aymen toys to Deeco, receivable one month later (8,000 toys at £2 each)	16,000

We shall consider each of these transactions in detail and subsequently represent them in T account format for clarity, with debits on the left and credits on the right of the middle line of the T. We will repeatedly refer to the earlier four key double-entry definitions in order to establish the entries required for each transaction.

Receipt of cheque from Mr Bean £50,000 – transaction 1
Ayco will have needed to open a bank account to pay in the money received from Mr Bean. This

represents a receipt of cash of £50,000 to Ayco, and so

Debit cash account   **£50,000**   **and credit what?**

This money represents the capital that Mr Bean, as the sole investor in the business, has invested in Ayco and so the account is called the capital account. So:

Debit cash account   **£50,000**
Credit capital account   **£50,000**

Worked Example A1.2

Purchase for cash the freehold of a shop £30,000 – transaction 2
This represents a cash payment for the purchase of a shop, something which is called a fixed asset: an asset acquired for retention by the entity for the purpose of providing a service to the business, and not held for resale in the normal course of trading.

Credit cash account   **£30,000**   **and debit what?**

A payment of cash of £30,000 is a credit to the cash account, and so:

Credit cash account   **£30,000**
Debit fixed assets – shop account   **£30,000**

Worked Example A1.3

Purchase for cash the shop fittings £5,000 – transaction 3
This represents a cash payment for the shop fittings, which are also fixed assets, but a different category of fixed assets from the freehold shop.

A payment of cash of £5,000 is a credit to the cash account, and so:

Credit cash account   **£5,000**
Debit fixed assets – fittings account   **£5,000**

Worked Example A1.4

Cash expenses on printing and stationery £200 – transaction 4
This represents a payment of cash of £200 by Ayco in the month, and so:

Credit cash account   **£200**   **and debit what?**

This money was paid out on day-to-day expenses that have been made to support the business, and is a charge for printing and stationery expenses. So:

Credit cash account	**£200**
Debit printing and stationery expenses account	**£200**

Worked Example A1.5

Purchases of stock, from Beeco, of Aymen toys, payable two months later £12,000 – transaction 5
This represents a purchase on credit from Beeco. An invoice is assumed to have been received from Beeco along with the receipt of stock. The invoice from Beeco is a purchase invoice for £12,000 to Ayco, and so:

Credit creditors (accounts payable) account   **£12,000**   and debit what?
This represents a purchase of stock which are goods held for resale, and so

Credit creditors account	**£12,000**
Debit stock account	**£12,000**

A purchase of stock may alternatively be initially debited to a purchases account and then subsequently transferred to a stocks account.

Worked Example A1.6

Sales of Aymen toys to Ceeco for cash £2,000 – transaction 6
This represents a sale for cash to Ceeco. An invoice will be issued by Ayco to Ceeco along with the delivery of stock. The invoice to Ceeco is a sales invoice for £2,000 from Ayco, and so:

Debit debtors (accounts receivable) account   **£2,000**   and credit what?

This represents sales of stock which are called sales, revenue or turnover, and so:

Debit debtors account	**£2,000**
Credit sales account	**£2,000**

But as a cash sale this sales invoice is being paid immediately with a cash receipt of £2,000, so:

Debit cash account   **£2,000**   and credit what?

This £2,000 is immediately paying the receivables, and so:

Debit cash account	**£2,000**
Credit debtors account	**£2,000**

which means that on this transaction the net balance of the receivables (debtors) account is zero.

This transaction may be short cut by directly crediting the sales account and debiting the cash account. However, it is normally recorded in the way described in order to create and record a VAT sales invoice.

Worked Example A1.7

Sales of Aymen toys to Deeco, receivable one month later £16,000 – transaction 7
This represents sales on credit to Deeco. An invoice will be issued by Ayco to Deeco along with the delivery of stock.

The invoice to Deeco is a sales invoice for £16,000 from Ayco, and so as above:

Debit debtors account	**£16,000**
Credit sales account	**£16,000**

This is different from the transaction in Worked Example A1.6 because the receivables will not be paid until the following month.

Closing stocks adjustment

In the Ayco example, one further accounting entry needs to be considered, which relates to stocks of toys sold during the period. It is called a **closing stocks** adjustment, which is illustrated in Worked Example A1.8.

Worked Example A1.8

We represented the purchase of 12,000 toys into the stock of Ayco as a debit of £12,000 to the stock account. Ayco sold 1,000 toys for cash and 8,000 toys on credit. The physical stock of 12,000 toys at 31 January 2005 has therefore been reduced to only 3,000 (12,000 – 1,000 – 8,000). We may value these units that are left in stock at cost, for the purpose of this example, at 3,000 × £1, or £3,000. Ayco sold a total of 9,000 units during January at a selling price of £2 per unit. These 9,000 units cost £1 each and so these sales have cost Ayco £9,000: cost of sales £9,000. A double-entry accounting transaction is necessary to represent this for two reasons: to show the cost of the 9,000 toys that matches the sale of 9,000 toys; to ensure that the stock account represents only the physical toys that are actually held in stock.

The entries for the original purchase of stock were:

Credit creditors account	**£12,000**
Debit stock account	**£12,000**

We know that the stock account should now be £9,000 less than the original £12,000, representing the £9,000 cost of sales. Therefore we need to credit the stock account to reduce it and debit something else. The something else is the cost of sales account.

Transaction 8

Credit stock account	**£9,000**
Debit cost of sales account	**£9,000**

Accounting adjustments

The diagram in Fig. A1.1 includes all the main types of accounting transactions that may be recorded in an accounting system. The shaded items represent the prime entries (the first record of transactions) and cash entries. The non-shaded items are the five main accounting adjustment entries.

The closing stocks adjustment, illustrated in Worked Example A1.8, is one of the five main accounting adjustment entries shown in Fig. A1.2, which may or may not be incorporated into the **trial balance**.

Accounting adjustments are made prior to preparation of the profit and loss account and balance sheet. The other four adjusting entries are **accruals** and **prepayments** (covered later in this appendix), depreciation, and bad and doubtful debts and the **doubtful debt provision** (which are covered together with further detail on closing stocks in Chapter 3).

Each of the T accounts for Ayco in Fig. A1.3 shows the detailed movement through the month and each account represents the balance on each account at 31 January 2005, the end of the first month of trading.

> **Progress check A1.2 Explain broadly what is meant by accounting adjustment entries.**

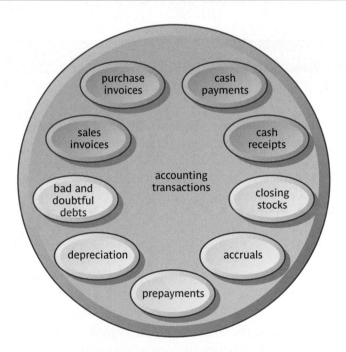

Figure A1.1 Accounting transactions

Books of account and the ledgers in action

We saw in the previous section how the principle of double-entry bookkeeping operates to record the detail of transactions. We represented these records in T accounts to provide some clarity in seeing how each entry has been made and the interrelation of the entries. In practice, accounting records are

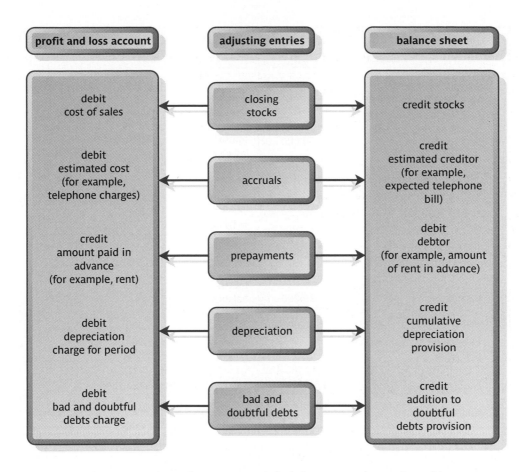

Figure A1.2 The five accounting adjustments and their impact on the profit and loss account and the balance sheet

kept along the same lines but in books of account and ledgers rather than T accounts on a piece of paper. The old-fashioned manually prepared ledgers maintained by companies have long since been superseded by **computerised accounting systems**. Nevertheless, the same principles apply and the same books of account and ledgers are maintained albeit in an electronic format.

The chart shown in Fig. A1.4 shows the relationship between the main ledger, the general ledger (or nominal ledger) and the other books of account, and subsidiary ledgers:

- **cash book** (receipts and payments)
- **purchase invoice daybook** and **purchase ledger** (or **accounts payable**)
- **sales invoice daybook** and **sales ledger** (or **accounts receivable**).

It also shows the main sources of data input for these ledgers and the basic reporting information produced out of these ledgers and books of account.

General ledger

In smaller businesses, wages and salaries data are usually recorded in the cash books and subsequently posted to the general ledger. In larger companies, wages and salaries usually have their own ledgers and control accounts in the general ledger.

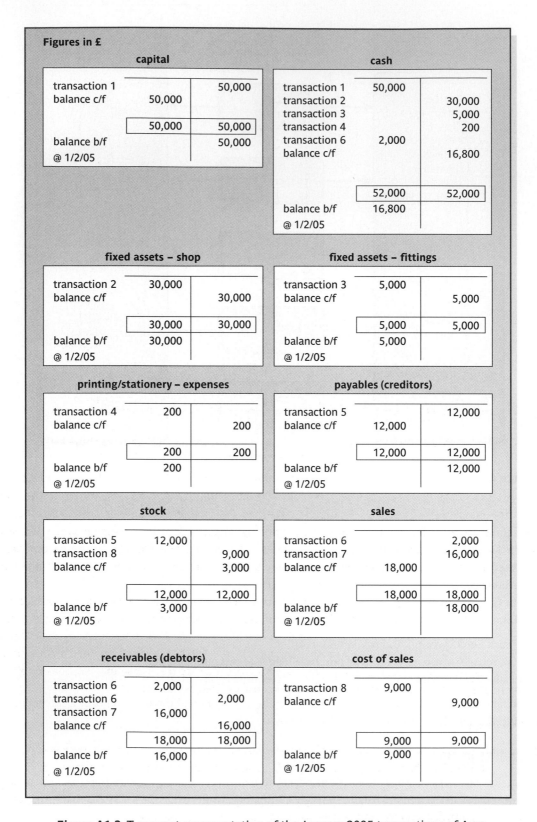

Figure A1.3 T account representation of the January 2005 transactions of Ayco

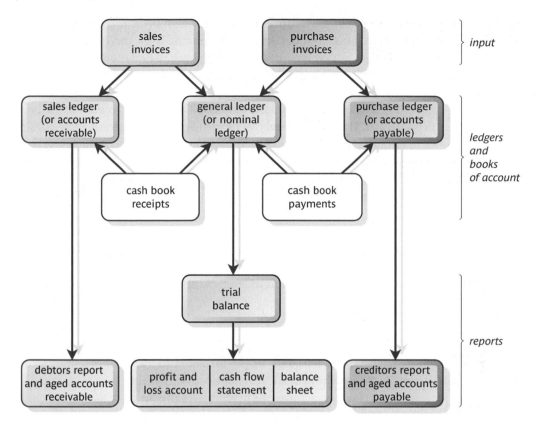

Figure A1.4 The general ledger and its relationship with the cash book, purchase ledger and sales ledger

The main ledger of any company, in which the results of all transactions made by the entity are recorded, is called the **general ledger** or nominal ledger. This ledger is set up to include all accounts whether they are assets, liabilities, sales (or revenues), or costs (or expenses). The detail of every transaction finds its way to this ledger, or is posted to it (to use the technical term), in much the same way as we saw in the T accounts. The general ledger may be said to be the collection of every T account within the entity.

Within the general ledger one account or more will be established to represent cash transactions (including cheques, drafts, bank transfers, etc.). These entries are posted to the general ledger from the analysis of entries made into the cash book. The cash book is a book of original entry maintained to show the detail of all receipts and payments made by the entity; it records the dates, values and unique references of all receipts and payments, and what they are for. These include, for example, payment of salaries, receipts from customers, purchase of fixed assets, etc.

Cash book

The cash book is a book of account that in theory should match exactly with the regular statements issued by the entity's bank. In practice, the cash book is prepared partly from company internally generated **cash payment** information and available information relating to **cash receipts**. Some transactions may appear in the bank account without prior notification, for example bank charges, and so the cash book may also be partly prepared from the bank statement.

There may always be differences in the balances between the cash book and the bank statement because cheques may have been issued but not yet presented to the bank and cash may have been received into the bank account but not yet recorded in the cash book. Regular preparation of a **bank reconciliation**, which identifies the differences between the cash book and the bank statement, is a necessary function of the finance department.

Each payment and each receipt is posted from the cash book to the cash account in the general ledger as a credit or debit to cash. The opposite entry, either debit or credit, is posted at the same time to its relevant account in the general ledger, for example, payables, printing and stationery expenses, receivables, etc. In the days when such ledgers were maintained manually such postings were made weekly or monthly. With computerised, integrated accounting systems postings may be made simultaneously to the cash book and the general ledger from the same source but avoiding any duplication of effort.

It is most important that the balance on the cash book, the net of all receipts and payments, at all times equals the balance of the cash book represented in the cash account within the general ledger, and that all the opposite entries have also been posted to their relevant accounts. In this way, the equality of total debits and total credits is maintained. The use of computerised accounting systems should guarantee this.

Purchase ledger

Payables are recorded in a ledger, the purchase ledger (or accounts payable) that represents all accounts payable by the entity. Within the general ledger one account or more (control accounts) will be established to represent payables transactions, the purchases by the entity for which invoices have been rendered by suppliers, or vendors. All supplier invoices are recorded in a purchase ledger and analysed into the various items of expense by allocating them to a specific general ledger account. These entries are debited to the appropriate general ledger accounts from the analysis of invoices made in the purchase ledger. The totals of these entries are credited to the account(s) representing accounts payable in the general ledger.

The purchase ledger is maintained to show the detail of all invoices received from suppliers. In addition to the purchase ledger's function of posting the totals of invoices to the accounts payable account in the general ledger, and the analysis of what the invoices represent to the appropriate accounts in the general ledger, it analyses all invoices and groups them by supplier.

Payments made to suppliers from the cash book which have been credited to the cash account and debited to the payables account in the general ledger are also recorded in detail by amount, date and supplier within the purchase ledger. In this way it can be seen that the total balances at any one time of all accounts in the purchase ledger equal the balance on the payables account in the general ledger.

Sales ledger

Receivables are recorded in another ledger – the sales ledger (or accounts receivable) which represents all accounts receivable by the entity. Within the general ledger one account or more will be established (control accounts) to represent receivables transactions – the sales by the entity for which invoices have been issued to customers. All customer invoices are recorded in a sales ledger and analysed into the various items of sale or revenue by allocating them to a specific general ledger account. These entries are credited to the appropriate general ledger accounts from the analysis of invoices made in the sales ledger. The totals of these entries are debited to the account(s) representing accounts receivable in the general ledger.

The sales ledger is maintained to show the detail of all invoices issued to customers. The totals of customer invoices are posted to the accounts receivable account in the general ledger. The analyses of what the invoices represent are posted to the appropriate accounts in the general ledger. The sales ledger may also enable each invoice to be analysed and grouped by customer.

Receipts from customers from the cash book which have been debited to the cash account and credited to the receivables account in the general ledger are also recorded in detail by amount, date and customer within the sales ledger. In this way the total balances at any one time of all accounts in the sales ledger equal the balance on the receivables account in the general ledger.

The cash accounts, payables and receivables accounts in the general ledger are referred to as control accounts because they provide control over the same transactions which are also represented in some further detail, and which must agree in total, in what are termed the books of account and subsidiary ledgers: the cash book, accounts payable (purchase ledger), and accounts receivable (sales ledger).

> **Progress check A1.3 What are the usual books of account and ledgers you would expect to be used in a company's accounting system?**

The trial balance

A trial balance is a list of account balances in a double-entry system. If the records have been correctly maintained, the sum of the debit balance accounts will be equal and opposite to the sum of the credit balance accounts, although certain errors such as omission of a transaction or erroneous entries will not be apparent in the trial balance.

Worked Example A1.9

If we turn again to the Ayco example, we can that see that each of the T accounts we have prepared represents the general (or nominal) ledger balances of the entity. These balances may be listed to form a trial balance for Ayco as at 31 January 2005.

The trial balance for Ayco as at 31 January 2005

	Debit £	Credit £
Capital		50,000
Cash	16,800	
Fixed assets – shop	30,000	
Fixed assets – fittings	5,000	
Printing and stationery expenses	200	
Payables		12,000
Stock	3,000	
Sales		18,000
Receivables	16,000	
Cost of sales	9,000	
	80,000	80,000

From this simple trial balance it is possible to derive three reports that tell us something about the business: the profit and loss account (or income statement); the balance sheet; the cash flow statement.

How do we know which items in the trial balance are balance sheet items and which are profit and loss items? Well, if an item is not a cost (expense) or a sales (revenue) item, then it must be an asset or a liability. The expenses and revenues must appear in the profit and loss account and the assets and liabilities must appear in the balance sheet. Even a computerised accounting system must be told the specific classification of a transaction.

Worked Example A1.10

Let's examine each of the items in the Ayco trial balance as at 31 January 2005.

	Debit £	Credit £
Capital		50,000
This represents the original money that the investor Mr Bean put into Ayco – not revenue/expense		
Cash	16,800	
This represents the total cash that Ayco has at its disposal at 31 January, an asset – not revenue/expense		
Fixed assets – shop	30,000	
This represents assets purchased out of cash to help run the business – not revenue/expense		
Fixed assets – fittings	5,000	
This represents assets purchased out of cash to help run the business – not revenue/expense		
Printing and stationery expenses	200	
This represents costs incurred on disposable items used in running the business through January – expense		
Payables		12,000
This represents debts which Ayco must pay in the next two months, a liability – not revenue/expense		
Stock	3,000	
This represents items held in stock to sell to customers over future periods, an asset – not revenue/expense		

Sales		18,000
This represents the value of toys delivered to customers in January – revenue		
Receivables	16,000	
This represents debts for which Ayco will receive payment next month, an asset – not revenue/expense		
Cost of sales	9,000	
This represents the cost of toys delivered to customers in January – expense		
	80,000	80,000

> **Progress check A1.4 What is a trial balance?**

Profit and loss account

The profit and loss account shows the profit or loss generated by an entity during an accounting period by deducting all costs from total sales. Within the trial balance we may extract the balances on the costs (expenses) and sales (revenues) accounts in order to construct the profit and loss account. The total sum of these accounts will then result in a balance which is profit or a loss, and which may be inserted back into a restated trial balance in summary form in place of all the individual profit and loss items which comprise that balance.

Worked Example A1.11

The expense and revenue items, or the profit and loss account items, may be extracted from Ayco's trial balance and summarised as follows:

	Debit £	Credit £
Sales		18,000
Cost of sales	9,000	
Printing and stationery expenses	200	
Balance representing a profit for January	8,800	
	18,000	18,000

Although the £8,800 is shown in the debit column to balance the account, it is in fact a credit balance that is carried forward, that is a balance resulting from £18,000 less debits of £9,200.

Ayco profit and loss account for January 2005

	£
Sales	18,000
less	
Cost of sales	9,000
Gross margin (gross profit)	9,000
Printing and stationery expenses	200
Net profit for January 2005	8,800

> **Progress check A1.5** Outline what a profit and loss account tells us about a company.

Balance sheet

The balance sheet of an entity discloses the assets (debit balances) and liabilities, and shareholders' capital (credit balances), and gains or losses as at a given date. A gain or profit is a credit balance, and a loss is a debit balance. The revised trial balance, which includes the net balance of profit or loss, then forms the basis for the balance sheet. The balance sheet may then be constructed by rearranging the balances into an established format.

Worked Example A1.12

The profit is a credit balance of £8,800, and if we substitute this back into Ayco's trial balance for the individual revenue and expense items we have:

	Debit	Credit
	£	£
Capital		50,000
Cash	16,800	
Fixed assets – shop	30,000	
Fixed assets – fittings	5,000	
Payables (or creditors)		12,000
Stock	3,000	
Receivables (or debtors)	16,000	
Profit for January		8,800
	70,800	70,800

To construct a balance sheet this needs to be rearranged into a more usual sort of format:

Ayco balance sheet as at 31 January 2005

	£	£		£	£
Assets			**Liabilities**		
Fixed assets		35,000	**Owner's investment**		
			Capital	50,000	
			Profit and loss account	8,800	
					58,800
Current assets			**Short-term liabilities**		
Debtors	16,000		Creditors		12,000
Stock	3,000				
Cash	16,800				
		35,800			
		70,800			70,800

Progress check A1.6 **Outline what a balance sheet tells us about a company.**

Cash flow statement

The final report, the **cash flow statement,** is simply a report on the detail of the movement within the cash account in Ayco's trial balance. This starts with the opening balance, shows the receipts and payments during the accounting period and results in the closing balance.

Worked Example A1.13

The final report, the cash flow report, may be constructed by looking at the elements that are included in Ayco's cash T account, that is the elements which make up the total movements in the cash account in the general ledger:

	Debit £	Credit £
Cash balance at 1 January 2005	–	
Receipt from Mr Bean – capital for business	50,000	
Payment for freehold shop		30,000
Payment for shop fittings		5,000
Payment for printing and stationery expenses		200
Receipt from customers	2,000	
Cash balance at 31 January 2005		16,800
	52,000	52,000

The £16,800 debit balance carried forward represents a positive cash position of £16,800.

The aim of the last few sections has been to explain the basics of double-entry bookkeeping, the sources of accounting data, and to provide an introduction to the accounting ledgers and books of account. This begins to show how the information from double-entry records may be usefully used. The inclusion of the rudimentary financial statements shown above illustrates the importance of the:

■ accuracy
■ timeliness
■ completeness

of the financial data included in the double-entry system.

> **Progress check A1.7 Outline what a cash flow statement tells us about a company.**

Accrual accounting and cash accounting

We have already covered a number of important accounting ideas and concepts, one of which is that profit does not necessarily equal cash. This was apparent from the Ayco worked examples. The net cash movement in that example for the month of January was an inflow, a positive of £16,800. However, the profit and loss account showed a gain, a positive of £8,800. The reason that they were not identical was first (as shown in the cash flow report) due to cash items other than those associated with trading, for example receipt of the original capital, and expenditure on fixed assets. Second, the trading or operational transactions were not all converted into cash within the month of January; they were held as accounts payable, stocks, and accounts receivable.

The approach that we took in the Ayco example demonstrated compliance with the **accruals concept**, or matching concept, the principle that revenue and costs are:

■ recognised as they are earned or incurred
■ matched with one another
■ dealt with in the profit and loss account of the period to which they relate, irrespective of the period of receipt or payment.

> **Progress check A1.8 In what way does a company's profit and loss account differ from the movements on its cash account during an accounting period?**

Accruals

It may be that an expense has been incurred within an accounting period, for which an invoice may or may not have been received. For example, electricity used, telephone charges incurred, or stationery supplies received and used. We have talked about the concept of matching costs with sales, or revenues. Costs not necessarily related to sales cannot be matched in that way. Such charges must be matched to the **accounting period** to which they relate, and therefore an estimate of the cost (an accrual) must be made and included as an accounting adjusting entry in the accounts for that period.

Figure A1.5 shows an invoice dated 15 April 2005 received by a company from its communications provider for charges of £2,000 for the period January to March 2005. At the end of April 2005 the company had not yet received its bill for the next quarter even though it had use of telephone lines and had incurred call charges. We may assume that the company's accounting year runs from January to

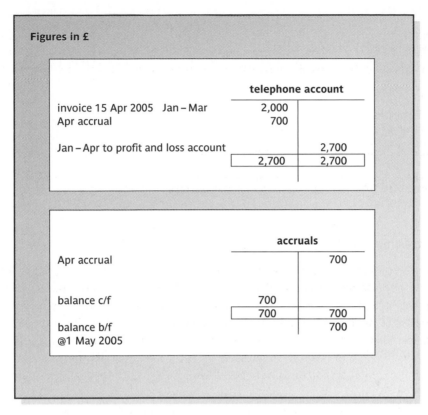

Figure A1.5 T account illustration of accounting for accruals

December. Therefore, before finalising its profit and loss account for January to April the company needed to estimate its telephone costs for April, which are shown as £700.

The estimate of £700 has been charged, or debited, to telephone costs in the profit and loss account, and a temporary creditor, an accrual, credited in the balance sheet for £700. The total telephone costs charged to the profit and loss account for January to April 2005 are therefore £2,700. The accrual carried forward at the end of April would normally be reversed and the position assessed again at the end of May, and the same procedure followed at the end of June. By the end of July the bill would normally be expected to have been received covering the period April to June and so no accrual will be necessary. However, an accrual will be required for the month of July.

Worked Example A1.14

From the following information we are required to prepare three-column accounts (in an Excel spreadsheet or in a Word table) to reflect the current balances on each account, which are then required to be adjusted for the accruals at 31 December 2005 to show the total transfer to the profit and loss account. We are also required to show a summary of the accruals as at 31 December 2005.

	£
Current balances at 31 December 2005	
Electricity	10,000
Gas	11,000
Telephone	5,000
Interest on overdraft	6,000
Accruals required at 31 December 2005	
Electricity	500
Gas	600
Telephone	500
Interest on overdraft	600

Accruals adjustments at 31 December 2005:

	Debit £	Credit £	Balance £
Electricity			
31 December 2005			10,000
Accrual 31 December 2005	500		10,500
Transfer to profit and loss account		(10,500)	0
Gas			
31 December 2005			11,000
Accrual 31 December 2005	600		11,600
Transfer to profit and loss account		(11,600)	0
Telephone			
31 December 2005			5,000
Accrual 31 December 2005	500		5,500
Transfer to profit and loss account		(5,500)	0
Interest payable on overdraft			
31 December 2005			6,000
Accrual 31 December 2005	600		6,600
Transfer to profit and loss account		(6,600)	0
Accruals 31 December 2005			
Electricity		(500)	(500)
Gas		(600)	(1,100)
Telephone		(500)	(1,600)
Interest payable on overdraft		(600)	(2,200)

The same sort of exercise is carried out within a company for all of the categories of expense for which accruals are likely to be required. Worked Example A1.15 explains how accruals may have been dealt with in Ayco.

Worked Example A1.15

The accruals concept could have been further illustrated in the Ayco scenario by the introduction of a number of additional factors. Assume, for example, that Ayco had used more than £200 of stationery in the month, say £1,000. We know that Ayco had been invoiced for and paid for £200 worth of stationery.

If £500 worth of the additional stationery had been used, and an invoice had been received but not processed through the ledgers, what would be the impact on Ayco? If £300 worth of the additional stationery had been used, and an invoice had not yet been received but was in the mail what would be the impact on Ayco?

The answer is that both would have to be debited to printing and stationery expenses for a total of £800, and credited not to payables but to accruals.

Accruals are treated in a similar way to payables but the invoices for these charges have not yet been processed by the entity. They are charges which are brought into the period because, although goods (or services) have been provided, they have not yet been included in the supplier's accounts.

Expense recognition is an important concept. Expenses should be recognised immediately they are known about. Ayco knew they had used stationery for which there was a cost even though an invoice may not have been processed. On the other hand revenues or profits should not be recognised until they are earned.

The net impact of the above on Ayco would have been a reduction in profit, a debit of £800 and an increase in liabilities, a credit of £800 to accruals. The accruals entries would need to be exactly reversed at the beginning of the following month to avoid a doubling up since the actual transactions will also be processed.

Prepayments

It may be that an expense has been incurred within an accounting period that related to future period(s). For example, business rates, rents, or vehicle licence fees paid in advance. As with accruals, these costs are not necessarily related to sales and cannot be matched with sales. Such charges must also be matched to the period to which they relate and therefore the proportion of the charges that relate to future periods (a prepayment) must be calculated and included as an adjustment in the accounts for that period. Figure A1.6 shows a charge of £6,000 that has been incurred by a company from its landlord on 1 January 2005 for rent for the period January to June 2005. At the end of April 2005 the company had paid rent not only for January to April, but rent in advance for May and June. Therefore, before finalising its profit and loss account for January to April the company needed to calculate the rent in advance for May and June, which is shown as £2,000.

The rent in advance of £2,000 has been credited to the rent account and a temporary debtor, a prepayment, created in the balance sheet for £2,000. The total rent costs charged to the profit and loss account for January to April 2005 are therefore £4,000. The prepayment carried forward at the end of April would normally be reversed and the position assessed again at the end of May, and the same procedure followed at the end of June. By the end of July a charge would normally be expected to have been received covering the period July to December and so a prepayment will be necessary at the end of July for the period August to December.

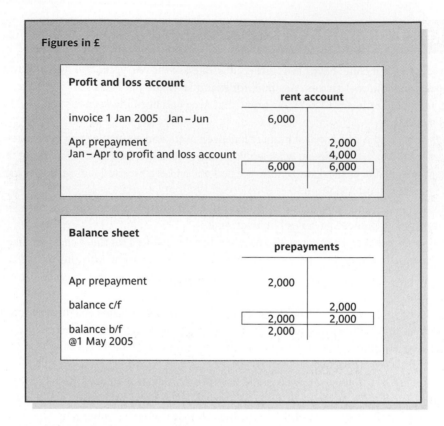

Figure A1.6 T account illustration of accounting for prepayments

Worked Example A1.16

From the following information we are required to prepare three-column accounts (in an Excel spreadsheet or in a Word table) to reflect the current balances on each account, which are then required to be adjusted for the prepayments, deferred income, and accrued income at 31 December 2005, to show the total transfer to the profit and loss account. We are also required to show a summary of the prepayments and accrued income, and accruals and deferred income as at 31 December 2005.

	£
Current balances at 31 December 2005	
Rent payable	12,000
Business rates	13,000
Interest receivable	7,000 (credit)
Rent receivable	8,000 (credit)
Prepayments, accrued income, and deferred income required at 31 December 2005	
Rent payable	700 (normally paid in advance)
Business rates	800 (normally paid in advance)
Interest receivable	700 (normally received in arrears)
Rent received	800 (normally received in advance)

Prepayments adjustments at 31 December 2005

	Debit £	Credit £	Balance £
Rent payable			
31 December			12,000
Prepayment 31 December 2005		(700)	11,300
Transfer to profit and loss account		(11,300)	0
Business rates			
31 December			13,000
Prepayment 31 December 2005		(800)	12,200
Transfer to profit and loss account		(12,200)	0
Interest receivable			
31 December			(7,000)
Accrued income 31 December 2005		(700)	(7,700)
Transfer to profit and loss account	7,700		0
Rent receivable			
31 December			(8,000)
Deferred income 31 December 2005	800		(7,200)
Transfer to profit and loss account	7,200		0
Prepayments and accrued income			
31 December 2005			0
Rent payable	700		700
Business rates	800		1,500
Interest receivable	700		2,200
Accruals and deferred income			
31 December 2005			0
Rent receivable		(800)	(800)

The same sort of exercise is carried out within a company for all of the categories of expense for which prepayments are likely to be required. Worked Example A1.17 explains how prepayments may have been dealt with in Ayco.

Worked Example A1.17

Assume, for example, that Ayco had received an invoice for £2,000 for advertising in January to be paid in March, but the advertising was not taking place until February. An invoice may have been received and processed through the ledgers, but what would be the impact on Ayco?

The answer is that payables would have been credited with £2,000 and advertising expenses debited with £2,000 in the month of January. However, because the advertising had not taken place, the charge of £2,000 would be considered as being in advance, or to use its technical term, a prepayment. The payables entry remains as a credit of £2,000, but an additional entry is required to credit advertising expenses with £2,000 and debit prepayments with £2,000.

A prepayment is expenditure on goods (or services) for future benefit, which is to be charged to future operations. Such amounts are similar to debtors and are included in current assets in the balance sheet.

The net impact of the above on Ayco would have been no charge to profit. The prepayment entry would need to be exactly reversed at the beginning of the following month.

> **Progress check A1.9** **What are accruals and prepayments and why are such adjusting entries needed?**

Accounting periods

In the Ayco worked examples we were introduced to the idea of an accounting period. An accounting period is that covered by the accounting statements of an entity. Different periods may be chosen within the financial year, for example 13 periods of four weeks, 12 periods using a four, four, five week quarter basis, or 12 calendar periods. The Ayco worked examples assumed 12 periods on a calendar basis. Once an accounting period basis has been chosen, consistency must be maintained. This is an example of both the **periodicity concept** and the **consistency concept** (see Chapter 1).

> **Progress check A1.10** **What is an accounting period?**

Summary of key points

- Double-entry bookkeeping is a convention, the two main objectives of which are to have a permanent record of transactions, and to show the effect of each transaction and the combined effect of all the transactions upon the financial position of the entity.
- Double-entry bookkeeping data are recorded as transactions described as 'debits' and 'credits'.
- The meaning of a debit and a credit may most usefully be remembered using the following rule, applying to entries reflected in the accounts of a company:

Cash receipt	=	debit cash account	and credit another account
Cash payment	=	credit cash account	and debit another account
Purchase invoice	=	credit accounts payable	and debit another account
Sales invoice	=	debit accounts receivable	and credit another account

- The main ledger held within the accounting system of a company is called the general ledger, or nominal ledger, in which the results of all transactions made by the company are recorded either in summary or in detail.
- The original books of account, and subsidiary ledgers: cash book (receipts and payments); purchase invoice daybook and purchase ledger (or accounts payable); sales invoice daybook and sales ledger (or accounts receivable), hold the details of transactions that are reflected in the general ledger.

- Wages and salaries data are recorded in the cash books and posted to the general ledger.
- Adjusting accounting entries, such as those relating to closing stock valuations, are made to the accounts prior to preparation of the profit and loss account and balance sheet.
- There are five main accounting adjustments that are made prior to preparation of the profit and loss account and balance sheet:
  - closing stocks
  - accruals: charges not yet received
  - prepayments: payments in advance (and income accrued)
  - depreciation
  - bad and doubtful debts.
- The balances on the individual accounts recorded within the general ledger may be summarised in a trial balance, the total of the debit balances being equal to the total of the credit balances.
- The profit and loss account of an entity shows the profit or loss generated by the entity during an accounting period by deducting all expenses from all revenues.
- The balance sheet of an entity discloses the assets (debit balances) and liabilities, and shareholders' capital (credit balances), and gains (credits) or losses (debits) as at a given date.
- The cash flow statement is a report on the detail of the movement within the cash account in the trial balance, starting with the opening balance and adding the receipts and deducting the payments during the accounting period, resulting in the closing balance.
- The accounting period chosen by a business is the period covered by its accounting statements.

Questions

QA1.1 What are the four basic business transactions and what are their corresponding debit and credit accounting entries under the convention of double-entry bookkeeping?

QA1.2 (i) Name each of the books of account and ledgers in an accounting system.
(ii) What are they used for?

QA1.3 Describe the use and purpose of the five main accounting adjusting entries.

QA1.4 (i) At a specific point in time, what does a company's trial balance show?
(ii) What may the trial balance not show?

QA1.5 How may the financial performance of a company be ascertained from its trial balance?

QA1.6 How may the financial position of a company be ascertained from its trial balance?

QA1.7 How may the cash position of a company be ascertained from its trial balance?

QA1.8 Why is the profit made during an accounting period not necessarily equal to the cash flow during that period?

QA1.9   In what ways do businesses adjust their accounts for accruals and prepayments?

QA1.10   What is the relevance of the accounting period?

Discussion points

DA1.1 'Managers who are non-accounting specialists don't need to learn about bookkeeping, debits and credits, etc.' Discuss.

DA1.2 Computerised accounts and information systems have speeded up the recording of accounting data and the presentation of information. What are the other advantages over manual accounting systems and what are the disadvantages?

Exercises

Solutions are provided in Appendix 3 to all exercise numbers highlighted in colour.

Level I

EA1.1 *Time allowed – 30 minutes*
Extracts from the ledgers of Hall Ltd have provided the following information for 2003 and 2004.

	£
Sales 2003	11,000
Sales 2004	12,000
Purchases 2003	7,100
Purchases 2004	8,300
Expenses 2003	2,500
Expenses 2004	2,800
Stock 1 January 2003	600
Stock 31 December 2003	700
Stock 31 December 2004	800
Obsolete stock in 31 December 2004 stock	200

You are required to prepare a basic profit and loss account for the years ended 31 December 2003 and 2004.

EA1.2 *Time allowed – 30 minutes*

(i)   **Explain why there are always problems at the year end in the assessment of the costs associated with electricity, gas and telephone.**

(ii) **Using the information below, prepare the appropriate year-end accounting entries.**

Electricity charges account balance at 15 December 2004: £10,000
Gas charges account balance at 20 December 2004: £5,000
Estimated consumption
Electricity 16 December to 31 December 2004: £300
Gas 21 December to 31 December 2004: £150

EA1.3 *Time allowed – 30 minutes*
Arthur Moment set up a table-making business, Forlegco, on 1 July 2005. He had £10,000 available to invest, which is the amount he estimated was required for setting up costs. In the first month of trading Forlegco entered into the following transactions:

	£
£10,000 from Arthur Moment	10,000
Purchase of hand tools for cash	2,000
Purchase of lathe, power saw and drill on one month's credit	6,000
Purchase of printing and stationery – invoice received for half the order	100

The total order is £200, and it was all delivered in July and used
Purchase of advertising flyers for cash 2,000 at 50p each, of which 1,000 will
   be used in July, and 500 in August and September
Purchases of timber, glue and varnish, from Woodco, payable within the
   month £1,500 – half of this stock will be on hand at 31 July 2005
Sales of tables to Gardenfurnco for settlement one month later (10 tables at
   £700 each)

You are required to present these transactions in T account format, and then prepare a trial balance for Forlegco for 31 July 2005.

EA1.4 *Time allowed – 30 minutes*
From the trial balance for Forlegco for 31 July 2005 (Exercise EA1.3):

(i)   **Prepare a simple profit and loss account for the month of July 2005.**
(ii)   **Has Forlegco made a profit in July?**
(iii) **If Forlegco has not made a profit, why not?**

EA1.5 *Time allowed – 30 minutes*
From the trial balance for Forlegco for 31 July 2005 (Exercise EA1.3) prepare a simple balance sheet at that date.

EA1.6 *Time allowed – 30 minutes*
From the trial balance for Forlegco for 31 July 2005 (Exercise EA1.3) prepare a simple cash flow statement for the month of July 2005.

EA1.7 *Time allowed – 30 minutes*
You are required to prepare the appropriate correcting entries in a company's accounts at 31 December 2004 for the following:

(i)   **A cheque paid for rent amounting to £2,400 has been entered into the car hire account in error.**
(ii)   **A cheque for £980 was received from a customer in full settlement of a balance of £1,000, but no accounting entry for the discount has been made.**
(iii) **A cheque paid for insurance on the company cars amounting to £1,200 has been entered in the cost of motor cars account in error.**
(iv)   **An invoice from a builder for £3,500 has been entered in the buildings cost account, but in fact it related to redecoration of the reception area of the office and should be treated as a building repair.**

Level II

EA1.8 *Time allowed – 60 minutes*

David (Dai) Etcoak decided to set up a drinks wholesale business, Etcoakco, on 1 December 2004. He had £100,000 available to invest, which is the amount he felt was required to set up the business. In the first month of trading Etcoakco entered into the following transactions:

	£
£100,000 from Dai Etcoak	100,000
Purchase for cash the freehold of a shop	50,000
Purchase for cash the shop fittings	7,000
Purchase of a labelling machine payable one month later	20,000
Cash expenses on printing and stationery	400
Purchases of stock, from Gasco, of bottles of pop, payable three months later (25,000 bottles at £1.25 each)	31,250
Sales of bottles of Etcoak to Boozah for settlement one month later (10,000 bottles at £2.30 each)	23,000
Sales of bottles of Etcoak to Disco30, receivable in the month (12,000 bottles at £2.30 each)	27,600

You are required to:

(i)   look at these transactions in detail and then present them in T account format, and

(ii)   state any assumptions you have made particularly relating to how you have valued stock transactions.

Also:

(iii)   Do you think £100,000 was enough money or too much to invest in the business?

(iv)   What alternative courses of action are open to Dai?

Appendix 2

FRSs, SSAPs, IASs and IFRSs

Financial Reporting Standards (FRSs) in force in the year 2005

FRS 1	Cash flow statements
FRS 2	Accounting for subsidiary undertakings
FRS 3	Reporting financial performance
FRS 4	Capital instruments
FRS 5	Reporting the substance of transactions
FRS 6	Acquisitions and mergers
FRS 7	Fair values in acquisition accounting
FRS 8	Related party disclosures
FRS 9	Associates and joint ventures
FRS 10	Goodwill and intangible assets
FRS 11	Impairment of fixed assets and goodwill
FRS 12	Provisions, contingent liabilities and contingent assets
FRS 13	Derivatives and other financial instruments: disclosures
FRS 14	Earnings per share
FRS 15	Tangible fixed assets
FRS 16	Current tax
FRS 17	Retirement benefits
FRS 18	Accounting policies
FRS 19	Deferred tax
FRS 20	Share-based payment
FRS 21	Events after the balance sheet date
FRS 22	Earnings per share
FRS 23	The effects of changes in foreign currency rates
FRS 24	Financial reporting in hyperinflationary economies
FRS 25	Financial instruments: disclosure and presentation
FRS 26	Financial instruments: measurement
FRSSE	Financial reporting standard for smaller entities

Statements of Standard Accounting Practice (SSAPs) in force in the year 2005

SSAP 4	Accounting for government grants
SSAP 5	Accounting for value added tax
SSAP 9	Stocks and long-term contracts
SSAP 13	Accounting for research and development
SSAP 19	Accounting for investment properties
SSAP 21	Accounting for leases and hire purchase contracts
SSAP 24	Accounting for pension costs
SSAP 25	Segmental reporting

International Accounting Standards (IASs) in force in the year 2005

IAS 1	Presentation of financial statements
IAS 2	Inventories
IAS 7	Cash flow statements
IAS 8	Accounting policies, changes in accounting estimates, and errors
IAS 10	Events after the balance sheet date
IAS 11	Construction contracts
IAS 12	Income taxes
IAS 14	Segment reporting
IAS 15	Information reflecting the effects of changing prices
IAS 16	Property, plant and equipment
IAS 17	Leases
IAS 18	Revenue
IAS 19	Employee benefits
IAS 20	Accounting for Government grants and disclosure of Government assistance
IAS 21	The effects of changes in foreign exchange rates
IAS 23	Borrowing costs
IAS 24	Related party disclosures
IAS 26	Accounting and reporting by retirement benefit plans
IAS 27	Consolidated and separate financial statements
IAS 28	Investments in associates
IAS 29	Financial reporting in hyperinflationary economies
IAS 30	Disclosures in the financial statements of banks and similar financial institutions
IAS 31	Interests in joint ventures
IAS 32	Financial instruments: disclosure and presentation
IAS 33	Earnings per share
IAS 34	Interim financial reporting
IAS 36	Impairment of assets
IAS 37	Provisions, contingent liabilities and contingent assets
IAS 38	Intangible assets
IAS 39	Financial instruments: recognition and measurement
IAS 40	Investment property
IAS 41	Agriculture

International Financial Reporting Standards (IFRSs) in force in the year 2005

Preface to	International financial reporting standards
IFRS 1	First-time adoption of international financial reporting standards
IFRS 2	Share-based payment
IFRS 3	Business combinations
IFRS 4	Insurance contracts
IFRS 5	Non-current assets held for sale and discontinued operations

Appendix 3

Solutions to selected exercises

Solutions are provided for the chapter-end exercise numbers highlighted in colour.

Chapter 2

E2.3 Trainer

Trainer plc
Balance sheet as at 31 December 2005

	£000	£000
Fixed assets		
Land and buildings		320
Plant and machinery		
Cost	200	
Depreciation	80	120
Current assets		
Stocks	100	
Debtors	100	
Bank	73	
	273	
Current liabilities		
Trade creditors	130	
Accruals	5	
Taxation	20	
	155	118
		558
Capital and reserves		
Ordinary shares		320
Profit and loss account		238
		558

Working	£000
Sales	1,000
Cost of sales	600
Gross profit	400
Expenses	(120)
Bad debt	(2)
Depreciation	(20)
Profit before tax	258
Taxation (also a short-term creditor within *Current liabilities*)	(20)
Net profit	238

E2.6 Gorban

Gorban Ltd
Balance sheet as at 31 December 2004

	Per TB £					
Fixed assets						
Tangible assets	235,000		29,368			264,368
Less: depreciation provision	30,165					30,165
	204,835					234,203
Current assets						
Stocks	51,420		48,000			99,420
Debtors	42,500				(10,342)	32,158
Doubtful debts provision	(1,725)			(1,870)		(3,595)
Bank and cash	67,050	(20,000)	(29,368)	50,000		67,682
	159,245					195,665
Current liabilities						
Creditors	35,112					35,112
Accruals		1,173				1,173
	35,112					36,285
Net current assets	124,133					159,380
Total assets less current liabilities	328,968					393,583
less						
Long-term liabilities						
Loan	20,000	(20,000)				
Net assets	308,968					393,583
Capital and reserves						
Share capital	200,000			50,000		250,000
Profit and loss account	108,968	(1,173)	48,000	(1,870)	(10,342)	143,583
	308,968					393,583

E2.7 Pip

Pip Ltd
Balance sheet as at 31 December 2005

	£000	£000	Working
Fixed assets			
Land and buildings	100,000		
Plant and equipment	100,000		[150,000 − 50,000]
		200,000	
Current assets			
Stocks	45,000		[50,000 − 5,000]
Debtors	45,000		[50,000 − 5,000]
Cash in hand and at bank	11,000		[10,000 + 1,000]
	101,000		

Current liabilities

Bank overdraft	10,000	
Trade creditors	81,000	
	91,000	
Net current assets		10,000
		210,000

Capital and reserves

Ordinary shares (issued)		100,000
Profit and loss account		110,000
		210,000

Note that the intangible assets, brands worth £10,000 in the opinion of the directors, have not been included in the balance sheet on the assumption that they are not purchased brands. Under FRS 10 only brand names that have been purchased may be capitalised and included in the balance sheet.

Chapter 3

E3.3 CDs

Overview

Stocks are regulated by the revised SSAP 9. Stocks should be valued at the lower of cost and net realisable value. Retailers can (and do) take the retail value of their stocks (by category) and deduct the gross profit (by category) as an estimate of cost.

- **(i)** This stock should be valued at £5,000 (cost) as the stock is selling consistently.
- **(ii)** This stock should not be in the balance sheet at any value, as it will not generate any cash in the future.
- **(iii)** As in (i) above this stock can be valued at £1,000 (cost) for balance sheet purposes. As there are more risks associated with holding single artist CDs the stock levels should be continually reviewed.
- **(iv)** In this situation the selling pattern has changed and the posters have stopped selling. The posters must not appear in the balance sheet as they will not generate any future cash.

E3.4 Partex

	2002	2003	2004
	£	£	£
(i) Balance sheet as at 31 December – Debtors			
Debtors including debts to be written-off	88,000	110,000	94,000
Write-off of debts to profit and loss account (1)	(4,000)	(5,000)	(4,000)
	84,000	105,000	90,000
Doubtful provision at 4% of debtors (2)	–	3,360	4,200
	(3,360)	(4,200)	(3,600)
Debtors at end of year	80,640	104,160	90,600

(ii)   Profit and loss account year ended 31 December – Bad and doubtful debts

Bad debts written-off (1)	4,000	5,000	4,000
Doubtful debt provision at 4% of debtors (2)	–	(3,360)	(4,200)
	3,360	4,200	3,600
Bad and doubtful debts charge for year	7,360	5,840	3,400

E3.5 Tartantrips

(i) Sum of the digits depreciation

The company needs to decide the economic life of the asset (say 10 years in this example) and its estimated residual value at the end of its life (£1m in this example).

Cost		£5,000,000
Residual value		£1,000,000
Amount to be written-off over 10 years		£4,000,000
Over 10 years the digits 10 + 9 + 8 ... 2 + 1 add up to 55		
Depreciation in year 1 is 10/55 × £4,000,000	=	£727,272
Depreciation in year 2 is 9/55 × £4,000,000	=	£654,545
Depreciation in year 3 is 8/55 × £4,000,000	=	£581,818
and so on until		
Depreciation in year 9 is 2/55 × £4,000,000	=	£145,546
Depreciation in year 10 is 1/55 × £4,000,000	=	£72,727
Total depreciation for 10 years		£4,000,000

(ii) Straight line depreciation

This method is very simple to operate. The company needs to decide on the economic life of the asset and its residual value at the end of its life (as above). The annual depreciation will be:

Depreciation per year is £4,000,000 divided by 10 years = £400,000 per year

It can be seen that there is a constant charge to the annual profit and loss account for each of the ten years for 'wear and tear' of the fixed asset.

(iii) Reducing balance depreciation

This method is quite different to the straight line method because the depreciation charge is much higher in the earlier years of the life of the asset. The same sort of estimates are required: economic life, residual value, which are used in a reducing balance formula to calculate each year's depreciation.

The reducing balance formula where d is the percentage depreciation to charge on the written down value of the asset at the end of each year is:

$d = 1 - \sqrt[10]{1,000,000/5,000,000} = 14.9\%$ (which may also be calculated using the Excel DB function)

Depreciation in year 1 is 14.9% of £5,000,000	=	£745,000
Depreciation in year 2 is 14.9% of £4,255,000	=	£633,995
Depreciation in year 3 is 14.9% of £3,621,005	=	£539,530
and so on until year 10		
The total depreciation for 10 years is		£4,000,000

E3.8 Retepmal

Retepmal Ltd
Profit and loss account for the year ended 31 March 2004

	£	£
Sales		266,000
Cost of Sales		
Opening stock 31 March 2003	15,000	
plus Purchases	150,000	
less Closing stock 31 March 2004	(25,000)	140,000
Gross profit		126,000
Distribution costs and administrative expenses		
[90,000 + 3,000 − 5,000 + 3,000]		91,000
Profit before tax		35,000
Tax		19,000
Profit after tax		16,000
Dividend		7,000
Net profit for the year		9,000

Balance sheet as at 31 March 2004

	£	£
Fixed assets [95,000 + 40,000 + 30,000 − 3,000]		162,000
Current assets		
Stocks	25,000	
Debtors	75,000	
Prepayments	5,000	
Cash and bank	35,000	
	140,000	
Current liabilities		
Trade creditors	54,000	
Accruals	3,000	
Taxation	19,000	
Dividend	7,000	
	83,000	
Net current assets		57,000
Net assets		219,000
Capital and reserves		
Ordinary share capital		80,000
Profit and loss account [130,000 + 9,000]		139,000
		219,000

Chapter 4

E4.1 Candyfloss

(i) Candyfloss cash flow 6 months to 30 June 2005 using the direct method

	£000	£000
Operating cash flow		76.0
Receipts from customers		
Payments		
Flowers suppliers	59.5	
Employees	5.0	
Other overheads		
Rent	4.0	
Operating expenses	7.0	75.5
Cash inflow from operations		0.5
Investing activities		
Purchase of lease	15.0	
Lease fees	1.0	
	16.0	
Purchase of van	14.5	(30.5)
Net cash outflow before financing		(30.0)
Financing		
Loan	3.0	
Issue of shares	18.0	21.0
Net cash outflow for period		(9.0)

(ii) Candyfloss profit and loss account for 6 months to 30 June 2005

	£000	£000	
Sales		84.0	[76.0 + 8.0]
Cost of flowers	54.0		[59.5 + 4.0 − 9.5]
Operating expenses	8.0		[7.0 + 1.0]
Wages	5.0	(67.0)	
Gross profit		17.0	
Overheads			
Rent	2.0		
Depreciation	1.5		[(14.5 − 2.5)/4 × 50% for the half year]
Bad debts	1.5	(5.0)	
Net profit for period		12.0	

(iii) The difference between the cash flow and profit for the period is
− £9,000 − £12,000 = −£21,000

Both cash and profit give an indication of performance.
The profit of £12,000 may be compared with the cash inflow from operations of £500.

	Profit	Operating Cash	Differences
	£000	£000	
Sales/receipts	84.0	76.0	sales 8 not yet paid by customers
Bad debts	(1.5)		sales assumed will never be paid
Flowers	(54.0)	(59.5)	9.5 in stock and 4 not yet paid for
Wages	(5.0)	(5.0)	
Operating expenses	(8.0)	(7.0)	1 not yet paid
Rent	(2.0)	(4.0)	2 rent paid in advance
Depreciation	(1.5)		1.5 not cash
	12.0	0.5	

(iv) A number of items in the profit and loss account are subjective and open to various different methods of valuation:

Bad debts	1.5	different subjective views as to whether customers may pay or not
Stocks	9.5	different valuation methods
Depreciation	1.5	different bases may be used

- additionally cash flow shows how much was paid out for the lease and for the van and what financing was obtained

- cash flow gives a clear picture of the financial performance, looked at alongside the balance sheet which shows the financial position at a point in time

- looking at the profit and loss account from period to period it is difficult to compare performance and with that of similar businesses because of different approaches to asset valuation.

E4.4 Medco

Medco Ltd
Cash flow statement for the year ended 31 December 2004
Reconciliation of operating profit to net cash flow from operating activities

	£
Operating profit	2,500
Depreciation charges	2,000
Loss on sale of fixed assets	500
Increase in stocks	(1,000)
Increase in debtors	(1,000)
Decrease in creditors	(2,000)
Net cash inflow from operating activities	1,000

Cash flow statement

	£
Net cash inflow from operating activities	1,000
Interest paid	(100)
Taxation paid	(400)
Capital expenditure	(10,500)
	(10,000)
Equity dividend paid	(750)
Management of liquid resources	(2,100)
Financing	6,000
Decrease in cash	(6,850)

Reconciliation of net cash flow to movement in net debt/funds

	£
Decrease in cash for the period	(6,850)
Cash inflow from increase in loans	(1,000)
Change in net debt	(7,850)
Net funds 1 January 2004	2,000
Net debt 31 December 2004	(5,850)

Note 1 to the cash flow statement – gross cash flows

	£	£
Returns on investments and servicing of finance		
Interest paid		(100)
Capital expenditure		
Payments to acquire tangible fixed assets	(12,500)	
Receipts from sales of tangible fixed assets	2,000	
		(10,500)
Financing		
Issue of ordinary shares	5,000	
Increase in loans	1,000	
		6,000

Note 2 to the cash flow statement – analysis of change in net debt

	At 1 Jan 2004	Cash flows	At 31 Dec 2004
	£	£	£
Cash and bank	5,000	(2,850)	2,150
Overdraft	(2,000)	(4,000)	(6,000)
Loans	(1,000)	(1,000)	(2,000)
Total	2,000	(7,850)	(5,850)

E4.6 Victoria

(i)

(a)

	£000
Increase in profit and loss account 2004 over 2003 from balance sheet	500
Add tax	320
Add dividends	480
Therefore profit before tax is	1,300

(b)

	£000
Profit before tax	1,300
Add debenture interest	100
Therefore operating profit is	1,400

(ii)

Victoria plc

Cash flow statement for the year ended 30 June 2004

Reconciliation of operating profit to net cash flow from operating activities

	£000
Operating profit	1,400
Depreciation	200
Increase in stocks	(1,400)
Increase in debtors	(680)
Decrease in creditors	(200)
Net cash outflow from operating activities	(680)

Cash flow statement

	£000
Net cash outflow from operating activities	(680)
Interest paid	(100)
Taxation paid (in respect of year 2003)	(300)
Capital expenditure	(2,100)
	(3,180)
Equity dividend paid	(360)
Financing: issue of ordinary shares	2,740
Decrease in cash	(800)

Note 2 to the cash flow statement – analysis of change in net debt

	At 30 Jun 2003 £000	Cash flows £000	At 30 Jun 2004 £000
Cash and bank	200	(200)	–
Overdraft	–	(600)	(600)
Debentures	(1,000)	–	(1,000)
Total	(800)	(800)	(1,600)

E4.7 Sparklers

Sparklers plc
Cash flow statement for the year ended 31 October 2004
Reconciliation of operating profit to net cash flow from operating activities

	£m
Operating profit	41.28
Depreciation charges	10.10
Loss on sale of fixed assets	1.40
Increase in stocks	(20.00)
Increase in debtors	(36.40)
Increase in creditors	8.40
Net cash inflow from operating activities	4.78

Cash flow statement

	£m
Net cash inflow from operating activities	4.78
Returns on investments and servicing of finance (note 1)	(0.48)
Taxation – corporation tax paid	(6.40)
Capital expenditure (note 1)	(21.60)
	(23.70)
Dividends paid	(10.20)
	(33.90)
Financing (note 1)	0.30
Decrease in cash	(33.60)

Reconciliation of net cash flow to movement in net debt (note 2)

	£m
Decrease in cash for the period	(33.60)
Cash flow from increase in debenture	(0.30)
Change in net debt	(33.90)
Net debt 1 November 2003	–
Net debt 31 October 2004	(33.90)

Note 1 to the cash flow statement – gross cash flows

	£m	£m
Returns on investments and servicing of finance		
Interest received	0.08	
Interest paid	(0.56)	
		(0.48)
Capital expenditure		
Payments to acquire tangible fixed assets	(23.60)	
Receipts from sales of tangible fixed assets	2.00	
		(21.60)

Financing

Increase in debentures   0.30

Note 2 to the cash flow statement – analysis of change in net debt

	At 1 Nov 2003 £m	Cash flows £m	At 31 Oct 2004 £m
Cash and bank	1.20	(1.20)	–
Overdraft	–	(32.40)	(32.40)
Debentures	(1.20)	(0.30)	(1.50)
Total	–	(33.90)	(33.90)

Working

	£m	£m
Depreciation		
Depreciation 31 October 2004		21.50
Depreciation at 31 October 2003	19.00	
Depreciation on assets sold in 2004	(7.60)	(11.40)
Charge for the year 2004		10.10
Loss on sale of assets		
Proceeds on sale		2.00
Net book value: cost	11.00	
depreciation	(7.60)	(3.40)
Loss on sale		(1.40)

Dividends paid

Dividends payable at 31 October 2003		6.00
Dividends declared for 2004: preference		0.20
ordinary interim		4.00
ordinary final		12.00
		22.20
Less dividends payable at 31 October 2004		12.00
Dividends paid during 2004		10.20

Purchase of fixed assets

Fixed assets balance 31 October 2004		47.80
Fixed assets balance 31 October 2003	35.20	
Cost of fixed assets sold	(11.00)	(24.20)
Fixed assets purchased		23.60

You should refer to the relevant sections in Chapter 4 to check your assessment of the reasons for the increased overdraft.

Chapter 5

E5.1 Priory

(i) Net debt to equity

	2004	2005	2006
Net debt	100	250	800
Equity	300	500	800
Debt/equity (%)	33%	50%	100%

(ii) Long-term loans to equity and long-term loans

	2004	2005	2006
Long-term loans	200	200	600
Equity + long-term loans	500	700	1,400
Gearing (%)	40%	29%	43%

E5.2 Freshco

Profitability ratios for Freshco plc for 2005 and the comparative ratios for 2004

Gross margin, GM

$$\text{Gross margin \% 2005} = \frac{\text{gross margin}}{\text{sales}} = \frac{£204 \times 100\%}{£894} = 22.8\%$$

$$\text{Gross margin \% 2004} = \frac{£166 \times 100\%}{£747} = 22.2\%$$

Profit before interest and tax, PBIT (or operating profit)

$$\text{PBIT \% 2005} = \frac{\text{operating profit}}{\text{sales}} = \frac{£103 \times 100\%}{£894} = 11.5\%$$

$$\text{PBIT \% 2004} = \frac{£87 \times 100\%}{£747} = 11.6\%$$

Net profit, PAT (return on sales, ROS)

$$\text{PAT \% 2005} = \frac{\text{net profit}}{\text{sales}} = \frac{£56 \times 100\%}{£894} = 6.3\%$$

$$\text{PAT \% 2004} = \frac{£54 \times 100\%}{£747} = 7.2\%$$

Return on capital employed, ROCE (return on investment, ROI)

$$\text{ROCE \% 2005} = \frac{\text{operating profit}}{\substack{\text{total assets − current liabilities} \\ \text{(average capital employed)}}} = \frac{£103 \times 100\%}{(£233 \times £233)/2} = \frac{£103 \times 100\%}{£233} = 44.2\%$$

$$\text{ROCE \% 2004} = \frac{£87 \times 100\%}{(£233 + £219)/2} = \frac{£87 \times 100\%}{£226} = 38.5\%$$

Return on equity, ROE

$$\text{ROE \% 2005} = \frac{\text{PAT}}{\text{equity}} = \frac{£56 \times 100\%}{£213} = 26.3\%$$

$$\text{ROE \% 2004} = \frac{£54 \times 100\%}{£166} = 32.5\%$$

Capital turnover

$$\text{Capital turnover 2005} = \frac{\text{sales}}{\text{average capital employed in year}} = \frac{£894}{£233} = 3.8 \text{ times}$$

$$\text{Capital turnover 2004} = \frac{£747}{£226} = 3.3 \text{ times}$$

Report on the profitability of Freshco plc

Sales for the year 2005 increased by 19.7% over the previous year, but it is not clear whether from increased volumes, new products, or higher selling prices.

Gross margin improved by 0.6% to 22.8% of sales, possibly from increased selling prices and/or from lower costs of production.

Operating profit dropped by 0.1% to 11.5% of sales despite the improvement in gross margin, because of higher levels of distribution costs and administrative expenses.

ROCE improved from 38.5% to 44.2%, indicating a more effective use of funds by Freshco.

Return on equity dropped by 6.2% to 26.3%. This was because profit after tax remained fairly static but equity was increased through an issue of shares and increases in general reserves and retained earnings.

Capital turnover for 2005 increased to 3.8 times from 3.3 in 2004, reflecting the significant increases in sales levels in 2005 over 2004.

E5.4 Freshco

Liquidity ratios for Freshco plc for 2005 and the comparative ratios for 2004

Current ratio

$$\text{Current ratio 2005} = \frac{\text{current assets}}{\text{current liabilities}} = \frac{£208}{£121} = 1.7 \text{ times}$$

$$\text{Current ratio 2004} = \frac{£191}{£107} = 1.8 \text{ times}$$

Acid test (quick ratio)

$$\text{Quick ratio 2005} = \frac{\text{current assets} - \text{stocks}}{\text{current liabilities}} = \frac{£208 - £124}{£121} = 0.7 \text{ times}$$

$$\text{Quick ratio 2004} = \frac{£191 - £100}{£107} = 0.8 \text{ times}$$

Defensive interval

$$\text{Defensive interval 2005} = \frac{\text{quick assets}}{\text{average daily cash from operations}} = \frac{£208 - £124}{(£80 + £894 - £70)/365} = 34 \text{ days}$$

$$\text{Defensive interval 2004} = \frac{£191 - £100}{(£60 + £747 - £80)/365} = 46 \text{ days}$$

Report on the liquidity of Freshco plc

The current ratio and the quick ratio have both dropped slightly to 1.7 times and 0.7 times respectively. However, the defensive interval has dropped significantly from 46 days to 34 days at which level the company could potentially survive if there were no further cash inflows.

Net cash flow from operations improved from £7m in 2004 to £8.1m in 2005. Investments in fixed assets were at lower levels in 2005 and matched by a reduction in long-term financing (debentures).

E5.8 Laurel

(i)

Profitability ratios for Hardy plc for 2005 and the comparative ratios for 2004 and 2003

Gross margin, GM

$$\text{Gross margin \% 2005} = \frac{\text{gross margin}}{\text{sales}} = \frac{£161 \times 100\%}{£456} = 35.3\%$$

$$\text{Gross margin \% 2004} = \frac{£168 \times 100\%}{£491} = 34.2\%$$

$$\text{Gross margin \% 2003} = \frac{£142 \times 100\%}{£420} = 34.0\%$$

Profit before interest and tax, PBIT (or operating profit)

$$\text{PBIT \% 2005} = \frac{\text{operating profit}}{\text{sales}} = \frac{£52 \times 100\%}{£456} = 11.4\%$$

$$\text{PBIT \% 2004} = \frac{£61 \times 100\%}{£491} = 12.4\%$$

$$\text{PBIT \% 2003} = \frac{£50 \times 100\%}{£420} = 11.9\%$$

Net profit, PAT (return on sales, ROS)

$$\text{PAT \% 2005} = \frac{\text{net profit}}{\text{sales}} = \frac{£20 \times 100\%}{£456} = 4.4\%$$

$$\text{PAT \% 2004} = \frac{£28 \times 100\%}{£491} = 5.7\%$$

$$\text{PAT \% 2003} = \frac{£25 \times 100\%}{£420} = 6.0\%$$

Return on capital employed, ROCE (return on investment, ROI)

$$\text{ROCE \% 2005} = \frac{\text{operating profit}}{\text{total assets} - \text{current liabilities}} = \frac{£52 \times 100\%}{(£284 + £292)/2} = \frac{£52 \times 100\%}{£288} = 18.1\%$$

$$\text{ROCE \% 2004} = \frac{£61 \times 100\%}{(£237 + £284)/2} = \frac{£61 \times 100\%}{£260.5} = 23.4\%$$

ROCE % 2003 is not available because we do not have the capital employed figure for 31 March 2002.

Return on equity, ROE

$$\text{ROE \% 2005} = \frac{\text{PAT}}{\text{equity}} = \frac{£20 \times 100\%}{£223} = 9.0\%$$

$$\text{ROE \% 2004} = \frac{£28 \times 100\%}{£215} = 13.0\%$$

$$\text{ROE \% 2003} = \frac{£25 \times 100\%}{£200} = 12.5\%$$

Capital turnover

$$\text{Capital turnover 2005} = \frac{\text{sales}}{\text{average capital employed in year}} = \frac{£456}{£288} = 1.6 \text{ times}$$

$$\text{Capital turnover 2004} = \frac{£491}{£260.5} = 1.9 \text{ times}$$

Capital turnover 2003 is not available because we do not have the capital employed figure for 31 March 2002.

Report on the profitability of Hardy plc

Sales for the year 2005 were 7.1% lower than sales in 2004, which were 16.9% above 2003. It is not clear whether these sales reductions were from lower volumes, fewer products, or changes in selling prices.

Gross margin improved from 34.0% in 2003 to 34.2% in 2004 to 35.3% in 2005, possibly from increased selling prices and/or from lower costs of production.

Operating profit to sales increased from 11.9% in 2003 to 12.4% in 2004 but then fell to 11.4% in 2005, despite the improvement in gross margin, because of higher levels of distribution costs and administrative expenses.

ROCE dropped from 23.4% to 18.1%, reflecting the lower level of operating profit. Return on equity increased from 12.5% in 1998 to 13.0% in 2004 but then fell sharply in 2005 to 9.0%. This was because of the large fall in profit after tax in 2005.

Capital turnover for 2005 was reduced from 1.9 times in 2004 to 1.6 in 2005, reflecting the fall in sales levels in 2005 over 2004.

Efficiency ratios for Hardy plc for 2005 and the comparative ratios for 2004 and 2003

Debtor days

$$\text{Debtor days 2005} = \frac{\text{trade debtors} \times 365}{\text{sales}} = \frac{\text{£80} \times 365}{\text{£456}} = 64 \text{ days}$$

$$\text{Debtor days 2004} = \frac{\text{£70} \times 365}{\text{£491}} = 52 \text{ days}$$

$$\text{Debtor days 2003} = \frac{\text{£53} \times 365}{\text{£420}} = 46 \text{ days}$$

Creditor days

$$\text{Creditor days 2005} = \frac{\text{trade creditors} \times 365}{\text{cost of sales}} = \frac{\text{£38} \times 365}{\text{£295}} = 47 \text{ days}$$

$$\text{Creditor days 2004} = \frac{\text{£38} \times 365}{\text{£323}} = 43 \text{ days}$$

$$\text{Creditor days 2003} = \frac{\text{£26} \times 365}{\text{£277}} = 34 \text{ days}$$

Stock days (stock turnover)

$$\text{Stock days 2005} = \frac{\text{stock value}}{\text{average daily cost of sales in period}} = \frac{\text{£147}}{\text{£295}/365} = 182 \text{ days (26.0 weeks)}$$

$$\text{Stock days 2004} = \frac{\text{£152}}{\text{£323}/365} = 172 \text{ days (24.5 weeks)}$$

$$\text{Stock days 2003} = \frac{\text{£118}}{\text{£277}/365} = 155 \text{ days (22.2 weeks)}$$

Operating cycle days

Operating cycle 2005 = stock days + debtor days − creditor days = 182 + 64 − 47 = 199 days
Operating cycle 2004 = 172 + 52 − 43 = 181 days
Operating cycle 2003 = 155 + 46 − 34 = 167 days

Operating cycle %

$$\text{Operating cycle \% 2005} = \frac{\text{working capital requirement}}{\text{sales}}$$

$$= \frac{(\text{£147} + \text{£80} - \text{£38}) \times 100\%}{\text{£456}} = 41.4\%$$

$$\text{Operating cycle \% 2004} = \frac{(\text{£152} + \text{£70} - \text{£38}) \times 100\%}{\text{£491}} = 37.5\%$$

$$\text{Operating cycle \% 2003} = \frac{(\text{£118} + \text{£53} - \text{£26})}{\text{£420}} = 34.5\%$$

Asset turnover

$$\text{Asset turnover } 2005 = \frac{\text{sales}}{\text{total assets}} = \frac{£456}{£385} = 1.18 \text{ times}$$

$$\text{Asset turnover } 2004 = \frac{£491}{£374} = 1.31 \text{ times}$$

$$\text{Asset turnover } 2003 = \frac{£420}{£303} = 1.39 \text{ times}$$

Report on the working capital performance of Hardy plc

Average customer settlement days worsened successively over the years 2003, 2004 and 2005 from 46 to 52 to 64 days. This was partly mitigated by some improvement in the average creditors settlement period which increased from 34 to 43 to 47 days over the same period. The average stock turnover period worsened from 155 to 172 to 182 days over 2003, 2004, and 2005. Therefore, mainly because of the poor debt collection performance and increasingly high stock levels, the operating cycle worsened from 167 days in 2003 to 181 days in 2004 and to 199 days in 2005 (operating cycle 34.5% to 37.5% to 41.4%). Asset turnover reduced from 1.39 to 1.31 times from 2003 to 2004 and then to 1.18 in 2005, reflecting the degree to which sales had dropped despite increasing levels of total assets.

Liquidity ratios for Hardy plc for 2005 and the comparative ratios for 2004 and 2003

Current ratio

$$\text{Current ratio } 2005 = \frac{\text{current assets}}{\text{current liabilities}} = \frac{£253}{£93} = 2.7 \text{ times}$$

$$\text{Current ratio } 2004 = \frac{£251}{£90} = 2.8 \text{ times}$$

$$\text{Current ratio } 2003 = \frac{£197}{£66} = 3.0 \text{ times}$$

Acid test (quick ratio)

$$\text{Quick ratio } 2005 = \frac{\text{current assets } - \text{ stocks}}{\text{current liabilities}} = \frac{£253 - £147}{£93} = 1.1 \text{ times}$$

$$\text{Quick ratio } 2004 = \frac{£251 - £152}{£90} = 1.1 \text{ times}$$

$$\text{Quick ratio } 2003 = \frac{£197 - £118}{£66} = 1.2 \text{ times}$$

Defensive interval

$$\text{Defensive interval } 2005 = \frac{\text{quick assets}}{\text{average daily cash from operations}}$$

$$= \frac{£253 - £147}{(£70 + £456 - £80)/365} = 87 \text{ days}$$

$$\text{Defensive interval } 2004 = \frac{£251 - £152}{(£53 + £491 - £70)/365} = 76 \text{ days}$$

The defensive interval for 2003 is not available because we do not have the trade debtors figure for 31 March 2002.

Report on the liquidity of Hardy plc

The current ratio and the quick ratio have both dropped over the 3 years from 3.0 to 2.7 times, and 1.2 times to 1.1 times respectively. The defensive interval has increased from 76 days to 87 days at which level the company could potentially survive if there were no further cash inflows.

(ii) There are a number of areas that require further investigation. The following five ratios may be particularly useful to assist this investigation:

- Return on capital employed, ROCE
- Debtor days
- Creditor days
- Stock days
- Current ratio.

(iii) The relevant information has not been provided to enable the following investment ratios to be calculated for Hardy plc, which would have improved the analysis of Hardy plc's performance:

Earnings per share, eps

Cannot be calculated because we do not have details of the number of ordinary shares in issue.

Dividend per share

Cannot be calculated because we do not have details of the number of ordinary shares in issue.

Dividend cover

Cannot be calculated because we have not been able to calculate earnings per share, eps, and dividend per share.

Dividend yield %

Cannot be calculated because we have not been able to calculate dividend per share, and we do not have the market prices of the company's shares.

Price/earnings ratio, P/E

Cannot be calculated because we have not been able to calculate earnings per share, and we do not have the market prices of the company's shares.

Capital expenditure to sales %

Cannot be calculated because we do not have details of capital expenditure.

Capital expenditure to gross fixed assets %

Cannot be calculated because we do not have details of capital expenditure.

Chapter 6

E6.11 Guinness

Guinness plc five-year profit and loss account

Horizontal analysis

	Year 5	Year 4	Year 3	Year 2	Year 1
Turnover	108.4	107.3	107.5	106.9	100.0
Gross profit	93.9	92.2	93.5	91.7	100.0
Other investment income	(470.8)	(195.8)	(370.8)	200.0	100.0
Profit before interest and tax (operating profit)	107.5	99.1	104.6	89.1	100.0
Net interest	48.5	55.9	63.7	92.2	100.0
Profit before tax	122.6	110.2	115.1	88.3	100.0
Tax on profit on ordinary activities	107.0	103.7	100.4	102.1	100.0
Profit on ordinary activities after tax	129.5	113.0	121.5	82.3	100.0
Minority interests	106.9	103.4	106.9	75.9	100.0
Profit for the financial year	130.7	113.5	122.3	82.6	100.0
Dividends	124.5	127.4	117.7	108.9	100.0
Retained profit	135.9	102.1	126.1	61.0	100.0
Earnings per share	124.9	104.6	113.2	81.5	100.0
Interest cover	220.4	177.6	163.3	95.9	100.0
Dividend cover	95.7	87.0	100.0	78.3	100.0

Guinness plc five-year profit and loss account

Vertical analysis

	Year 5	Year 4	Year 3	Year 2	Year 1
Turnover	100.0	100.0	100.0	100.0	100.0
Gross profit	20.3	20.1	20.4	20.1	23.4
Other investment income	2.4	1.0	1.9	(1.0)	(0.6)
Profit before interest and tax (operating profit)	22.7	21.1	22.3	19.1	22.9
Net interest	(2.1)	(2.4)	(2.8)	(4.0)	(4.7)
Profit before tax	20.6	18.7	19.5	15.1	18.2
Tax on profit on ordinary activities	(5.5)	(5.4)	(5.2)	(5.3)	(5.5)
Profit on ordinary activities after tax	15.1	13.4	14.3	9.8	12.7
Minority interests	(0.7)	(0.6)	(0.7)	(0.5)	(0.7)
Profit for the financial year	14.5	12.7	13.7	9.3	12.0
Dividends	(6.2)	(6.5)	(5.9)	(5.5)	(5.4)
Retained profit	8.2	6.3	7.7	3.8	6.6

Sales

The horizontal analysis shows an increase in sales of 8.4% over the five years, most of which was gained from year two over year one. Since year two, sales have not increased materially.

Gross profit

The horizontal analysis shows a drop in gross profit of 6.1% of sales over the five years. The vertical analysis shows that gross profit at 23.4% of sales in year one has dropped to 20.3% of sales in year five. The group may have been suffering from increased competition as its brands failed to continue to maintain their profitability.

Operating profit

The horizontal analysis shows an increase in operating profit of 7.5% of sales over the five years, despite the drop in gross profit levels. This is due to the extremely large gains in investment income. The vertical analysis shows that operating profit has been maintained fairly level over the five years at 22.9% of sales in year one to 22.7% of sales in year five.

Interest payable

The horizontal analysis shows a drop in interest payable by year five to less than half the level in year one. The vertical analysis bears this out, showing interest payable of 2.1% of sales in year five compared with 4.7% of sales in year one. The group's borrowings were probably significantly reduced as little expansion has taken place, indicated by a reliance on mature markets and a lack of new ideas. The increased interest cover confirms the loan repayments.

Profit for the financial year

The horizontal analysis reflects a small increase in profit levels from 12.0% of sales in year one to 14.5% of sales in year five. The vertical analysis shows a steady increase in profit over the years except for a drop in year two, because of the negative investment income and high interest payments in that year.

Dividends

The level of dividends has been up and down over the years but year five is slightly higher at 6.2% of sales than year one which was 5.4% of sales, as shown in the vertical analysis. Dividend cover has been maintained at around two times.

Earnings per share

The horizontal analysis shows an increase of almost 25% in earnings per share in year five compared with year one, having recovered from a dip in earnings in year four.

Chapter 7

E7.1 Share options

Past governments have made employer/employee share option schemes tax efficient and therefore schemes are now very common amongst plcs.

Many plcs have found that their share prices react to specific management policies and decisions, for example takeovers and disposals of businesses. Users of financial information can assess these decisions, knowing of the options awarded to the directors.

Many plcs have found that they can only keep/attract high calibre managers by including share options in their remuneration packages.

Investing institutions demand more and more information regarding directors' remuneration. This can influence their basic hold/buy/sell decisions. The financial press frequently includes criticism of specific companies.

E7.2 Perks

Directors do not necessarily own the company they work for; the shareholders do.

Any monies (expenses) that a director takes from the company will affect the annual profit.

Annual dividends are paid from the annual profits. The shareholders approve the accounts at the AGM, which includes remuneration of the directors.

If the directors hide information regarding their remuneration and benefits from the shareholders, then that part of the accounts may not show a true and fair view of the situation.

E7.3 Contracts

Before the new corporate governance code was introduced, shareholders found that their directors had powers that were increasing, especially regarding length of contract and compensation for loss of office.

The Cadbury and Greenbury committees recommended that directors' contracts should be no longer than (first) three years (Cadbury) and then one year (Greenbury). These committees had looked at the evidence presented to them. Hampel (1998) provided that the contracts should be one year or less.

The financial press regularly comments on the compensation paid to a director, where company performance has been acknowledged to be poor. There is always reference to the length of outstanding directors' contracts.

Shareholders can decide whether to hold/buy/sell shares if they have advance information on the type of contracts being awarded to the executive directors of their company.

UK financial institutions have also become pro-active regarding the length of directors' contracts issue. They have noted that in the past too many highly paid directors were awarding themselves contracts in which compensation for loss of office was very expensive to pay. Currently it often costs companies potentially over £1m to buy out a chief executive from just a one-year contract.

E7.7 Tomkins

Equity shareholders are the owners of the company, and the level of their dividends usually varies with levels of profits earned by the company.

Directors are appointed by the shareholders, and remunerated for their efforts. Major multinational companies are difficult to manage successfully over a long period of time. The remuneration of directors should reflect that difficulty.

The information that has been given about Tomkins plc shows that there was an executive director who earned a basic salary of just below £1 million a year, an amount which most shareholders would like to see disclosed in the accounts and discussed at the AGM.

The bonus of £443,000 would also have generated some interest amongst the institutions and individual shareholders. Institutions (and the UK Government) are seen to put pressure on directors if they feel pay awards are excessive.

The consultancy agreement for a non-executive director may also have been of interest to the various users of the notes to the accounts.

Chapter 8

E8.3 Lucky Jim

If shareholders' equity is E and the net financial debt D then the relative proportions of equity and debt in the total financing are:

$$\frac{E}{E+D} \text{ and } \frac{D}{E+D}$$

$$\frac{E}{E+D} = 2/3$$

$$\frac{D}{E+D} = 1/3$$

Cost of equity e = 18%
Return on financial debt d = 12%
WACC = (2/3 × 18%) + (1/3 × 12%) = 12% + 4% = 16%

$$\text{The present value of future cash flows in perpetuity} = \frac{\text{annual cash flows}}{\text{annual discount rate}\%}$$

$$= \frac{\pounds35,000}{0.16} = \pounds218,750$$

Net present value, NPV = £218,750 − £200,000 = £18,750

Using WACC to discount the cash flows of the project, the result is a positive NPV of £18,750 and therefore the project should be undertaken.

E8.4 Supermarket

	2004	2003	2002
Adjusted net assets	£5,000m	£4,769m	£4,377m
Market value	£17,808m	£11,531m	£11,995m
MVA	£12,808m	£6,762m	£7,618m

E8.5 Yor

(i)

Yor plc
Profit and loss account for the year ended 30 September 2005

Figures in £m

	Debentures	Shares
PBIT	15.6	15.6
Interest payable	(1.6)	(1.2)
Profit before tax	14.0	14.4
Tax on profit on ordinary activities	(3.5)	(3.6)
Profit on ordinary activities after tax	10.5	10.8
Retained profit at 1 October 2004	10.6	10.6
	21.1	21.4
Dividends	(3.3)	(4.6)
Retained profit at 30 September 2005	17.8	16.8

(ii)

Yor plc
Capital and reserves as at 30 September 2005

Figures in £m

	Debentures	Shares
Share capital (£1 ordinary shares)	10.0	14.0
Share premium (4m × £1.50)		6.0
Profit and loss account	17.8	16.8
	27.8	36.8
Loans	30.0	20.0

(iii)

$$\text{earnings per share } 2004 = \frac{\text{profit available for ordinary shareholders}}{\text{number of ordinary shares in issue}} = \frac{£7.8m}{10m}$$

$$= 78p$$

(iv)

using debentures

$$\text{earnings per share } 2005 = \frac{£10.5m}{10m} = £1.05$$

using shares

$$\text{earnings per share } 2005 = \frac{£10.8m}{10m} = 77p$$

(v)

$$\text{dividend per share } 2004 = \frac{\text{total dividends paid to ordinary shareholders}}{\text{number of ordinary shares in issue}} = \frac{£3.0m}{10m}$$

$$= 30p$$

(vi)

using debentures

$$\text{dividend per share } 2005 = \frac{£3.3m}{10m} = 33p$$

using shares

$$\text{dividend per share } 2005 = \frac{£4.6m}{14m} = 33p$$

(vii)

$$\text{gearing} = \frac{\text{long-term debt}}{\text{equity + long-term debt}}$$

2004	**using debentures 2005**	**using shares 2005**
$\dfrac{£20.0m}{£20.6m + £20.0m} = 49.3\%$	$\dfrac{£30.0m}{£27.8m + £30.0m} = 51.9\%$	$\dfrac{£20.0m}{£36.8m + £20.0m} = 35.2\%$

(viii)
Summary of results

Figures in £m

		using debentures	using shares
	2004	**2005**	**2005**
Profit after tax	7.8	10.5	10.8
Dividends	(3.0)	(3.3)	(4.6)
Retained profit for year	4.8	7.2	6.2

The use of debentures to finance the new project will increase the 2004/2005 profit after tax, and available for dividends, by £2.7m or 34.6%, whereas if shares were used the increase would be £3.0m or 38.5%. Earnings per share will be increased to £1.05 (+27p) and decreased to 77p (−1p) respectively. However, retained profit would be increased by £2.4m (50%) and £1.4m (29.2%) respectively. The difference is because the gain from the lower interest cost in using shares is more than offset by the increase in dividends.

Dividend per share will be increased from 30p to 33p per share regardless of which method of financing is used.

Gearing at 30 September 2004 was 49.3%. If debentures are used to finance the new project then gearing will increase to 51.9%, but if shares are used to finance the new project then gearing will decrease to 35.2%. This represents a higher financial risk for the company with regard to its commitments to making a high level of interest payments. The company is therefore vulnerable to a downturn in business and also the possibility of its loans being called in and possible liquidation of the company.

Appendix 1

EA1.1 Hall

Hall Ltd
Profit and loss account for the year ended 31 December 2004

	2004	2003
	£	£
Sales	12,000	11,000
Cost of sales	8,000	7,000
Gross profit	4,000	4,000
Expenses	3,000	2,500
Net profit	1,000	1,500

Working
2003
Cost of sales: opening stock £600 + purchases £7,100 less closing stock £700

2004
Cost of sales: opening stock £700 + purchases £8,300 less closing stock £800 less the obsolete stock of £200
Cost of sales for 2004 must exclude obsolete stock as it has not been sold
Expenses £2,800 plus the obsolete stock £200

EA1.2 Accruals

(i)

The invoices for the common utilities rarely coincide with accounting period ends. To ensure that costs up to the year end are appropriately included, an adjustment is required for the consumption between the invoice date and year end.

(ii)

	Debit £	Credit £
Profit and loss account		
Electricity to 15 December 2004	10,000	
Accruals for charges 16 to 31 December 2004	300	
Total electricity costs for the year 2004	10,300	
Gas to 20 December 2004	5,000	
Accruals for charges 21 to 31 December 2004	150	
Total gas costs for the year 2004	5,150	
Balance sheet		
Electricity accrual at 31 December 2004		(300)
Gas accrual at 31 December 2004		(150)
Total accruals at 31 December 2004		(450)

EA1.7 Correcting Entries

31 December 2004

	Debit £	Credit £
(i)		
Profit and loss account		
Rent	2,400	
Profit and loss account		
Car hire		(2,400)
Correction of account error		
(ii)		
Profit and loss account		
Discount allowed		(20)
Balance sheet		
Sales ledger control account	20	
Customer settlement discount		
(iii)		
Profit and loss account		
Car insurance	1,200	
Balance sheet		
Motor vehicle fixed assets account		(1,200)
Correction of account error		

(iv)

Profit and loss account

Building repairs	3,500

Balance sheet

Buildings fixed assets account	(3,500)
Correction of account error	

EA1.8 Etcoakco

(i)

	Debit £	Credit £		Debit £	Credit £
	Capital			**Cash**	
Transaction 1		100,000	Transaction 1	100,000	
Balance c/f	100,000		Transaction 2		150,000
	100,000	100,000	Transaction 3		7,000
Balance b/f		100,000	Transaction 5		400
@ 1/1/05			Transaction 10	27,600	
			Balance c/f		70,200
				127,600	127,600
			Balance b/f	70,200	
			@ 1/1/05		
	Fixed assets – shop			**Fixed assets – fittings/equipment**	
Transaction 2	50,000		Transaction 3	7,000	
			Transaction 4	20,000	
Balance c/f		50,000	Balance c/f		27,000
	50,000	50,000		27,000	27,000
Balance b/f	50,000		Balance b/f	27,000	
@ 1/1/05			@ 1/1/05		
	Printing/stationery expenses			**Payables**	
Transaction 5	400		Transaction 4		20,000
			Transaction 6		31,250
Balance c/f		400	Balance c/f	51,250	
	400	400		51,250	51,250
Balance b/f	400		Balance b/f		51,250
@ 1/1/05			@ 1/1/05		
	Stock			**Sales**	
Transaction 6	31,250		Transaction 7		23,000
Transaction 9		27,500	Transaction 8		27,600
Balance c/f		3,750	Balance c/f	50,600	
	31,250	31,250		50,600	50,600
Balance b/f	3,750		Balance b/f		50,600
@ 1/1/05			@ 1/1/05		

	Receivables			**Cost of sales**	
Transaction 7	23,000		Transaction 9	27,500	
Transaction 8	27,600		Balance c/f		27,500
Transaction 10		27,600		27,500	27,500
Balance c/f		23,000	Balance b/f	27,500	
	50,600	50,600	@ 1/1/05		
Balance b/f	23,000				
@ 1/1/05					

Solutions to parts **(ii)**, **(iii)** and **(iv)** may provide an introduction to stock valuation, cost of sales and sources of funds, covered in Chapters 2, 3 and 8.

Glossary of key terms

accountancy The practice or profession of accounting.

accounting The classification and recording of monetary transactions, the presentation and interpretation of the results of those transactions in order to assess performance over a period and the financial position at a given date, and the monetary projection of future activities arising from alternative planned courses of action.

accounting adjustments Accounting entries that do not arise from the basic transactions of cash and invoices. Adjusting entries are made for depreciation, bad and doubtful debts, closing stocks, prepayments, and accruals.

accounting concepts The principles underpinning the preparation of accounting information. Fundamental accounting concepts are the broad basic assumptions which underlie the periodic financial accounts of business enterprises.

accounting period The time period covered by the accounting statements of an entity.

accounting policies The specific accounting bases selected and consistently followed by an entity as being, in the opinion of the management, appropriate to its circumstances and best suited to present fairly its results and financial position (FRS 18 and Companies Act).

accounting standard Authoritative statement of how particular types of transaction and other events should be reflected in financial statements. Compliance with accounting standards will normally be necessary for financial statements to give a true and fair view (ASB).

Accounting Standards Board (ASB) A UK standard-setting body set up in 1990 to develop, issue and withdraw accounting standards. Its aims are to 'establish and improve standards of financial accounting and reporting, for the benefit of users, preparers and auditors of financial information'.

accounts payable Also called trade creditors, is the money owed to suppliers for goods and services.

accounts receivable Also called trade debtors, is the money owed to entities by customers.

accruals Allowances made for costs and expenses payable within one year of the balance sheet date but for which no invoices have yet been recorded.

accruals concept The principle that revenues and costs are recognised as they are earned or incurred, and so matched with each other, and dealt with in the profit and loss account of the period to which they relate, irrespective of the period of receipt or payment. Where a conflict arises, this concept is subservient to the prudence concept.

acid test Quick assets (current assets excluding stocks) divided by current liabilities measures the ability of the business to pay creditors in the short term.

activity based costing (ABC) An approach to costing and monitoring of activities which involves tracing resource consumption and costing final outputs. Resources are assigned to activities and activities to cost objects based on consumption estimates. The latter utilise cost drivers to attach activity costs to outputs.

amortisation In the same way that depreciation applies to the charging of the cost of tangible fixed assets over their useful economic lives, amortisation is the systematic write-off of the cost of an intangible asset, relating particularly to the passage of time, for example leasehold premises (FRS 11 and FRS 15).

annual report and accounts A set of statements which may comprise a management report (in the case of companies, a directors' report), an operating and financial review (OFR), and the financial statements of the entity.

asset A right or other access to future economic benefits controlled by an entity as a result of past transactions or events (FRS 5).

asymmetric digital subscriber line (ADSL) An ADSL is the specific technology for making broadband transmissions on the existing telephone network (the main alternative for broadband transmission being cable technology). ADSL is potentially 40 times faster than a 56 kilobyte modem.

audit A systematic examination of the activities and status of an entity, based primarily on investigation and analysis of its systems, controls and records. A statutory annual audit of a company is defined by the ASB as an independent examination of, and expression of an opinion on, the financial statements of the enterprise.

Auditing Practices Board (APB) A body formed in 1991 by an agreement between the six members of the Consultative Committee of Accountancy Bodies, to be responsible for developing and issuing professional standards for auditors in the United Kingdom and the Republic of Ireland.

auditor A professionally qualified accountant who is appointed by, and reports independently to, the shareholders, providing an objective verification to shareholders and other users that the financial statements have been prepared properly and in accordance with legislative and regulatory requirements; that they present the information truthfully and fairly; and that they conform to the best accounting practice in their treatment of the various measurements and valuations.

audit report An objective verification to shareholders and other users that the financial statements have been prepared properly and in accordance with legislative and regulatory requirements; that they present the information truthfully and fairly and that they conform to the best accounting practice in their treatment of the various measurements and valuations.

BACS (bankers automated clearing services) An electronic bulk clearing system generally used by banks and building societies for low-value and/or repetitive items such as standing orders, direct debits and automated credits such as salary payments.

bad debt A debt which is considered to be uncollectable and is, therefore, written off either as a charge to the profit and loss account or against an existing doubtful debt provision.

balance sheet A statement of the financial position of an entity at a given date disclosing the assets, liabilities and accumulated funds such as shareholders' contributions and reserves, prepared to give a true and fair view of the financial state of the entity at that date.

bank reconciliation A detailed statement reconciling, at a given date, the cash balance in an entity's cash book with that reported in a bank statement.

beta factor (β) The measure of the volatility of the return on a share relative to the market. If a share price were to rise or fall at double the market rate, it would have a beta factor of 2. Conversely, if the share price moved at half the market rate, the beta factor would be 0.5.

bit A bit is short for binary digit, either 1 or 0 in the binary number system, and is the smallest unit of information handled by a computer, represented physically by an element such as a single pulse sent through a circuit or a small spot on a magnetic disc. Bits are normally seen in groups of eight, which is termed a byte, to represent more meaningful information including the letters of the alphabet and the digits 0 to 9.

bookkeeping Recording of monetary transactions, appropriately classified, in the financial records of an entity, either by manual means or otherwise.

broadband The method of sending and receiving data over high speed networks which is most commonly associated with a much faster way of connecting computers to the Internet than possible via conventional dial-up. Broadband is continually operational (not tying up the telephone line) and enables quicker loading of web pages, and transfer of files and email.

browser Users generally navigate through information on the Internet with the aid of a program called a browser, or client. A browser presents text, images, sound or other information objects on a user's computer screen in the form of a page, which is obtained from a www server.

budget A quantified statement, for a defined period of time, which may include planned revenues, expenses, assets, liabilities and cash flows.

business entity concept The concept that financial accounting information relates only to the activities of the business entity and not to the activities of its owners.

byte A byte is used to represent computer information including the letters of the alphabet and the digits 0 to 9, and is a unit of information consisting of 8 bits.

cable modem A cable modem transmits data at very high speeds, typically between 1 and 3 megabytes per second (or higher) compared with a telephone modem's Internet connection at 56 kilobytes per second. A cable modem can also be used to provide a television with channels for Internet access.

Cadbury Committee Report of the Cadbury Committee (December 1992) on the Financial Aspects of Corporate Governance, set up to consider issues in relation to financial reporting and accountability, and to make recommendations on good practice, relating to:

- responsibilities of executive and non-executive directors
- establishment of company audit committees
- responsibility of auditors
- links between shareholders, directors, and auditors
- any other relevant matters.

The report established a Code of Best Practice, now succeeded by the Combined Code of Practice.

capital asset pricing model (CAPM) A theory which predicts that the expected risk premium for an individual share will be proportional to its beta, such that the expected risk premium on a share = beta × the expected risk premium in the market. Risk premium is defined as the expected incremental return for making a risky investment rather than a safe one.

capital expenditure The cost of acquiring, producing or enhancing fixed assets.

cash Cash in hand and deposits repayable on demand with any bank or other financial institution. Cash includes cash in hand and deposits denominated in foreign currency (FRS 1).

cash book A book of original entry that includes details of all receipts and payments made by an entity. The details normally include transaction date, method of payment or receipt, amount paid or received, bank statement value (if different), name of payee or payer, general ledger allocation and coding.

cash flow statement A statement that summarises the inflows and outflows of cash for a period, classified under the following standard headings (FRS 1):

- operating activities
- returns on investment and servicing of finance
- taxation
- investing activities
- liquid funds
- equity dividends
- financing.

cash interest cover Net cash inflow from operations plus interest received, divided by interest paid, calculates the number of times the interest payable is covered by cash flow available for such payments.

cash payment A cash payment is the transfer of funds from a business to a recipient (for example, trade creditor or employee).

cash receipt A cash receipt is the transfer of funds to a business from a payer (for example, a customer).

client-server A client-server is a form of network architecture in which each computer on a network is either a client or a server. Servers are powerful computers dedicated to managing disc drives, printers or network traffic. Clients are PCs or workstations, from which users are able to run application programs. Clients rely on servers for resources such as data, devices and sometimes processing power.

closing stocks All trading companies buy stock with the intention of reselling, at a profit, to a customer. At the end of each accounting period, the company will have unsold stock that will be sold during a subsequent accounting period. That unsold stock is termed 'closing stock' and is deducted from opening stock plus purchases (to derive cost of sales), and will appear in the balance sheet as stocks (within current assets).

Combined Code of Practice The successor to the Cadbury Code, established by the Hampel Committee. The code consists of a set of principles of corporate governance and detailed code provisions embracing the work of the Cadbury, Greenbury and Hampel Committees. Section 1 of the code contains the principles and provisions applicable to UK listed companies, while section 2 contains the principles and provisions applicable to institutional shareholders in their relationships with companies.

computer-aided design (CAD) CAD is a general term referring to software applications and the method used in art, architecture, engineering and manufacturing to design and provide precision drawings, for example buildings, machinery, components and other items, using a computer VDU. CAD enables the interactive design and testing of a product or component.

computer-aided engineering (CAE) CAE, the broad term used by the electronic design automation (EDA) industry for the use of computers to design, analyse, and manufacture products and processes, includes computer-aided design (CAD – the use of a computer for drafting and modelling designs), and computer-aided manufacturing (CAM).

computer-aided manufacturing (CAM) CAM relates to the use of computers for managing manufacturing processes, through software designed to control each of the tasks involved.

computer-integrated manufacturing (CIM) CIM is the use of computers to give instructions that automatically set up, run and monitor the performance of manufacturing equipment and processes. The use of robotic plant and equipment provides computer software to monitor the manufactured product and directly control processes, which ensures high quality manufacturing output of defect-free components and products.

computerised accounting system This is a system that maintains business transactions on a computer on a long-term basis.

conceptual frameworks of accounting The statements of principles, which provide generally accepted guidance for the development of new financial information reporting practices and the review of current reporting practices.

consistency concept The principle that there is uniformity of accounting treatment of like items within each accounting period and from one period to the next.

consolidated accounts The consolidated financial statements which present financial information for the group as a single economic entity, prepared using a process of adjusting and combining financial information from the individual financial statements of a parent undertaking and its subsidiary undertakings (FRS 2).

contingent liability A possible obligation that arises from past events and whose existence will be confirmed only by the occurrence of one or more uncertain future events not wholly within the entity's control; or

A present obligation that arises from past events but is not recognised because: it is not probable that a transfer of benefits will be required to settle the obligation; or, the amount of the obligation cannot be measured with sufficient reliability (FRS 12).

continuing operations Operations not satisfying all the conditions relating to discontinued operations (see below).

convertible loan A loan which gives the holder the right to convert to other securities, normally ordinary shares, at a pre-determined date and at a pre-determined price or ratio.

corporate governance The system by which companies are directed and controlled. Boards of directors are responsible for the governance of their companies. The shareholders' role in governance is to appoint the directors and the auditors and to satisfy themselves that an appropriate governance structure is in place.

corporate social responsibility (CSR) CSR is the decision-making and implementation process that guides all company activities in the protection and promotion of international human rights, labour and environmental standards and compliance with legal requirements within its operations and in its relations to the societies and communities where it operates. CSR involves a commitment to contribute to the economic, environmental and social sustainability of communities through the on-going engagement of stakeholders, the active participation of communities impacted by company activities and the public reporting of company policies and performance in the economic, environmental and social arenas (www.bench-marks.org).

corporation tax Tax chargeable on companies resident in the UK, or trading in the UK through a branch or agency, as well as on certain unincorporated associations (FRS 16).

cost The amount of expenditure (actual or notional) incurred on, or attributable to, a specified thing or activity. To cost something is to ascertain the cost of a specified thing or activity. Cost also relates to a resource sacrificed or forgone, expressed in a monetary value.

cost of quality (COQ) The cost of quality may be defined as the additional cost incurred in non-added value activities and events in a business in fully satisfying customers' agreed requirements for products and services delivered. It is the cost both of not doing the right things and not doing things right first time.

cost of sales The sum of direct cost of sales, adjusted for closing stocks, plus manufacturing overhead attributable to the sales. Direct costs include the wages and salaries costs of time worked on products, and the costs of materials used in production. Manufacturing overheads include the wages and salaries costs of employees not directly working on production, and materials and expenses incurred on activities not directly used in production but necessary to carry out production. Examples are cleaning materials and electricity costs.

creative accounting A form of accounting which, while complying with all regulations, nevertheless gives a biased (generally favourable) impression of a company's performance.

creditor A person or an entity to whom money is owed as a consequence of the receipt of goods or services in advance of payment.

creditor days Average trade creditors divided by average daily purchases on credit terms indicates the average time taken, in calendar days, to pay for supplies received on credit.

cross-sectional analysis Cross-sectional analysis provides a means of providing a standard against which performance can be measured and uses ratios to compare different businesses at the same points in time (see inter-firm comparison).

current assets Cash or other assets, for example stocks, debtors and short-term investments, held for conversion into cash in the normal course of trading.

current liabilities Liabilities which fall due for payment within one year. They include that part of long-term loans due for repayment within one year.

current ratio Current assets divided by current liabilities is an overall measure of liquidity.

database management system (DBMS) A database is any collection of data organised for storage in a computer memory and designed for access by authorised users. Data may be in the form of text, numbers, or encoded graphics.

debenture The written acknowledgement of a debt by a company, usually given under its seal, and normally containing provisions as to payment of interest and the terms of repayment of principal. A debenture may be secured on some or all of the assets of the company or its subsidiaries.

debt One of the alternative sources of capital for a company, also called long-term debt or loans.

debt/equity ratio A gearing ratio that relates to financial gearing, which is the relationship between a company's borrowings, which includes both prior charge capital and long-term debt, and its ordinary shareholders' funds (share capital plus reserves).

debtor days Average trade debtors divided by average daily sales on credit terms indicates the average time taken, in calendar days, to receive payment from credit customers.

debtors Money that is owed to the company by customers, usually called trade debtors.

defensive interval Quick assets (current assets excluding stocks) divided by average daily cash from operations shows how many days a business could survive at its present level of operating activity if no inflow of cash was received from sales or other sources.

depreciation A measure of the wearing out, consumption or other reduction in the useful economic life of a fixed asset, whether arising from use, effluxion of time or obsolescence through technological or market changes (FRS 11 and FRS 15). Depreciation should be allocated so as to charge a fair proportion of the total cost (or valuation) of the asset to each accounting period expected to benefit from its use.

depreciation provision The amount of depreciation that has cumulatively been charged to the profit and loss account, relating to a fixed asset, from the date of its acquisition. Fixed assets are stated in the balance sheet at their net book value (or written down value), which is usually their historical cost less the cumulative amount of depreciation at the balance sheet date.

direct method A method of calculating cash flow as the net of operating cash receipts and payments that is summarised for inclusion in the cash flow statement. It is a time-consuming process that is not straightforward and is not widely used by UK companies.

director A person elected under the company's articles of association to be responsible for the overall direction of the company's affairs. Directors usually act collectively as a board and carry out such functions as are specified in the articles of association or the Companies Acts, but they may also act individually in an executive capacity.

discontinued operations Operations of the reporting entity that are sold or terminated and that satisfy certain criteria (FRS 3):

- the sale or termination is completed either in the period or before the earlier of three months after the commencement of the subsequent period and the date on which the financial statements are approved
- if a termination, the former activities have ceased permanently
- the sale or termination has a material effect on the nature and focus of the reporting entity's operations, and represents a material reduction in its operating facilities resulting from its withdrawal from a particular market (whether class of business or geographical) or from a material reduction in turnover in the reporting entity's continuing markets
- the assets, liabilities, results of operations and activities are clearly distinguishable physically, operationally and for financial reporting purposes.

discounted cash flow (DCF) The discounting of the projected net cash flows of a capital project to ascertain its present value, using a yield or internal rate of return (IRR), net present value (NPV) or discounted payback.

dividend An amount payable to shareholders from profits or distributable reserves. Dividends are normally paid in cash, but scrip dividends, paid by the issue of additional shares, are permissible. Listed companies usually declare two dividends each year, an interim dividend based on the mid-year profits, and a final dividend based on annual profit.

dividend cover Earnings per share divided by dividend per share indicates the number of times the profits attributable to the equity shareholders cover the actual dividends payable for the period.

double-entry bookkeeping The system of bookkeeping based on the principle that every financial transaction involves the simultaneous receiving and giving of value, and is therefore recorded twice.

doubtful debt A debt for which there is some uncertainty as to whether or not it will be settled, and for which there is a possibility that it may eventually prove to be bad. A doubtful debt provision may be created for such a debt by charging it as an expense to the profit and loss account.

doubtful debt provision An amount charged against profit and deducted from debtors to allow for the estimated non-recovery of a proportion of the debts.

dual aspect concept The rule that provides the basis for double-entry bookkeeping, reflecting the practical reality that every transaction always includes both the giving and receiving of something.

earnings per share (eps) Profit after tax less preference share dividends divided by the number of ordinary shares in issue measures the return per share of earnings available to shareholders.

EBITDA Earnings before interest, tax, depreciation, and amortisation.

E-business E-business uses electronic technology to change or automate business processes and includes a range of tools and techniques such as e-commerce, business intelligence, customer relationship management, supply chain management, and enterprise planning.

E-commerce E-commerce is a more narrowly focused term, being one aspect of e-business, broadly involving the sharing of business information and performing business transactions. It may include electronic data interchange (EDI), mobile telephone technology, electronic supplier links, Internet, intranet, extranet, electronic catalogue buying, and email.

economic value added (EVA™) Profit after tax adjusted for distortions in operating performance (such as goodwill, extraordinary losses, and operating leases) less a charge for the amount of capital employed to create that profit (calculated from the adjusted book value of net assets times the company's weighted average cost of capital) (Stern Stewart).

electronic data interchange (EDI) EDI is the secure electronic exchange of business documents such as invoices, fund transfer requests or purchase orders between trading partners. EDI is vital for efficient e-commerce between trading partners. It allows businesses to automate routine transactions and to guarantee transaction integrity. There are several sector-specific EDI standards in use internationally. Initially, private networks were used to send and receive messages, but since the mid-1990s EDI over the Internet has been widely adopted and complexity and cost issues have been greatly reduced.

electronic funds transfer (EFT) EFT works in a similar way to EDI (which deals with the electronic transfer of documents), but with a different set of standards, and is used to transmit funds. EFT may be made between organisations and their employees, suppliers, customers, and any other third parties.

electronic point of sale (EPOS) EPOS systems process sales transactions electronically and scan and capture real-time product information at the point of sale. The systems range from networked cash registers in retail and wholesale outlets with links to business computer systems, to larger systems that link point of sale information with warehousing, suppliers ordering systems, customer databases and online web stores.

Email Electronic mail, or email, enables any person with Internet access to send and receive written messages, files, still and moving images, to and from any other person with Internet access, anywhere in the world, and almost instantaneously.

encryption Encryption is a process used to encode data that is entered into a system, and therefore provides security through preventing unauthorised access to data while it is being stored or transmitted and before it reaches its required destination.

enterprise resource planning (ERP) ERP software spans across functional boundaries. ERP packages comprise individual modules that are process-focused and supporting, for example, accounting, finance, stocks management, design, engineering, supply chain management, manufacturing, quality management, human resource management, planning, sales, and distribution. ERP packages provide flexible systems that are totally integrated and enable use of the Internet for information flows between suppliers, customers and other third parties, on a local and a global basis.

environmental reporting A statement included within the annual report and accounts that sets out the environmental policies of the company and an explanation of its environmental management systems and responsibilities. The environmental report may include reporting on the performance of the business on environmental matters in qualitative terms regarding the extent to which it meets national and international standards. It may also include a quantitative report on the performance of the business on environmental matters against targets, together with an assessment of the financial impact.

equity The total investment of the shareholders in the company, the total wealth. Equity comprises capital, premiums, and retained earnings.

euro The common currency of the European Union, which came into being on 1 January 1999. Financial transactions and/or financial reporting of member states may now be undertaken in either the functional domestic currencies, or in euros.

exceptional items Material items which derive from events or transactions that fall within the ordinary activities of the reporting entity individually or, if a similar type, in aggregate and which need to be disclosed separately by virtue of their size or incidence if the financial statements are to give a true and fair view (FRS 3).

extranet An extranet is a mechanism based on Internet and web technology for businesses to communicate both privately and selectively with their customers. It is effectively a part of the business's intranet that is extended to users outside the business.

extraordinary items Material items possessing a high degree of abnormality that arise from events or transactions that fall outside the ordinary activities of the reporting entity and which are not expected to recur. They do not include exceptional items, nor do they include prior period items merely because they relate to a prior period (FRS 3).

failure mode and effect analysis (FMEA) FMEA is used to identify the most important possible modes of failure during the design and development stage of a product so that action may be taken to reduce the risks of those occurrences.

finance director The finance director of an organisation is actively involved in broad strategic and policy-making activities involving financial considerations. The finance director provides the board of directors with advice on financing, capital expenditure, acquisitions, dividends, the implications of changes in the economic environment, and the financial aspects of legislation. The finance director is responsible for the planning and control functions, the financial systems, financial reporting, and the management of funds.

finance lease A lease is a contract between a lessor and a lessee for the hire of a specific asset. The lessor retains ownership of the asset but gives the right to the use of the asset to the lessee for an agreed period in return for the payment of specified rentals (SSAP 21). A finance lease transfers substantially all the risks and rewards of ownership of the asset to the lessee.

financial accounting Financial accounting is the function responsible for the periodic external reporting, statutorily required, for shareholders. It also provides such similar information as required for Government and other interested third parties, such as potential investors, employees, lenders, suppliers, customers, and financial analysts.

financial instrument Any contract that gives rise to both a financial asset of one entity and a financial liability or equity instrument of another entity. Financial instruments include both primary financial instruments – such as bonds, debtors, creditors and shares – and derivative financial instruments whose value derives from the underlying assets.

financial management The management of all the processes associated with the efficient acquisition and deployment of both short- and long-term financial resources. Within an organisation financial management assists operations management to reach their financial objectives.

Financial Reporting Standards (FRSs) The accounting standards of practice published by the Accounting Standards Board since 1 August 1990, and which are gradually replacing the Standard Statements of Accounting Practice (SSAPs), which were published by the Accounting Standards Committee up to 1 August 1990.

financial statements Summaries of accounts, whether to internal or external parties, to provide information for interested parties. The three key financial statements are: profit and loss account; balance sheet; cash flow statement. Other financial statements are: report of the auditors; statement of recognised gains and losses; reconciliation of movements in shareholders' funds.

financing The section of the cash flow statement that shows the long-term funds raised by or repaid by the company during the year.

finished product Finished product or finished goods are manufactured goods ready for sale or despatch.

firewall A firewall is software and/or hardware that is used to isolate a computer network from unauthorised external use.

first in first out (FIFO) Assumes that the oldest items or costs are the first to be used. It is commonly applied to the pricing of issues of materials, based on using first the costs of the oldest materials in stock, irrespective of the sequence in which actual material usage takes place. Closing stocks are therefore valued at relatively current costs.

fixed assets Any asset, tangible or intangible, acquired for retention by an entity for the purpose of providing a service to the business, and not held for resale in the normal course of trading. This includes, for example, equipment, machinery, furniture, fittings, computers, software, and motor vehicles that the company has purchased to enable it to meet its strategic objectives; such items are not renewed within the operating cycle.

flotation A flotation (or a new issue) is the obtaining of a listing by a company on a stock exchange, through the offering of its shares to the general public, financial institutions or private sector businesses.

fraudulent trading An offence committed by persons who are knowingly party to the continuance of a company trading in circumstances where creditors are defrauded or for other fraudulent purposes. Generally, this means that the company incurs more debts at a time when it is known that those debts will not be met. Persons responsible for so acting are personally liable without limitation for the debts of the company. The offence also carries criminal penalties.

gearing Financial gearing calculations can be made in a number of ways. Gearing is generally seen as the relationship between a company's borrowings, which include both prior charge capital (capital having a right of interest or preference shares having fixed dividends) and long-term debt, and its ordinary shareholders' funds (share capital plus reserves).

general ledger Also called the nominal ledger, contains all accounts relating to assets, expenses, revenue and liabilities.

gigabyte A gigabyte or Gb is a measure of capacity equal to one billion bytes. It can often be used to mean either 1,000 megabytes or 1,024 megabytes.

going concern concept The assumption that the entity will continue in operational existence for the forseeable future.

goodwill The difference between the value of a business as a whole and the aggregate of the fair values of the separable net assets (FRS 10). Goodwill is normally recognised on the purchase of a business, when the price paid for the net assets acquired exceeds their fair values. Where the fair value of the separable net assets exceeds the value of the business as a whole, the difference is termed negative goodwill.

graphic user interface (GUI) A GUI is a development of operating systems that now enable users to command the computer by using a mouse to click on icons, rather than using the keyboard to type instructions. Icons are small pictorial representations of objects, denoting a particular function or program, which are displayed on the computer screen.

gross margin (GM) Gross margin (or gross profit) is the difference between sales and the total cost of sales.

groupware Groupware is software that allows individuals to coordinate efforts and collaborate on various tasks and projects.

hacker A hacker is a malicious intruder who has gained unauthorised access to a computer system. Hacking may occur in the systems of individuals, and in both large and small organisations by current or past employees as well as outsiders, simply to cause damage or for fraudulent purposes.

Hampel Committee The 1998 report of the Hampel Committee on Corporate Governance was set up to conduct a review of the Cadbury Code and its implications:
- review of the role of directors
- matters arising from the Greenbury Study Group on directors' remuneration
- role of shareholders and auditors
- other relevant matters.

The Hampel Committee was responsible for the corporate governance Combined Code of Practice.

historical cost concept A basis of accounting prescribed by the Companies Act for published accounts that uses a system of accounting in which all values are based on the historical costs incurred.

horizontal analysis (or **common size analysis**) An analysis of the profit and loss account (or balance sheet) that allows a line-by-line analysis of the accounts with those of the previous year. It may provide over a number of years a trend of changes showing either growth or decline in these elements of the accounts through calculation of annual percentage growth rates in profits, sales, stock or any other item.

hybrid finance A financial instrument that has the characteristics of both debt and equity.

indirect method A method of calculating cash flow which uses the starting point of operating profit, since it is the operating activities of sales and costs that normally give rise to the majority of cash inflows and cash outflows of an entity. Operating profit for the period must then be adjusted for depreciation, as well as movements in stock, debtors and creditors over the same period to derive the net cash flow from operating activities.

inflation A general increase in the price level over time. In a period of hyperinflation the rate at which the price level rises has become extremely high, and possibly out of control.

initial public offering (IPO) An IPO is a company's first public sale of its shares. Shares offered in an IPO are often, but not always, those of young, small companies seeking outside equity capital and a public market for their shares. Investors purchasing shares in IPOs generally must be prepared to accept considerable risks for the possibility of large gains.

insolvency The inability of a company, partnership or individual to pay creditors' debts in full after realisation of all the assets of the business.

intangible assets Assets, except for investments in subsidiary companies, which do not have a physical identity and include software, patents, trademarks, and goodwill (FRS 10).

integrated services digital network (ISDN) An ISDN provides digital data services over traditional analogue telephone lines in the same way as ADSL. An ISDN allows users to send and receive data at very high speeds and can carry both voice and/or data transmission on the same line. The use of ISDN appears to be declining as the use of broadband increases.

interest cover Profit before interest and tax divided by interest payable, calculates the number of times the interest payable is covered by profits available for such payments. It is particularly important for lenders to determine the vulnerability of interest payments to a drop in profit.

inter-firm comparison Systematic and detailed comparison of the performance of different companies generally operating in a common industry. Normally the information distributed by the scheme administrator (to participating companies only) is in the form of ratios, or in a format, which prevents the identity of individual scheme members from being identified.

internal audit An independent appraisal function established within an organisation to examine and evaluate its activities as a service to the organisation. The objective of internal auditing is to assist members of the organisation in the effective discharge of their responsibilities. To this end, internal auditing furnishes them with analyses, appraisals, recommendations, counsel and information concerning the activities reviewed (Institute of Internal Auditors – UK).

internal control As defined in the Cadbury Report, it is the whole system of controls, financial or otherwise, established in order to provide reasonable assurance of:
- effective and efficient operation
- internal financial control
- compliance with laws and regulations.

internal rate of return (IRR) The annual percentage return achieved by a project, at which the sum of the discounted cash inflows over the life of the project is equal to the sum of the discounted cash outflows.

International Accounting Standard (IAS) The international financial reporting standards issued by the IASC, which are very similar to the SSAPs and FRSs, which are used in the UK.

International Accounting Standards Board (IASB) The IASB is the body that is responsible for setting and publishing International Financial Reporting Standards (IFRSs). It was formed on 1 April 2001 and succeeded the International Accounting Standards Committee (IASC) which had been formed in 1973. The parent body of the IASB is the International Accounting Standards Committee Foundation, which was incorporated in the USA in March 2001, and was also responsible for issuing International Accounting Standards (IASs).

International Financial Reporting Standard (IFRS) The international financial reporting standards issued by the IASB, which incorporate the IASs, issued by the IASC. IASs are very similar to the SSAPs and FRSs, which are used in the UK.

Internet The Internet or the net is a worldwide system of computer networks, a network of networks in which users at any one computer can, if they have permission, exchange information with any other computer. The Internet is distinguished by its use of a set of protocols called TCP/IP, which means transmission control protocol/Internet protocol.

Internet service provider (ISP) An ISP is a company, which provides Internet access to other companies or individuals. An ISP maintains connections to other networks and ISPs, acting as a router for Internet traffic between a customer's computer and any other machine also connected to the Internet. The Internet connections are typically ADSL, cable, and dial-up.

intranet An intranet is a network within an organisation that uses Internet technologies to enable users to find, use, and share documents and web pages. Businesses also use intranets to communicate with employees. A firewall is used to isolate the network.

intrusion detection software Intrusion detection software is designed to detect intrusion or entrance to systems by monitoring the entire computer system continuously and notifying users if the system has been entered without authorisation or if the system is being used inappropriately.

investment Any application of funds which is intended to provide a return by way of interest, dividend or capital appreciation.

just in time (JIT) The management philosophy that incorporates a 'pull' system of producing or purchasing components and products in response to customer demand, which contrasts with a 'push' system where stocks act as buffers between each process within and between purchasing, manufacturing, and sales.

kilobyte A kilobyte or Kb is a measure of capacity equal to 1,024 bytes. For example, 15 Kb equates approximately to one A4 page of text.

knowledge management software The enormous developments in IT have resulted in the creation of unprecedented amounts of data and information that is widely and easily accessible – far more than can be realistically retrieved and used. The use of knowledge management software has become increasingly important to ensure that the information that is required may be accessed, and that the information that is really useful is obtained and used effectively.

last in first out (LIFO) Assumes that the last item of stock received is the first to be used. In the UK it is a little-used method of pricing the issue of material using the purchase price of the latest unit in stock. It is used more often in the USA as a method of valuing stock using indices to charge most recent prices against profits.

leave of the court This is where the court will make a decision after hearing all the relevant information.

liabilities An entity's obligations to transfer economic benefits as a result of past transactions or events (FRS 5).

limited company (Ltd) A Ltd company is one in which the liability of members for the company's debts is limited to the amount paid and, if any, unpaid on the shares taken up by them.

liquid resources Liquid resources, or liquid assets, are cash, and other assets readily convertible into cash, for example short-term investments.

loan capital Also called debt, relates to debentures and other long-term loans to a business.

local area network (LAN) A LAN is a group of computers, printers or other hardware that are all connected in a reasonably small geographic location like an office or home, which makes it possible for the connected users to share files and applications that usually reside on a server or some type of shared computer.

management accounting The application of the principles of accounting and financial management to create, protect, preserve and increase value so as to deliver that value to the stakeholders of profit and not-for-profit enterprises, both public and private. Management accounting is an integral part of management, requiring the identification, generation, presentation, interpretation and use of information relevant to:

- formulating business strategy
- planning and controlling activities
- decision-making
- efficient resource usage
- performance improvement and value enhancement
- safeguarding tangible and intangible assets
- corporate governance and internal control.

manufacturing resource planning (MRPII) An expansion of material requirements planning (MRPI) to give a broader approach than MRPI to the planning and scheduling of resources, embracing areas such as finance, logistics, engineering and marketing.

market value added (MVA) The difference between the market value of the company and the adjusted book values of its assets.

materiality concept Information is material if its omission or misstatement could influence the economic decisions of users taken on the basis of the financial statements. Materiality depends on the size of the item or error judged in the particular circumstances of its omission or misstatement. Thus, materiality provides a threshold or cut-off point rather than being a primary qualitative characteristic that information must have if it is to be useful.

materials requirement planning (MRP1 or MRP) A system that converts a production schedule into a listing of the materials and components required to meet that schedule, so that adequate stock levels are maintained and items are available when needed.

megabyte A megabyte or Mb is a measure of capacity equal to 1,048,576 bytes. For example, 1 Mb equates approximately to the text of an average paperback novel, and 5 Mb equates approximately to the complete works of Shakespeare.

modem Modems (derived from MOdulator/DEModulator) are electronic devices for converting between serial data from a computer and an audio signal suitable for transmission over a telephone line connected to another modem, distinguished primarily by the maximum data rate they support. Data rates can range from 75 bits per second up to 56,000 bits per second and beyond, with data from the user (i.e. flowing from the local terminal or computer via the modem to the telephone line) sometimes at a lower rate than the other direction, on the assumption that the user cannot type more than a few characters per second.

money measurement concept Most quantifiable data is capable of being converted, using a common denominator of money, into monetary terms. The money measurement concept holds that accounting deals only with those items capable of being translated into monetary terms, which imposes a limit on the scope of accounting reporting to such items.

net assets The excess of the book value of assets over liabilities, including loan capital. This is equivalent to net worth, which is used to describe the paid-up share capital and reserves.

net debt The total borrowings of the company net of liquid resources. Net debt excludes non-equity shares because, although similar to borrowings, they are not actually liabilities of the entity. Net debt excludes debtors and creditors because, whilst they are short-term claims on and sources of finance to the entity, their main role is as part of the entity's trading activities.

net present value (NPV) The difference between the sums of the projected discounted cash inflows and outflows attributable to a capital investment or other long-term project.

net profit (or profit after tax) Profit before tax (PBT) less corporation tax.

net realisable value The amount for which an asset could be disposed, less any direct selling costs (SSAP 9).

new economy The current new economy, in which IT plays a significant role, enables producers of both the tangible (computers, shoes, etc.) and intangible (services, ideas, etc.) to compete efficiently in global markets.

non-executive director A director who does not have a particular function to perform within the company's management. The usual involvement is to attend board meetings only.

non-related company A company in which a business has a long-term investment, but over which it has no control or influence. If control exists then the company is deemed to be a subsidiary.

off balance sheet financing The funding of operations in such a way that the relevant assets and liabilities are not disclosed in the balance sheet of the company concerned.

online Online is the condition of being connected to a network of computers or other devices and the term is usually used to describe someone who is currently connected to the Internet.

operating cycle The operating cycle, or working capital cycle, is calculated by deducting creditor days from stock days plus debtor days. It represents the period of time which elapses between the point at which cash begins to be expended on the production of a product and the collection of cash from the customer.

operating gearing The relationship of fixed costs to total costs. The greater the proportion of fixed costs, the higher the operating gearing, and the greater the advantage to the business of increasing sales volume. If sales drop, a business with high operating gearing may face a problem from its high level of fixed costs.

operating lease A lease is a contract between a lessor and a lessee for the hire of a specific asset. The lessor retains ownership of the asset but gives the right to the use of the asset to the lessee for an agreed period in return for the payment of specified rentals (SSAP 21). An operating lease is a lease other than a finance lease, where the lessor retains most of the risks and rewards of ownership.

operating profit Gross profit, or gross margin, plus/less all operating revenues and costs, regardless of the financial structure of the company and whatever exceptional events occurred during the period.

ordinary shares Shares which entitle the holders to the remaining divisible profits (and, in a liquidation, the assets) after prior interests, for example creditors and prior charge capital, have been satisfied.

password A password is a unique identifier known only to a specific individual, and used by them every time they are required to log into a computer system. Passwords do not ensure 100 per cent security, but to ensure that they provide the highest level of security possible they should not be obviously guessed words or numbers, and should be changed regularly, and protected from unauthorised users.

periodicity concept The requirement to produce financial statements at set time intervals. This requirement is embodied, in the case of UK companies, in the Companies Act 1985.

post balance sheet events Favourable and unfavourable events, which occur between the balance sheet date and the date on which the financial statements are approved by the board of directors.

preference shares Shares carrying a fixed rate of dividend, the holders of which, subject to the conditions of issue, have a prior claim to any company profits available for distribution. Preference shares may also have a prior claim to the repayment of capital in the event of a winding up.

prepayments Prepayments include prepaid expenses for services not yet used, for example rent in advance or electricity charges in advance, and also accrued income. Accrued income relates to sales of goods or services that have occurred and have been included in the profit and loss account for the trading period but have not yet been invoiced to the customer.

present value The cash equivalent now of a sum receivable or payable at a future date.

price/earnings ratio (P/E) The market price per ordinary share divided by earnings per share shows the number of years it would take to recoup an equity investment from its share of the attributable equity profit.

profit and loss account (or **income statement**) The profit and loss account shows the profit or loss generated by an entity during an accounting period by deducting all expenses from all revenues. It measures whether or not the company has made a profit or loss on its operations during the period, through producing and selling its goods or services.

profit before tax (PBT) Operating profit plus or minus net interest.

provision Amount charged against profit to provide for an expected liability or loss even though the amount or date of the liability or loss is uncertain (FRS 12).

prudence concept The principle that revenue and profits are not anticipated, but are included in the profit and loss account only when realised in the form either of cash or of other assets, or the ultimate cash realisation can be assessed with reasonable certainty; provision is made for all known liabilities (expenses and losses) whether the amount of these is known with certainty or is a best estimate in the light of information available.

public limited company (plc) A plc is a company limited by shares or by guarantee, with a share capital, whose memorandum states that it is public and that it has complied with the registration procedures for such a company. A public company is distinguished from a private company in the following ways: a minimum issued share capital of £50,000; public limited company, or plc, at the end of the name; public company clause in the memorandum; freedom to offer securities to the public.

purchase invoice A document received from a supplier by an entity showing the description, quantity, prices and values of goods or services received.

purchase invoice daybook A list of supplier invoices recording their dates, gross values, values net of VAT, the dates of receipt of the invoices, the names of suppliers, and the general ledger allocation and coding.

purchase ledger The purchase ledger contains all the personal accounts of each individual supplier or vendor, and records every transaction with each supplier since the start of their relationship with the company.

qualified accountant A member of the accountancy profession, and in the UK a member of one of the six professional accountancy bodies: CIMA; ICAEW; ICAS; ICAI; ACCA; CIPFA.

raw materials Goods purchased for incorporation into products for sale.

realisation concept The principle that increases in value should only be recognised on realisation of assets by arms-length sale to an independent purchaser.

receiver A person appointed by secured creditors or by the court to take control of company property, usually following the failure of the company to pay principal sums or interest due to debenture holders whose debt is secured by fixed or floating charges over the assets of the company. The receiver takes control of the charged assets and may operate the company's business with a view to selling it as a going concern. In practice receivership is closely followed by liquidation.

Registrar of Companies Government official agency that is responsible for initial registration of new companies and for collecting and arranging public access to the annual reports of all limited companies.

repayable on demand This refers to the definition of cash where there is a loss of interest if cash is withdrawn within 24 hours.

reporting entity A public or private limited company required to file its annual report and accounts with the Registrar of Companies.

reserves Retained profits or surpluses. In a not-for-profit entity these are described as accumulated funds. Reserves may be distributable or non-distributable.

residual income (RI) Profit before tax less an imputed interest charge for invested capital, which may be used to assess the performance of a division or a branch of a business.

retained profits Profits that have not been paid out as dividends to shareholders, but retained for future investment by the company.

return on capital employed (ROCE) ROCE, or return on investment (ROI), is the profit before interest and tax divided by average capital employed. It indicates the profit-generating capacity of capital employed.

return on investment (ROI) See return on capital employed (ROCE).

revenue expenditure Expenditure on the manufacture of goods, the provision of services or on the general conduct of the entity, which is charged to the profit and loss account in the accounting period of sale. This includes repairs and depreciation of fixed assets as distinct from the provision of these assets.

rights issue The raising of new capital by giving existing shareholders the right to subscribe to new shares or debentures in proportion to their current holdings. These shares are usually issued at a discount to the market price. A shareholder not wishing to take up a rights issue may sell the rights.

risk A condition in which there exists a quantifiable dispersion in the possible outcomes from any activity. For example: credit risk – the risk that a borrower may default on his obligations; currency risk – the possibility of loss or gain due to future changes in exchange rates.

risk management The process of understanding and managing the risks that the organisation is inevitably subject to in attempting to achieve its corporate objectives. For management purposes, risks are usually divided into categories such as: operational; financial; legal compliance; information; personnel.

sales Also called turnover or revenue, sales are amounts derived from the provision of goods or services falling within the company's ordinary activities, after deduction of sales returns, trade discounts, value added tax, and any other taxes based on the amounts so derived (Companies Act 1985/1989).

sales invoice A document prepared by an entity showing the description, quantity, prices and values of goods delivered or services rendered to a customer.

sales invoice daybook A list of customer invoices recording their dates, gross values, values net of VAT, the names of customers, and the general ledger allocation and coding.

sales ledger The sales ledger contains all the personal accounts of each individual customer, and records every transaction with each customer since the start of their relationship with the company.

scrip issue (or bonus issue) The capitalisation of the reserves of a company by the issue of additional shares to existing shareholders, in proportion to their holdings. Such shares are normally fully paid-up with no cash called for from the shareholders.

segmental reporting The inclusion in a company's report and accounts of analysis of turnover, profits and net assets by class of business and by geographical segments (Companies Act 1985/89 and SSAP 25).

separate valuation concept In determining the aggregate amount of any asset or liability, the amount of each individual asset or liability comprising the aggregate must be determined separately (Companies Act 1985).

server A server means two things: (a) a computer: or (b) a software program. (a) A server is a computer on a network that is dedicated to a particular purpose and which stores all information and performs the critical functions for that purpose. The most common example is a file server, which is a computer and a storage device dedicated to storing files. A print server is a computer, which manages one or more printers. A network server is a computer that manages network traffic. (b) A server is a program, which provides some service to other computer programs in the same computer or in other computers. An example is web server software, which transmits web pages over the Internet when it receives a web browsers' request for a page.

share A fixed identifiable unit of capital which has a fixed nominal or face value, which may be quite different from the market value of the share.

share capital Capital is the number of existing shares in the company multiplied by the nominal value of the shares.

share premium The difference in price between the original nominal value and the price new investors will have to pay for shares issued by the company.

small to medium-sized enterprise (SME) An SME is currently defined as an enterprise which has fewer that 250 occupied persons and which has either an annual turnover not exceeding 50 million euro, or an annual balance sheet total not exceeding 43 million euro.

spam Spam is unsolicited junk email sent to large numbers of people to promote products or services, and also refers to inappropriate promotional or commercial postings to discussion groups or bulletin boards.

spreadsheet A spreadsheet is a type of computer software package developed in the late 1970s and used in a variety of business operations. The spreadsheet is named after the accountant's manual spreadsheet in which text or numbers or formulae are displayed in rows and columns. Spreadsheet programs enable information to be introduced that automatically and speedily affects entries across the entire spreadsheet. Complex spreadsheet programs exist that enable the transfer of spreadsheet information through word processing techniques and there are also three-dimensional spreadsheets for multi-department, multi-division, and multi-company budgeting, planning and modelling.

statement of affairs Details submitted to the Official Receiver during the winding-up of a company identifying the assets and liabilities of the company. The details are prepared by the company directors, or other persons specified by the Official Receiver, and must be submitted within 14 days of the winding-up order or the appointment of a provisional liquidator.

Statement of Principles (SOP) for Financial Reporting The UK conceptual framework of accounting issued by the Accounting Standards Board in 1999.

Statements of Standard Accounting Practice (SSAPs) The accounting standards of practice published by the Accounting Standards Committee up to 1 August 1990.

statistical process control (SPC) SPC aims at achieving good quality during manufacture, through prevention rather than detection, by providing charts that plot performance (e.g. the length of steel rod compared with its specified length). If the process goes out of control, i.e. produces products outside specified upper and lower control limits, then it can be stopped before many or any defectives are produced.

stock days Stocks value divided by average daily cost of sales calculates the number of days' stocks at the current usage rate.

stocks Stocks, according to SSAP 9, are goods held for future use comprising
- goods or other assets purchased for resale
- consumable stores
- raw materials and components purchased for incorporation into products for sale
- products and services, in intermediate stages of completion (work in progress)
- long-term contracts
- finished goods.

subsidiary companies A subsidiary company, defined by the Companies Act 1985/1989, is a company for which another company – the parent company – is:
- directly a member of it and controls the composition of its board of directors; or
- holds or controls, either by itself or in agreement with other shareholders, a majority of the voting rights; or
- has the right to exercise a dominant influence over it.

substance over form concept Where a conflict exists, the structuring of reports should give precedence to the representation of financial reality over strict adherence to the requirements of the legal reporting structure.

SWOT analysis Performing a SWOT analysis is a means of gaining a clear picture of the Strengths, Weaknesses, Opportunities, and Threats, which made the organisation what it is. SWOT analysis can apply across diverse management functions and activities, but is particularly appropriate to the early stages of formulating strategy.

systematic risk (or **market risk**) Some investments are by their very nature more risky than others. This is nothing to do with chance variations in actual compared with expected returns; it is inherent risk that cannot be diversified away.

treasury management The corporate handling of all financial matters, the generation of external and internal funds for business, the management of currencies and cash flows, and the complex strategies, policies and procedures of corporate finance.

trial balance The list of account balances in a double-entry accounting system. If the records have been correctly maintained, the sum of the debit balances will equal the sum of the credit balances, although certain errors such as the omission of a transaction or erroneous entries will not be disclosed by a trial balance.

true and fair view The requirement for financial statements prepared in compliance with the Companies Act to 'give a true and fair view' overrides any other requirements. Although not precisely defined in the Companies Act this is generally accepted to mean that accounts show a true and fair view if they are unlikely to mislead a user of financial information in giving a false impression of the company.

turnover Also called sales or revenue, are amounts derived from the provision of goods or services falling within the company's ordinary activities, after deduction of sales returns, trade discounts, value added tax, and any other taxes based on the amounts so derived (Companies Act 1985).

uniform resource locator (url) A url is a reference or address to a resource on the Internet e.g. http://www.mcgraw-hill.co.uk/textbooks/davies.

unsystematic risk Risk that can be diversified away.

value added statement An alternative presentation of the traditional profit and loss account that measures the wealth created by a company through its activities, through value added by the business rather than the profit earned by the business. It shows how value added is distributed among the relevant parties: employees; lenders; shareholders; Government; and the amount to provide maintenance and expansion of the business.

vendor managed inventory (VMI) The management of stocks on behalf of a customer by the supplier, the supplier taking responsibility for the management of stocks within a framework that is mutually agreed by both parties. Examples are seen in separate supermarket racks maintained and stocked by merchandising groups for such items as spices, and car parts distributors topping up the shelves of dealers/garages, where the management of the stocks, racking and shelves is carried out by the merchandising group or distributor.

vertical analysis An analysis of the profit and loss account (or balance sheet) in which each item is expressed as a percentage of the total. The vertical analysis provides evidence of structural changes in the business such as increased profitability through more efficient production.

virus A computer virus is a program that usually infects the other executable programs in the computer by inserting in those files copies of itself, so that when the file is loaded into memory copies will be executed allowing them to infect still more files. Computer viruses are designed to replicate themselves and to spread from one location to another without the knowledge of the users, and usually have a very damaging effect on operational and application software.

voluntary winding-up A voluntary winding-up of a company occurs where the company passes a resolution that it shall liquidate and the court is not involved in the process. A voluntary winding-up may be made by the members (the shareholders) of the company or by its creditors, if the company has failed to declare its solvency.

website A website is a related collection of World Wide Web (www) files with a unique address (url).

weighted average cost of capital (WACC) The average cost of the company's finance (equity, debentures, bank loans) weighted according to the proportion each element bears to the total pool of capital. Weighting is usually based on market valuations, current yields and costs after tax.

wide area network (WAN) A WAN is a geographically dispersed telecommunications network, having a much broader structure than a LAN. A WAN may be privately owned or rented but usually involves the inclusion of public or shared user networks.

window dressing A creative accounting practice in which changes in short-term funding have the effect of disguising or improving the reported liquidity position of the reporting organisation.

workflow software Workflow software is used to document, define and graphically represent business processes and is used to analyse and automate such processes.

working capital Also called net current assets, is the capital available for conducting day-to-day operations of an organisation; normally the excess of current assets over current liabilities.

working capital requirement Stocks plus debtors plus prepayments less creditors and accruals. This investment in the operating cycle represents the financial resources specifically required for the company to purchase and create stocks and while it waits for payments from its customers.

work in progress (WIP) Products or services in intermediate stages of completion.

worm Computer worms are the same as computer viruses except that they do not replicate themselves, and they are created to change or delete data within a system. A virus is sometimes called a worm particularly if it is composed of separate segments distributed across the network.

wrongful trading Wrongful trading occurs where a director knows or ought to have known before the commencement of winding-up that there was no reasonable prospect of the company avoiding insolvency and he/she does not take every step to minimise loss to creditors. If the court is satisfied of this it may (i) order the director to contribute to the assets of the business, and (ii) disqualify him/her from further involvement in corporate management for a specified period (Insolvency Act 1986).

Index

Definitions of terms with page numbers highlighted in **colour** are shown in the Glossary.
The names of companies mentioned in the book are in **bold** type.